CASANOVA
GULA

MATT FRACTION
FÁBIO MOON

colors by Cris Peter
letters by Dustin Harbin

CASANOVA VOL. 2: GULA. Contains material originally published in magazine form as CASANOVA: GULA #1-4. First printing 2011. ISBN# 978-0-7851-4863-0. Published by MARVEL WORLDWIDE, INC., a subsidiary of MARVEL ENTERTAINMENT, LLC. OFFICE OF PUBLICATION: 135 West 50th Street, New York, NY 10020. Copyright © 2011 MILKFED CRIMINAL MASTERMINDS, INC. All rights reserved. $14.99 per copy in the U.S. and $16.50 in Canada (GST #R127032852); Canadian Agreement #40668537. "Casanova" and all characters featured herein and the distinctive names and likenesses thereof, and all related indicia are trademarks of MILKFED CRIMINAL MASTERMINDS, INC. No similarity between any of the names, characters, persons, and/or institutions in this magazine with those of any living or dead person or institution is intended, and any such similarity that may exist is purely coincidental. ICON and the Icon logo are trademarks of Marvel Characters, Inc. **Printed in the U.S.A. Manufactured between 6/2/11 and 6/21/2011 by QUAD/GRAPHICS, DUBUQUE, IA, USA.**

10 9 8 7 6 5 4 3 2 1

Representation: Law Offices of Harris Miller II, P.C.

ICON Edition

Editor	Alejandro Arbona
Senior Editor	Stephen Wacker
Collection Editor	Jennifer Grünwald

book design
Gabriel Bá

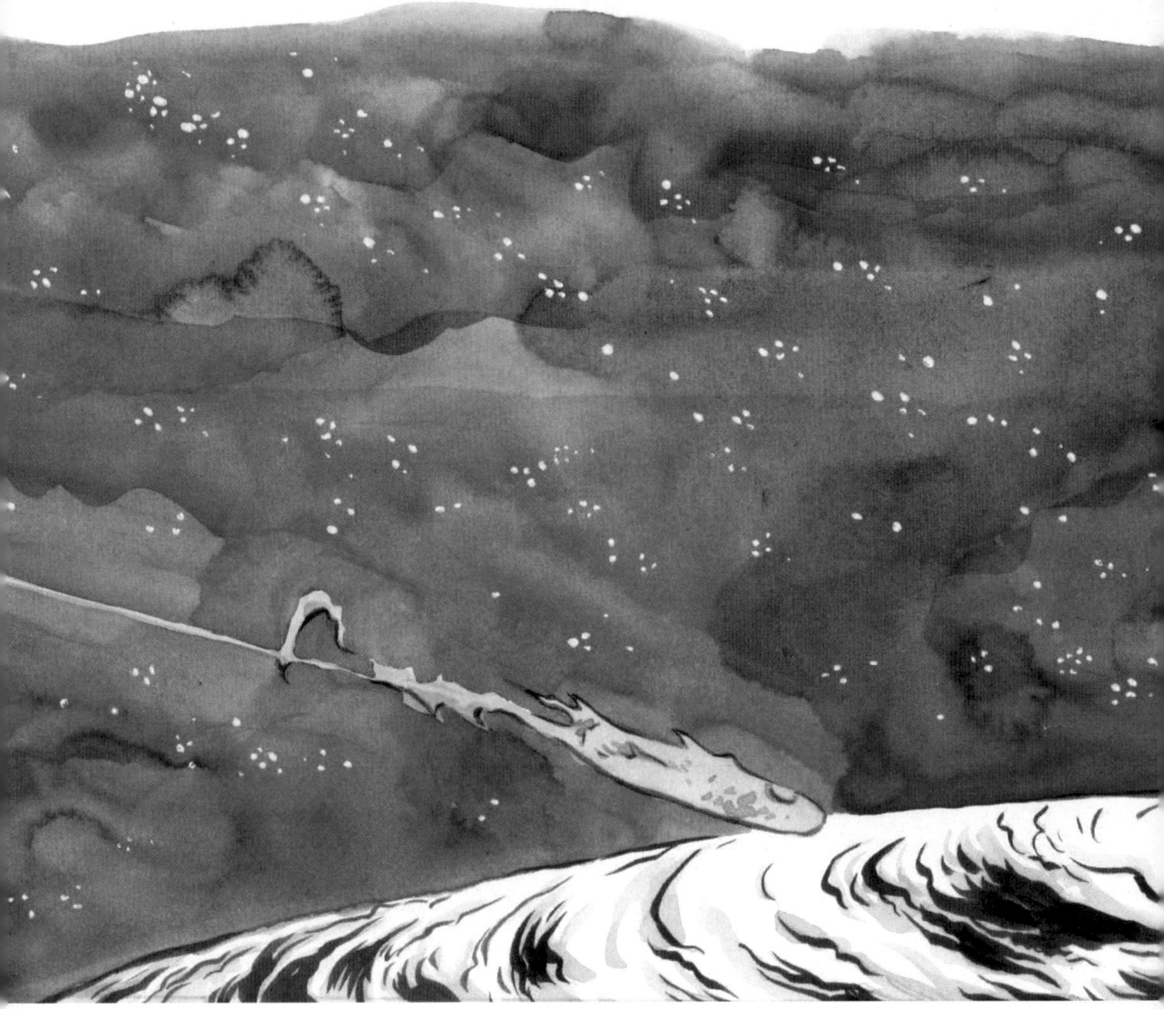

Matt Fraction:
For Kel
Who heard it first
Who held it longest
Who kept it like a secret and never flinched.
Sorry about dinner.

Fábio Moon:
Dedicated to Gabriel Bá, who drew this bad-ass comic in the first place, setting such high standards, and it made me jealous to the point that I had to go and draw it as well.

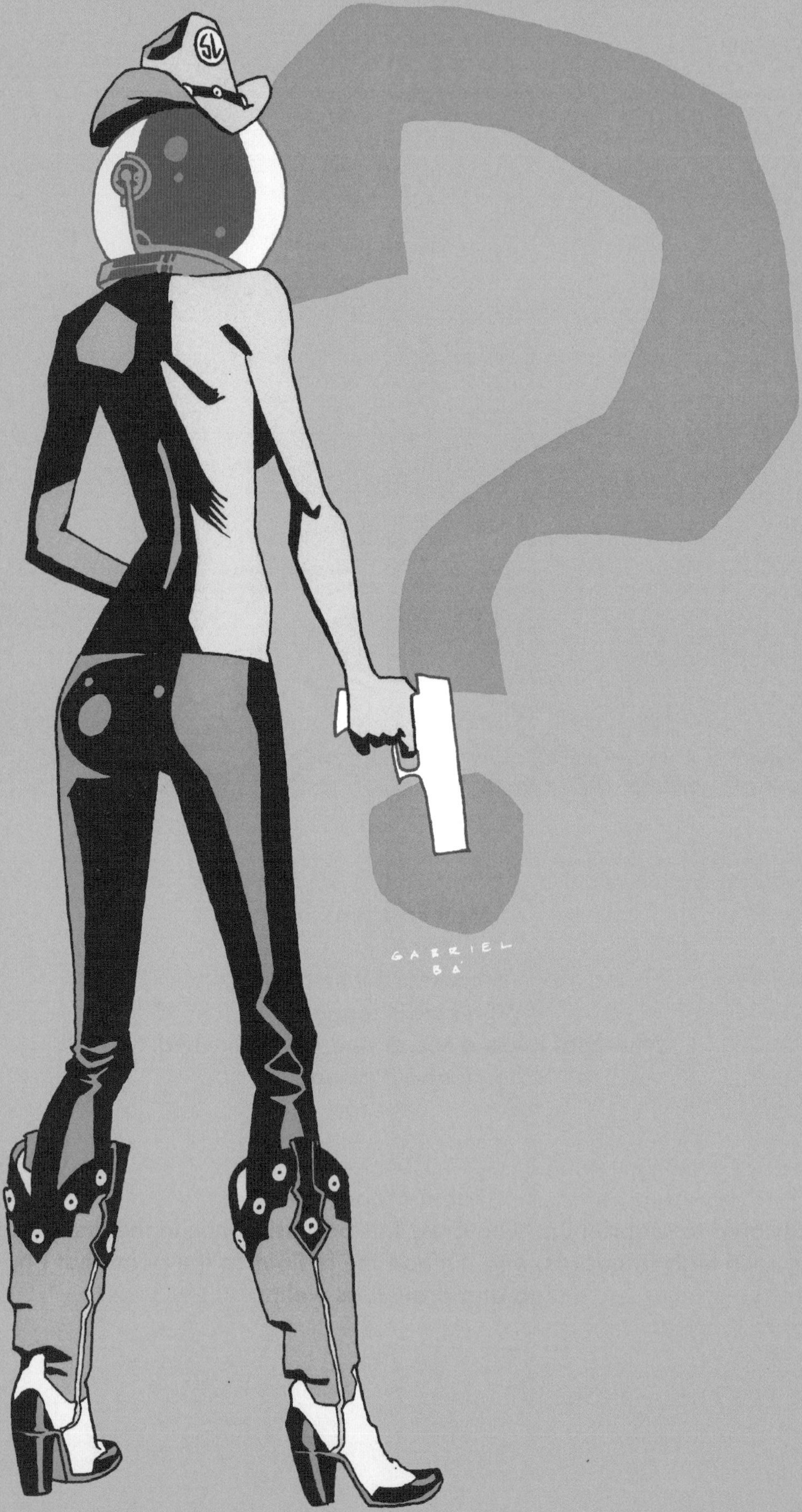
GABRIEL
BÁ

"Only a traitor undresses his
metaphors as if they
were whores."
John Darnielle, 2005.

"There was the distinct feeling that
'nothing was true' anymore and that
the future was not as clear-cut as it had
seemed. Nor, for that matter, was the
past. Therefore, everything was up for
grabs. If we needed any truths, we
could construct them ourselves. The
main platform would be, other than our
shoes, 'We are the future now.'"
David Bowie, 2002.

"You'll stay on the fucking label.
Hare Krishna."
George Harrison,
in a letter to Paul McCartney, 1970.

CHAPTER 1
IN MEDIAS RES

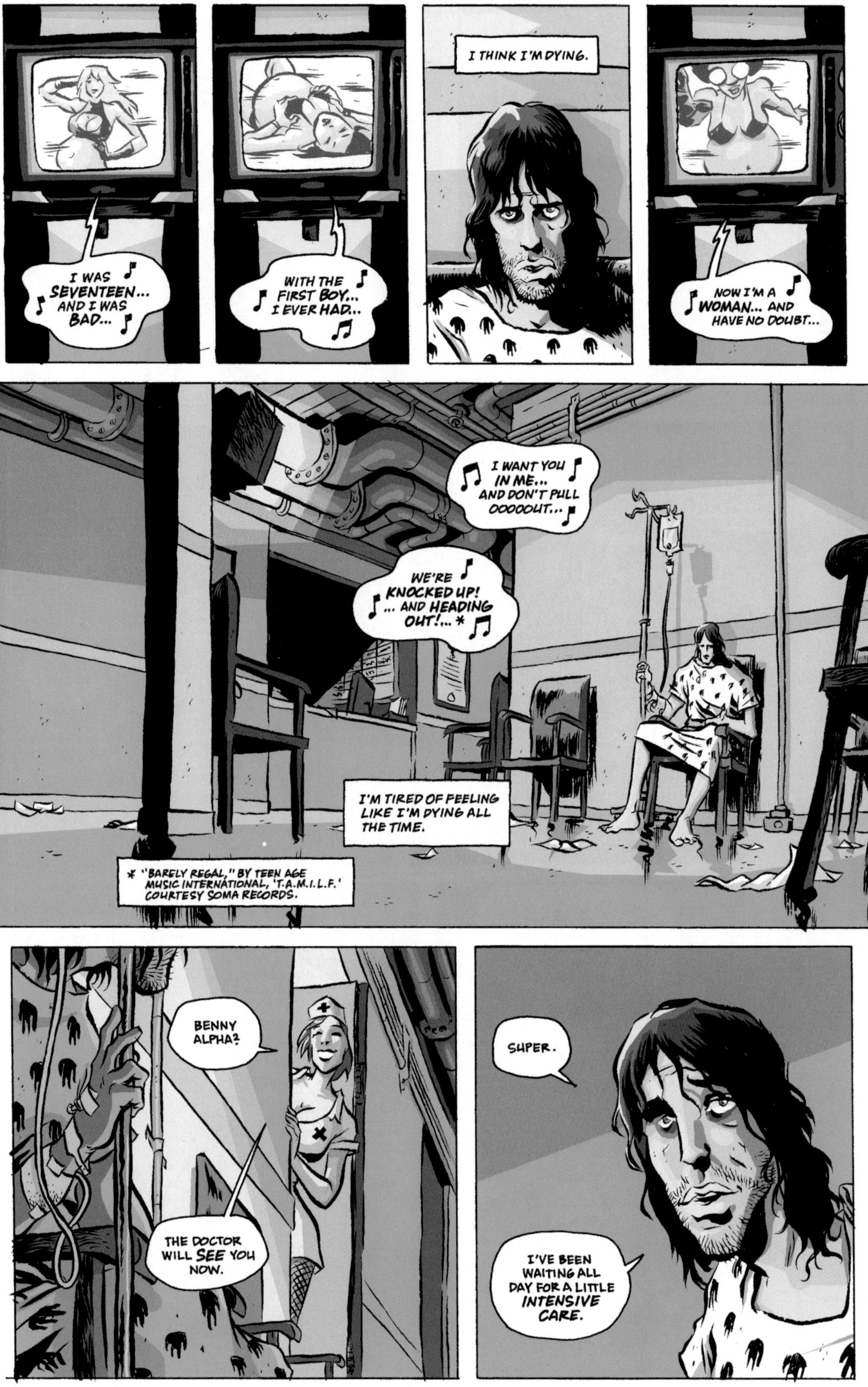
I WAS SEVENTEEN... AND I WAS BAD...
WITH THE FIRST BOY... I EVER HAD...
I THINK I'M DYING.
NOW I'M A WOMAN... AND HAVE NO DOUBT...
I WANT YOU IN ME... AND DON'T PULL OOOOOUT...
WE'RE KNOCKED UP! ... AND HEADING OUT!... *
I'M TIRED OF FEELING LIKE I'M DYING ALL THE TIME.
* "BARELY REGAL," BY TEEN AGE MUSIC INTERNATIONAL, 'T.A.M.I.L.F.' COURTESY SOMA RECORDS.
BENNY ALPHA?
THE DOCTOR WILL SEE YOU NOW.
SUPER.
I'VE BEEN WAITING ALL DAY FOR A LITTLE INTENSIVE CARE.

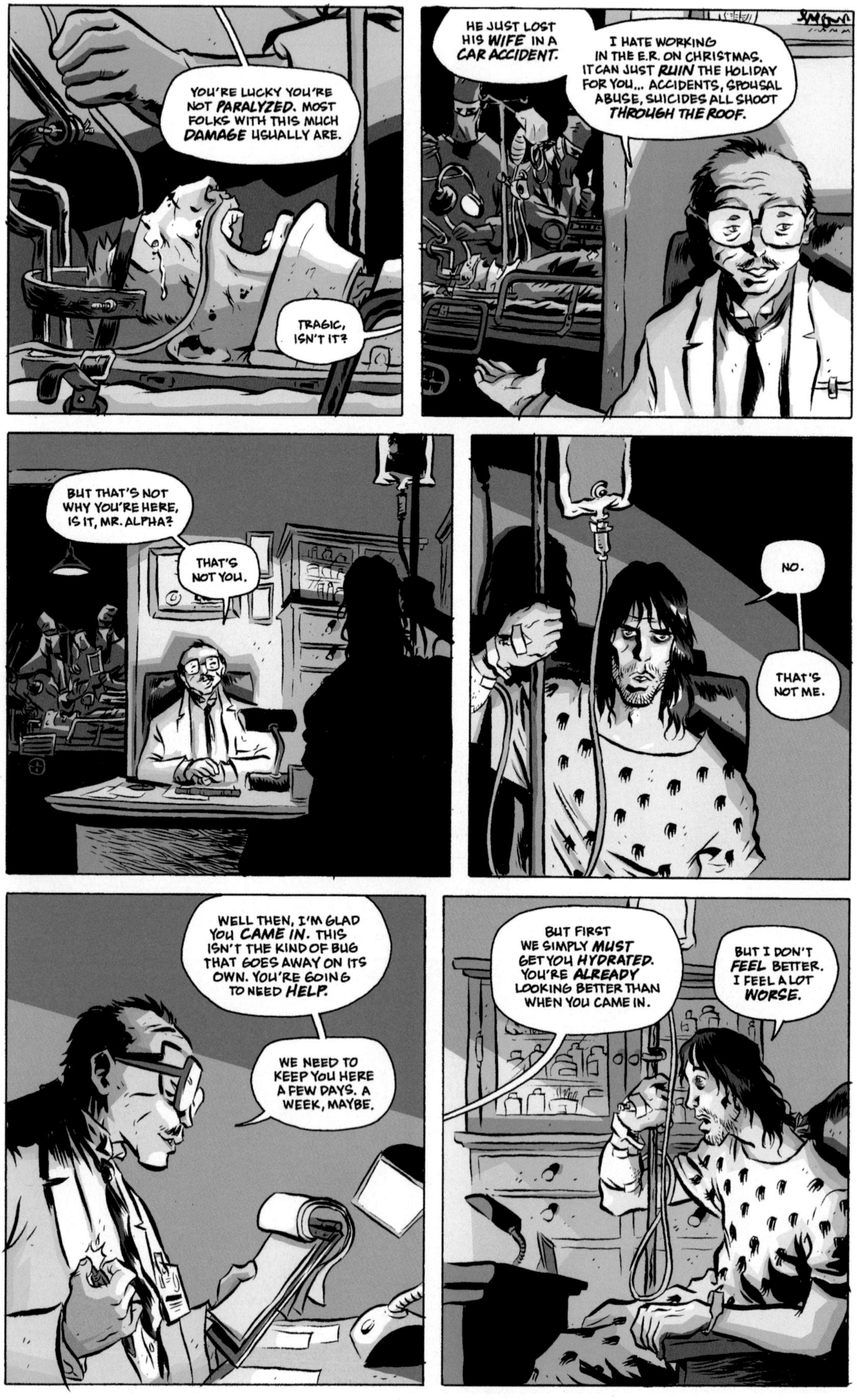
YOU'RE LUCKY YOU'RE NOT PARALYZED. MOST FOLKS WITH THIS MUCH DAMAGE USUALLY ARE.
TRAGIC, ISN'T IT?
HE JUST LOST HIS WIFE IN A CAR ACCIDENT.
I HATE WORKING IN THE E.R. ON CHRISTMAS. IT CAN JUST RUIN THE HOLIDAY FOR YOU... ACCIDENTS, SPOUSAL ABUSE, SUICIDES ALL SHOOT THROUGH THE ROOF.
BUT THAT'S NOT WHY YOU'RE HERE, IS IT, MR. ALPHA?
THAT'S NOT YOU.
NO.
THAT'S NOT ME.
WELL THEN, I'M GLAD YOU CAME IN. THIS ISN'T THE KIND OF BUG THAT GOES AWAY ON ITS OWN. YOU'RE GOING TO NEED HELP.
WE NEED TO KEEP YOU HERE A FEW DAYS. A WEEK, MAYBE.
BUT FIRST WE SIMPLY MUST GET YOU HYDRATED. YOU'RE ALREADY LOOKING BETTER THAN WHEN YOU CAME IN.
BUT I DON'T FEEL BETTER. I FEEL A LOT WORSE.

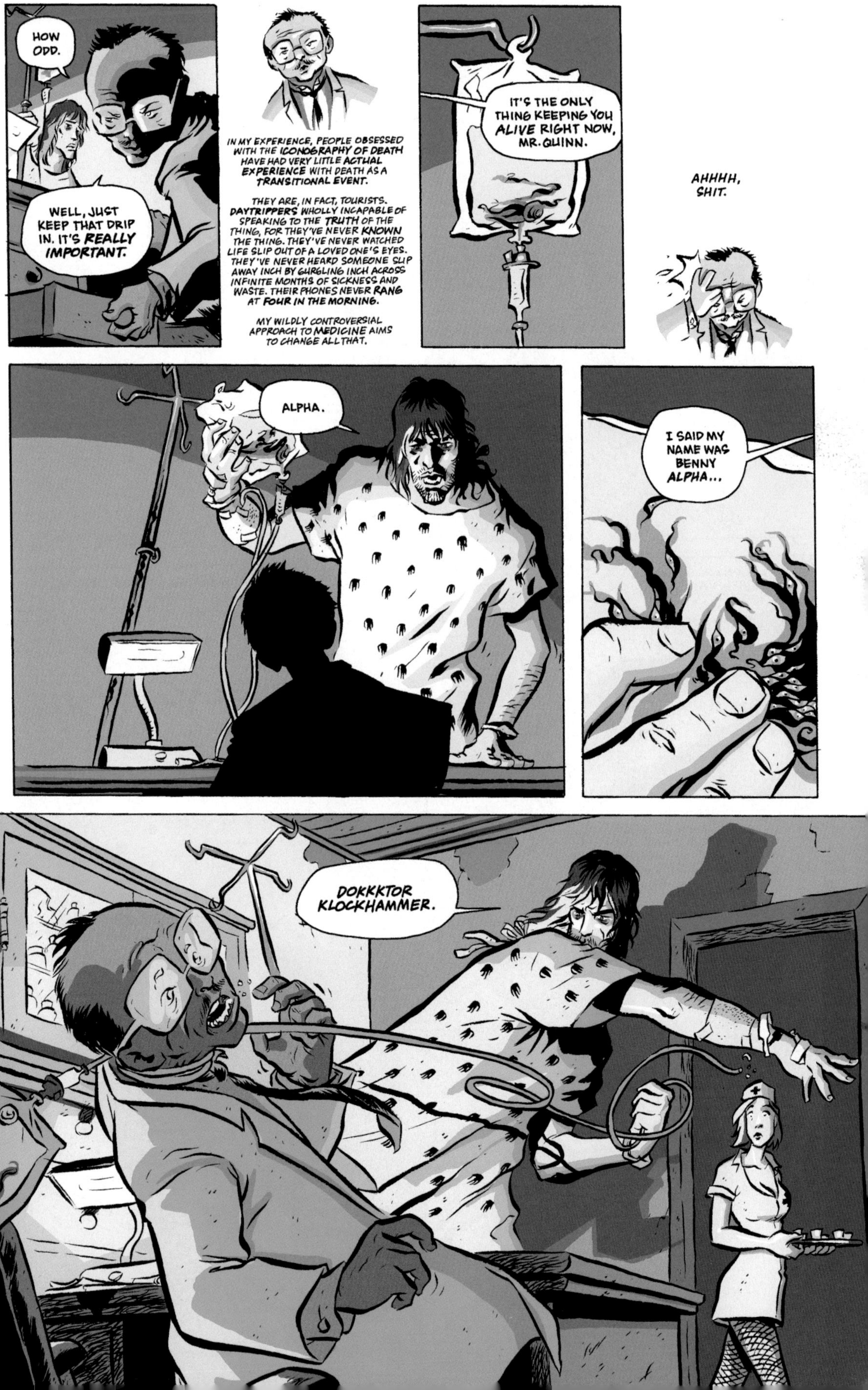
HOW ODD.
WELL, JUST KEEP THAT DRIP IN. IT'S REALLY IMPORTANT.
IN MY EXPERIENCE, PEOPLE OBSESSED WITH THE ICONOGRAPHY OF DEATH HAVE HAD VERY LITTLE ACTUAL EXPERIENCE WITH DEATH AS A TRANSITIONAL EVENT.
THEY ARE, IN FACT, TOURISTS. DAYTRIPPERS WHOLLY INCAPABLE OF SPEAKING TO THE TRUTH OF THE THING, FOR THEY'VE NEVER KNOWN THE THING. THEY'VE NEVER WATCHED LIFE SLIP OUT OF A LOVED ONE'S EYES. THEY'VE NEVER HEARD SOMEONE SLIP AWAY INCH BY GURGLING INCH ACROSS INFINITE MONTHS OF SICKNESS AND WASTE. THEIR PHONES NEVER RANG AT FOUR IN THE MORNING.
MY WILDLY CONTROVERSIAL APPROACH TO MEDICINE AIMS TO CHANGE ALL THAT.
IT'S THE ONLY THING KEEPING YOU ALIVE RIGHT NOW, MR. QUINN.
AHHHH, SHIT.
ALPHA.
I SAID MY NAME WAS BENNY ALPHA...
DOKKKTOR KLOCKHAMMER.

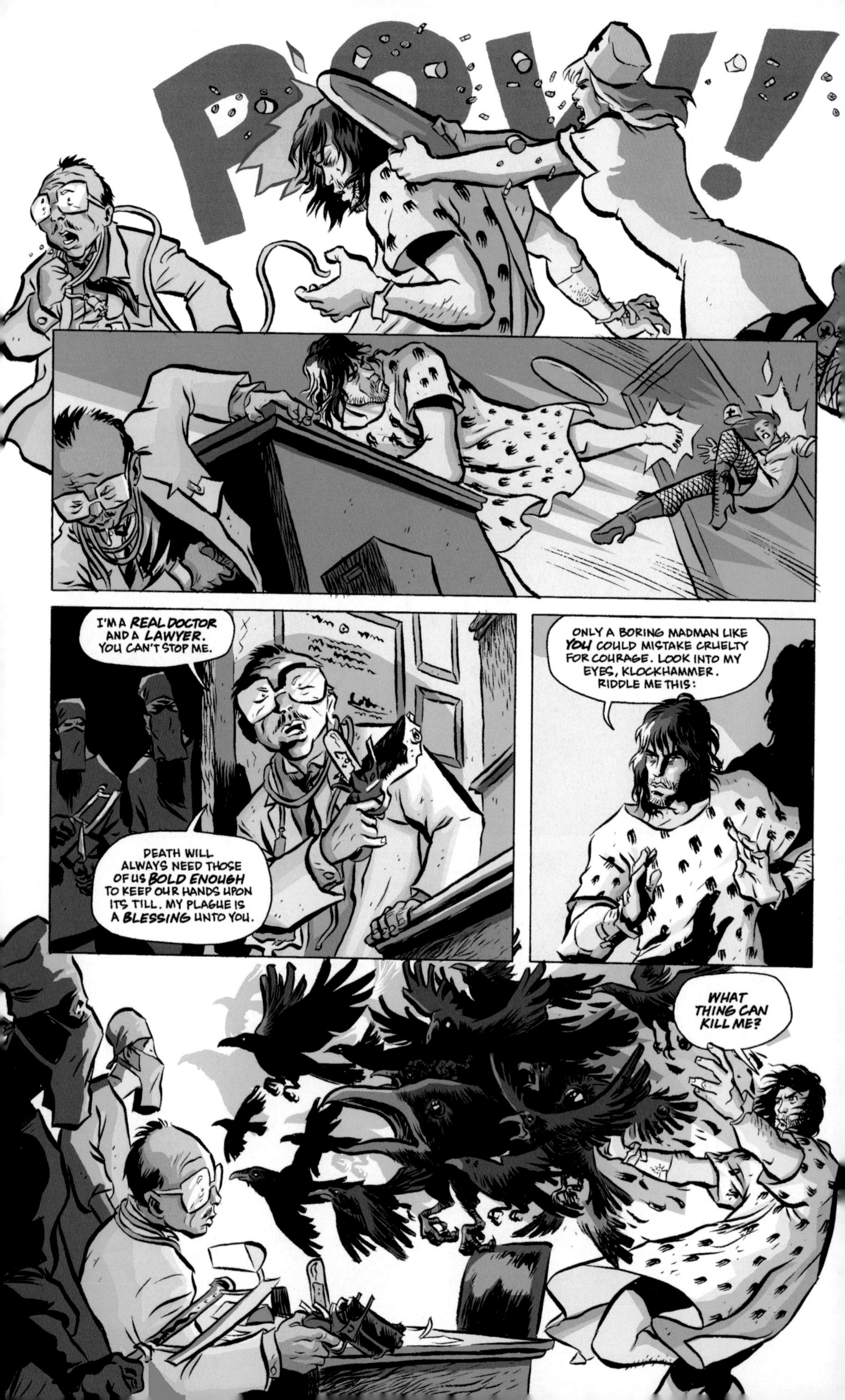
POW!!
I'M A REAL DOCTOR AND A LAWYER. YOU CAN'T STOP ME.
DEATH WILL ALWAYS NEED THOSE OF US BOLD ENOUGH TO KEEP OUR HANDS UPON ITS TILL. MY PLAGUE IS A BLESSING UNTO YOU.
ONLY A BORING MADMAN LIKE YOU COULD MISTAKE CRUELTY FOR COURAGE. LOOK INTO MY EYES, KLOCKHAMMER. RIDDLE ME THIS:
WHAT THING CAN KILL ME?

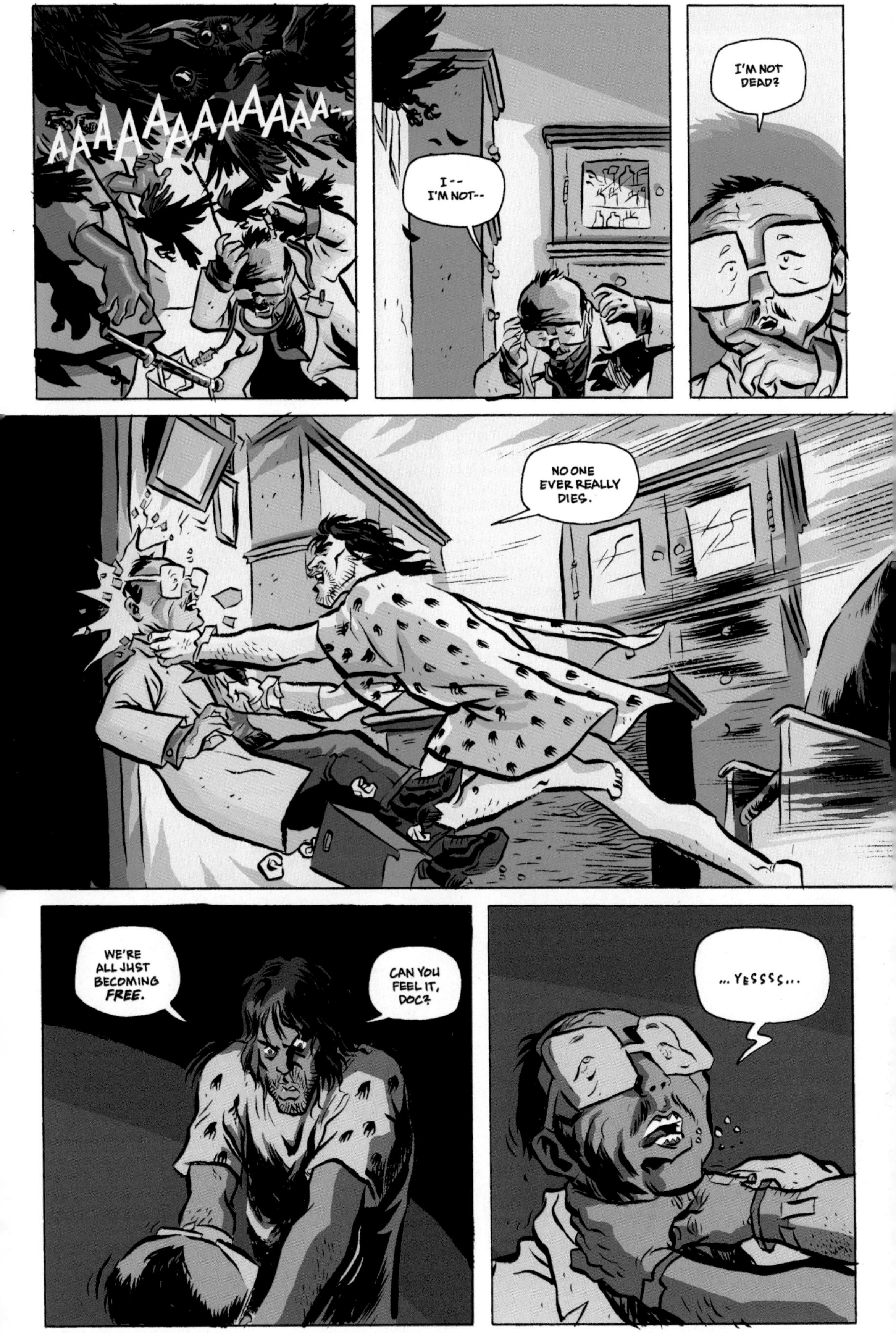
AAAAAAAAAAAA--
I--
I'M NOT--
I'M NOT DEAD?
NO ONE EVER REALLY DIES.
WE'RE ALL JUST BECOMING FREE.
CAN YOU FEEL IT, DOC?
...YESSSS...

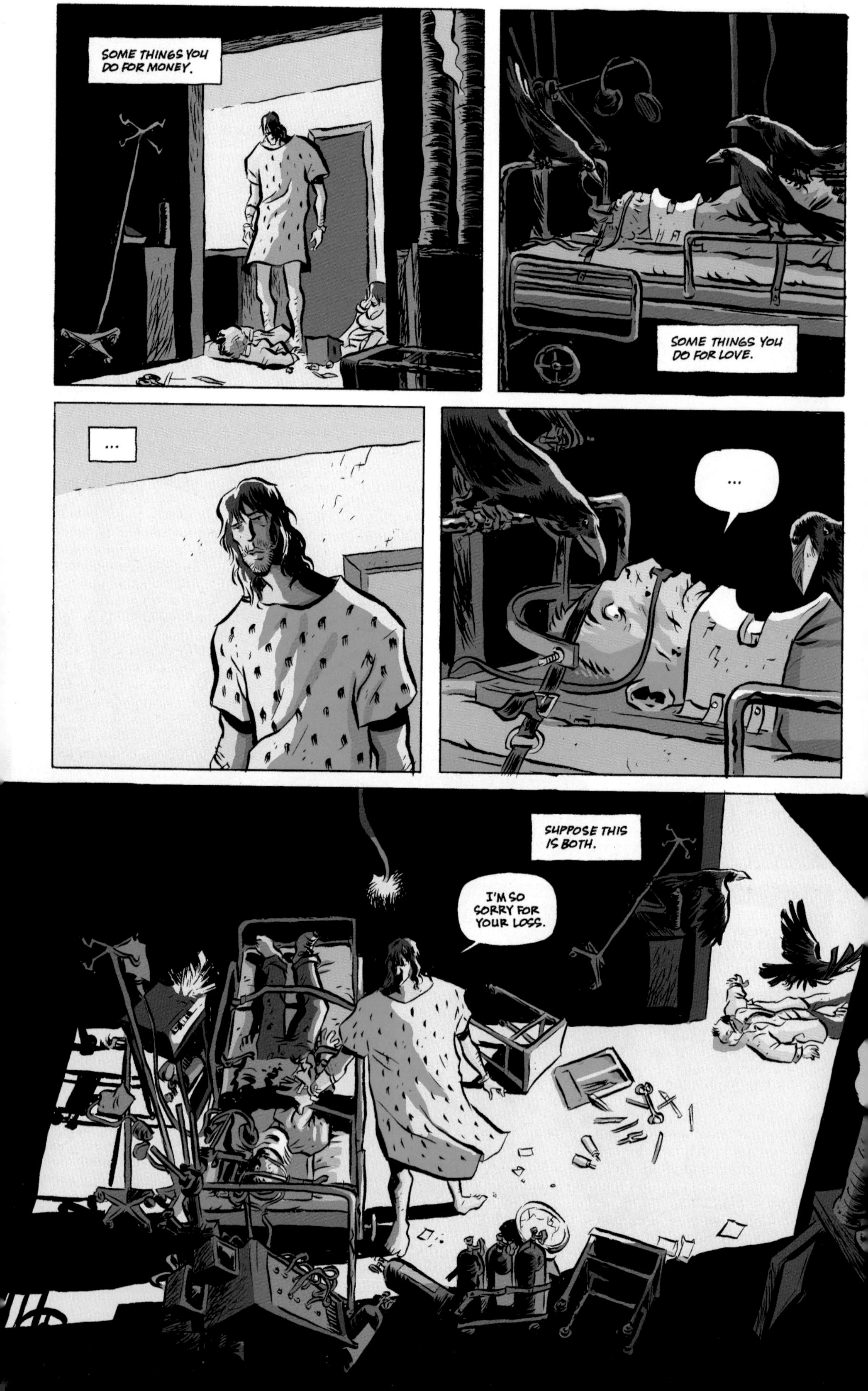

SOME THINGS YOU DO FOR MONEY.
SOME THINGS YOU DO FOR LOVE.
...
...
SUPPOSE THIS IS BOTH.
I'M SO SORRY FOR YOUR LOSS.

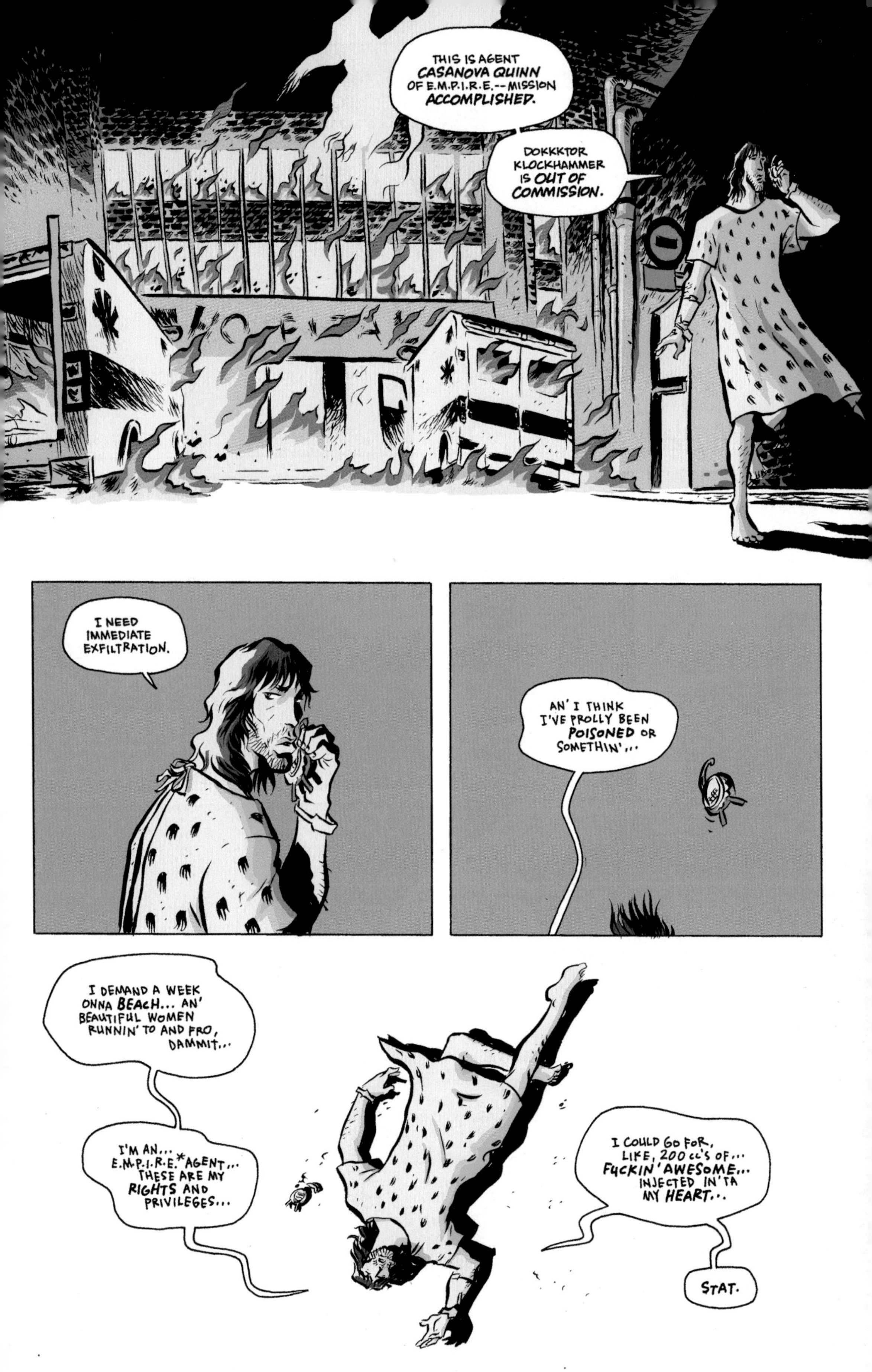
THIS IS AGENT CASANOVA QUINN OF E.M.P.I.R.E.--MISSION ACCOMPLISHED.
DOKKKTOR KLOCKHAMMER IS OUT OF COMMISSION.
I NEED IMMEDIATE EXFILTRATION.
AN' I THINK I'VE PROLLY BEEN POISONED OR SOMETHIN'...
I DEMAND A WEEK ONNA BEACH... AN' BEAUTIFUL WOMEN RUNNIN' TO AND FRO, DAMMIT...
I'M AN... E.M.P.I.R.E.* AGENT... THESE ARE MY RIGHTS AND PRIVILEGES...
I COULD GO FOR, LIKE, 200 CC'S OF... FUCKIN' AWESOME... INJECTED IN'TA MY HEART...
STAT.

* EXTRA-MILITARY POLICE, INTELLIGENCE, RESCUE, AND ESPIONAGE!

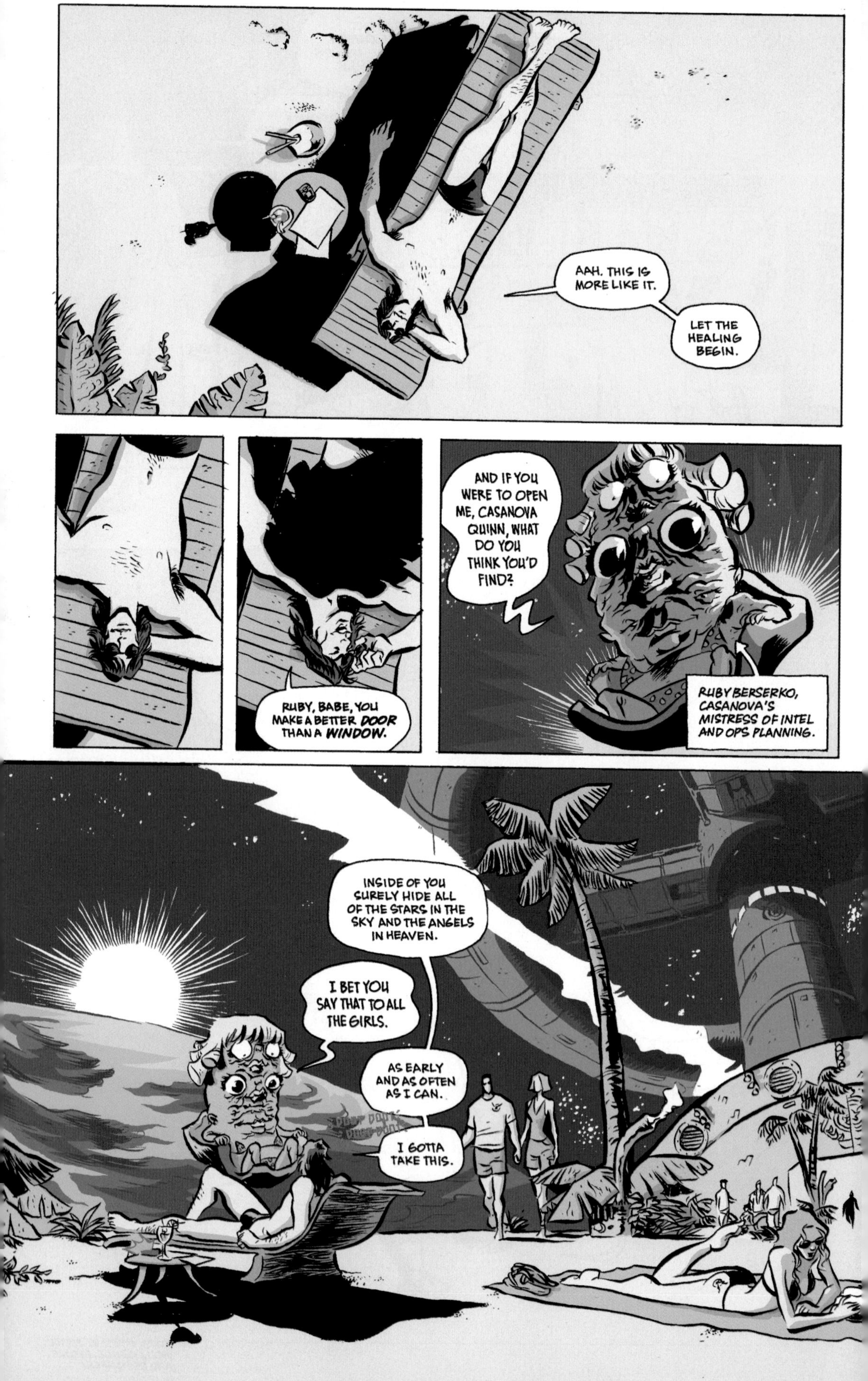

AAH. THIS IS MORE LIKE IT.
LET THE HEALING BEGIN.
RUBY, BABE, YOU MAKE A BETTER DOOR THAN A WINDOW.
AND IF YOU WERE TO OPEN ME, CASANOVA QUINN, WHAT DO YOU THINK YOU'D FIND?
RUBY BERSERKO, CASANOVA'S MISTRESS OF INTEL AND OPS PLANNING.
INSIDE OF YOU SURELY HIDE ALL OF THE STARS IN THE SKY AND THE ANGELS IN HEAVEN.
I BET YOU SAY THAT TO ALL THE GIRLS.
AS EARLY AND AS OFTEN AS I CAN.
I GOTTA TAKE THIS.

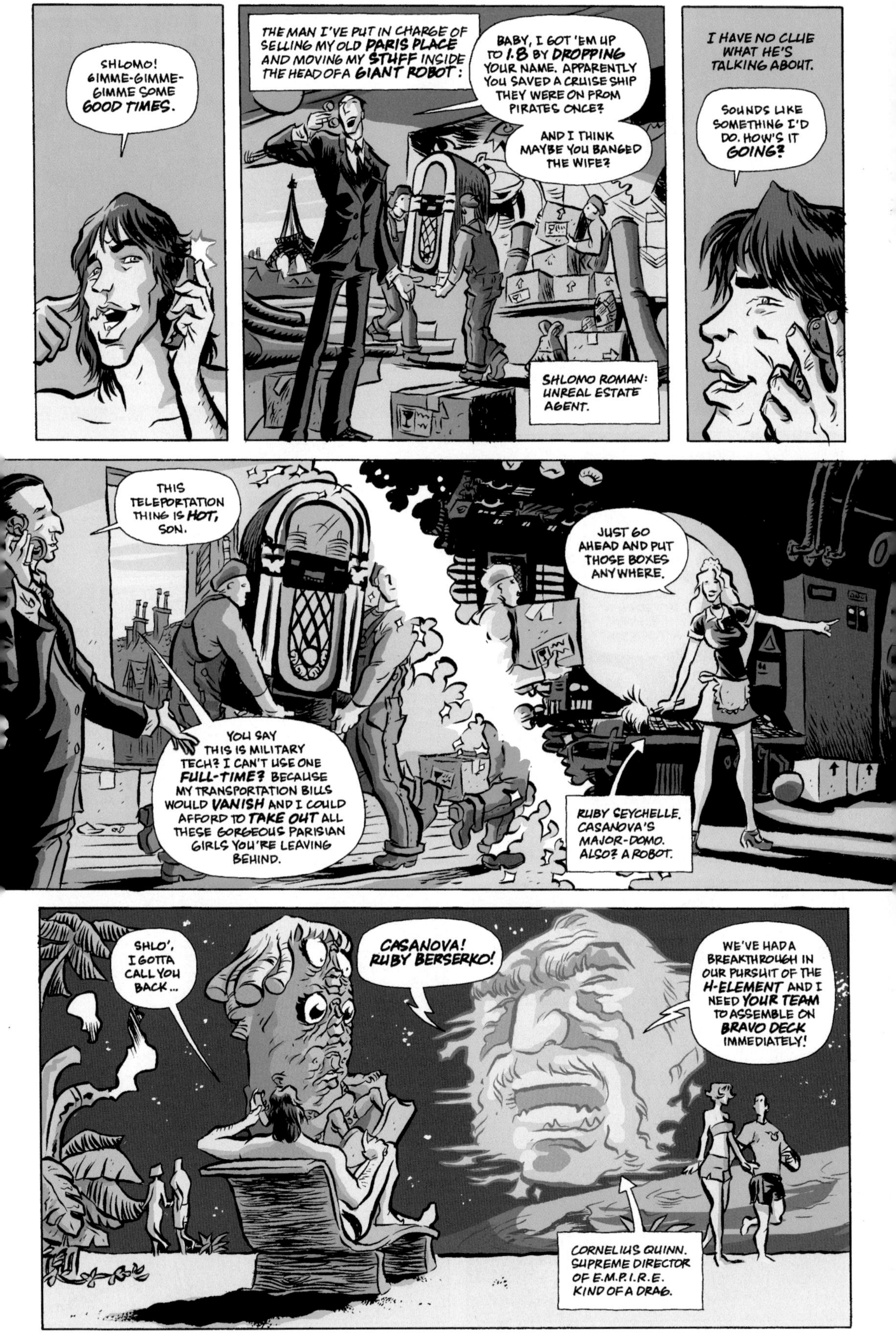
SHLOMO! GIMME-GIMME-GIMME SOME GOOD TIMES.
THE MAN I'VE PUT IN CHARGE OF SELLING MY OLD PARIS PLACE AND MOVING MY STUFF INSIDE THE HEAD OF A GIANT ROBOT:
BABY, I GOT 'EM UP TO 1.8 BY DROPPING YOUR NAME. APPARENTLY YOU SAVED A CRUISE SHIP THEY WERE ON FROM PIRATES ONCE?
AND I THINK MAYBE YOU BANGED THE WIFE?
SHLOMO ROMAN: UNREAL ESTATE AGENT.
I HAVE NO CLUE WHAT HE'S TALKING ABOUT.
SOUNDS LIKE SOMETHING I'D DO. HOW'S IT GOING?
THIS TELEPORTATION THING IS HOT, SON.
YOU SAY THIS IS MILITARY TECH? I CAN'T USE ONE FULL-TIME? BECAUSE MY TRANSPORTATION BILLS WOULD VANISH AND I COULD AFFORD TO TAKE OUT ALL THESE GORGEOUS PARISIAN GIRLS YOU'RE LEAVING BEHIND.
JUST GO AHEAD AND PUT THOSE BOXES ANYWHERE.
RUBY SEYCHELLE. CASANOVA'S MAJOR-DOMO. ALSO? A ROBOT.
SHLO', I GOTTA CALL YOU BACK...
CASANOVA! RUBY BERSERKO!
WE'VE HAD A BREAKTHROUGH IN OUR PURSUIT OF THE H-ELEMENT AND I NEED YOUR TEAM TO ASSEMBLE ON BRAVO DECK IMMEDIATELY!
CORNELIUS QUINN. SUPREME DIRECTOR OF E.M.P.I.R.E. KIND OF A DRAG.

IT WAS WORSE THAN WE THOUGHT-- KLOCKHAMMER WAS USING THE **ELECTROMAGNETIC SUPERCHARGE** RELEASED UPON **DYING** TO POWER AN EXPERIMENTAL **H-ELEMENT GENERATOR.**

AND THE ONLY REASON HE'D BE DEVELOPING AN **EXPERIMENTAL** GENERATOR WOULD BE THAT A **PRACTICAL** ONE ALREADY **EXISTS.**

SABINE SEYCHELLE. ROBOT MANUFACTURER TURNED E.M.P.I.R.E. TECH AND STRATEGY DESIGNER. CHAOTIC-GOOD.

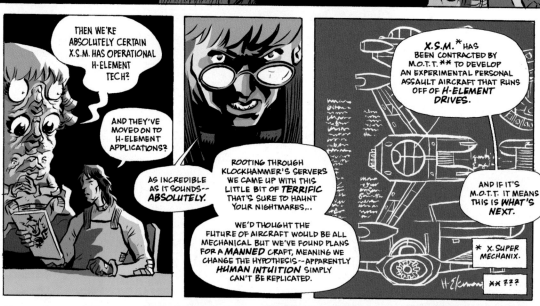

THEN WE'RE ABSOLUTELY CERTAIN X.S.M. HAS OPERATIONAL H-ELEMENT TECH?

AND THEY'VE **MOVED ON** TO H-ELEMENT APPLICATIONS?

AS INCREDIBLE AS IT SOUNDS-- **ABSOLUTELY.**

ROOTING THROUGH KLOCKHAMMER'S SERVERS WE CAME UP WITH THIS LITTLE BIT OF **TERRIFIC** THAT'S SURE TO HAUNT YOUR NIGHTMARES...

WE'D THOUGHT THE FUTURE OF AIRCRAFT WOULD BE ALL MECHANICAL BUT WE'VE FOUND PLANS FOR A **MANNED** CRAFT, MEANING WE CHANGE THE HYPOTHESIS-- APPARENTLY **HUMAN INTUITION** SIMPLY CAN'T BE REPLICATED.

X.S.M. * HAS BEEN CONTRACTED BY M.O.T.T. ** TO DEVELOP AN EXPERIMENTAL PERSONAL ASSAULT AIRCRAFT THAT RUNS OFF OF **H-ELEMENT DRIVES.**

AND IF IT'S M.O.T.T. IT MEANS THIS IS **WHAT'S NEXT.**

* X. SUPER MECHANIX.

** ???

THIS AIRCRAFT **MUST NOT** BE BUILT.

RUBY, YOU'LL WORK **OPS** WITH US; CASS AND KAITO, YOU'RE THE GROUND TEAM. YOU THINK YOU CAN HANDLE IT?

I LOVE MY JOB.

KAITO BEST. JUNIOR AGENT, CASANOVA'S SIDEKICK. CRAZY KUNG-FU.

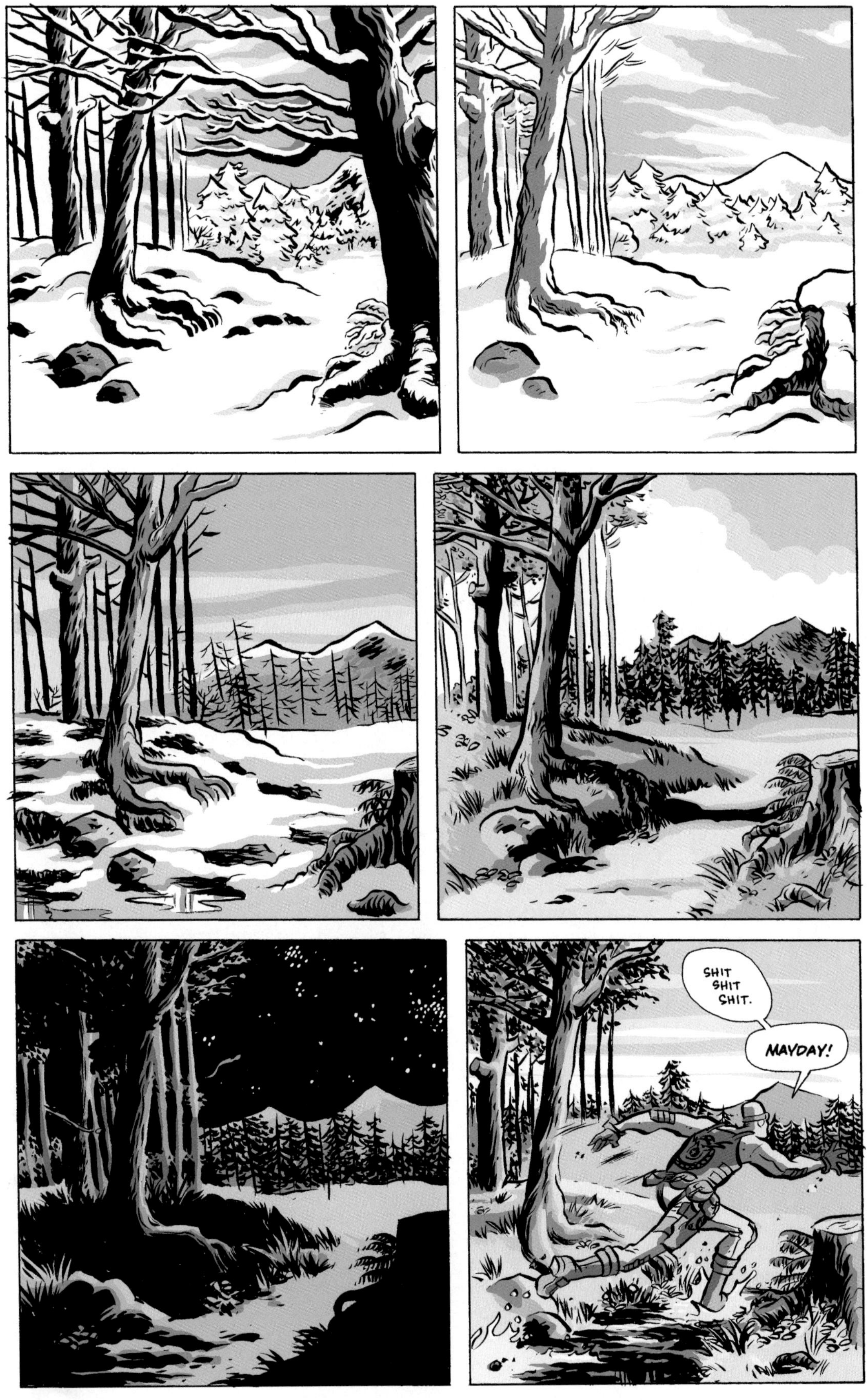
SHIT
SHIT
SHIT.
MAYDAY!

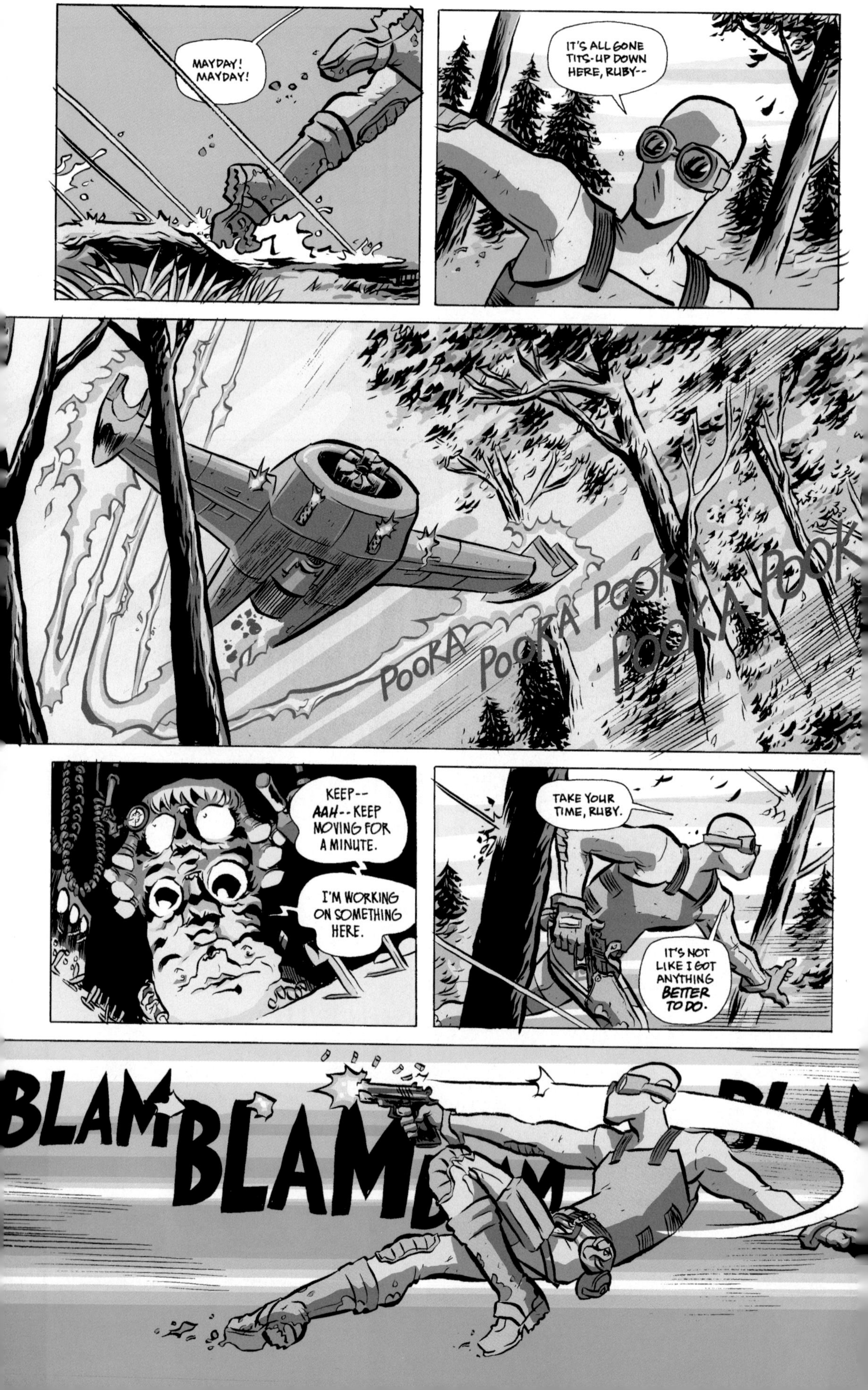
MAYDAY! MAYDAY!
IT'S ALL GONE TITS-UP DOWN HERE, RUBY--
POORA POOKA POOKA POOKA POOK
KEEP-- AAH-- KEEP MOVING FOR A MINUTE.
I'M WORKING ON SOMETHING HERE.
TAKE YOUR TIME, RUBY.
IT'S NOT LIKE I GOT ANYTHING BETTER TO DO.
BLAM BLAM

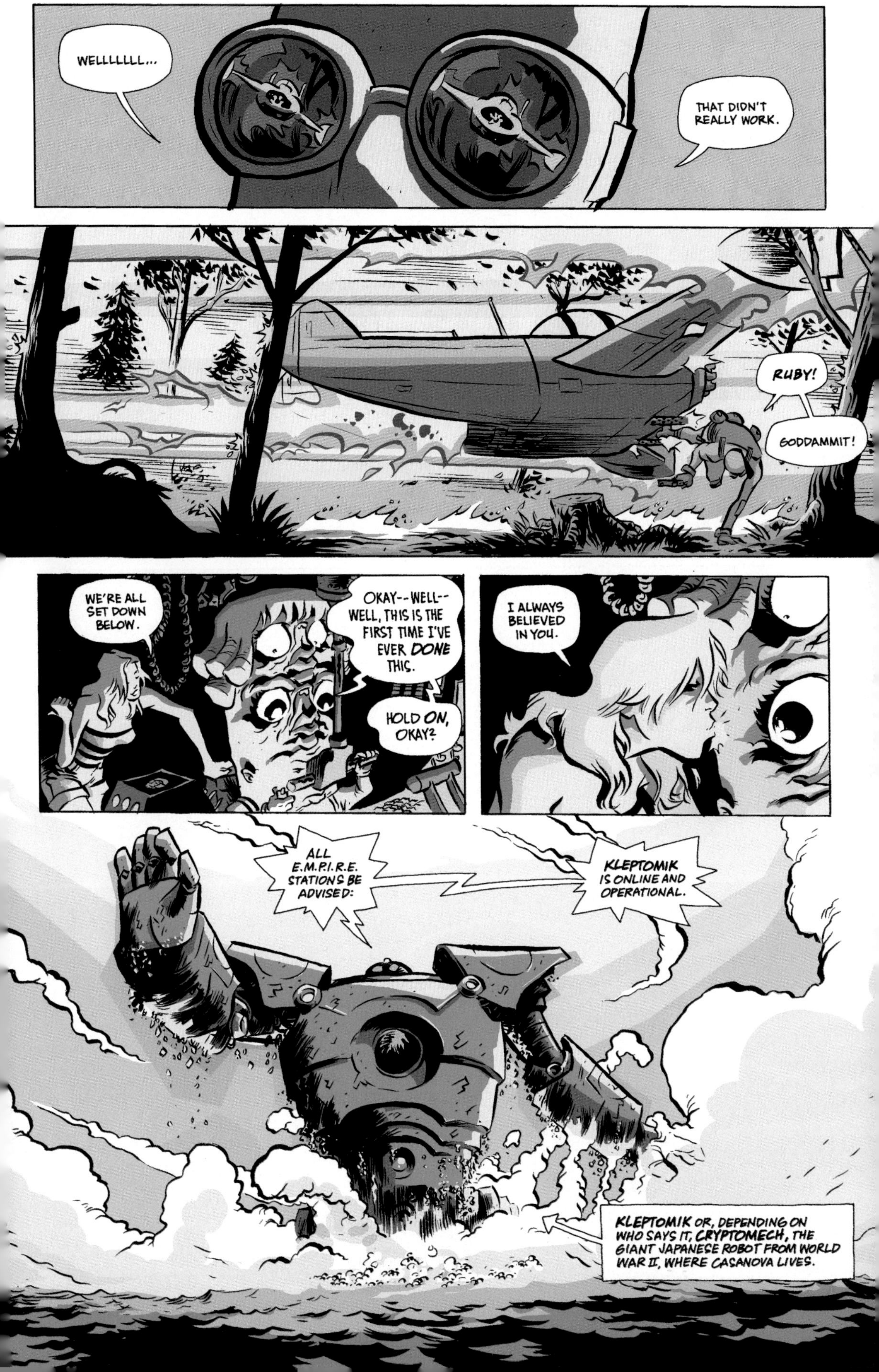
WELLLLLLLL...
THAT DIDN'T REALLY WORK.
RUBY!
GODDAMMIT!
WE'RE ALL SET DOWN BELOW.
OKAY--WELL--WELL, THIS IS THE FIRST TIME I'VE EVER DONE THIS.
HOLD ON, OKAY?
I ALWAYS BELIEVED IN YOU.
ALL E.M.P.I.R.E. STATIONS BE ADVISED:
KLEPTOMIK IS ONLINE AND OPERATIONAL.
KLEPTOMIK OR, DEPENDING ON WHO SAYS IT, CRYPTOMECH, THE GIANT JAPANESE ROBOT FROM WORLD WAR II, WHERE CASANOVA LIVES.

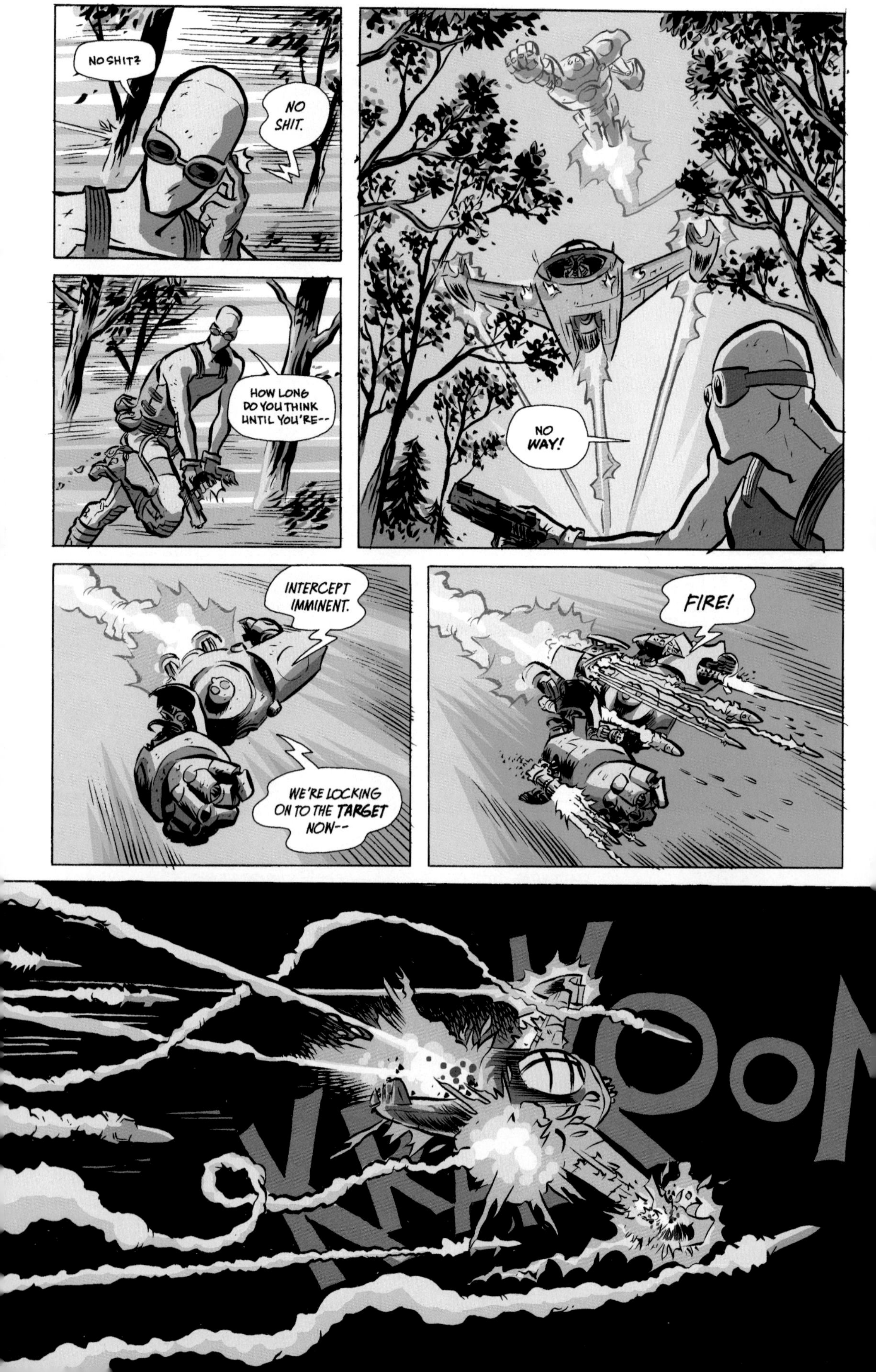
NO SHIT?
NO SHIT.
HOW LONG DO YOU THINK UNTIL YOU'RE--
NO WAY!
INTERCEPT IMMINENT.
WE'RE LOCKING ON TO THE TARGET NOW--
FIRE!

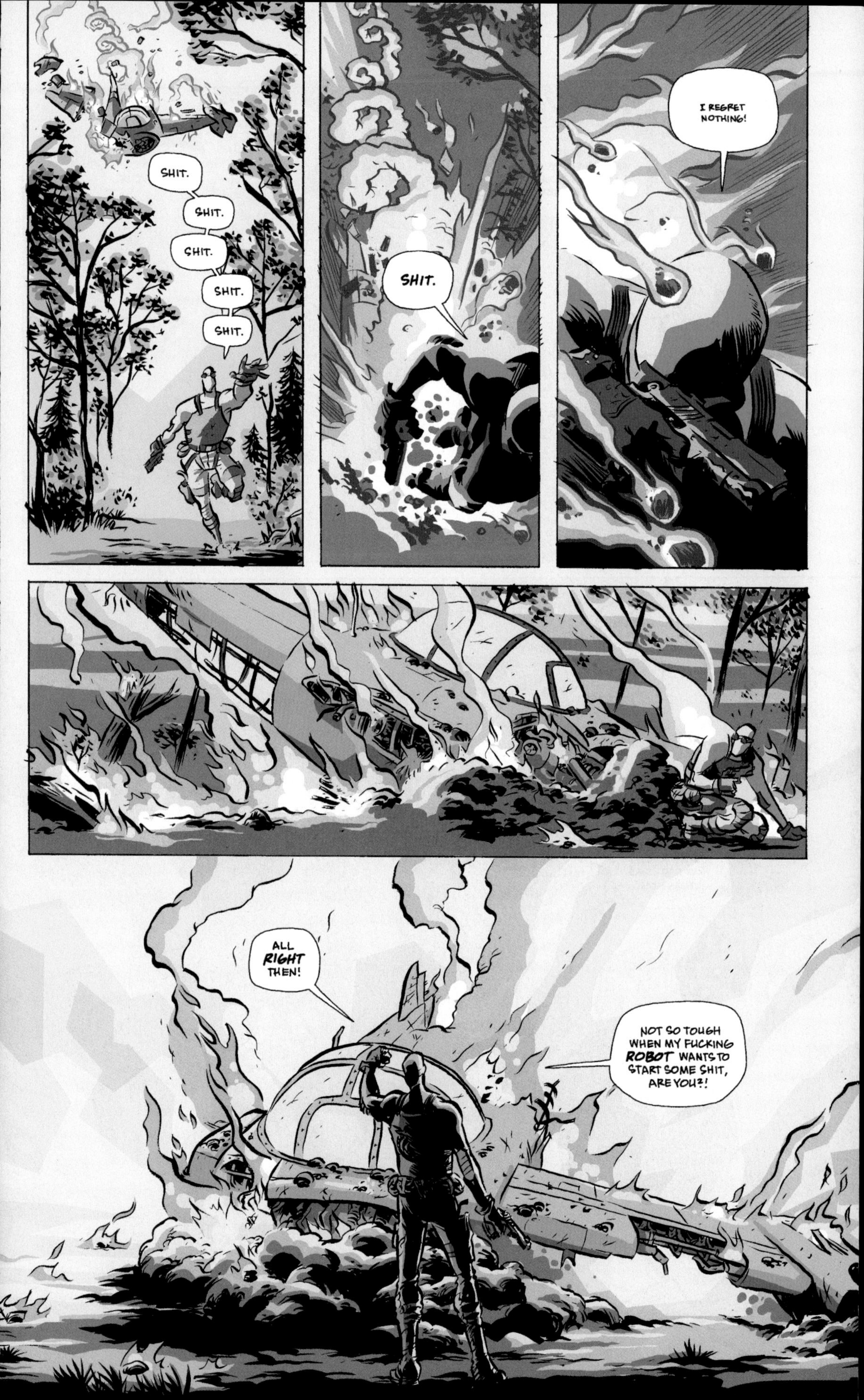
SHIT.
SHIT.
SHIT.
SHIT.
SHIT.
SHIT.
I REGRET NOTHING!
ALL RIGHT THEN!
NOT SO TOUGH WHEN MY FUCKING ROBOT WANTS TO START SOME SHIT, ARE YOU?!

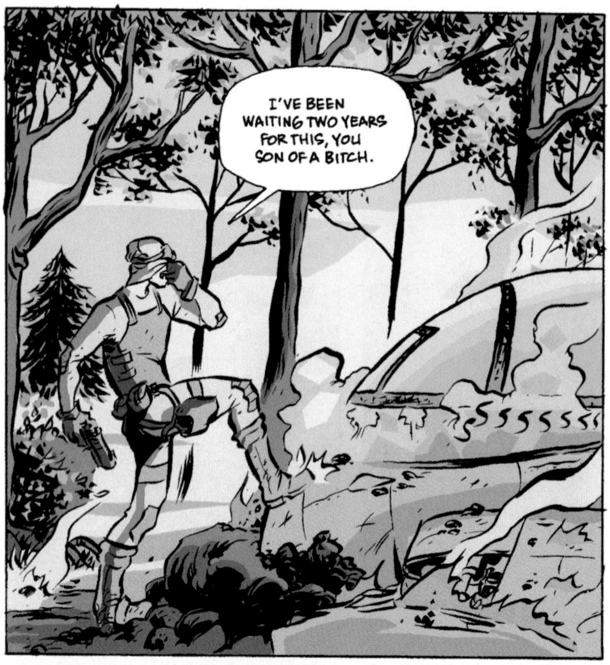
I'VE BEEN WAITING TWO YEARS FOR THIS, YOU SON OF A BITCH.

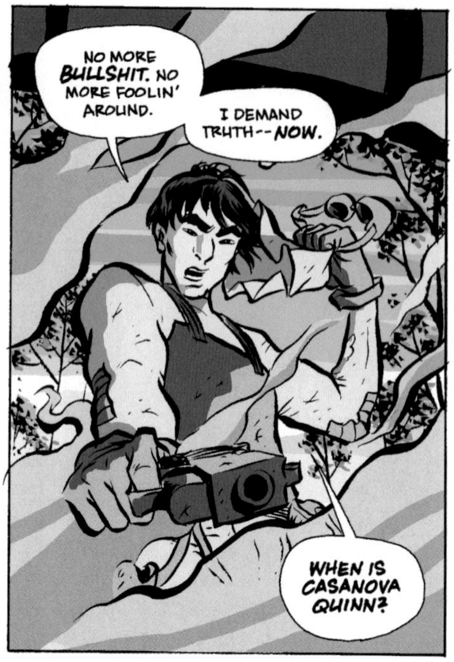
NO MORE BULLSHIT. NO MORE FOOLIN' AROUND.
I DEMAND TRUTH--NOW.
WHEN IS CASANOVA QUINN?

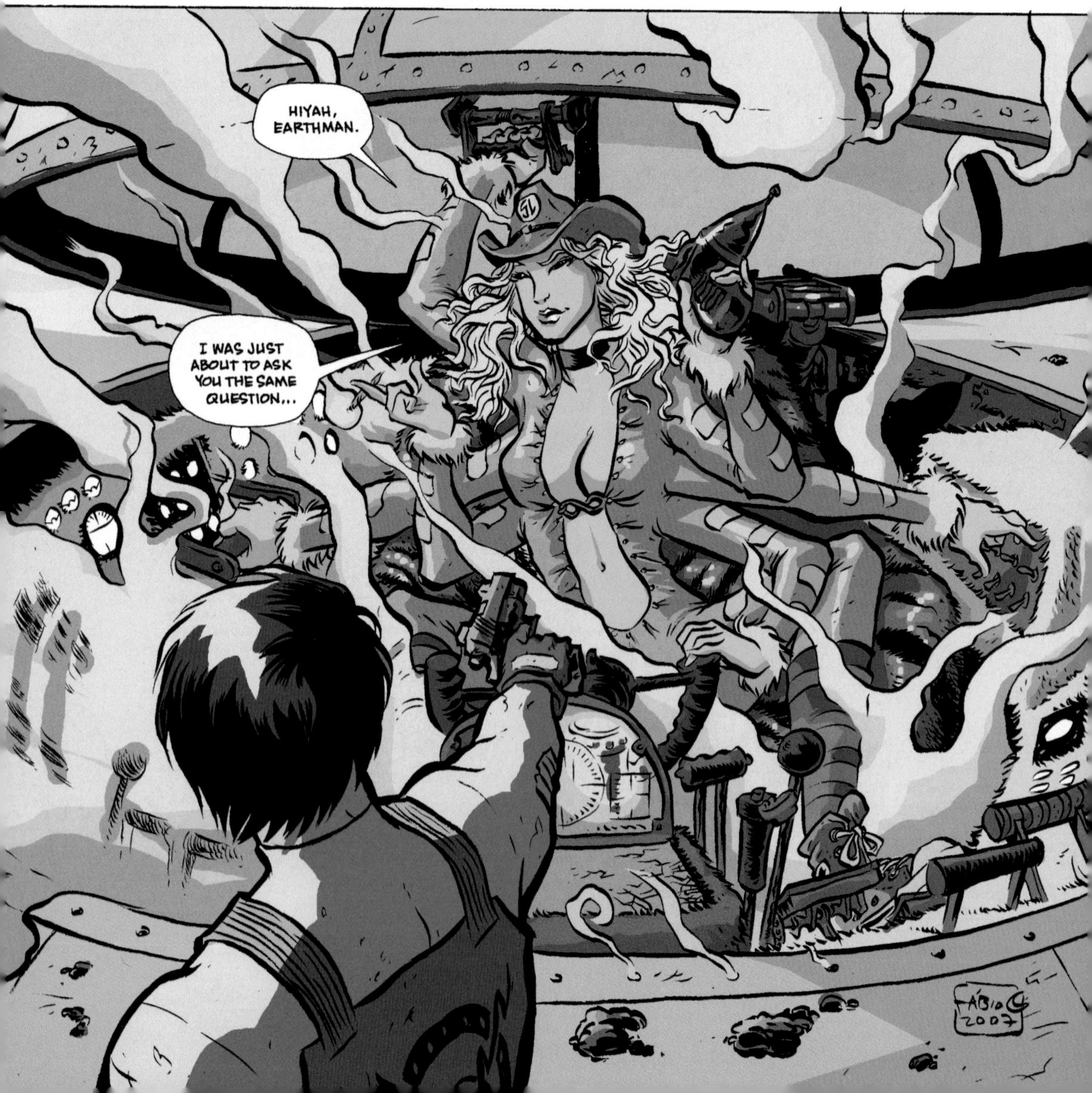
HIYAH, EARTHMAN.
I WAS JUST ABOUT TO ASK YOU THE SAME QUESTION...
FÁBIO 2007

CHAPTER 2
WHEN THE WOLF COMES HOME

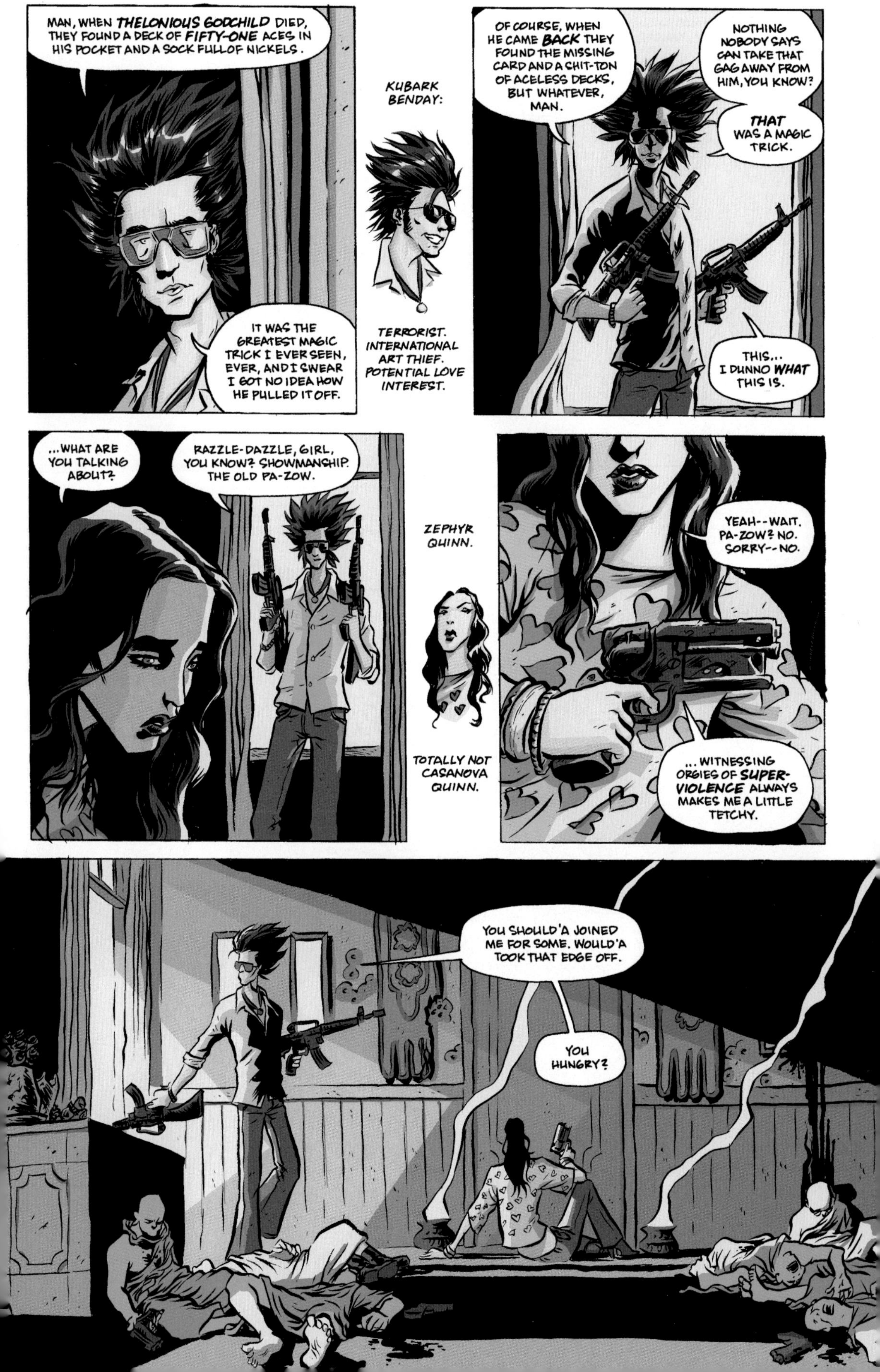
MAN, WHEN THELONIOUS GODCHILD DIED, THEY FOUND A DECK OF FIFTY-ONE ACES IN HIS POCKET AND A SOCK FULL OF NICKELS.
IT WAS THE GREATEST MAGIC TRICK I EVER SEEN, EVER, AND I SWEAR I GOT NO IDEA HOW HE PULLED IT OFF.
KUBARK BENDAY:
TERRORIST. INTERNATIONAL ART THIEF. POTENTIAL LOVE INTEREST.
OF COURSE, WHEN HE CAME BACK THEY FOUND THE MISSING CARD AND A CHIT-TON OF ACELESS DECKS, BUT WHATEVER, MAN.
NOTHING NOBODY SAYS CAN TAKE THAT GAG AWAY FROM HIM, YOU KNOW?
THAT WAS A MAGIC TRICK.
THIS... I DUNNO WHAT THIS IS.
...WHAT ARE YOU TALKING ABOUT?
RAZZLE-DAZZLE, GIRL, YOU KNOW? SHOWMANSHIP. THE OLD PA-ZOW.
ZEPHYR QUINN.
TOTALLY NOT CASANOVA QUINN.
YEAH--WAIT. PA-ZOW? NO. SORRY--NO.
...WITNESSING ORGIES OF SUPER-VIOLENCE ALWAYS MAKES ME A LITTLE TETCHY.
YOU SHOULD'A JOINED ME FOR SOME. WOULD'A TOOK THAT EDGE OFF.
YOU HUNGRY?

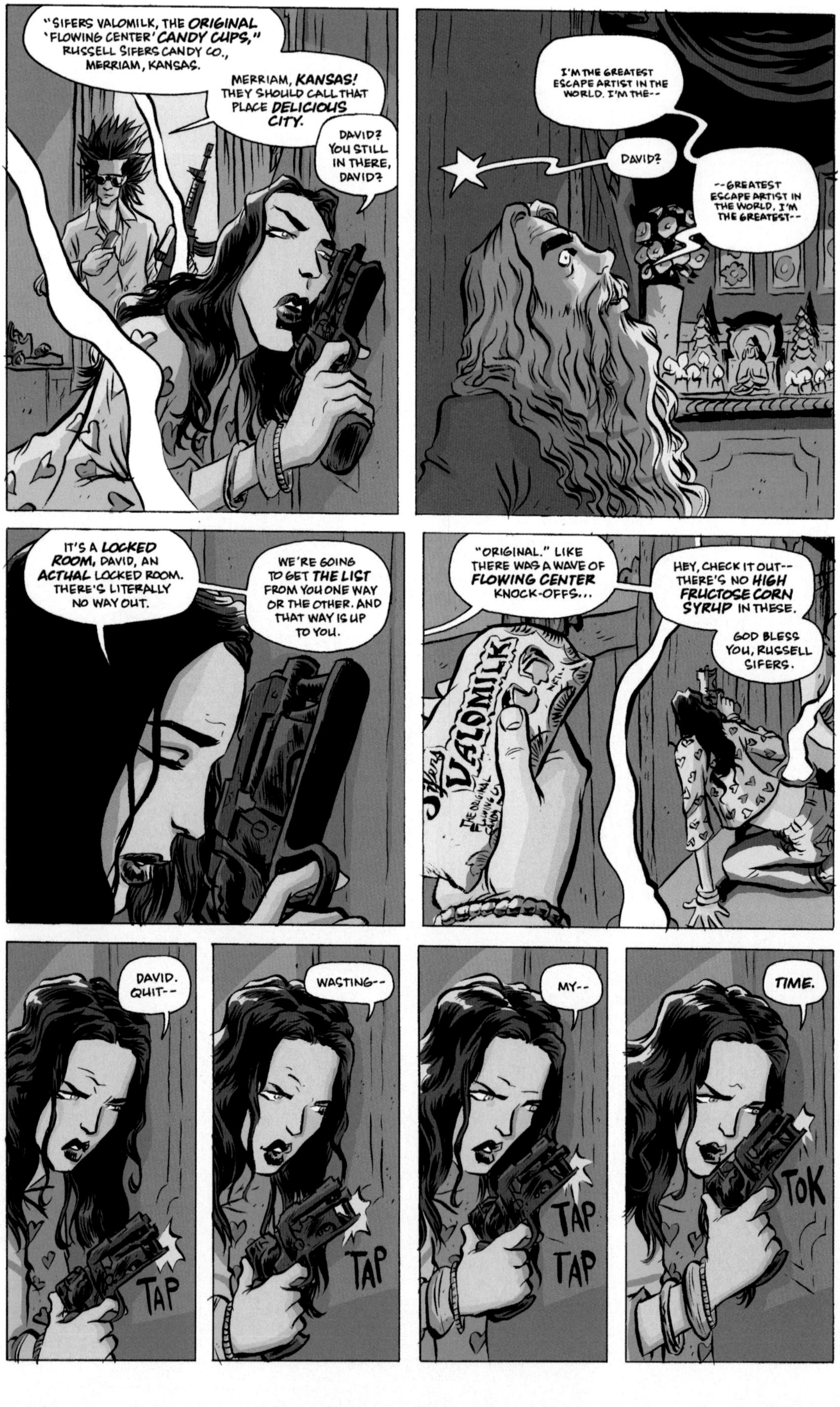
"SIFERS VALOMILK, THE ORIGINAL 'FLOWING CENTER' CANDY CUPS," RUSSELL SIFERS CANDY CO., MERRIAM, KANSAS.
MERRIAM, KANSAS! THEY SHOULD CALL THAT PLACE DELICIOUS CITY.
DAVID? YOU STILL IN THERE, DAVID?
I'M THE GREATEST ESCAPE ARTIST IN THE WORLD. I'M THE--
DAVID?
--GREATEST ESCAPE ARTIST IN THE WORLD, THE GREATEST--
IT'S A LOCKED ROOM, DAVID, AN ACTUAL LOCKED ROOM. THERE'S LITERALLY NO WAY OUT.
WE'RE GOING TO GET THE LIST FROM YOU ONE WAY OR THE OTHER. AND THAT WAY IS UP TO YOU.
"ORIGINAL." LIKE THERE WAS A WAVE OF FLOWING CENTER KNOCK-OFFS...
HEY, CHECK IT OUT-- THERE'S NO HIGH FRUCTOSE CORN SYRUP IN THESE.
GOD BLESS YOU, RUSSELL SIFERS.
VALOMILK
DAVID. QUIT--
TAP
WASTING--
TAP
MY--
TAP
TAP
TIME.
TOK

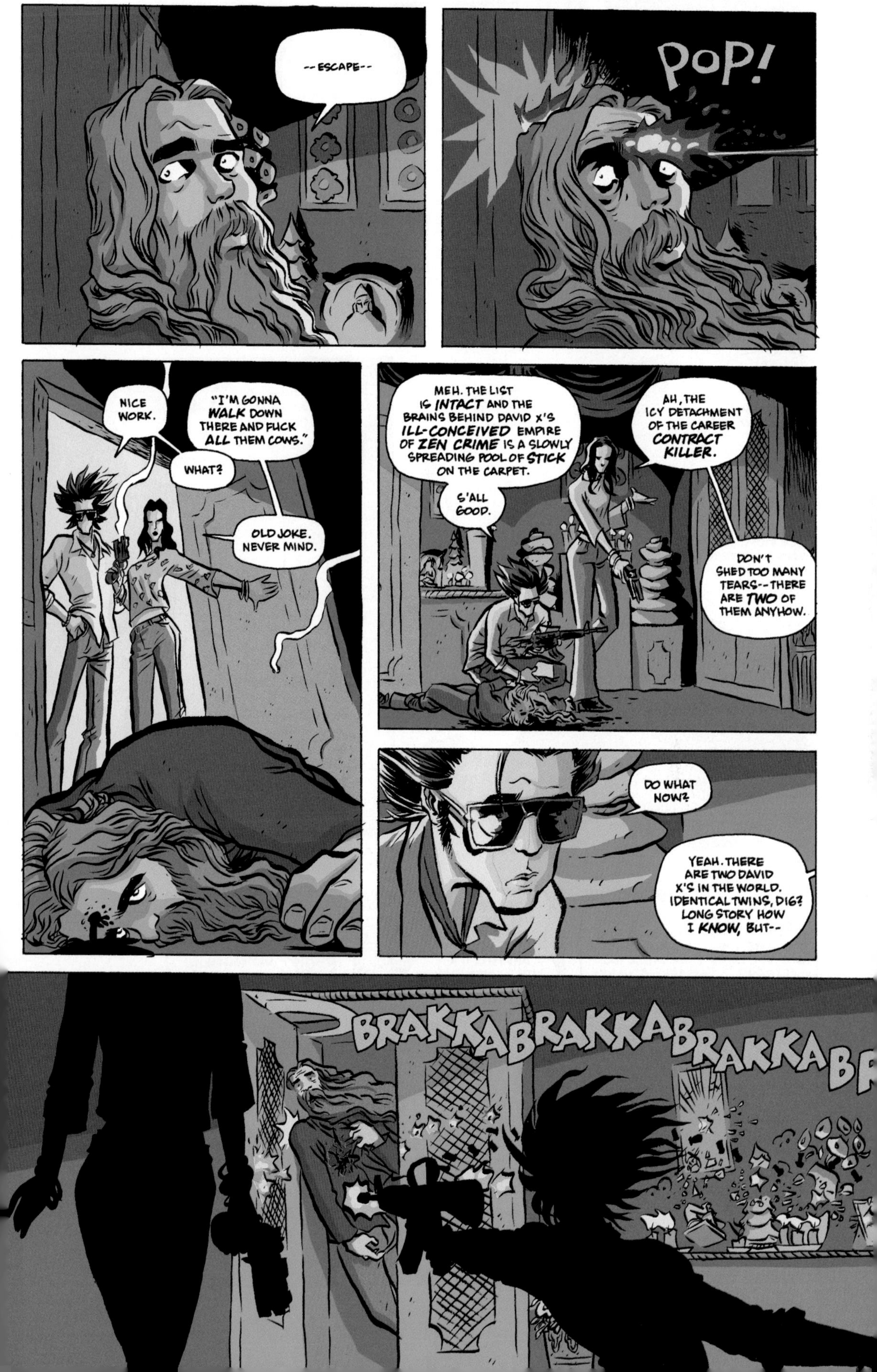
--ESCAPE--
POP!
NICE WORK.
"I'M GONNA WALK DOWN THERE AND FUCK ALL THEM COWS."
WHAT?
OLD JOKE. NEVER MIND.
MEH. THE LIST IS INTACT AND THE BRAINS BEHIND DAVID X'S ILL-CONCEIVED EMPIRE OF ZEN CRIME IS A SLOWLY SPREADING POOL OF STICK ON THE CARPET.
S'ALL GOOD.
AH, THE ICY DETACHMENT OF THE CAREER CONTRACT KILLER.
DON'T SHED TOO MANY TEARS--THERE ARE TWO OF THEM ANYHOW.
DO WHAT NOW?
YEAH. THERE ARE TWO DAVID X'S IN THE WORLD. IDENTICAL TWINS, DIG? LONG STORY HOW I KNOW, BUT--
BRAKKABRAKKABRAKKABR

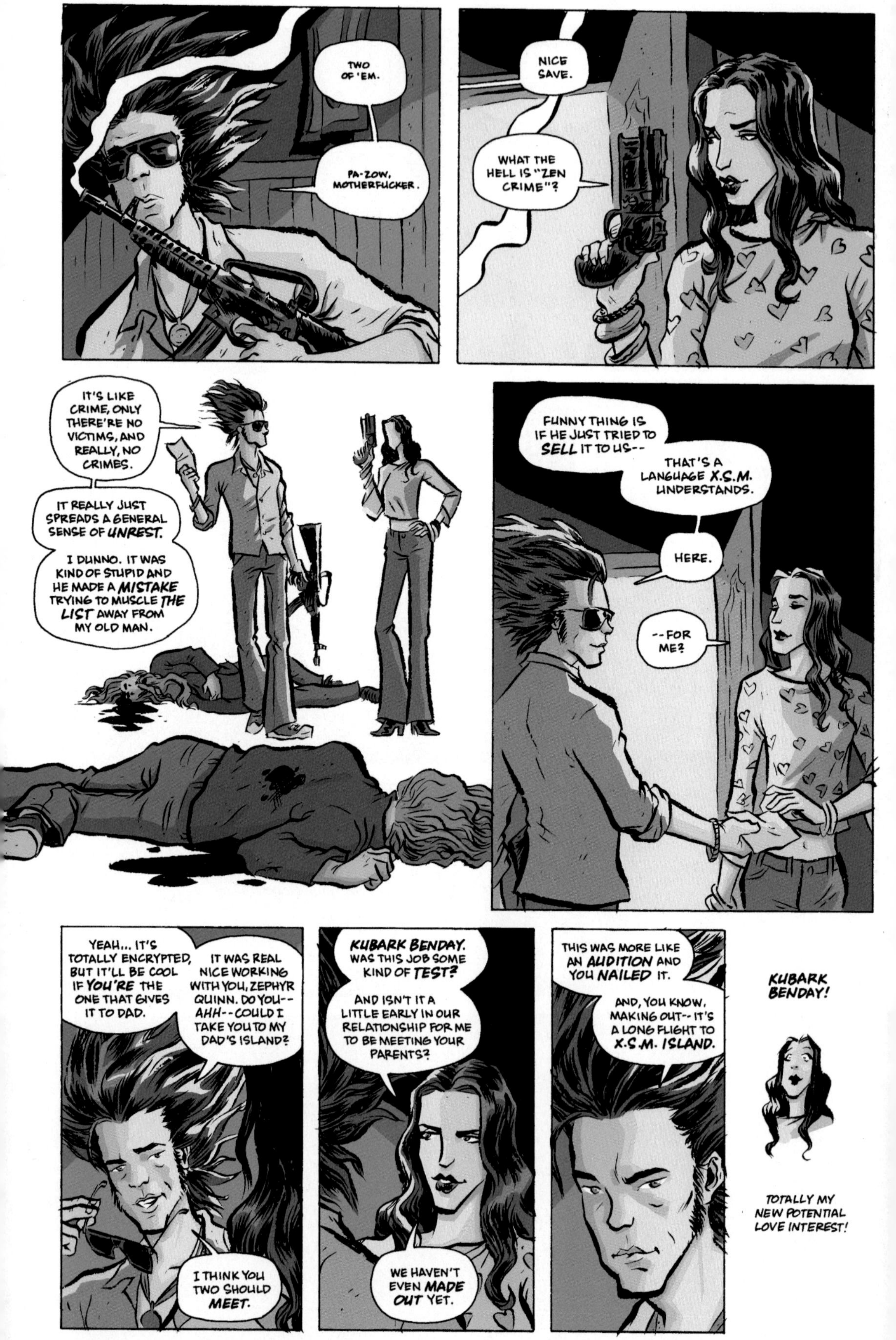
TWO OF 'EM.
PA-ZOW, MOTHERFUCKER.
NICE SAVE.
WHAT THE HELL IS "ZEN CRIME"?
IT'S LIKE CRIME, ONLY THERE'RE NO VICTIMS, AND REALLY, NO CRIMES.
IT REALLY JUST SPREADS A GENERAL SENSE OF UNREST.
I DUNNO. IT WAS KIND OF STUPID AND HE MADE A MISTAKE TRYING TO MUSCLE THE LIST AWAY FROM MY OLD MAN.
FUNNY THING IS IF HE JUST TRIED TO SELL IT TO US--
THAT'S A LANGUAGE X.S.M. UNDERSTANDS.
HERE.
--FOR ME?
YEAH... IT'S TOTALLY ENCRYPTED, BUT IT'LL BE COOL IF YOU'RE THE ONE THAT GIVES IT TO DAD.
IT WAS REAL NICE WORKING WITH YOU, ZEPHYR QUINN. DO YOU-- AHH--COULD I TAKE YOU TO MY DAD'S ISLAND?
I THINK YOU TWO SHOULD MEET.
KUBARK BENDAY. WAS THIS JOB SOME KIND OF TEST?
AND ISN'T IT A LITTLE EARLY IN OUR RELATIONSHIP FOR ME TO BE MEETING YOUR PARENTS?
WE HAVEN'T EVEN MADE OUT YET.
THIS WAS MORE LIKE AN AUDITION AND YOU NAILED IT.
AND, YOU KNOW, MAKING OUT-- IT'S A LONG FLIGHT TO X.S.M. ISLAND.
KUBARK BENDAY!
TOTALLY MY NEW POTENTIAL LOVE INTEREST!

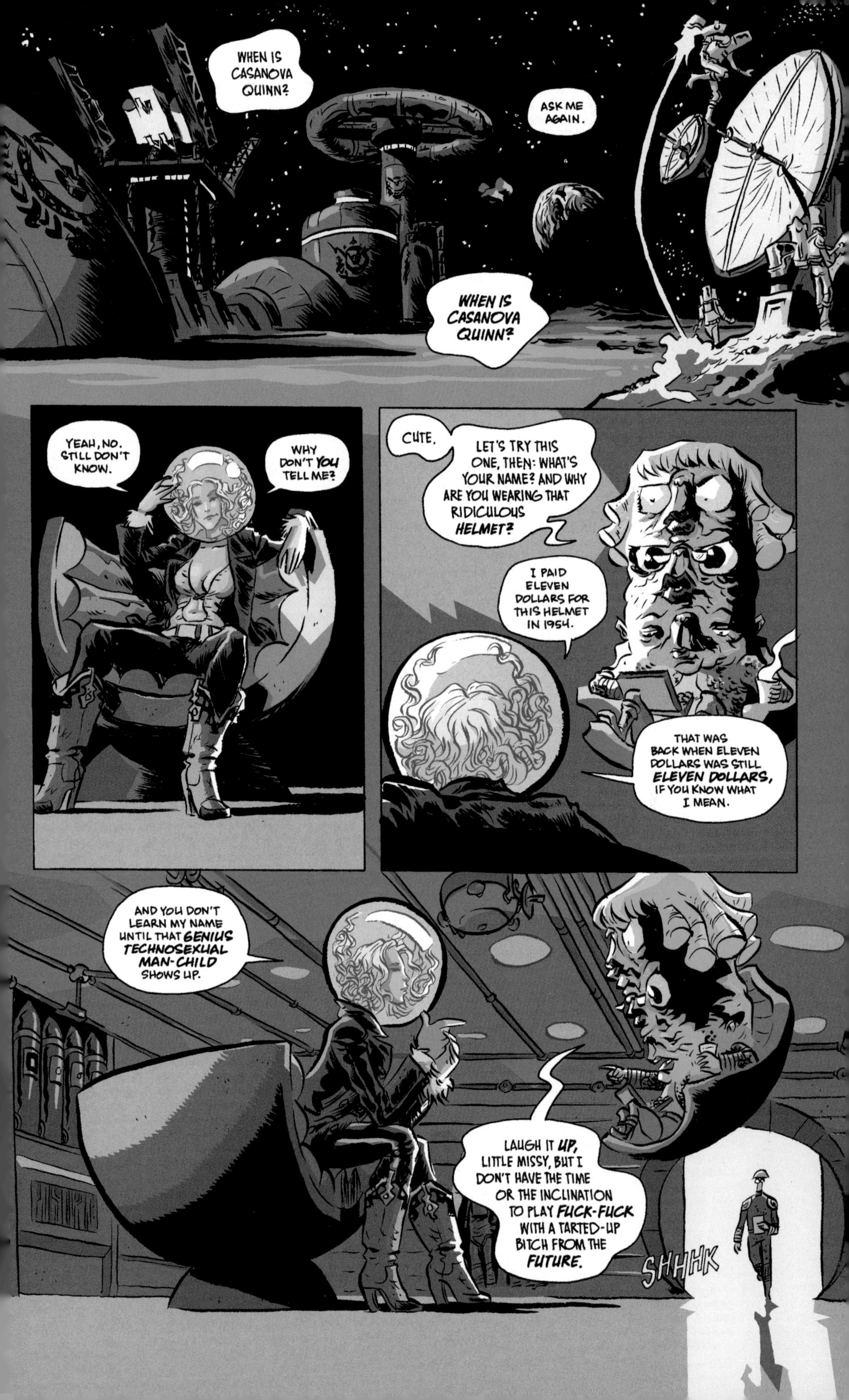

WHEN IS CASANOVA QUINN?
ASK ME AGAIN.
WHEN IS CASANOVA QUINN?
YEAH, NO. STILL DON'T KNOW.
WHY DON'T YOU TELL ME?
CUTE.
LET'S TRY THIS ONE, THEN: WHAT'S YOUR NAME? AND WHY ARE YOU WEARING THAT RIDICULOUS HELMET?
I PAID ELEVEN DOLLARS FOR THIS HELMET IN 1954.
THAT WAS BACK WHEN ELEVEN DOLLARS WAS STILL ELEVEN DOLLARS, IF YOU KNOW WHAT I MEAN.
AND YOU DON'T LEARN MY NAME UNTIL THAT GENIUS TECHNOSEXUAL MAN-CHILD SHOWS UP.
LAUGH IT UP, LITTLE MISSY, BUT I DON'T HAVE THE TIME OR THE INCLINATION TO PLAY FUCK-FUCK WITH A TARTED-UP BITCH FROM THE FUTURE.
SHHHK

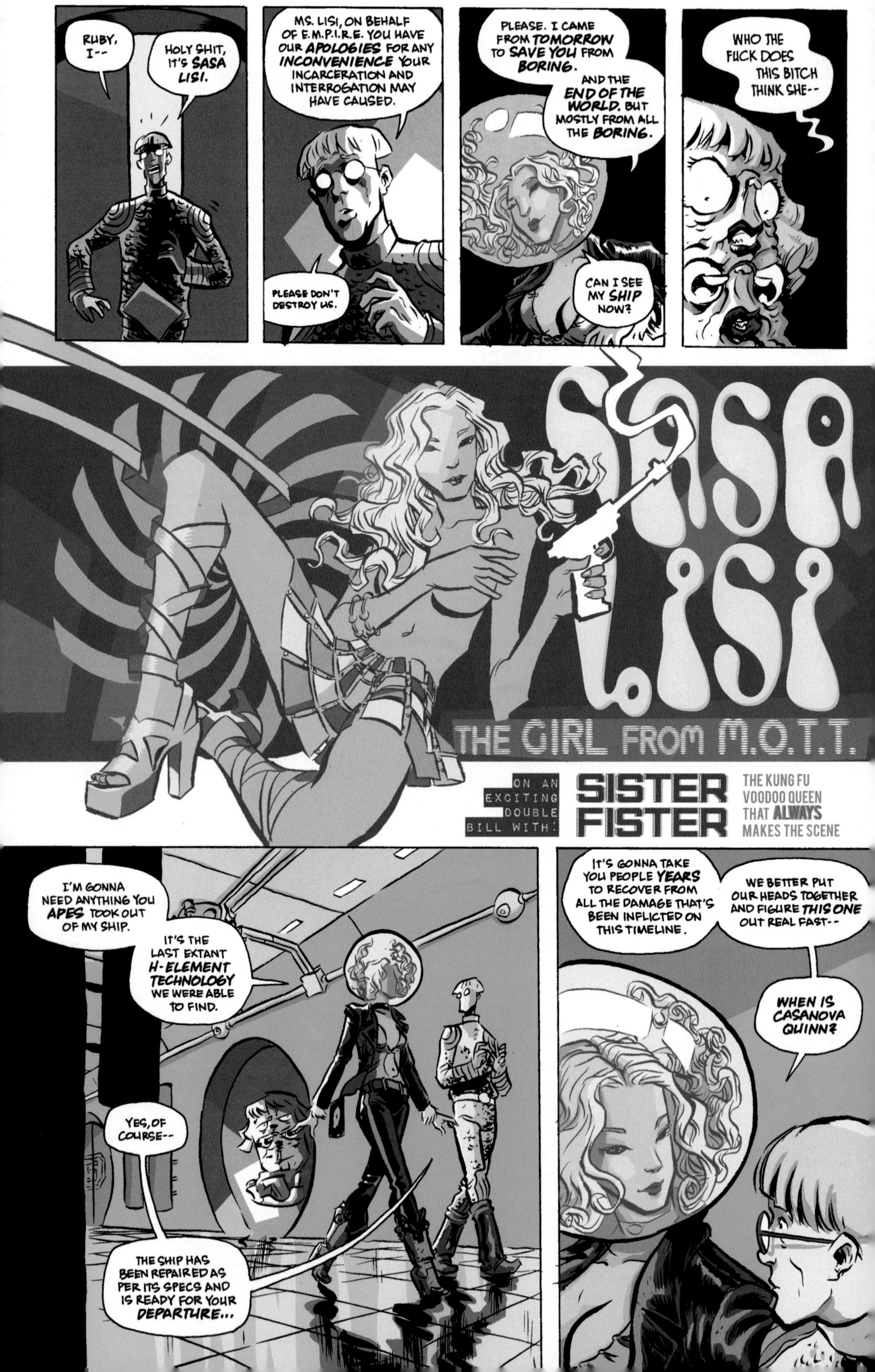

RUBY, I--
HOLY SHIT, IT'S SASA LISI.
MS. LISI, ON BEHALF OF E.M.P.I.R.E. YOU HAVE OUR APOLOGIES FOR ANY INCONVENIENCE YOUR INCARCERATION AND INTERROGATION MAY HAVE CAUSED.
PLEASE DON'T DESTROY US.
PLEASE. I CAME FROM TOMORROW TO SAVE YOU FROM BORING.
AND THE END OF THE WORLD. BUT MOSTLY FROM ALL THE BORING.
CAN I SEE MY SHIP NOW?
WHO THE FUCK DOES THIS BITCH THINK SHE--
SASA LISI
THE GIRL FROM M.O.T.T.
ON AN EXCITING DOUBLE BILL WITH:
SISTER FISTER
THE KUNG FU VOODOO QUEEN THAT ALWAYS MAKES THE SCENE
I'M GONNA NEED ANYTHING YOU APES TOOK OUT OF MY SHIP.
IT'S THE LAST EXTANT H-ELEMENT TECHNOLOGY WE WERE ABLE TO FIND.
YES, OF COURSE--
THE SHIP HAS BEEN REPAIRED AS PER ITS SPECS AND IS READY FOR YOUR DEPARTURE...
IT'S GONNA TAKE YOU PEOPLE YEARS TO RECOVER FROM ALL THE DAMAGE THAT'S BEEN INFLICTED ON THIS TIMELINE.
WE BETTER PUT OUR HEADS TOGETHER AND FIGURE THIS ONE OUT REAL FAST--
WHEN IS CASANOVA QUINN?

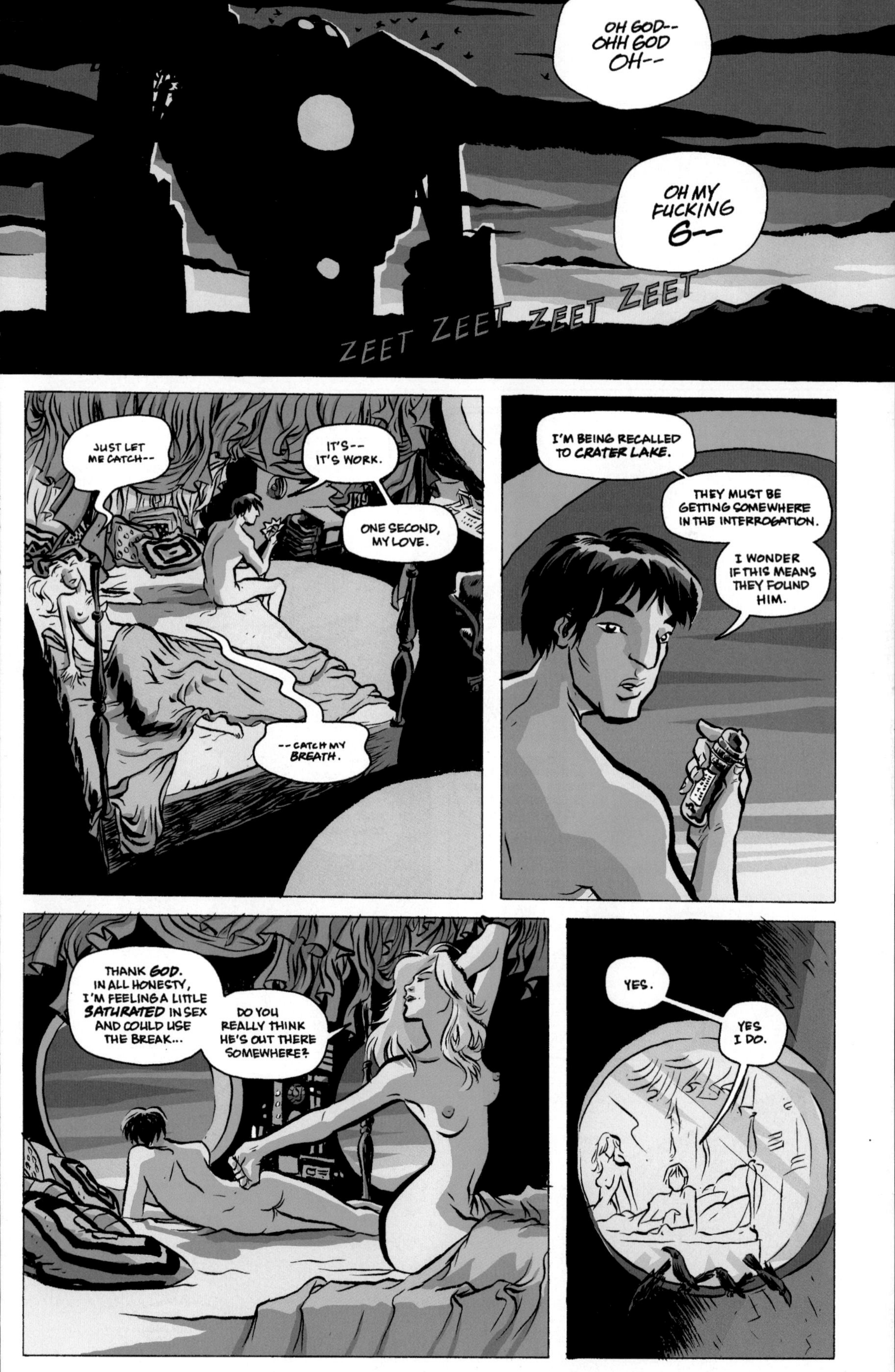
OH GOD--
OHH GOD
OH--
OH MY FUCKING G--
ZEET ZEET ZEET ZEET
JUST LET ME CATCH--
IT'S-- IT'S WORK.
ONE SECOND, MY LOVE.
--CATCH MY BREATH.
I'M BEING RECALLED TO CRATER LAKE.
THEY MUST BE GETTING SOMEWHERE IN THE INTERROGATION.
I WONDER IF THIS MEANS THEY FOUND HIM.
THANK GOD. IN ALL HONESTY, I'M FEELING A LITTLE SATURATED IN SEX AND COULD USE THE BREAK...
DO YOU REALLY THINK HE'S OUT THERE SOMEWHERE?
YES.
YES I DO.

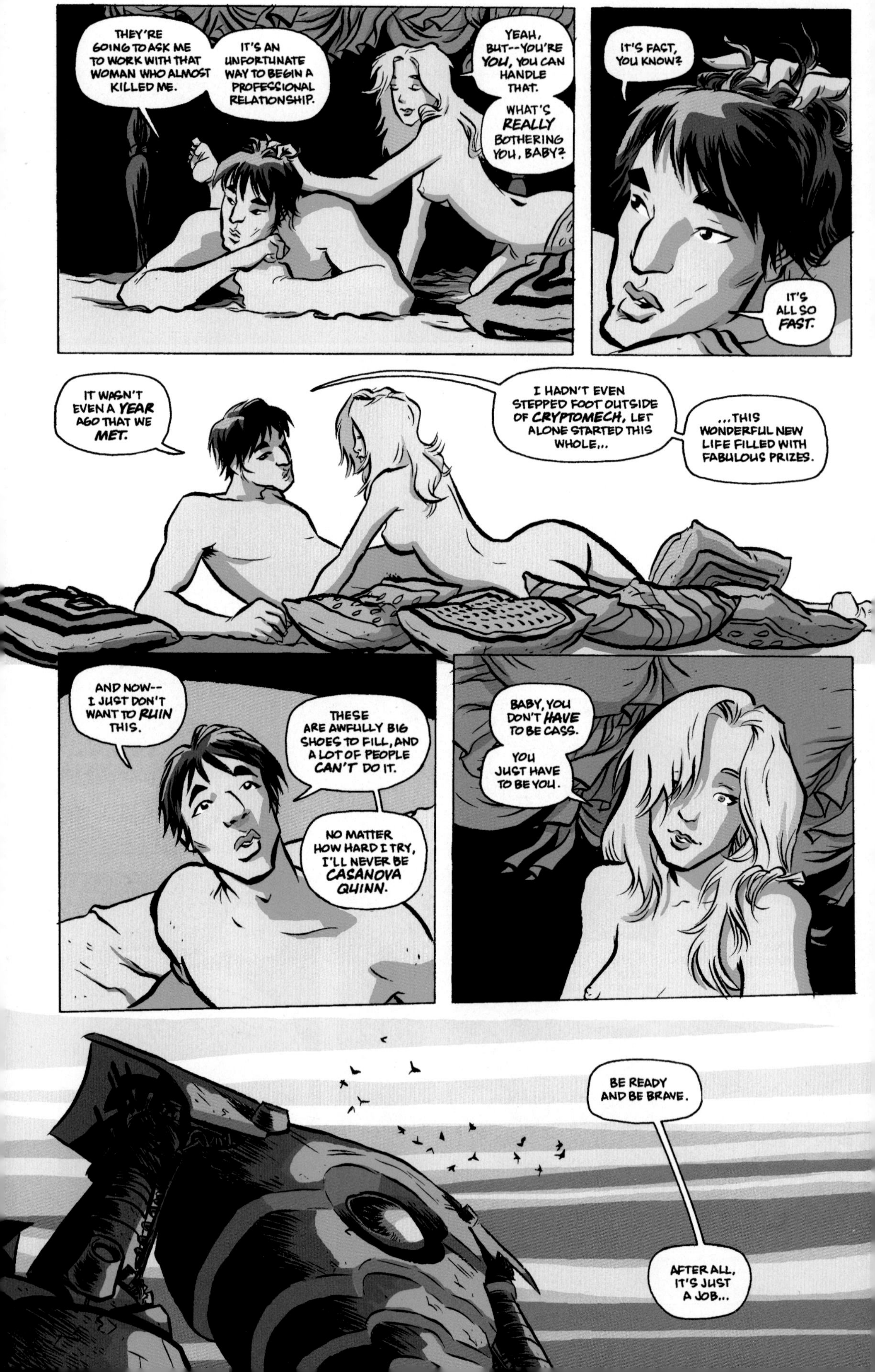
THEY'RE GOING TO ASK ME TO WORK WITH THAT WOMAN WHO ALMOST KILLED ME.
IT'S AN UNFORTUNATE WAY TO BEGIN A PROFESSIONAL RELATIONSHIP.
YEAH, BUT--YOU'RE YOU, YOU CAN HANDLE THAT.
WHAT'S REALLY BOTHERING YOU, BABY?
IT'S FACT, YOU KNOW?
IT'S ALL SO FAST.
IT WASN'T EVEN A YEAR AGO THAT WE MET.
I HADN'T EVEN STEPPED FOOT OUTSIDE OF CRYPTOMECH, LET ALONE STARTED THIS WHOLE...
...THIS WONDERFUL NEW LIFE FILLED WITH FABULOUS PRIZES.
AND NOW-- I JUST DON'T WANT TO RUIN THIS.
THESE ARE AWFULLY BIG SHOES TO FILL, AND A LOT OF PEOPLE CAN'T DO IT.
NO MATTER HOW HARD I TRY, I'LL NEVER BE CASANOVA QUINN.
BABY, YOU DON'T HAVE TO BE CASS.
YOU JUST HAVE TO BE YOU.
BE READY AND BE BRAVE.
AFTER ALL, IT'S JUST A JOB...

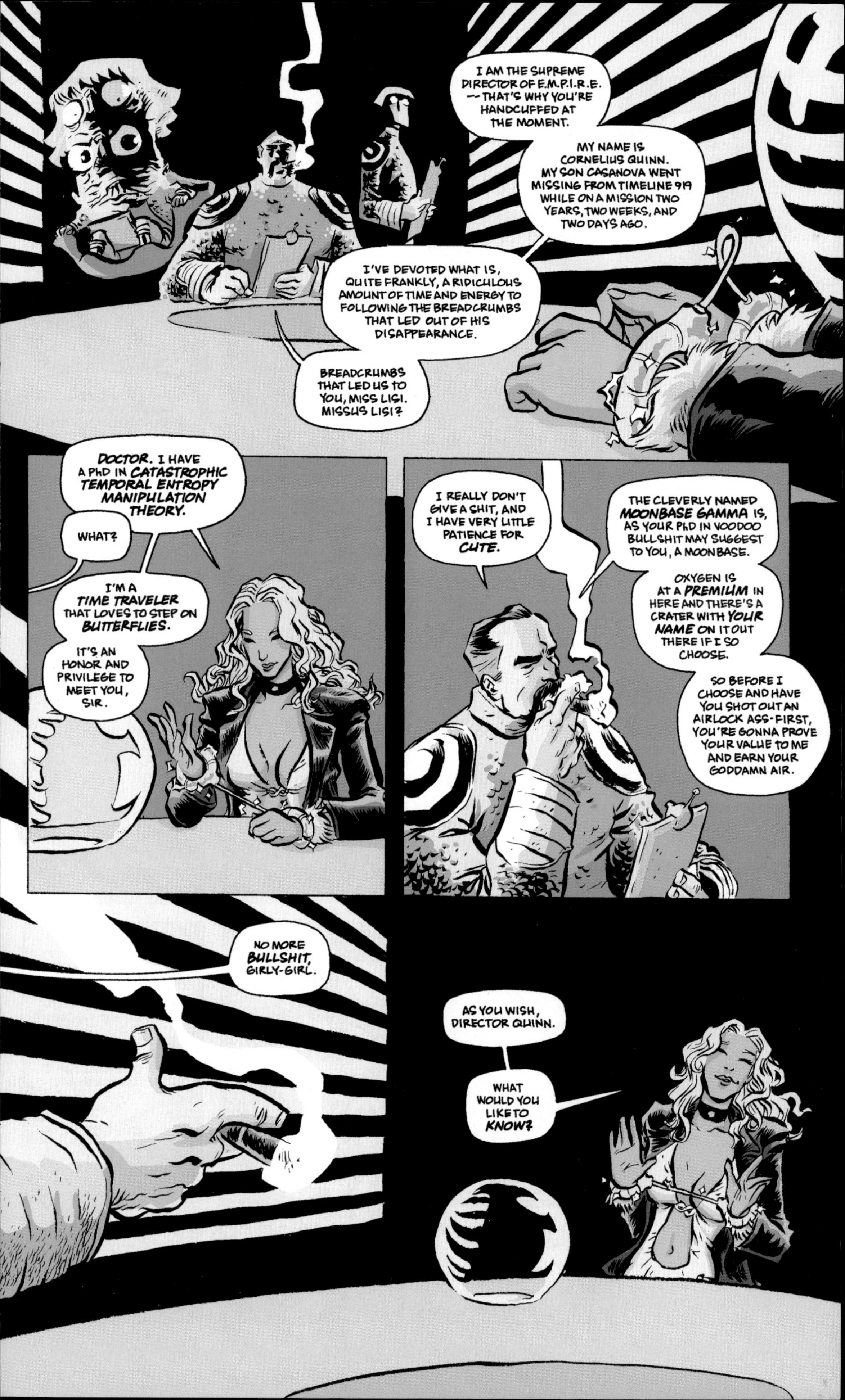
I AM THE SUPREME DIRECTOR OF E.M.P.I.R.E. -- THAT'S WHY YOU'RE HANDCUFFED AT THE MOMENT.
MY NAME IS CORNELIUS QUINN. MY SON CASANOVA WENT MISSING FROM TIMELINE 919 WHILE ON A MISSION TWO YEARS, TWO WEEKS, AND TWO DAYS AGO.
I'VE DEVOTED WHAT IS, QUITE FRANKLY, A RIDICULOUS AMOUNT OF TIME AND ENERGY TO FOLLOWING THE BREADCRUMBS THAT LED OUT OF HIS DISAPPEARANCE.
BREADCRUMBS THAT LED US TO YOU, MISS LISI. MISSUS LISI?
DOCTOR. I HAVE A PhD IN CATASTROPHIC TEMPORAL ENTROPY MANIPULATION THEORY.
WHAT?
I'M A TIME TRAVELER THAT LOVES TO STEP ON BUTTERFLIES.
IT'S AN HONOR AND PRIVILEGE TO MEET YOU, SIR.
I REALLY DON'T GIVE A SHIT, AND I HAVE VERY LITTLE PATIENCE FOR CUTE.
THE CLEVERLY NAMED MOONBASE GAMMA IS, AS YOUR PhD IN VOODOO BULLSHIT MAY SUGGEST TO YOU, A MOONBASE.
OXYGEN IS AT A PREMIUM IN HERE AND THERE'S A CRATER WITH YOUR NAME ON IT OUT THERE IF I SO CHOOSE.
SO BEFORE I CHOOSE AND HAVE YOU SHOT OUT AN AIRLOCK ASS-FIRST, YOU'RE GONNA PROVE YOUR VALUE TO ME AND EARN YOUR GODDAMN AIR.
NO MORE BULLSHIT, GIRLY-GIRL.
AS YOU WISH, DIRECTOR QUINN.
WHAT WOULD YOU LIKE TO KNOW?

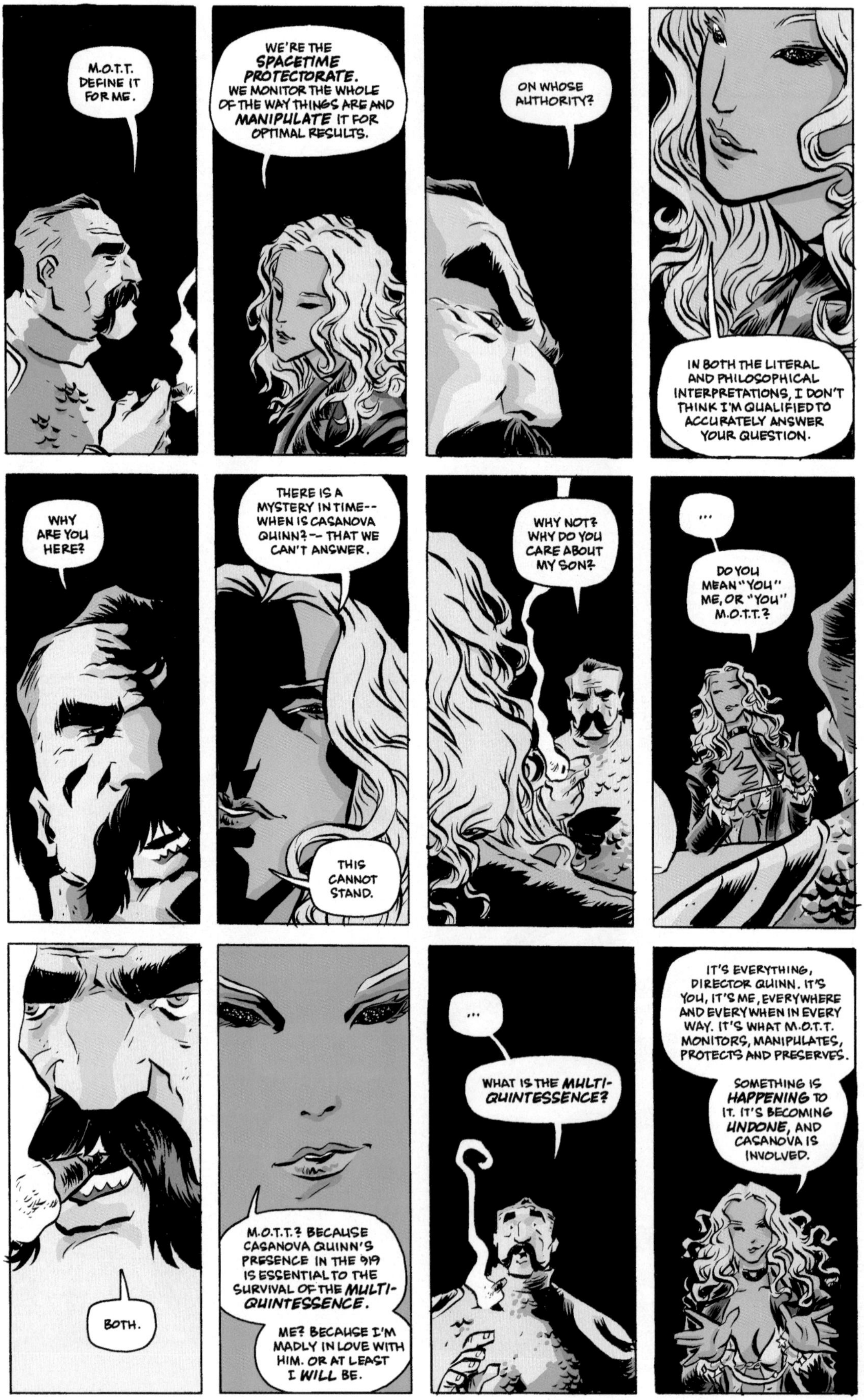
M.O.T.T. DEFINE IT FOR ME.
WE'RE THE SPACETIME PROTECTORATE. WE MONITOR THE WHOLE OF THE WAY THINGS ARE AND MANIPULATE IT FOR OPTIMAL RESULTS.
ON WHOSE AUTHORITY?
IN BOTH THE LITERAL AND PHILOSOPHICAL INTERPRETATIONS, I DON'T THINK I'M QUALIFIED TO ACCURATELY ANSWER YOUR QUESTION.
WHY ARE YOU HERE?
THERE IS A MYSTERY IN TIME-- WHEN IS CASANOVA QUINN?-- THAT WE CAN'T ANSWER.
THIS CANNOT STAND.
WHY NOT? WHY DO YOU CARE ABOUT MY SON?
...
DO YOU MEAN "YOU" ME, OR "YOU" M.O.T.T.?
BOTH.
M.O.T.T.? BECAUSE CASANOVA QUINN'S PRESENCE IN THE 919 IS ESSENTIAL TO THE SURVIVAL OF THE MULTI-QUINTESSENCE.
ME? BECAUSE I'M MADLY IN LOVE WITH HIM. OR AT LEAST I WILL BE.
...
WHAT IS THE MULTI-QUINTESSENCE?
IT'S EVERYTHING, DIRECTOR QUINN. IT'S YOU, IT'S ME, EVERYWHERE AND EVERYWHEN IN EVERY WAY. IT'S WHAT M.O.T.T. MONITORS, MANIPULATES, PROTECTS AND PRESERVES.
SOMETHING IS HAPPENING TO IT. IT'S BECOMING UNDONE, AND CASANOVA IS INVOLVED.

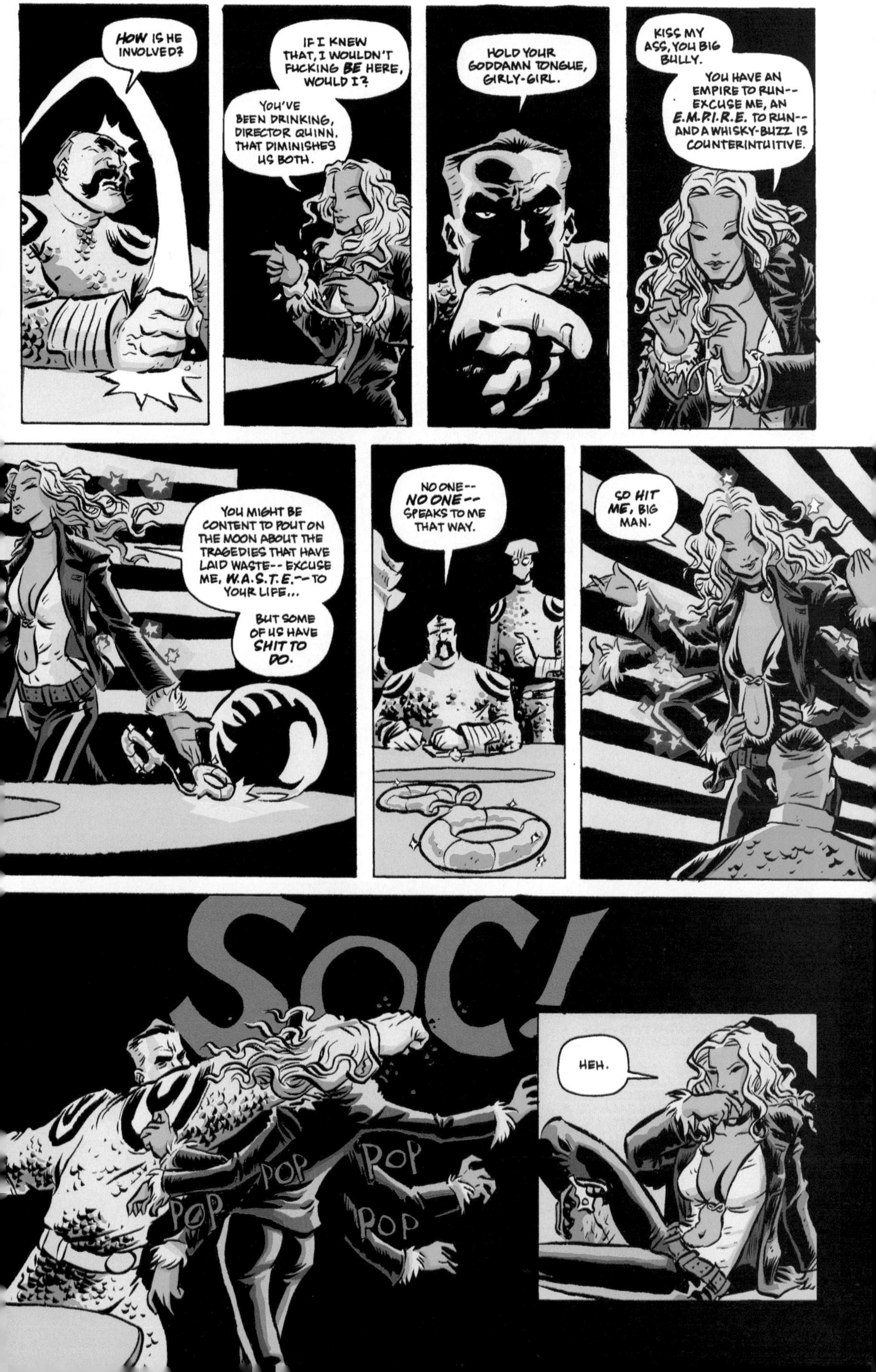
HOW IS HE INVOLVED?
IF I KNEW THAT, I WOULDN'T FUCKING BE HERE, WOULD I?
YOU'VE BEEN DRINKING, DIRECTOR QUINN. THAT DIMINISHES US BOTH.
HOLD YOUR GODDAMN TONGUE, GIRLY-GIRL.
KISS MY ASS, YOU BIG BULLY.
YOU HAVE AN EMPIRE TO RUN-- EXCUSE ME, AN E.M.P.I.R.E. TO RUN-- AND A WHISKY-BUZZ IS COUNTERINTUITIVE.
YOU MIGHT BE CONTENT TO POUT ON THE MOON ABOUT THE TRAGEDIES THAT HAVE LAID WASTE-- EXCUSE ME, W.A.S.T.E.-- TO YOUR LIFE...
BUT SOME OF US HAVE SHIT TO DO.
NO ONE-- NO ONE-- SPEAKS TO ME THAT WAY.
SO HIT ME, BIG MAN.
SOC!
POP
POP
POP
POP
HEH.

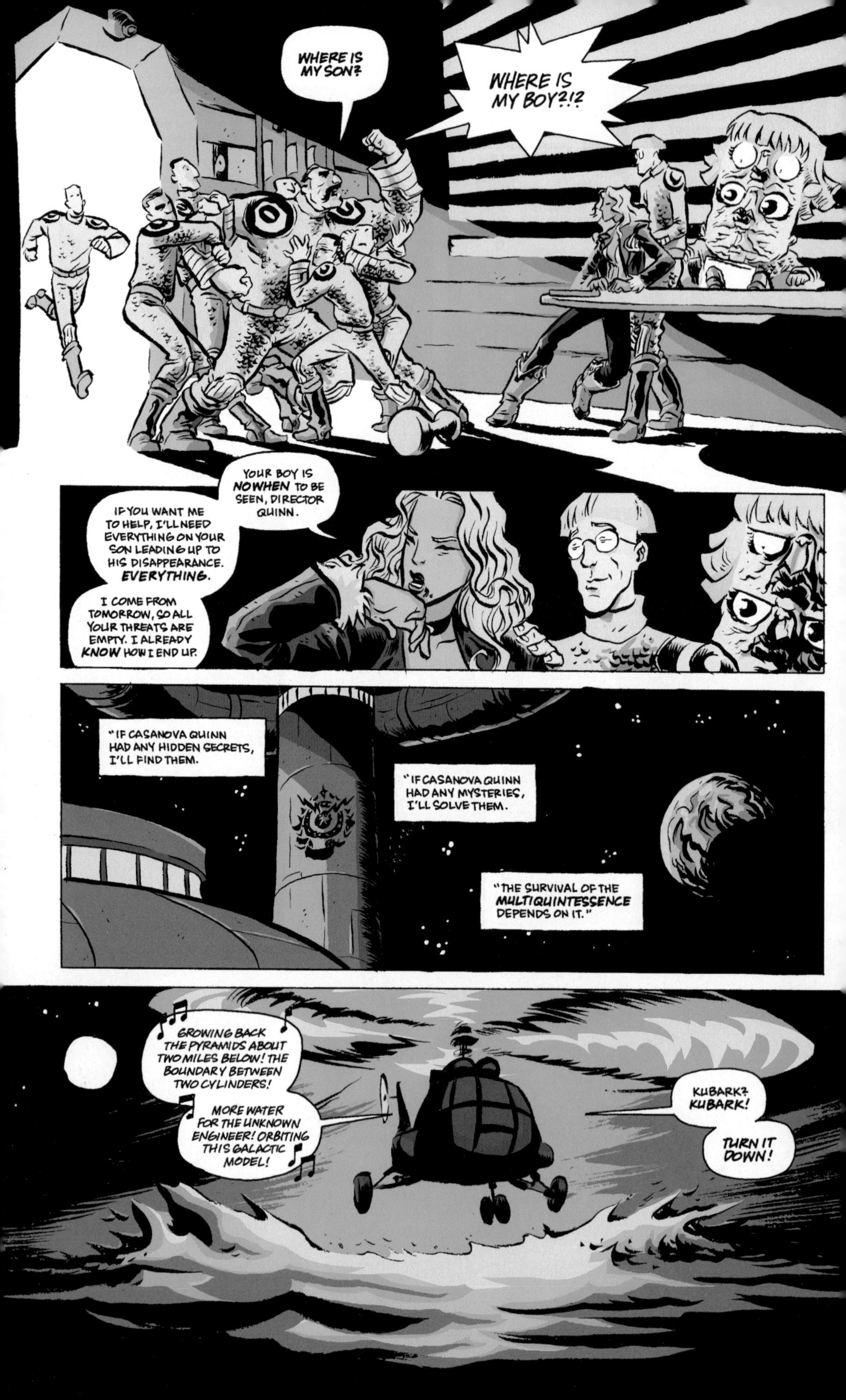
WHERE IS MY SON?
WHERE IS MY BOY?!?
YOUR BOY IS NOWHEN TO BE SEEN, DIRECTOR QUINN.
IF YOU WANT ME TO HELP, I'LL NEED EVERYTHING ON YOUR SON LEADING UP TO HIS DISAPPEARANCE. EVERYTHING.
I COME FROM TOMORROW, SO ALL YOUR THREATS ARE EMPTY. I ALREADY KNOW HOW I END UP.
"IF CASANOVA QUINN HAD ANY HIDDEN SECRETS, I'LL FIND THEM.
"IF CASANOVA QUINN HAD ANY MYSTERIES, I'LL SOLVE THEM.
"THE SURVIVAL OF THE MULTIQUINTESSENCE DEPENDS ON IT."
GROWING BACK THE PYRAMIDS ABOUT TWO MILES BELOW! THE BOUNDARY BETWEEN TWO CYLINDERS!
MORE WATER FOR THE UNKNOWN ENGINEER! ORBITING THIS GALACTIC MODEL!
KUBARK? KUBARK!
TURN IT DOWN!

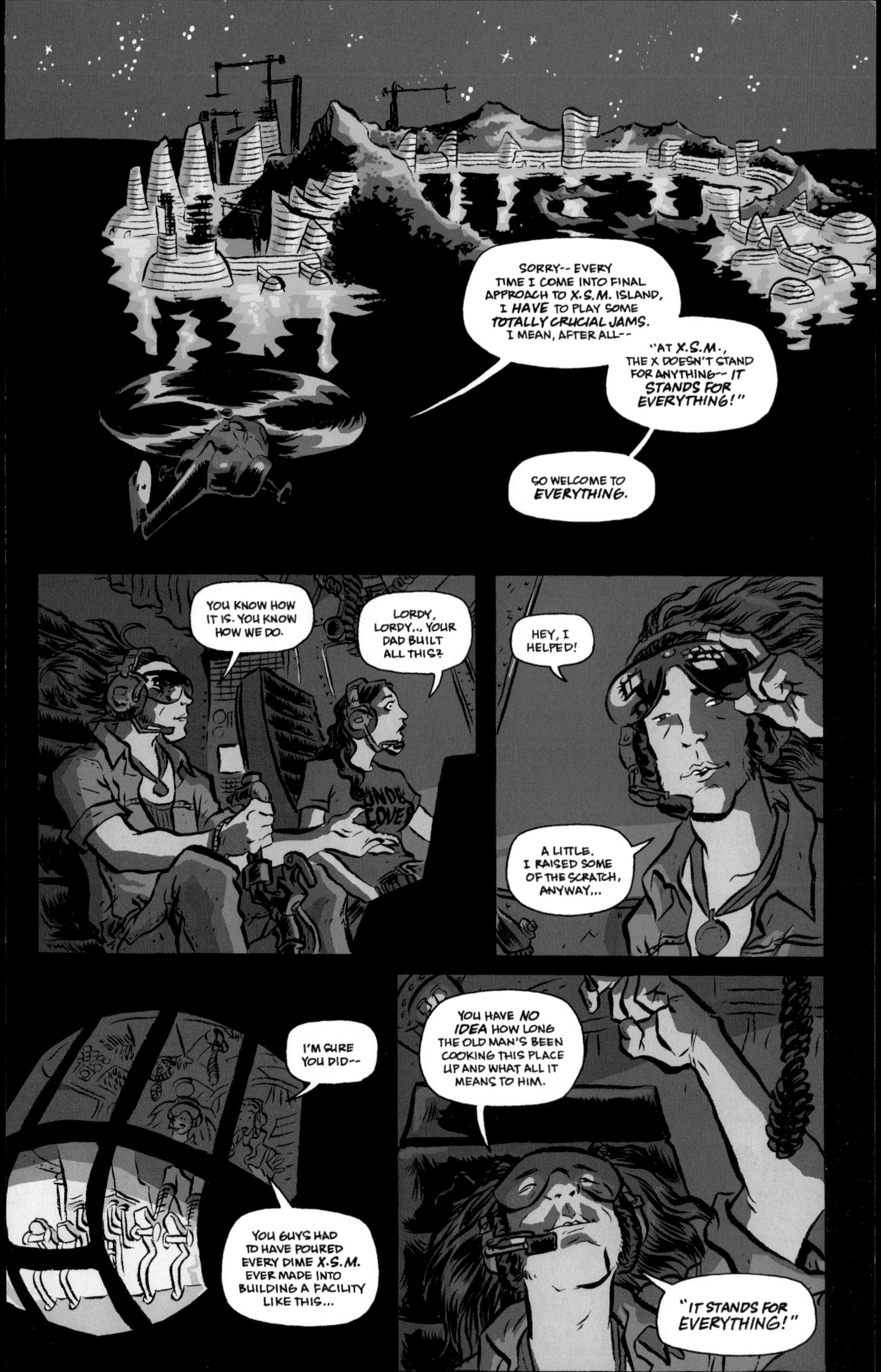
SORRY-- EVERY TIME I COME INTO FINAL APPROACH TO X.S.M. ISLAND, I *HAVE* TO PLAY SOME *TOTALLY CRUCIAL JAMS.* I MEAN, AFTER ALL--
"AT *X.S.M.*, THE X DOESN'T STAND FOR ANYTHING-- *IT STANDS FOR EVERYTHING!"*
SO WELCOME TO *EVERYTHING.*
YOU KNOW HOW IT IS. YOU KNOW HOW WE DO.
LORDY, LORDY... YOUR DAD BUILT ALL THIS?
HEY, I HELPED!
A LITTLE. I RAISED SOME OF THE SCRATCH, ANYWAY...
I'M SURE YOU DID--
YOU GUYS HAD TO HAVE POURED EVERY DIME *X.S.M.* EVER MADE INTO BUILDING A FACILITY LIKE THIS...
YOU HAVE *NO IDEA* HOW LONG THE OLD MAN'S BEEN COOKING THIS PLACE UP AND WHAT ALL IT MEANS TO HIM.
"IT STANDS FOR EVERYTHING!"

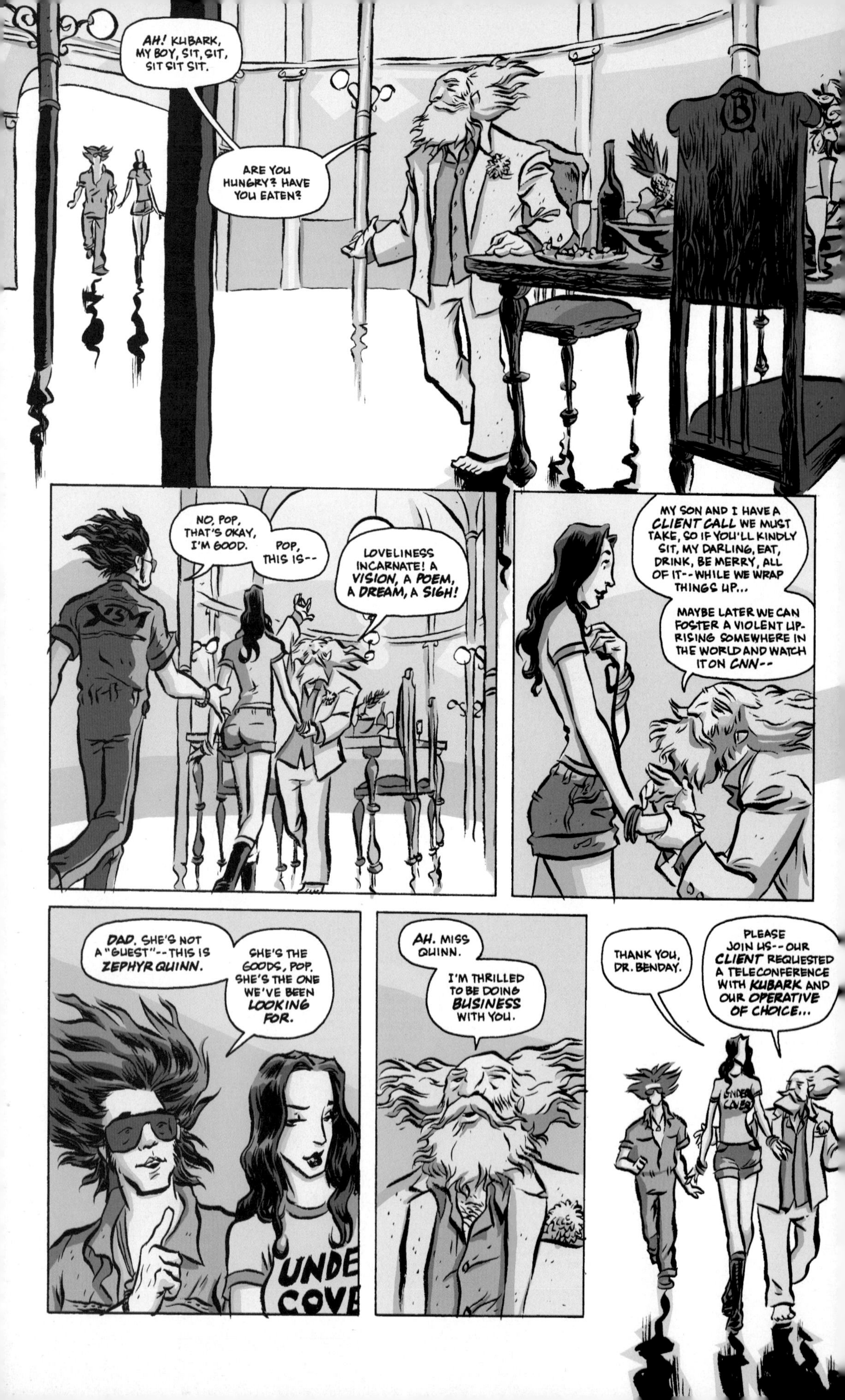
AH! KUBARK, MY BOY, SIT, SIT, SIT SIT SIT.
ARE YOU HUNGRY? HAVE YOU EATEN?
NO, POP, THAT'S OKAY, I'M GOOD.
POP, THIS IS--
LOVELINESS INCARNATE! A VISION, A POEM, A DREAM, A SIGH!
MY SON AND I HAVE A CLIENT CALL WE MUST TAKE, SO IF YOU'LL KINDLY SIT, MY DARLING, EAT, DRINK, BE MERRY, ALL OF IT--WHILE WE WRAP THINGS UP...
MAYBE LATER WE CAN FOSTER A VIOLENT UPRISING SOMEWHERE IN THE WORLD AND WATCH IT ON CNN--
DAD. SHE'S NOT A "GUEST"--THIS IS ZEPHYR QUINN.
SHE'S THE GOODS, POP. SHE'S THE ONE WE'VE BEEN LOOKING FOR.
AH. MISS QUINN.
I'M THRILLED TO BE DOING BUSINESS WITH YOU.
THANK YOU, DR. BENDAY.
PLEASE JOIN US--OUR CLIENT REQUESTED A TELECONFERENCE WITH KUBARK AND OUR OPERATIVE OF CHOICE...

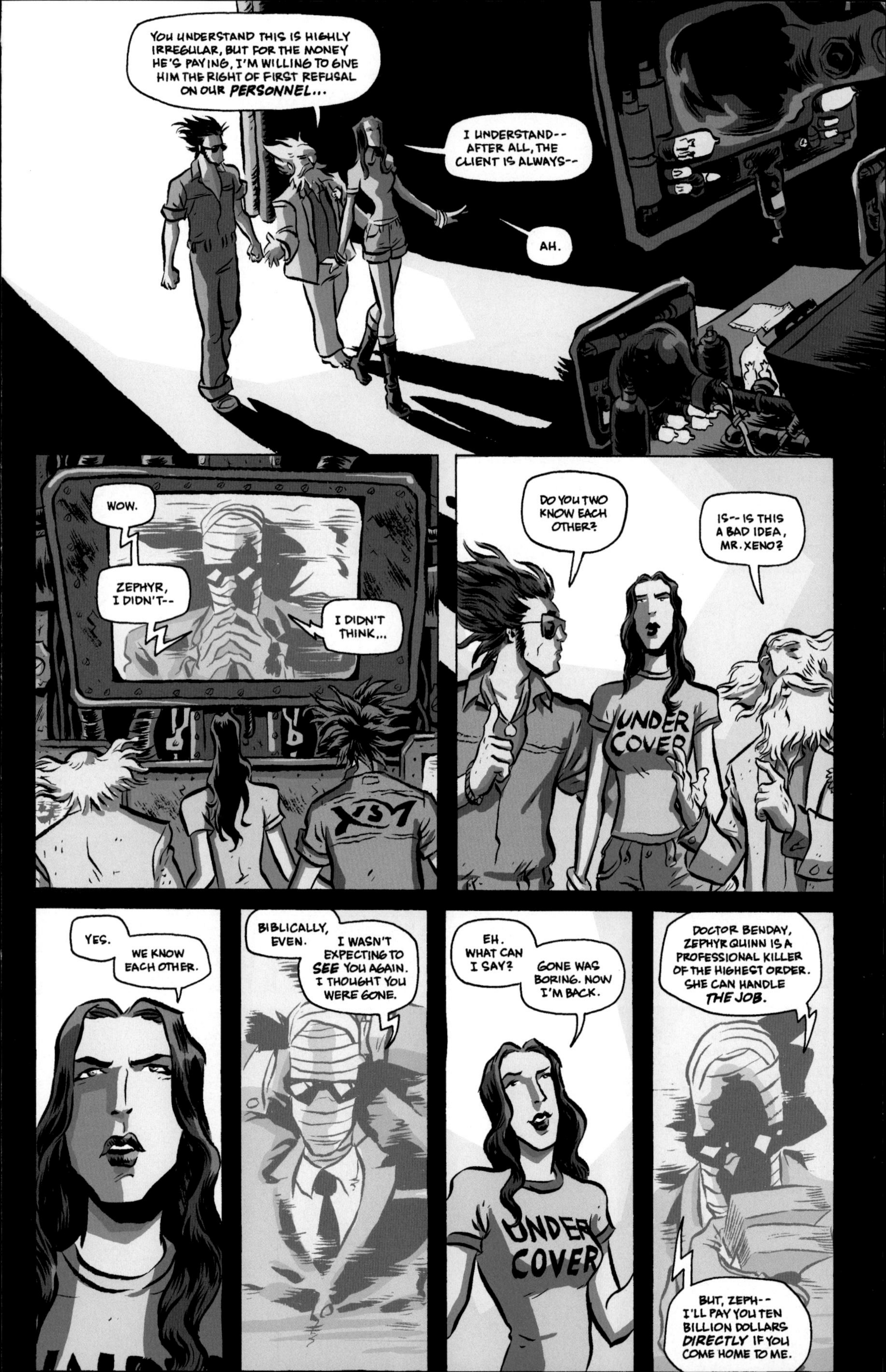
YOU UNDERSTAND THIS IS HIGHLY IRREGULAR, BUT FOR THE MONEY HE'S PAYING, I'M WILLING TO GIVE HIM THE RIGHT OF FIRST REFUSAL ON OUR PERSONNEL...
I UNDERSTAND-- AFTER ALL, THE CLIENT IS ALWAYS--
AH.
WOW.
ZEPHYR, I DIDN'T--
I DIDN'T THINK...
DO YOU TWO KNOW EACH OTHER?
IS-- IS THIS A BAD IDEA, MR. XENO?
UNDER COVER
YES.
WE KNOW EACH OTHER.
BIBLICALLY, EVEN.
I WASN'T EXPECTING TO SEE YOU AGAIN. I THOUGHT YOU WERE GONE.
EH. WHAT CAN I SAY?
GONE WAS BORING. NOW I'M BACK.
UNDER COVER
DOCTOR BENDAY, ZEPHYR QUINN IS A PROFESSIONAL KILLER OF THE HIGHEST ORDER. SHE CAN HANDLE THE JOB.
BUT, ZEPH-- I'LL PAY YOU TEN BILLION DOLLARS DIRECTLY IF YOU COME HOME TO ME.

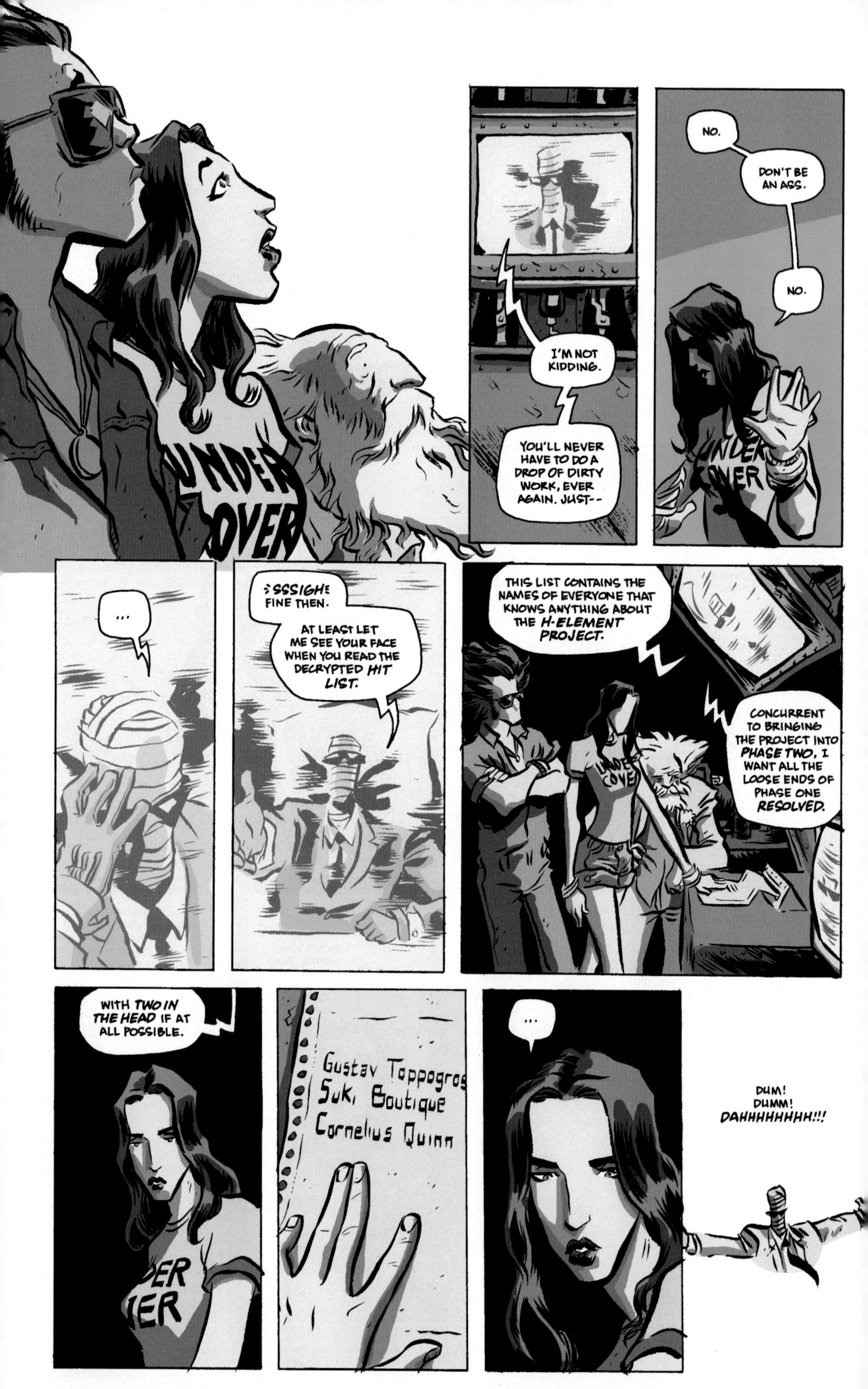
I'M NOT KIDDING.
YOU'LL NEVER HAVE TO DO A DROP OF DIRTY WORK, EVER AGAIN. JUST--
NO.
DON'T BE AN ASS.
NO.
...
:SSSIGH: FINE THEN.
AT LEAST LET ME SEE YOUR FACE WHEN YOU READ THE DECRYPTED HIT LIST.
THIS LIST CONTAINS THE NAMES OF EVERYONE THAT KNOWS ANYTHING ABOUT THE H-ELEMENT PROJECT.
CONCURRENT TO BRINGING THE PROJECT INTO PHASE TWO, I WANT ALL THE LOOSE ENDS OF PHASE ONE RESOLVED.
WITH TWO IN THE HEAD IF AT ALL POSSIBLE.
Gustav Toppogros
Suki, Boutique
Cornelius Quinn
...
DUM!
DUMM!
DAHHHHHHHH!!!

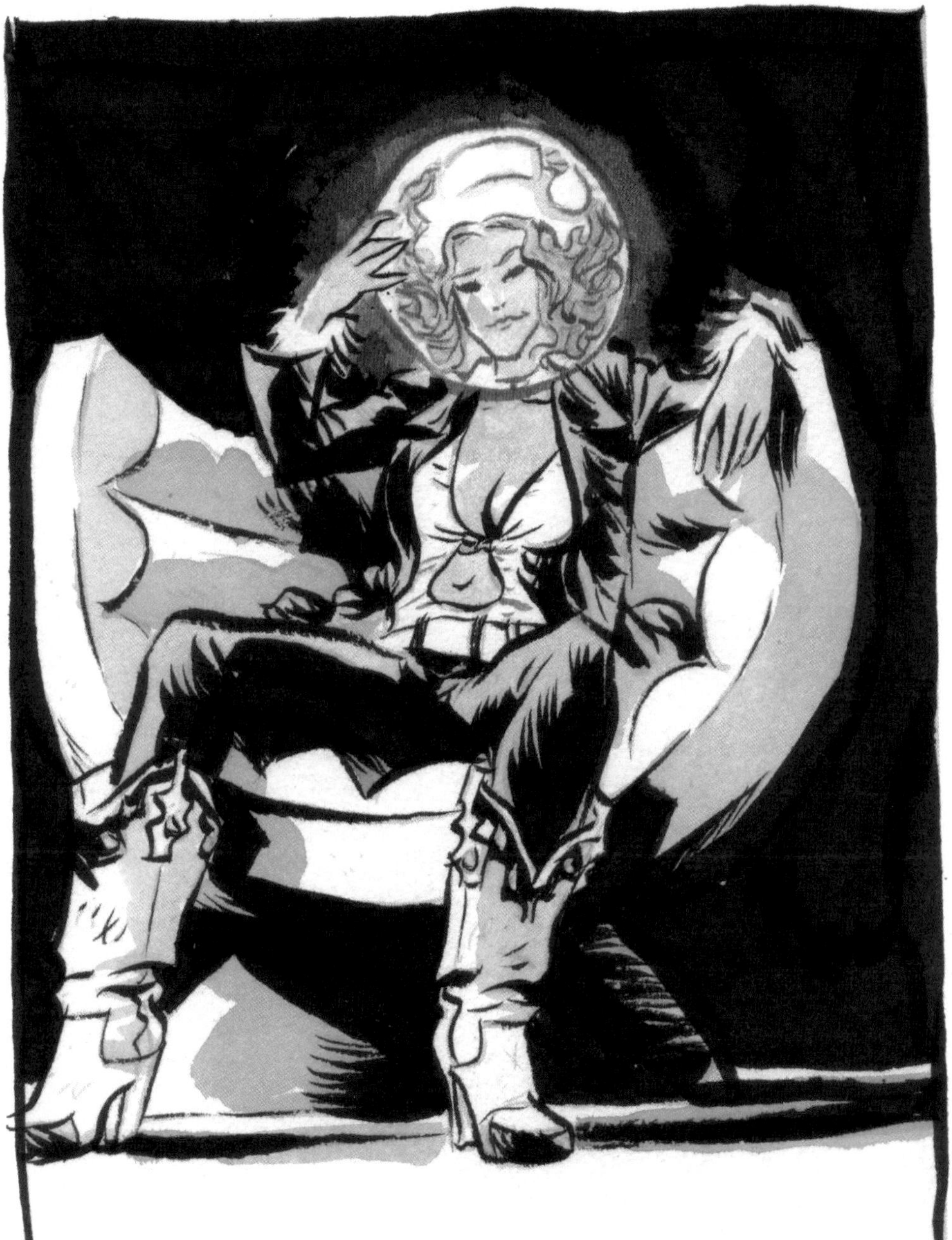

CHAPTER 3
SEVENTEEN

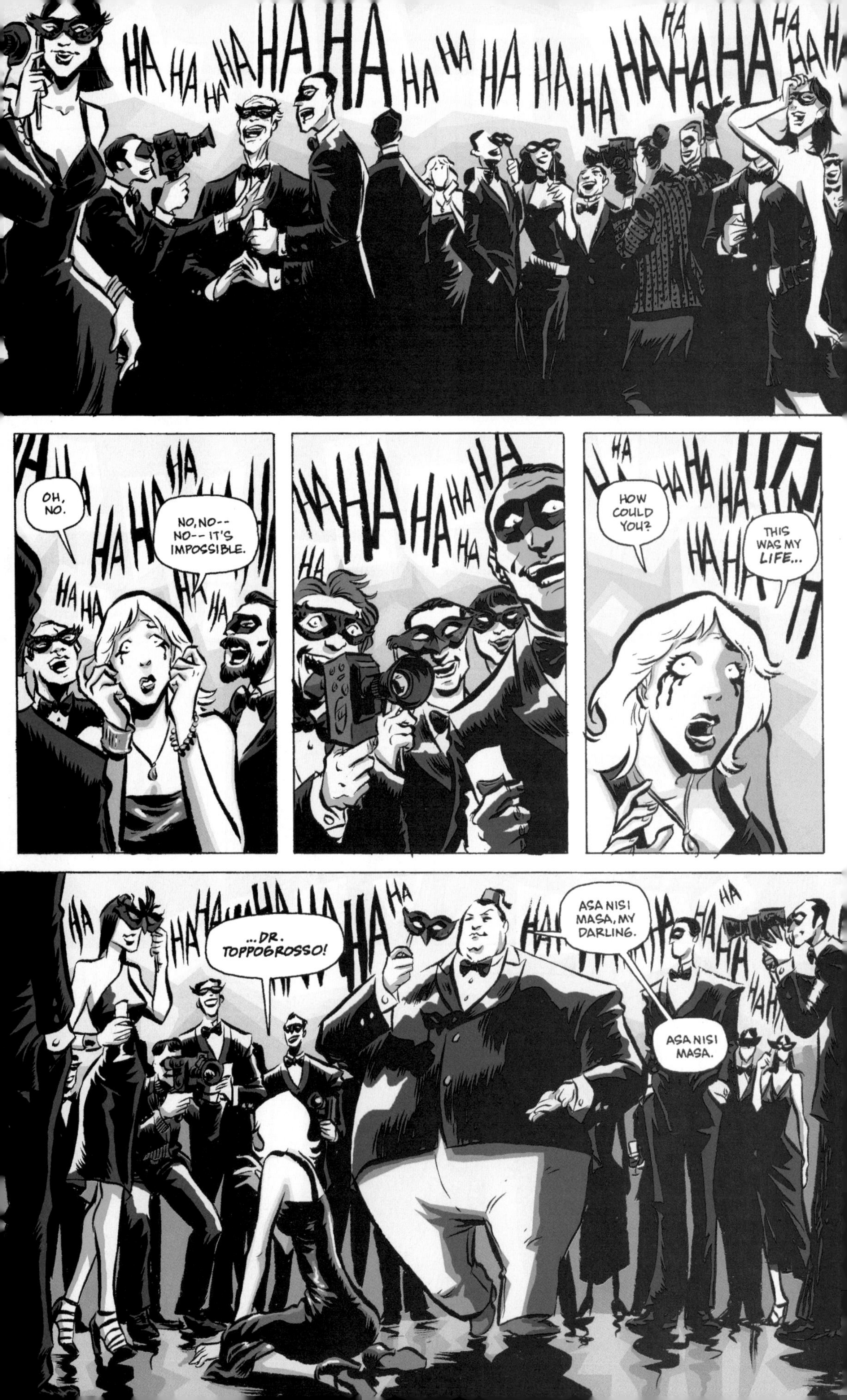

OH, NO.
NO, NO-- NO-- IT'S IMPOSSIBLE.
HOW COULD YOU?
THIS WAS MY LIFE...
...DR. TOPPOGROSSO!
ASA NISI MASA, MY DARLING.
ASA NISI MASA.

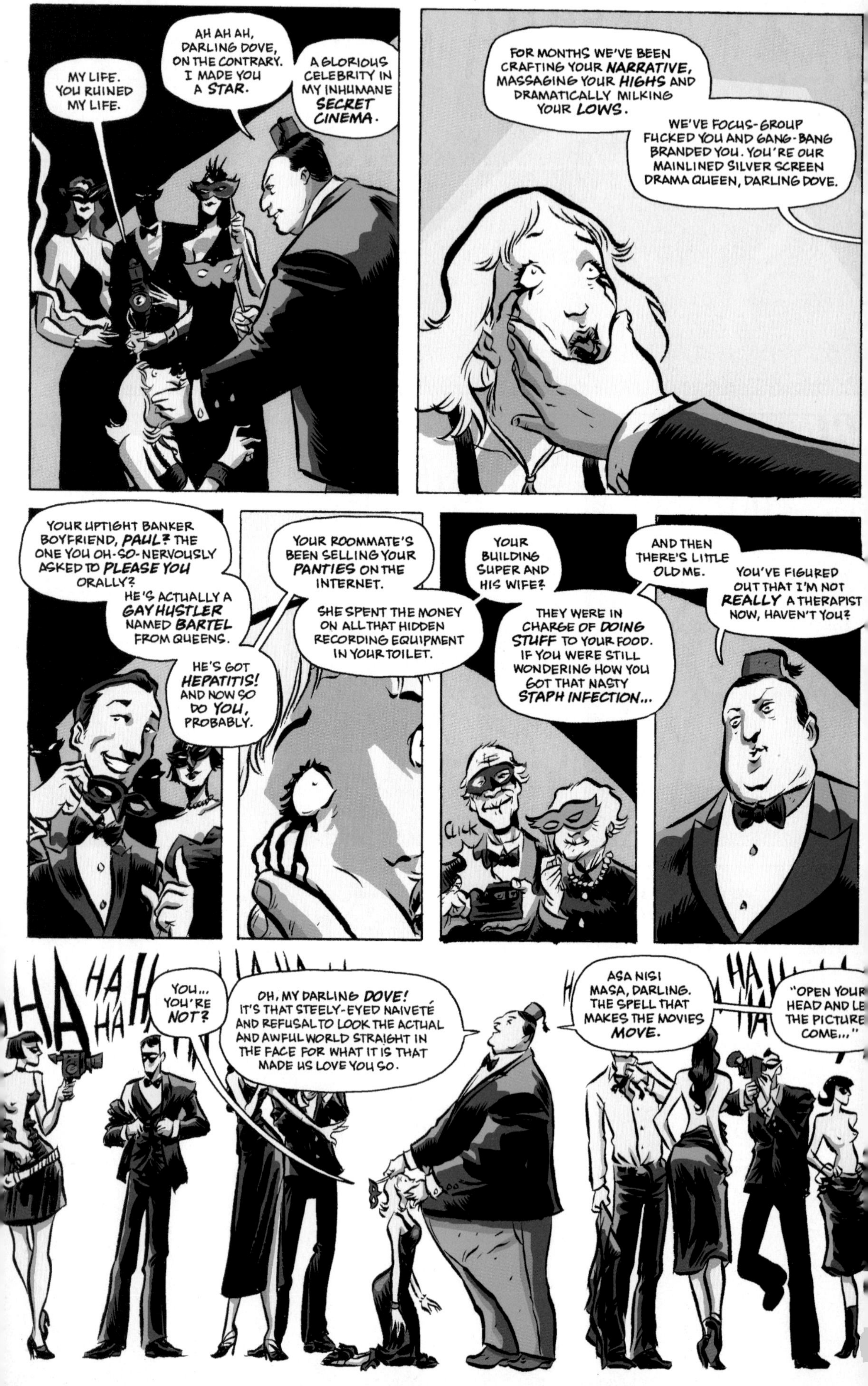

MY LIFE. YOU RUINED MY LIFE.
AH AH AH, DARLING DOVE, ON THE CONTRARY. I MADE YOU A STAR.
A GLORIOUS CELEBRITY IN MY INHUMANE SECRET CINEMA.
FOR MONTHS WE'VE BEEN CRAFTING YOUR NARRATIVE, MASSAGING YOUR HIGHS AND DRAMATICALLY MILKING YOUR LOWS.
WE'VE FOCUS-GROUP FUCKED YOU AND GANG-BANG BRANDED YOU. YOU'RE OUR MAINLINED SILVER SCREEN DRAMA QUEEN, DARLING DOVE.
YOUR UPTIGHT BANKER BOYFRIEND, PAUL? THE ONE YOU OH-SO-NERVOUSLY ASKED TO PLEASE YOU ORALLY?
HE'S ACTUALLY A GAY HUSTLER NAMED BARTEL FROM QUEENS.
HE'S GOT HEPATITIS! AND NOW SO DO YOU, PROBABLY.
YOUR ROOMMATE'S BEEN SELLING YOUR PANTIES ON THE INTERNET.
SHE SPENT THE MONEY ON ALL THAT HIDDEN RECORDING EQUIPMENT IN YOUR TOILET.
YOUR BUILDING SUPER AND HIS WIFE?
THEY WERE IN CHARGE OF DOING STUFF TO YOUR FOOD. IF YOU WERE STILL WONDERING HOW YOU GOT THAT NASTY STAPH INFECTION...
CLICK
AND THEN THERE'S LITTLE OLD ME.
YOU'VE FIGURED OUT THAT I'M NOT REALLY A THERAPIST NOW, HAVEN'T YOU?
HA HA HA
YOU... YOU'RE NOT?
OH, MY DARLING DOVE! IT'S THAT STEELY-EYED NAIVETÉ AND REFUSAL TO LOOK THE ACTUAL AND AWFUL WORLD STRAIGHT IN THE FACE FOR WHAT IT IS THAT MADE US LOVE YOU SO.
ASA NISI MASA, DARLING. THE SPELL THAT MAKES THE MOVIES MOVE.
"OPEN YOUR HEAD AND LE THE PICTURE COME..."

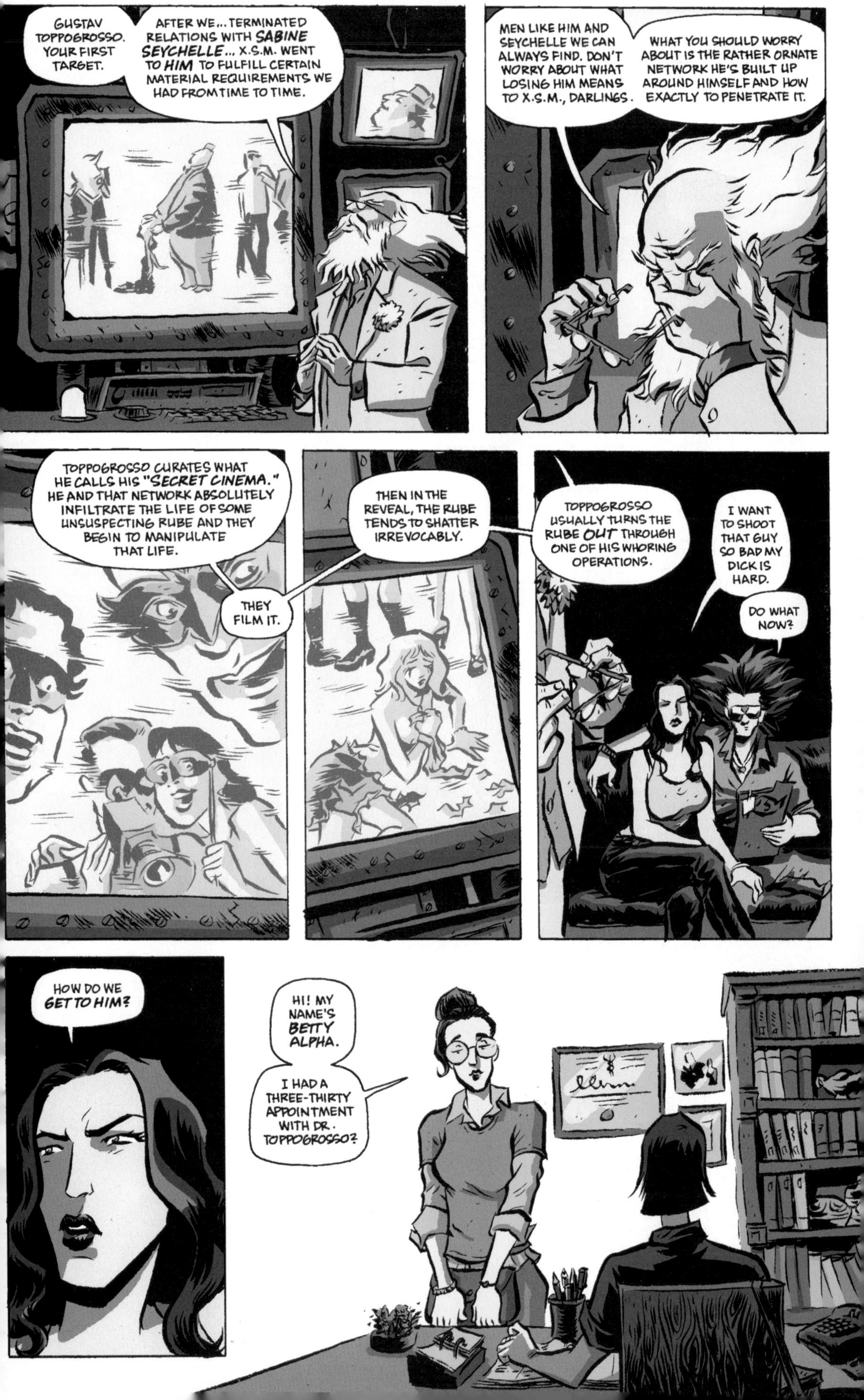
GUSTAV TOPPOGROSSO. YOUR FIRST TARGET.
AFTER WE... TERMINATED RELATIONS WITH SABINE SEYCHELLE... X.S.M. WENT TO HIM TO FULFILL CERTAIN MATERIAL REQUIREMENTS WE HAD FROM TIME TO TIME.
MEN LIKE HIM AND SEYCHELLE WE CAN ALWAYS FIND. DON'T WORRY ABOUT WHAT LOSING HIM MEANS TO X.S.M., DARLINGS.
WHAT YOU SHOULD WORRY ABOUT IS THE RATHER ORNATE NETWORK HE'S BUILT UP AROUND HIMSELF AND HOW EXACTLY TO PENETRATE IT.
TOPPOGROSSO CURATES WHAT HE CALLS HIS "SECRET CINEMA." HE AND THAT NETWORK ABSOLUTELY INFILTRATE THE LIFE OF SOME UNSUSPECTING RUBE AND THEY BEGIN TO MANIPULATE THAT LIFE.
THEY FILM IT.
THEN IN THE REVEAL, THE RUBE TENDS TO SHATTER IRREVOCABLY.
TOPPOGROSSO USUALLY TURNS THE RUBE OUT THROUGH ONE OF HIS WHORING OPERATIONS.
I WANT TO SHOOT THAT GUY SO BAD MY DICK IS HARD.
DO WHAT NOW?
HOW DO WE GET TO HIM?
HI! MY NAME'S BETTY ALPHA.
I HAD A THREE-THIRTY APPOINTMENT WITH DR. TOPPOGROSSO?

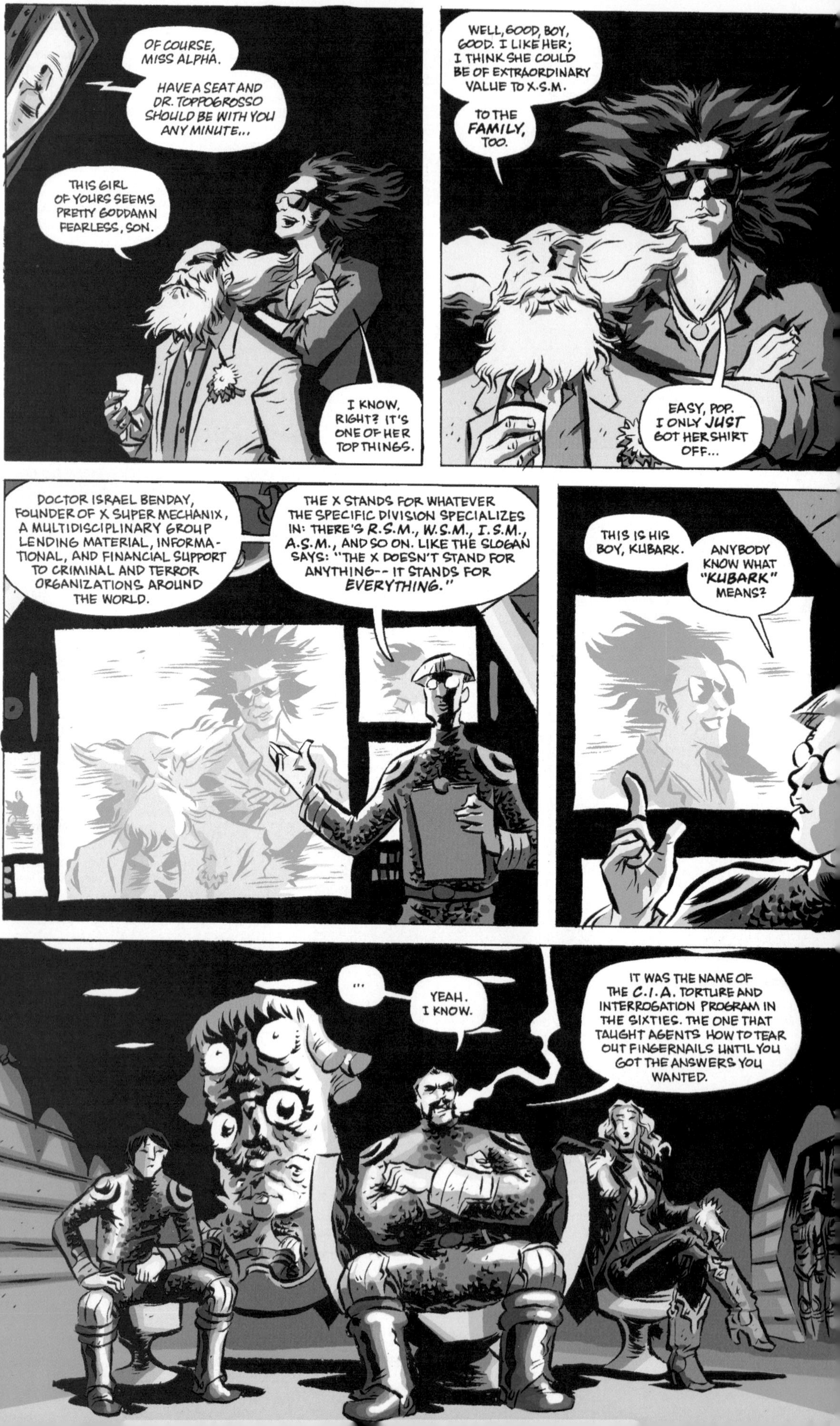
OF COURSE, MISS ALPHA.
HAVE A SEAT AND DR. TOPPOGROSSO SHOULD BE WITH YOU ANY MINUTE...
THIS GIRL OF YOURS SEEMS PRETTY GODDAMN FEARLESS, SON.
I KNOW, RIGHT? IT'S ONE OF HER TOP THINGS.
WELL, GOOD, BOY, GOOD. I LIKE HER; I THINK SHE COULD BE OF EXTRAORDINARY VALUE TO X.S.M.
TO THE FAMILY, TOO.
EASY, POP. I ONLY JUST GOT HER SHIRT OFF...
DOCTOR ISRAEL BENDAY, FOUNDER OF X SUPER MECHANIX, A MULTIDISCIPLINARY GROUP LENDING MATERIAL, INFORMATIONAL, AND FINANCIAL SUPPORT TO CRIMINAL AND TERROR ORGANIZATIONS AROUND THE WORLD.
THE X STANDS FOR WHATEVER THE SPECIFIC DIVISION SPECIALIZES IN: THERE'S R.S.M., W.S.M., I.S.M., A.S.M., AND SO ON. LIKE THE SLOGAN SAYS: "THE X DOESN'T STAND FOR ANYTHING-- IT STANDS FOR EVERYTHING."
THIS IS HIS BOY, KUBARK.
ANYBODY KNOW WHAT "KUBARK" MEANS?
...
YEAH. I KNOW.
IT WAS THE NAME OF THE C.I.A. TORTURE AND INTERROGATION PROGRAM IN THE SIXTIES. THE ONE THAT TAUGHT AGENTS HOW TO TEAR OUT FINGERNAILS UNTIL YOU GOT THE ANSWERS YOU WANTED.

THAT'S RIGHT, DIRECTOR QUINN. WOULD YOU CARE TO SHARE WITH US HOW YOU CAME TO KNOW THAT?

BECAUSE I WROTE IT.

I WROTE IT *WITH* IZZY BENDAY.

THAT'S RIGHT. THE SAME TRAINING AND EXPERIENCES THAT MADE YOU *YOU*, SIR, ALSO MADE HIM *HIM*.

"WE WERE IN *THE A.C.A.D.E.M.Y.* TOGETHER. WE WERE FIELD OPS TOGETHER. WE WERE *MEN IN BLACK* TOGETHER-- AND THEN SOMETHING HAPPENED.

"IZZY SNAPPED.

"HE LOST HIS WIFE IN CHILDBIRTH-- KUBARK'S MOTHER-- AND THEN HE LOST HIS MIND.

"ANYTHING BENDAY CAN EXPLOIT, HE WILL.

"ANY WAY PEOPLE CAN KILL PEOPLE, BENDAY MAKES IT POSSIBLE."

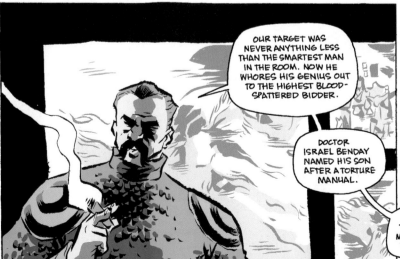

OUR TARGET WAS NEVER ANYTHING LESS THAN THE SMARTEST MAN IN THE ROOM. NOW HE WHORES HIS GENIUS OUT TO THE HIGHEST BLOOD-SPATTERED BIDDER.

DOCTOR ISRAEL BENDAY NAMED HIS SON AFTER A TORTURE MANUAL.

THAT'S THE KIND OF MAN MY FRIEND HAS BECOME.

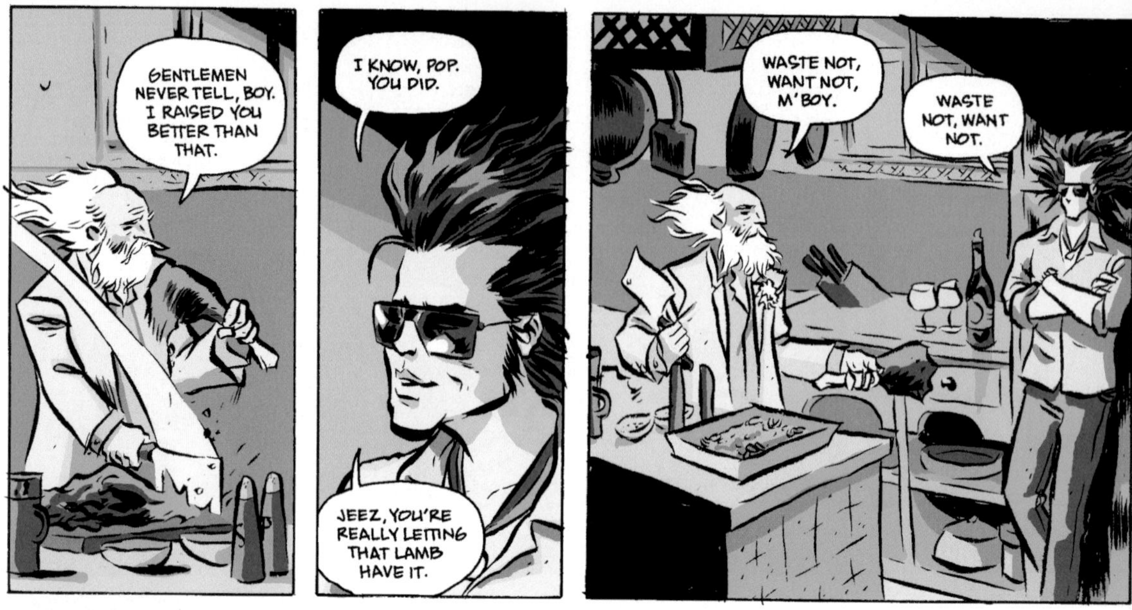
GENTLEMEN NEVER TELL, BOY. I RAISED YOU BETTER THAN THAT.
I KNOW, POP. YOU DID.
JEEZ, YOU'RE REALLY LETTING THAT LAMB HAVE IT.
WASTE NOT, WANT NOT, M' BOY.
WASTE NOT, WANT NOT.

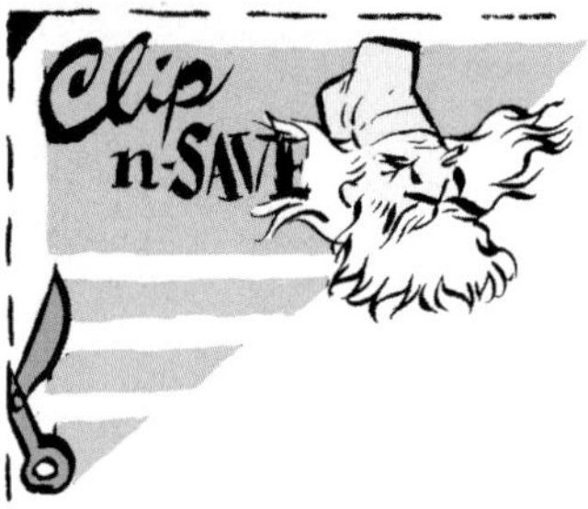
Clip n-SAVE

Epaule d'Agneau Confite de Benday

One shoulder of Lamb, bone in
(3 lbs, no more than 3 1/2)
Extra-virgin Olive Oil
1 tbsp. Thyme
1 tbsp. Basil
1 tbsp. Marjoram
2-3 tbsp. Rosemary (fresh)
1 head of Garlic
1/2 cup Dry White Wine
Sea Salt
Fresh Cracked Pepper

Rub the lamb with olive oil, then rub herbs across the meat, adding the rosemary last. Wrap in butcher's paper and refrigerate overnight. Let meat sit out as oven preheats to 250°F. Clove the garlic. Put the garlic cloves in the bottom of a heavy iron pot with a good lid. Put the lamb in the pot and sprinkle it with the salt and pepper. Pour the wine into the pot. Close the pot and put it in the oven for 4 hours. Flip the lamb every half-hour, basting it each time. If the juice runs low--and it will if your lid doesn't fit properly--add more wine.

The lamb is ready when tender, dark, and fragrant. Serve at moonrise near an open window above night-blooming jasmine.

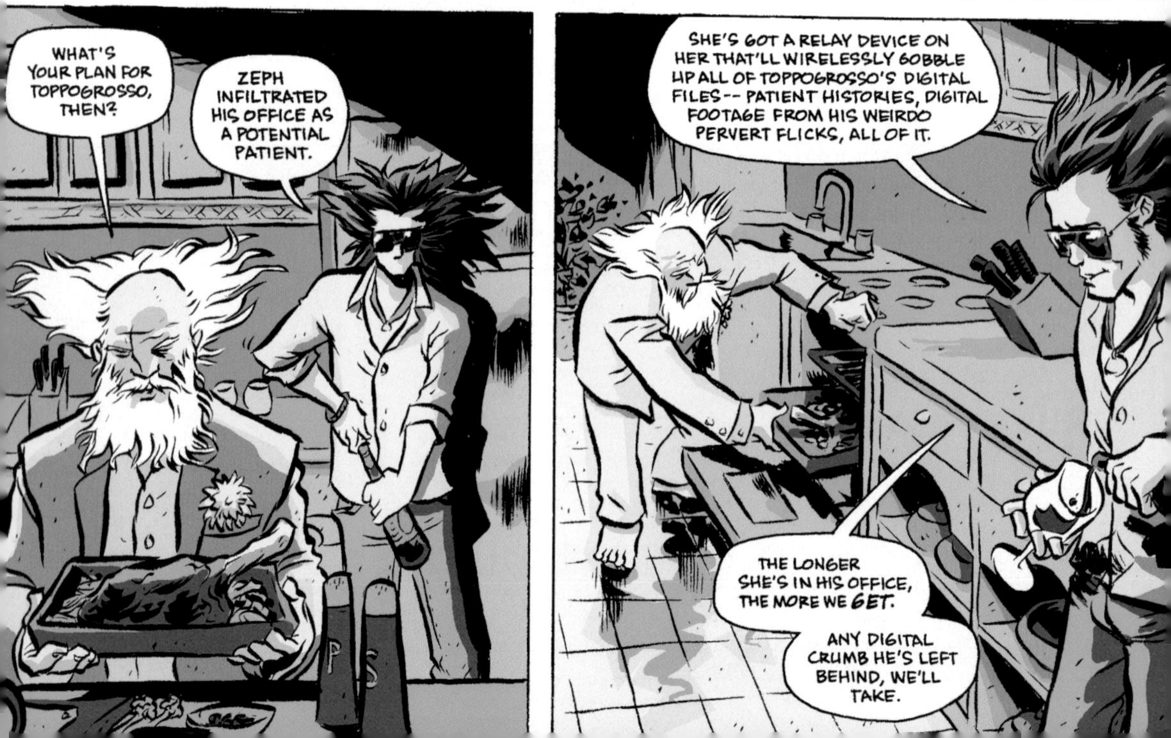
WHAT'S YOUR PLAN FOR TOPPOGROSSO, THEN?
ZEPH INFILTRATED HIS OFFICE AS A POTENTIAL PATIENT.
SHE'S GOT A RELAY DEVICE ON HER THAT'LL WIRELESSLY GOBBLE UP ALL OF TOPPOGROSSO'S DIGITAL FILES-- PATIENT HISTORIES, DIGITAL FOOTAGE FROM HIS WEIRDO PERVERT FLICKS, ALL OF IT.
THE LONGER SHE'S IN HIS OFFICE, THE MORE WE GET.
ANY DIGITAL CRUMB HE'S LEFT BEHIND, WE'LL TAKE.

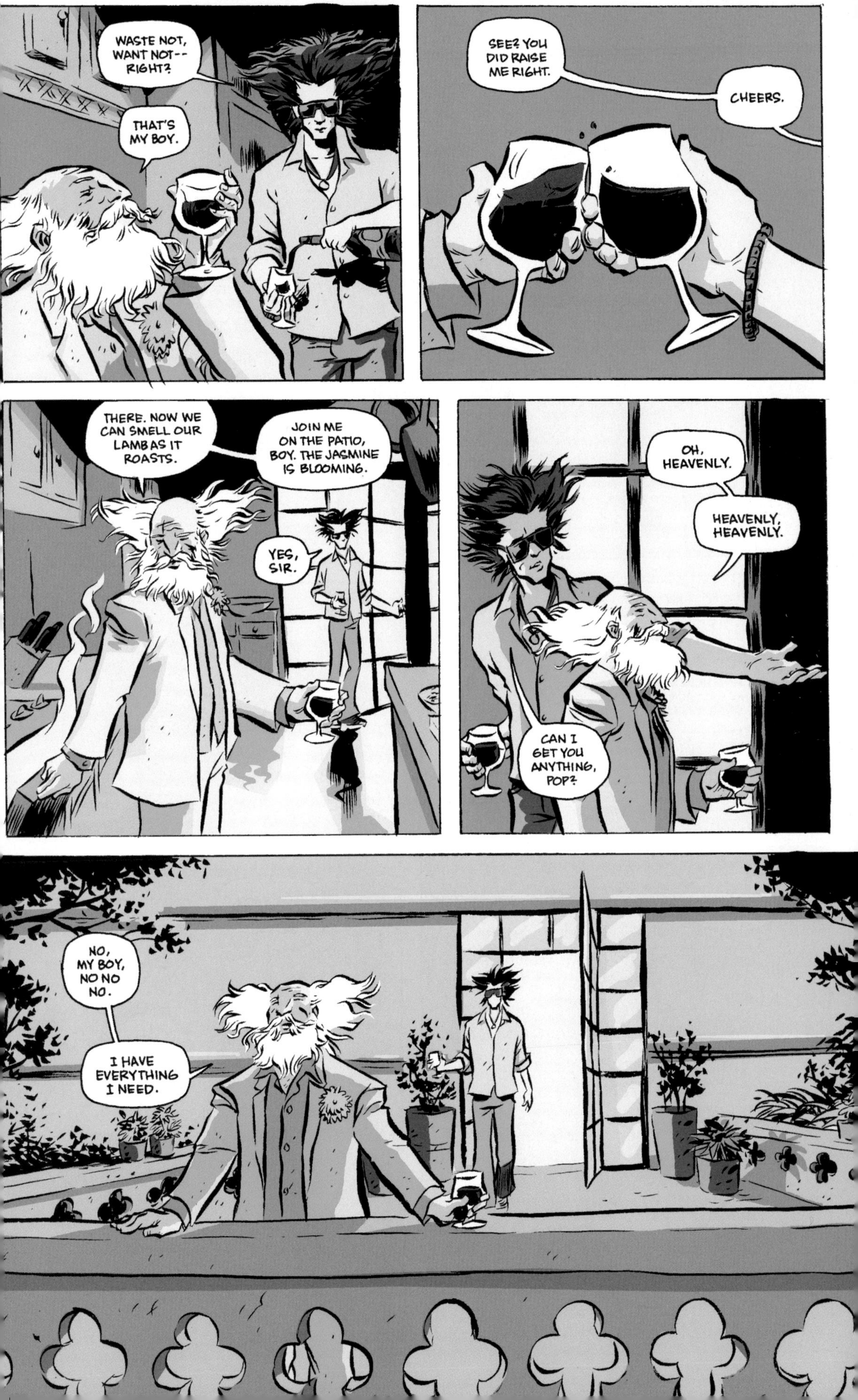
WASTE NOT, WANT NOT-- RIGHT?
THAT'S MY BOY.
SEE? YOU DID RAISE ME RIGHT.
CHEERS.
THERE. NOW WE CAN SMELL OUR LAMB AS IT ROASTS.
JOIN ME ON THE PATIO, BOY. THE JASMINE IS BLOOMING.
YES, SIR.
OH, HEAVENLY.
HEAVENLY, HEAVENLY.
CAN I GET YOU ANYTHING, POP?
NO, MY BOY, NO NO NO.
I HAVE EVERYTHING I NEED.

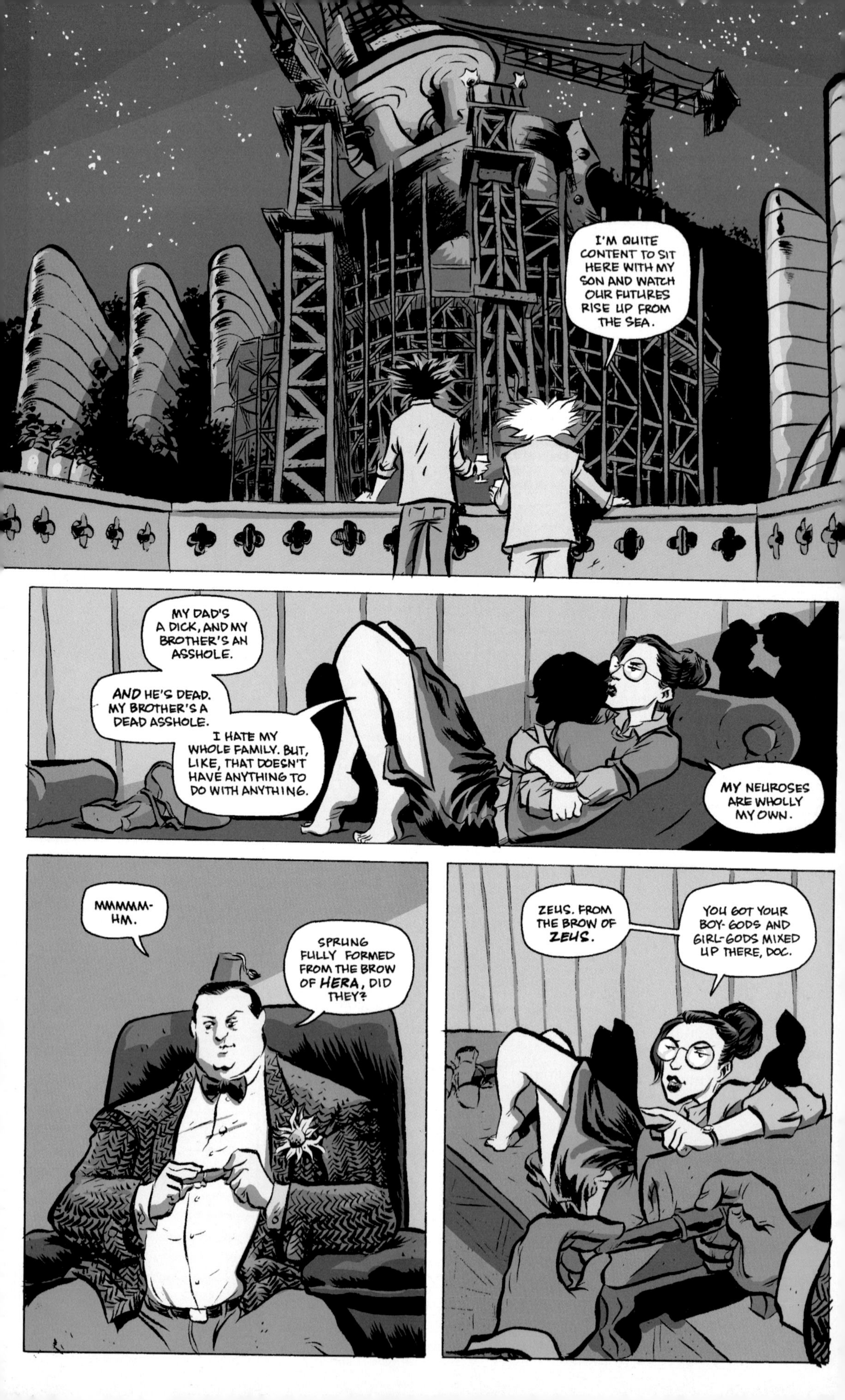
I'M QUITE CONTENT TO SIT HERE WITH MY SON AND WATCH OUR FUTURES RISE UP FROM THE SEA.
MY DAD'S A DICK, AND MY BROTHER'S AN ASSHOLE.
AND HE'S DEAD. MY BROTHER'S A DEAD ASSHOLE.
I HATE MY WHOLE FAMILY. BUT, LIKE, THAT DOESN'T HAVE ANYTHING TO DO WITH ANYTHING.
MY NEUROSES ARE WHOLLY MY OWN.
MMMMM-HM.
SPRUNG FULLY FORMED FROM THE BROW OF HERA, DID THEY?
YOU GOT YOUR BOY-GODS AND GIRL-GODS MIXED UP THERE, DOC.
ZEUS. FROM THE BROW OF ZEUS.

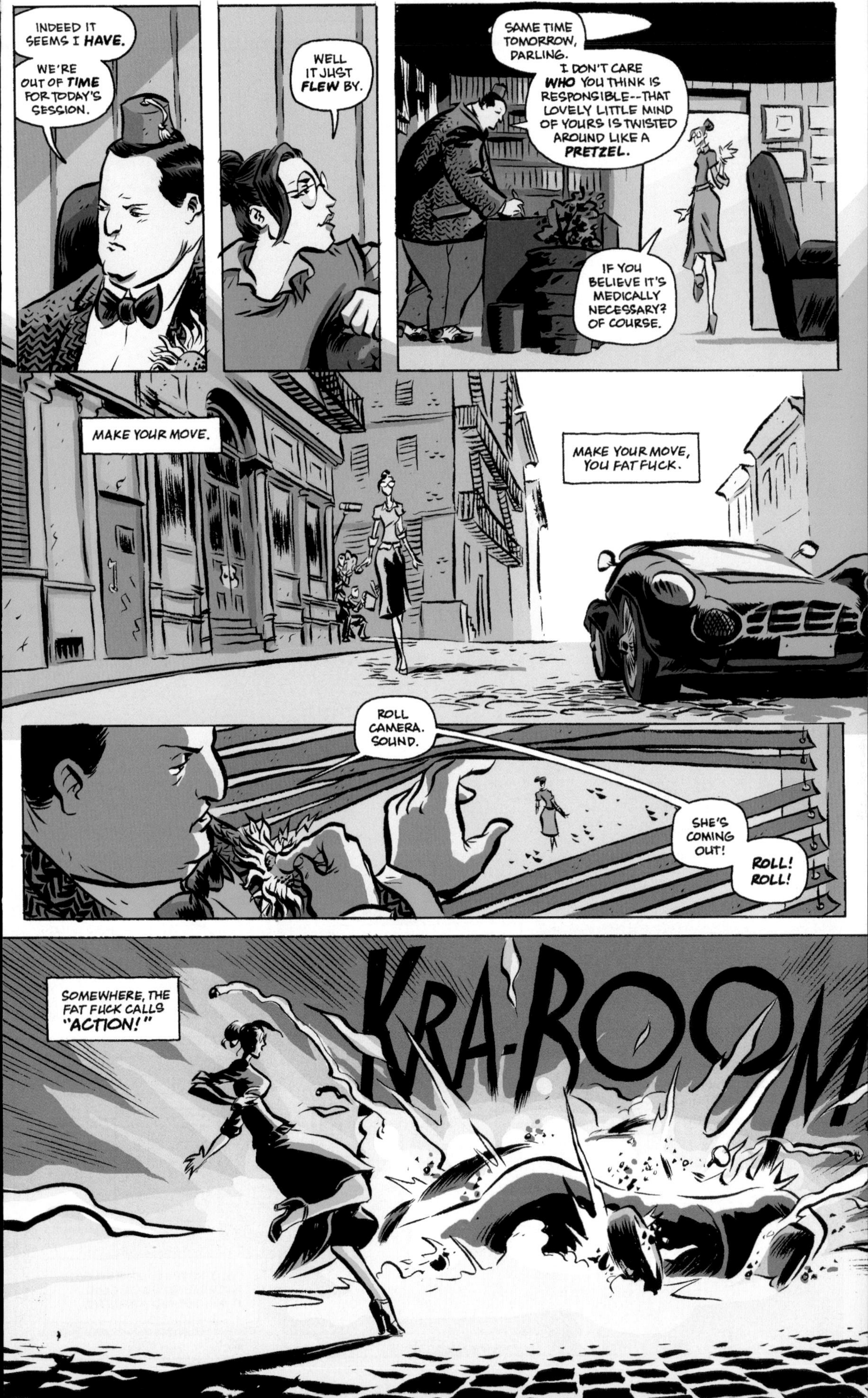

INDEED IT SEEMS I HAVE.
WE'RE OUT OF TIME FOR TODAY'S SESSION.
WELL IT JUST FLEW BY.
SAME TIME TOMORROW, DARLING.
I DON'T CARE WHO YOU THINK IS RESPONSIBLE--THAT LOVELY LITTLE MIND OF YOURS IS TWISTED AROUND LIKE A PRETZEL.
IF YOU BELIEVE IT'S MEDICALLY NECESSARY? OF COURSE.
MAKE YOUR MOVE.
MAKE YOUR MOVE, YOU FAT FUCK.
ROLL CAMERA. SOUND.
SHE'S COMING OUT!
ROLL! ROLL!
SOMEWHERE, THE FAT FUCK CALLS "ACTION!"
KRA-ROOM

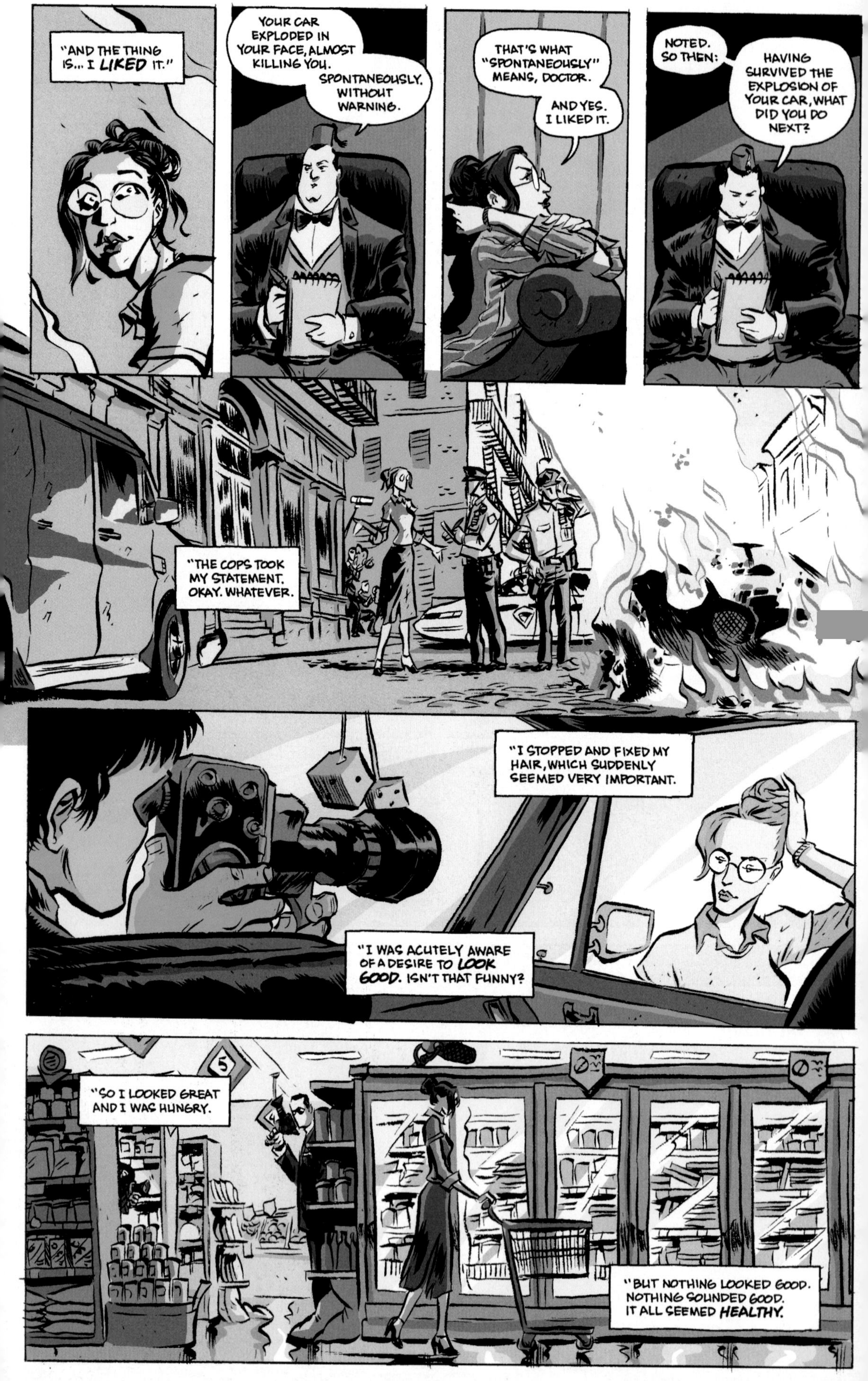
"AND THE THING IS... I LIKED IT."
YOUR CAR EXPLODED IN YOUR FACE, ALMOST KILLING YOU.
SPONTANEOUSLY. WITHOUT WARNING.
THAT'S WHAT "SPONTANEOUSLY" MEANS, DOCTOR.
AND YES. I LIKED IT.
NOTED. SO THEN:
HAVING SURVIVED THE EXPLOSION OF YOUR CAR, WHAT DID YOU DO NEXT?
"THE COPS TOOK MY STATEMENT. OKAY. WHATEVER.
"I STOPPED AND FIXED MY HAIR, WHICH SUDDENLY SEEMED VERY IMPORTANT.
"I WAS ACUTELY AWARE OF A DESIRE TO LOOK GOOD. ISN'T THAT FUNNY?
"SO I LOOKED GREAT AND I WAS HUNGRY.
"BUT NOTHING LOOKED GOOD. NOTHING SOUNDED GOOD. IT ALL SEEMED HEALTHY.

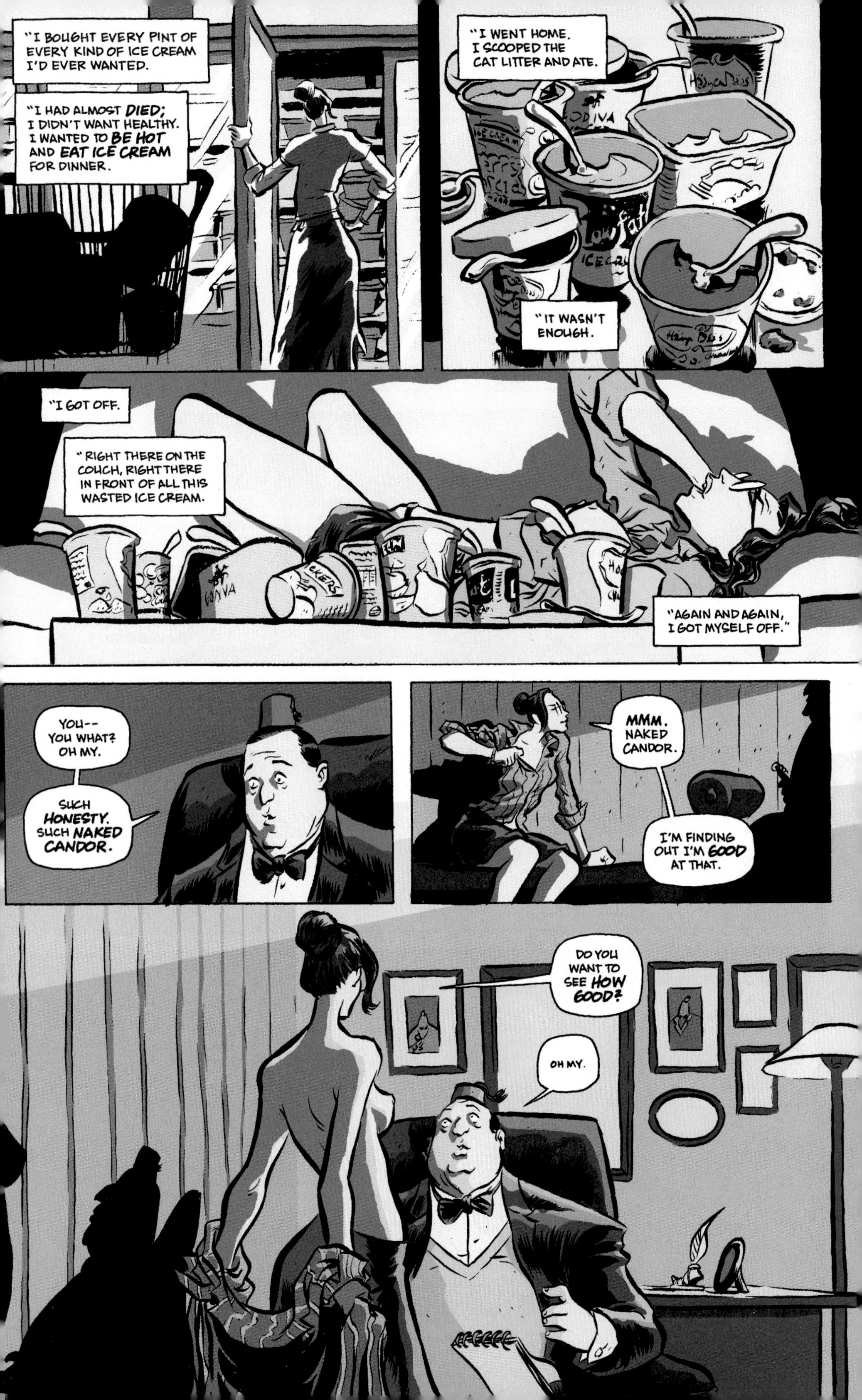

"I BOUGHT EVERY PINT OF EVERY KIND OF ICE CREAM I'D EVER WANTED.
"I HAD ALMOST DIED; I DIDN'T WANT HEALTHY. I WANTED TO BE HOT AND EAT ICE CREAM FOR DINNER.
"I WENT HOME. I SCOOPED THE CAT LITTER AND ATE.
"IT WASN'T ENOUGH.
"I GOT OFF.
"RIGHT THERE ON THE COUCH, RIGHT THERE IN FRONT OF ALL THIS WASTED ICE CREAM.
"AGAIN AND AGAIN, I GOT MYSELF OFF."
YOU-- YOU WHAT? OH MY.
SUCH HONESTY. SUCH NAKED CANDOR.
MMM. NAKED CANDOR.
I'M FINDING OUT I'M GOOD AT THAT.
DO YOU WANT TO SEE HOW GOOD?
OH MY.

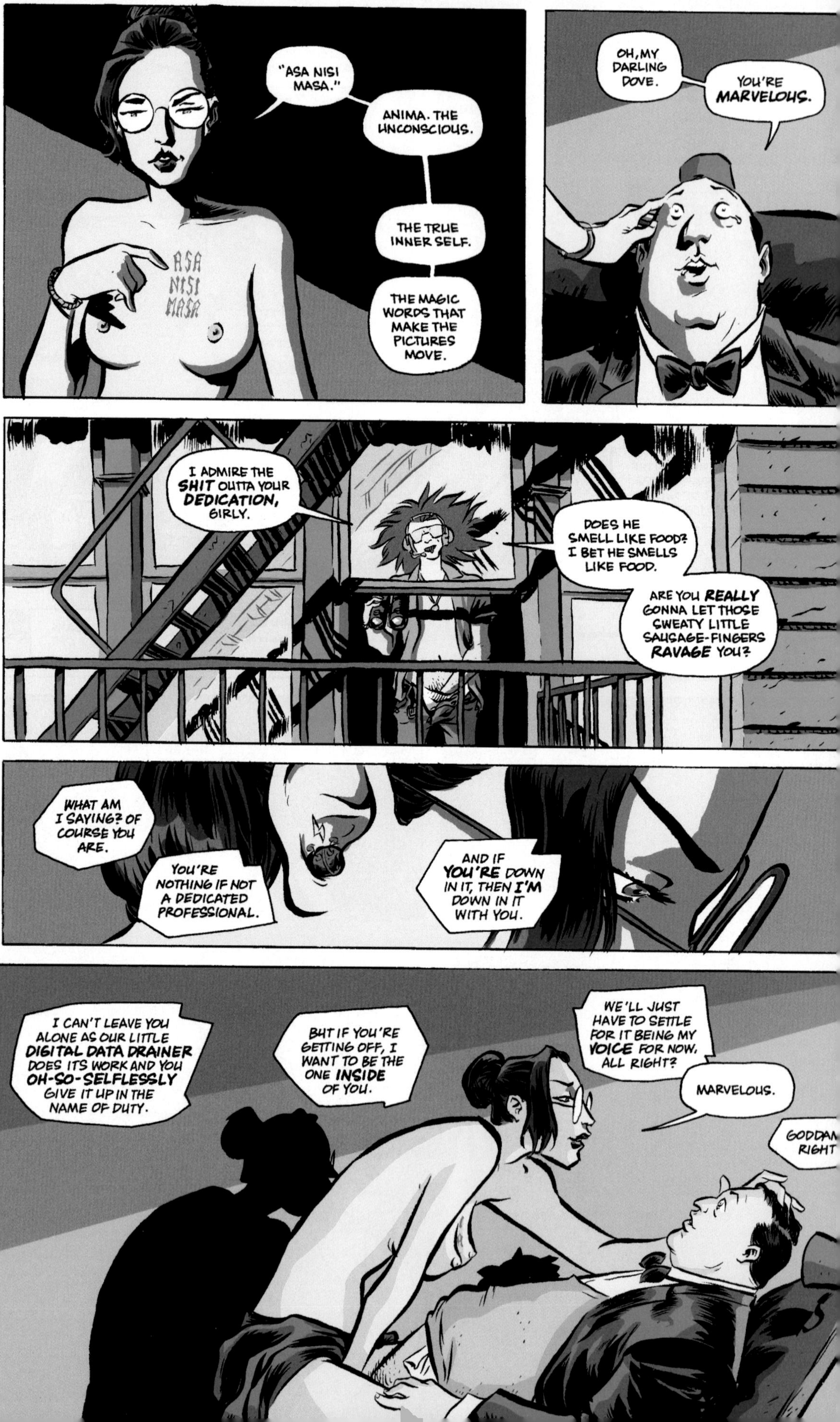
"ASA NISI MASA."
ANIMA. THE UNCONSCIOUS.
THE TRUE INNER SELF.
THE MAGIC WORDS THAT MAKE THE PICTURES MOVE.
ASA NISI MASA
OH, MY DARLING DOVE.
YOU'RE **MARVELOUS.**
I ADMIRE THE **SHIT** OUTTA YOUR **DEDICATION,** GIRLY.
DOES HE SMELL LIKE FOOD? I BET HE SMELLS LIKE FOOD.
ARE YOU **REALLY** GONNA LET THOSE SWEATY LITTLE SAUSAGE-FINGERS **RAVAGE** YOU?
WHAT AM I SAYING? OF COURSE YOU ARE.
YOU'RE NOTHING IF NOT A DEDICATED PROFESSIONAL.
AND IF **YOU'RE** DOWN IN IT, THEN **I'M** DOWN IN IT WITH YOU.
I CAN'T LEAVE YOU ALONE AS OUR LITTLE **DIGITAL DATA DRAINER** DOES ITS WORK AND YOU **OH-SO-SELFLESSLY** GIVE IT UP IN THE NAME OF DUTY.
BUT IF YOU'RE GETTING OFF, I WANT TO BE THE ONE **INSIDE** OF YOU.
WE'LL JUST HAVE TO SETTLE FOR IT BEING MY **VOICE** FOR NOW, ALL RIGHT?
MARVELOUS.
GODDAM RIGHT

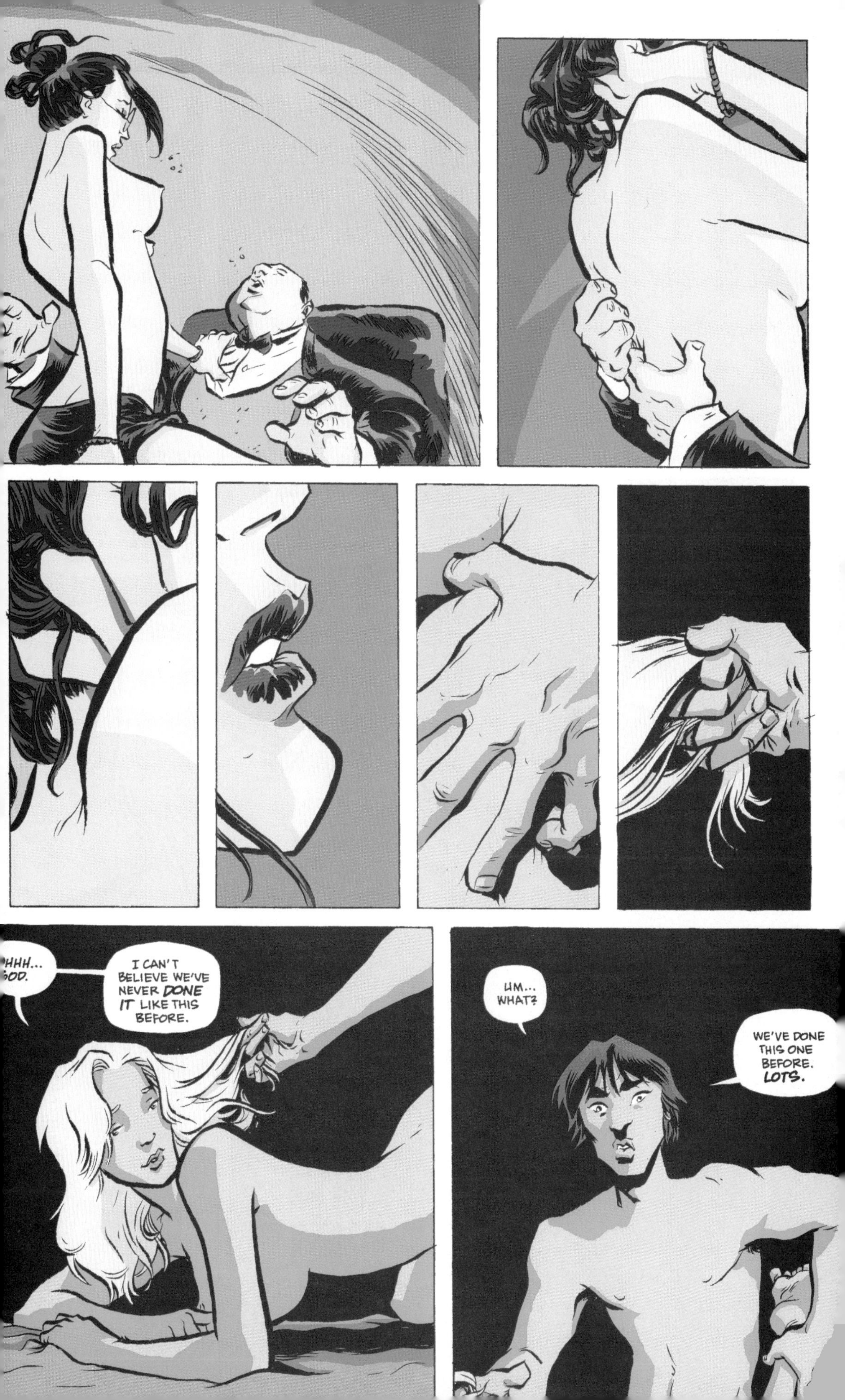
HHH... OD.
I CAN'T BELIEVE WE'VE NEVER DONE IT LIKE THIS BEFORE.
UM... WHAT?
WE'VE DONE THIS ONE BEFORE. LOTS.

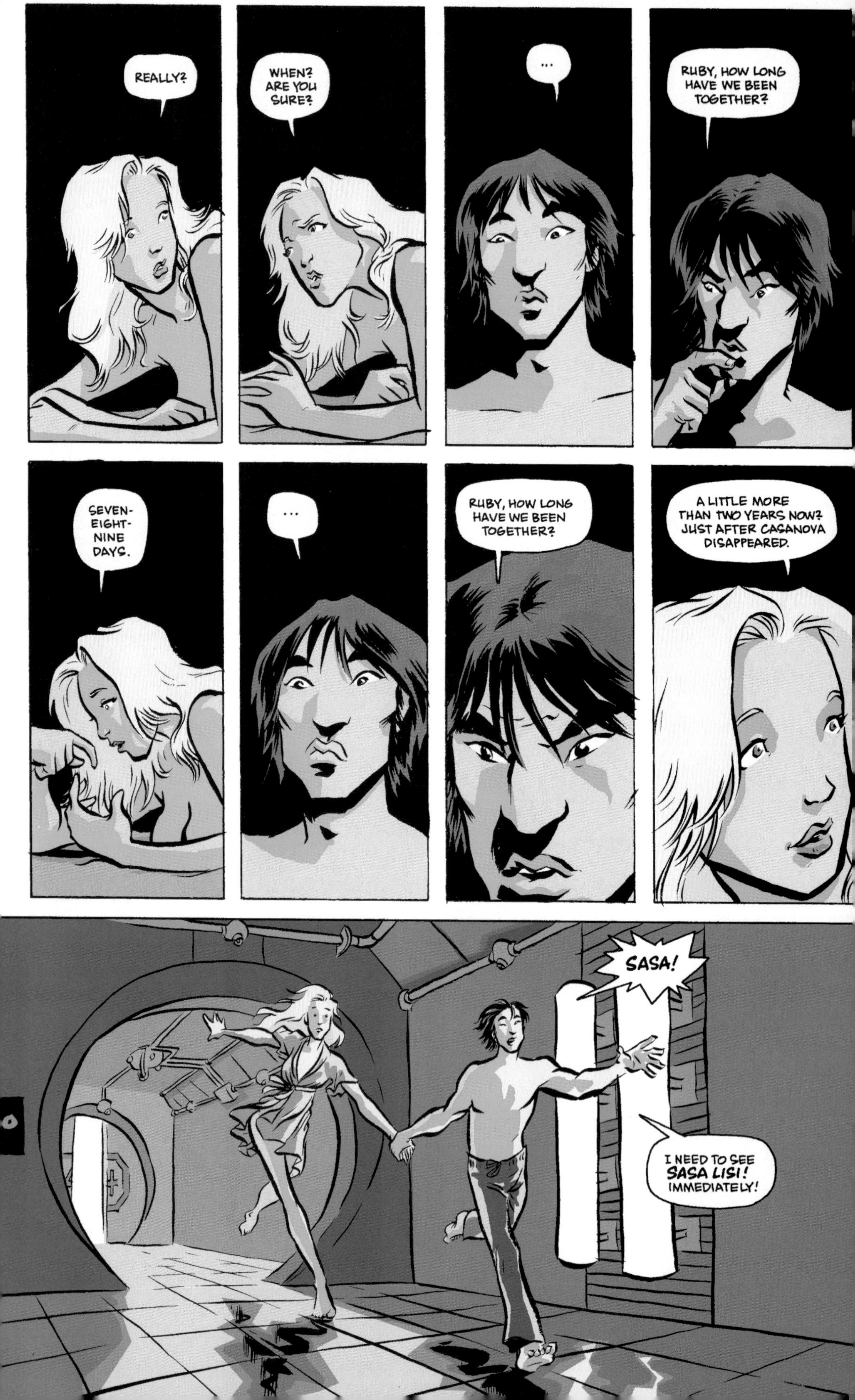
REALLY?
WHEN? ARE YOU SURE?
...
RUBY, HOW LONG HAVE WE BEEN TOGETHER?
SEVEN-EIGHT-NINE DAYS.
...
RUBY, HOW LONG HAVE WE BEEN TOGETHER?
A LITTLE MORE THAN TWO YEARS NOW? JUST AFTER CASANOVA DISAPPEARED.
SASA!
I NEED TO SEE SASA LISI! IMMEDIATELY!

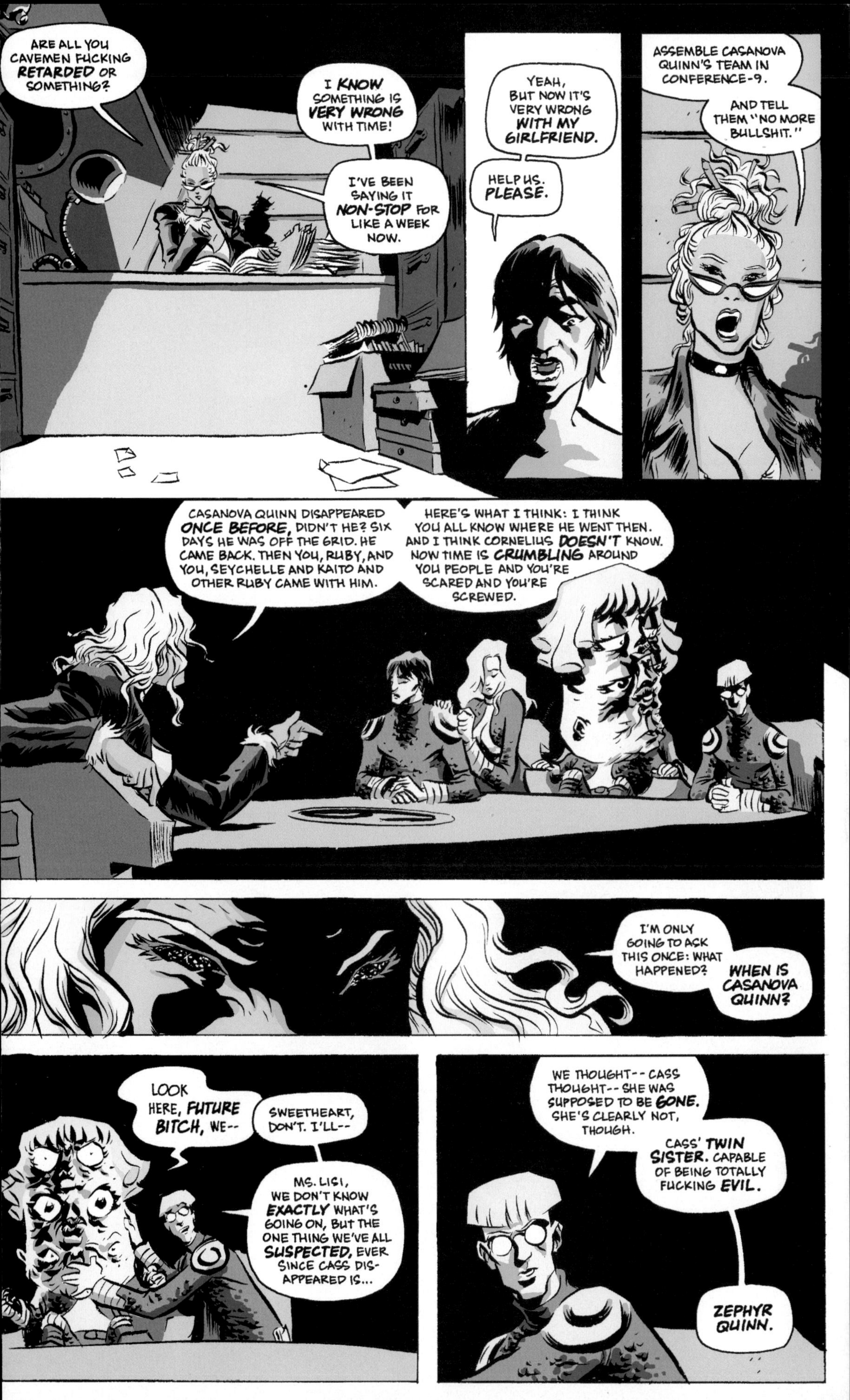
ARE ALL YOU CAVEMEN FUCKING RETARDED OR SOMETHING?
I KNOW SOMETHING IS VERY WRONG WITH TIME!
I'VE BEEN SAYING IT NON-STOP FOR LIKE A WEEK NOW.
YEAH, BUT NOW IT'S VERY WRONG WITH MY GIRLFRIEND.
HELP US. PLEASE.
ASSEMBLE CASANOVA QUINN'S TEAM IN CONFERENCE-9.
AND TELL THEM "NO MORE BULLSHIT."
CASANOVA QUINN DISAPPEARED ONCE BEFORE, DIDN'T HE? SIX DAYS HE WAS OFF THE GRID. HE CAME BACK. THEN YOU, RUBY, AND YOU, SEYCHELLE AND KAITO AND OTHER RUBY CAME WITH HIM.
HERE'S WHAT I THINK: I THINK YOU ALL KNOW WHERE HE WENT THEN. AND I THINK CORNELIUS DOESN'T KNOW. NOW TIME IS CRUMBLING AROUND YOU PEOPLE AND YOU'RE SCARED AND YOU'RE SCREWED.
I'M ONLY GOING TO ASK THIS ONCE: WHAT HAPPENED?
WHEN IS CASANOVA QUINN?
LOOK HERE, FUTURE BITCH, WE--
SWEETHEART, DON'T. I'LL--
MS. LISI, WE DON'T KNOW EXACTLY WHAT'S GOING ON, BUT THE ONE THING WE'VE ALL SUSPECTED, EVER SINCE CASS DIS-APPEARED IS...
WE THOUGHT-- CASS THOUGHT-- SHE WAS SUPPOSED TO BE GONE. SHE'S CLEARLY NOT, THOUGH.
CASS' TWIN SISTER. CAPABLE OF BEING TOTALLY FUCKING EVIL.
ZEPHYR QUINN.

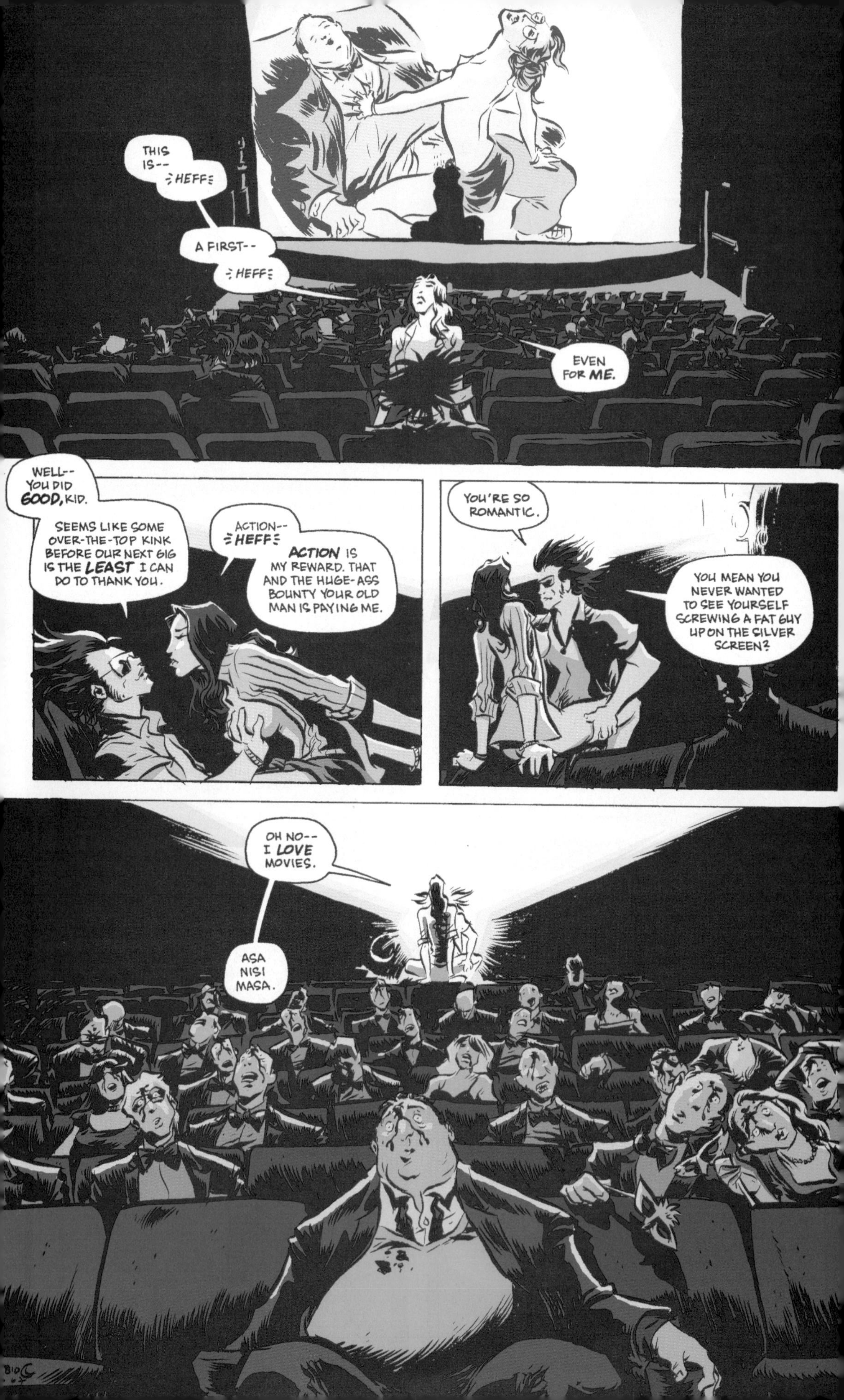
THIS IS--
HEFF
A FIRST--
HEFF
EVEN FOR **ME.**
WELL-- YOU DID **GOOD,** KID.
SEEMS LIKE SOME OVER-THE-TOP KINK BEFORE OUR NEXT GIG IS THE **LEAST** I CAN DO TO THANK YOU.
ACTION--
HEFF
ACTION IS MY REWARD. THAT AND THE HUGE-ASS BOUNTY YOUR OLD MAN IS PAYING ME.
YOU'RE SO ROMANTIC.
YOU MEAN YOU NEVER WANTED TO SEE YOURSELF SCREWING A FAT GUY UP ON THE SILVER SCREEN?
OH NO-- I **LOVE** MOVIES.
ASA NISI MASA.

CHAPTER 4
NAOMI I MOAN

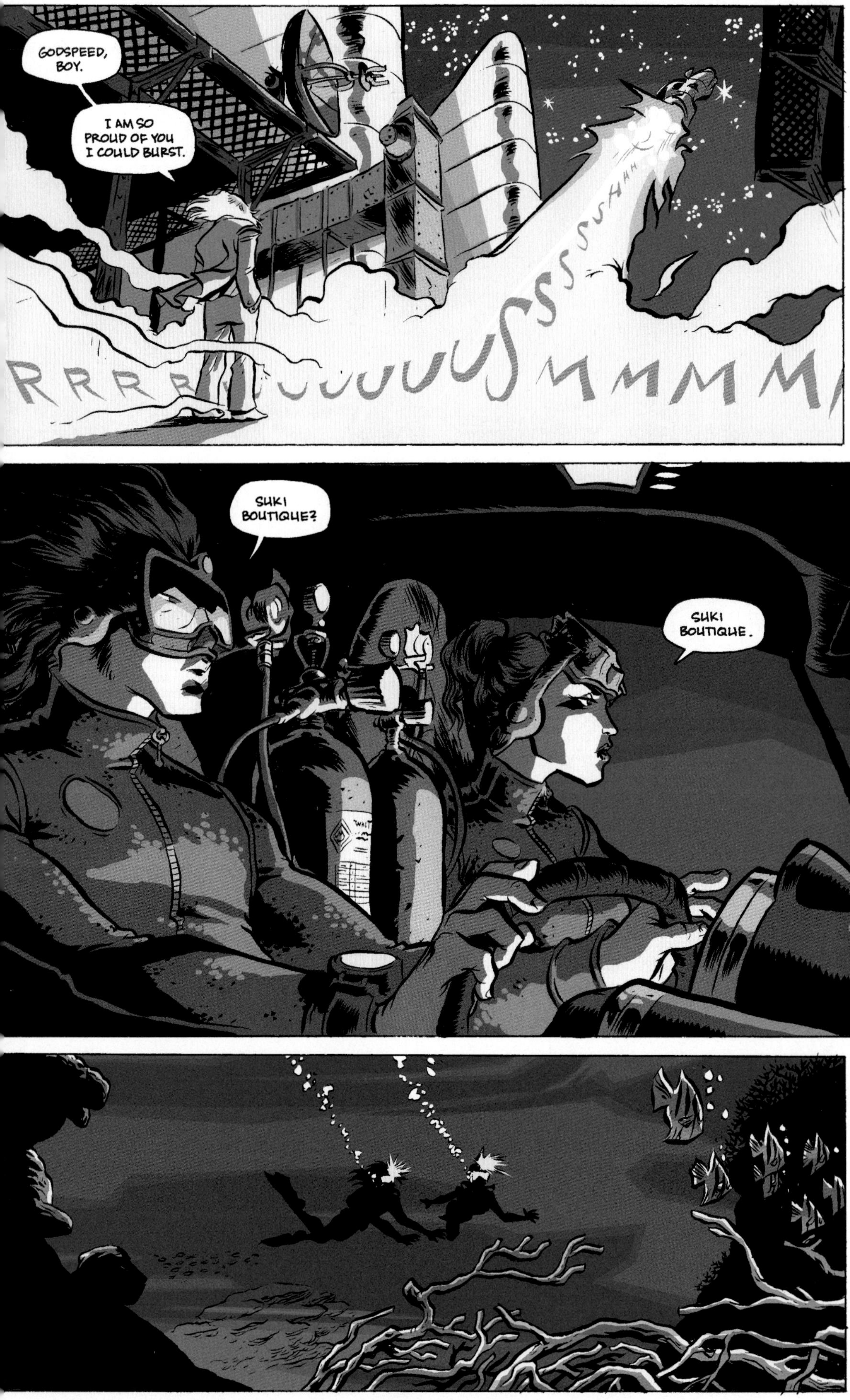
GODSPEED, BOY.
I AM SO PROUD OF YOU I COULD BURST.
RRRRUUUUUUSMMMMM
SUKI BOUTIQUE?
SUKI BOUTIQUE.

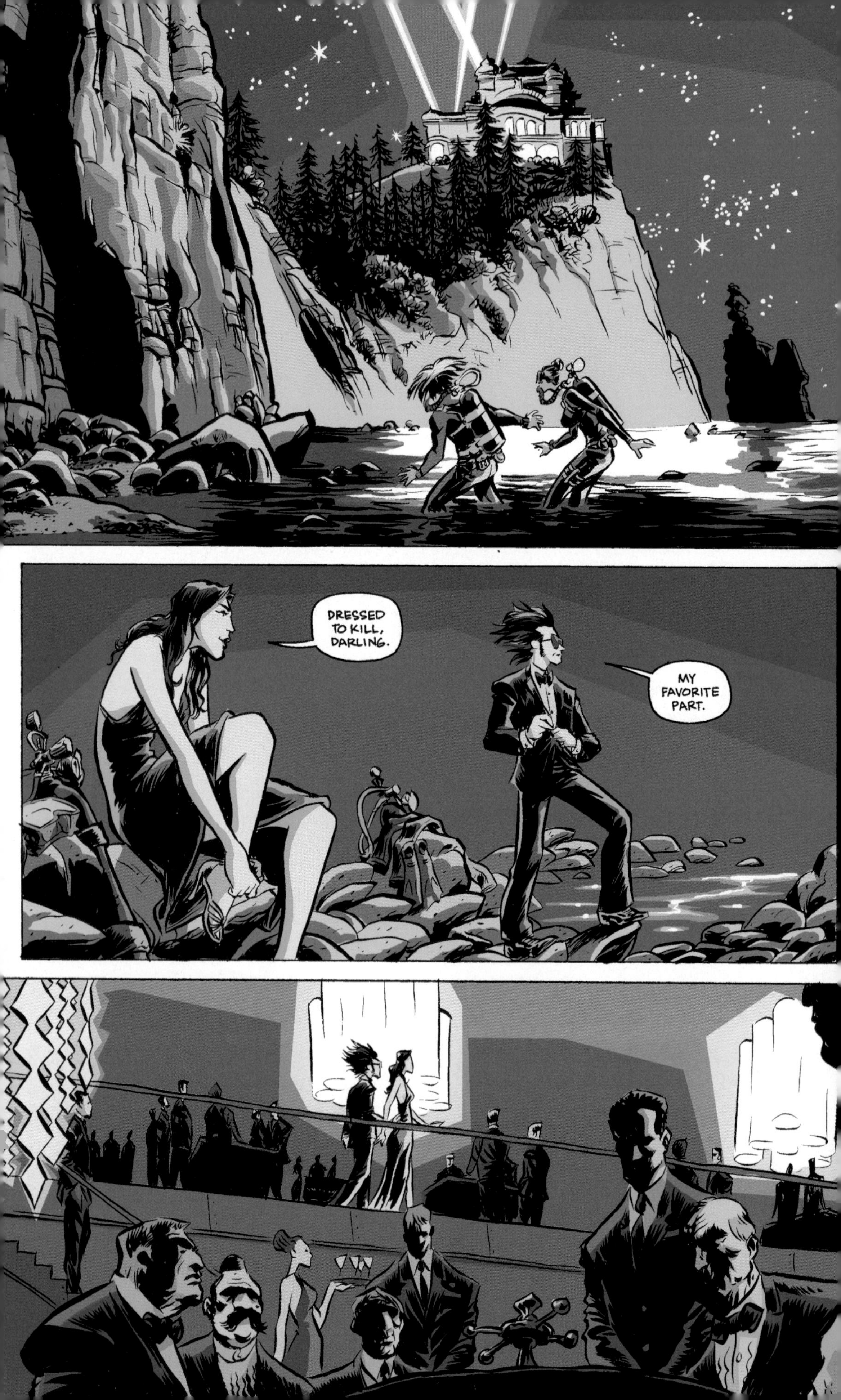
DRESSED TO KILL, DARLING.
MY FAVORITE PART.

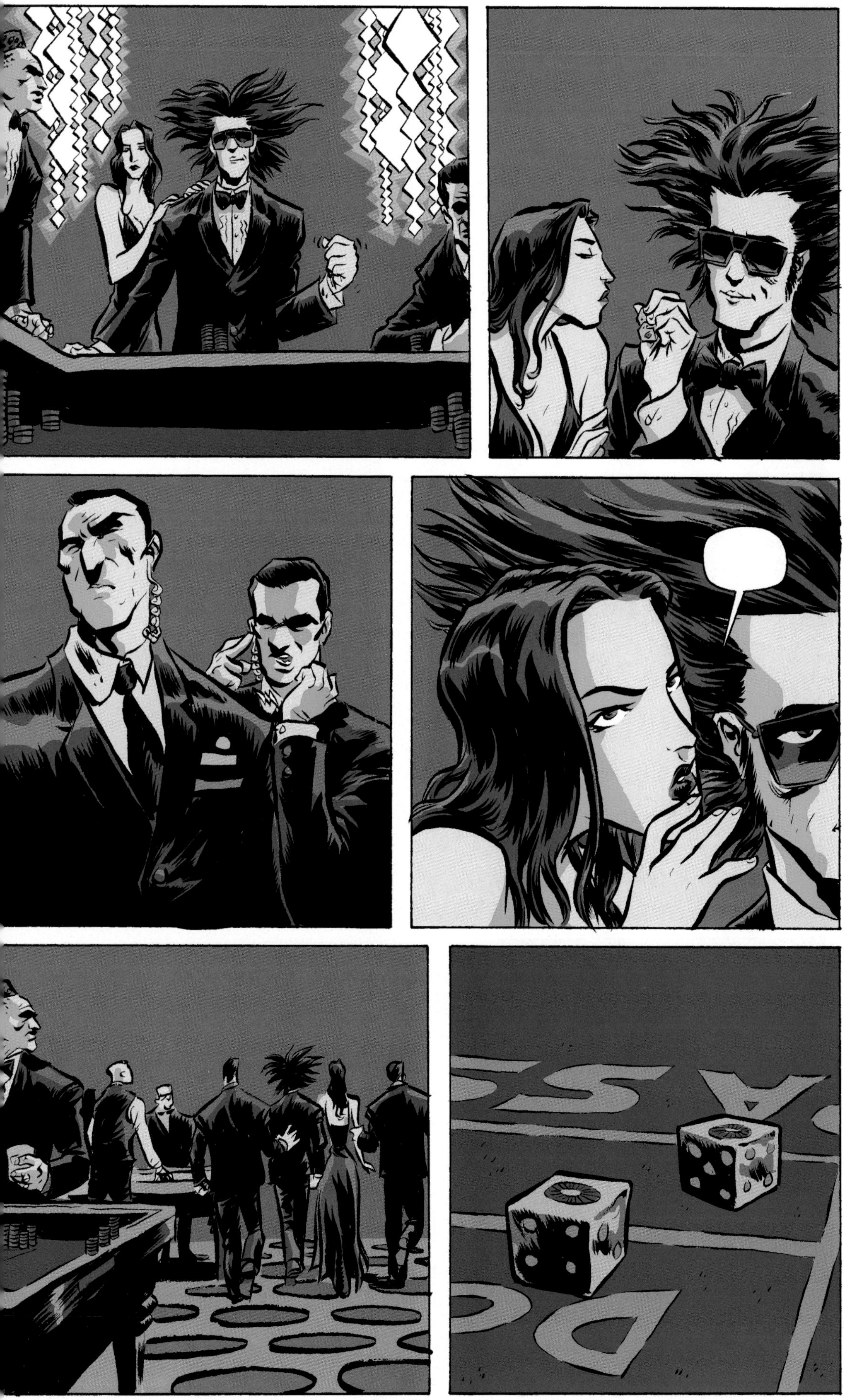

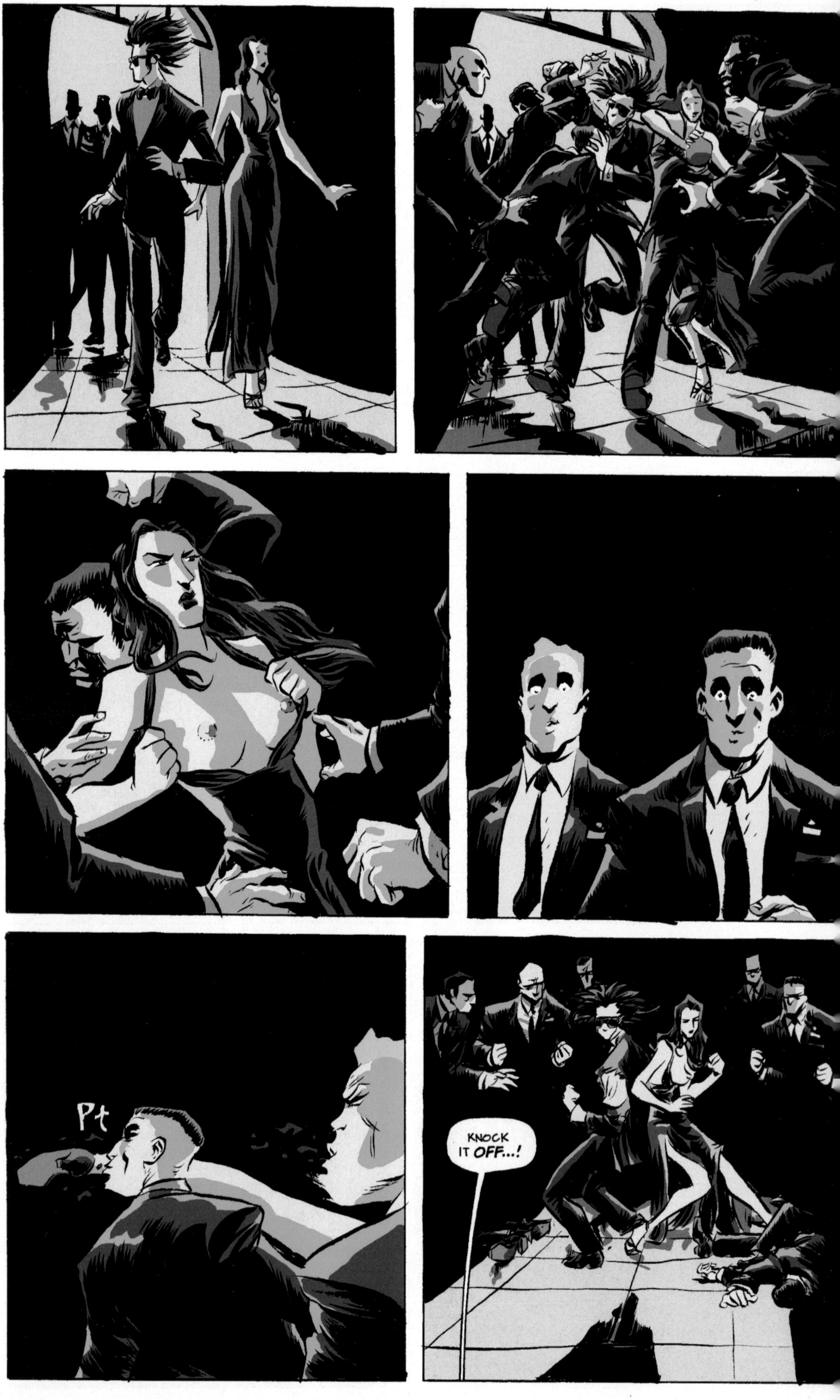
Pt
KNOCK IT OFF...!

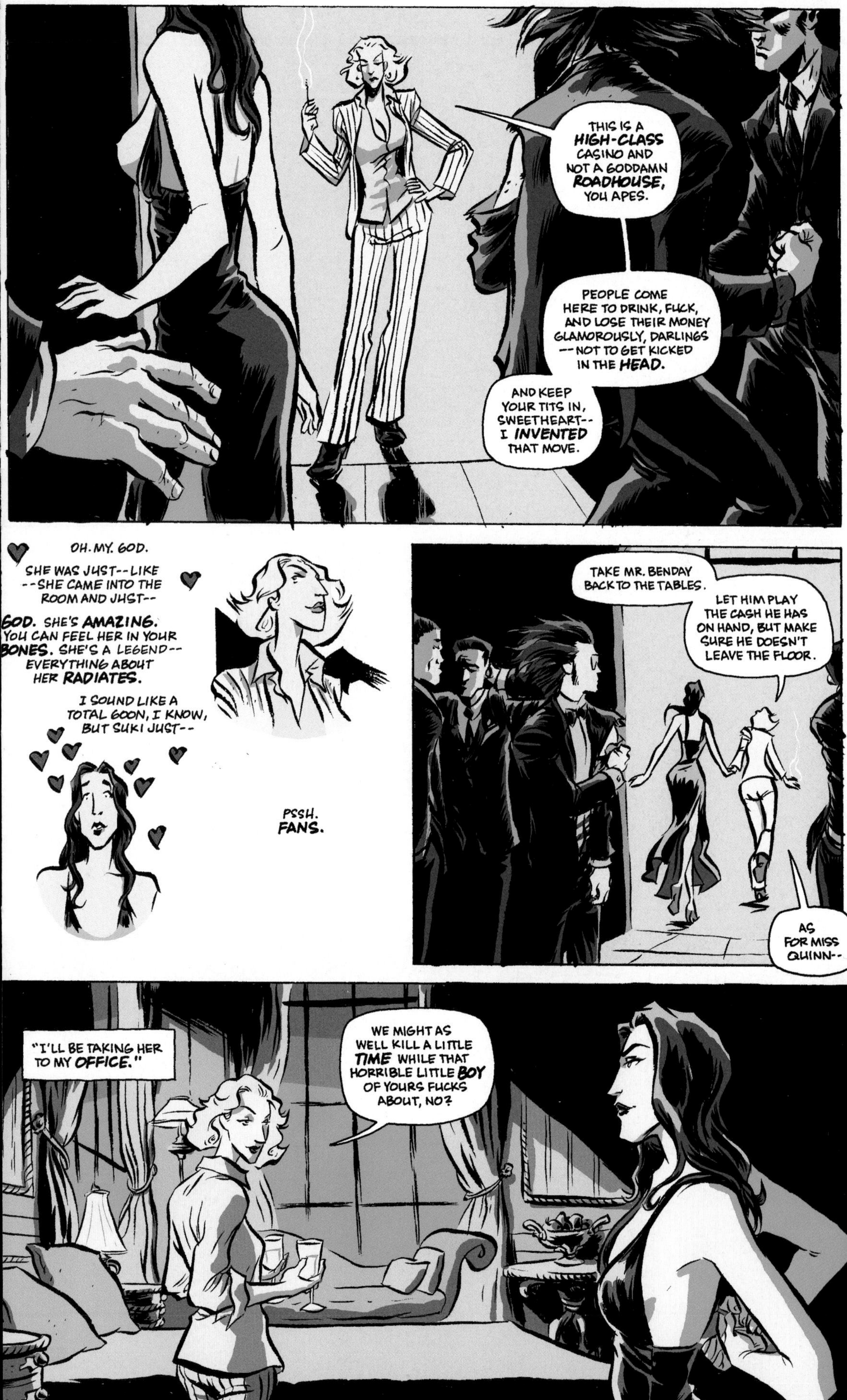

THIS IS A HIGH-CLASS CASINO AND NOT A GODDAMN ROADHOUSE, YOU APES.
PEOPLE COME HERE TO DRINK, FUCK, AND LOSE THEIR MONEY GLAMOROUSLY, DARLINGS --NOT TO GET KICKED IN THE HEAD.
AND KEEP YOUR TITS IN, SWEETHEART-- I INVENTED THAT MOVE.
OH. MY. GOD.
SHE WAS JUST--LIKE --SHE CAME INTO THE ROOM AND JUST--
GOD. SHE'S AMAZING. YOU CAN FEEL HER IN YOUR BONES. SHE'S A LEGEND-- EVERYTHING ABOUT HER RADIATES.
I SOUND LIKE A TOTAL GOON, I KNOW, BUT SUKI JUST--
PSSH. FANS.
TAKE MR. BENDAY BACK TO THE TABLES.
LET HIM PLAY THE CASH HE HAS ON HAND, BUT MAKE SURE HE DOESN'T LEAVE THE FLOOR.
AS FOR MISS QUINN--
"I'LL BE TAKING HER TO MY OFFICE."
WE MIGHT AS WELL KILL A LITTLE TIME WHILE THAT HORRIBLE LITTLE BOY OF YOURS FUCKS ABOUT, NO?

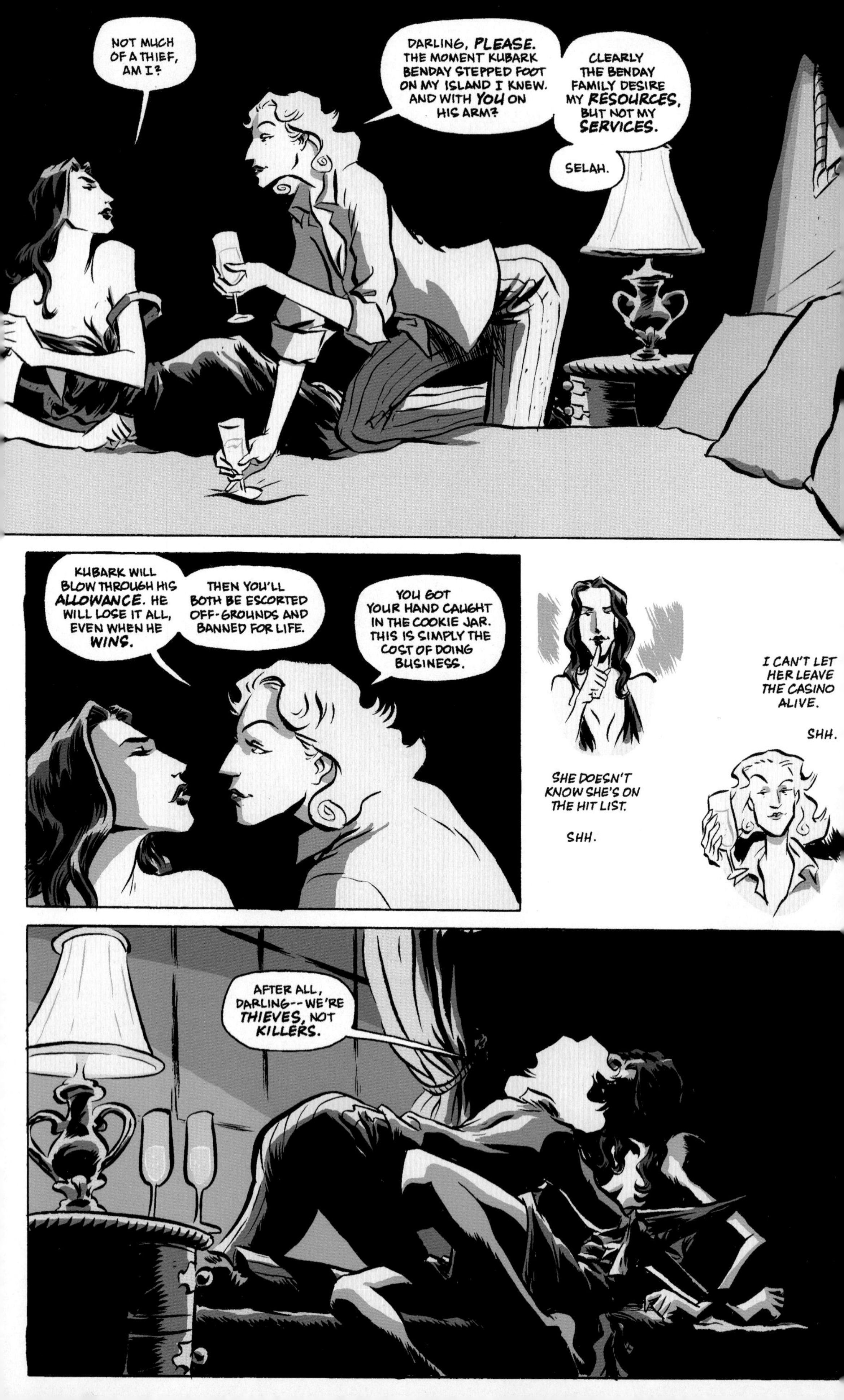
NOT MUCH OF A THIEF, AM I?
DARLING, PLEASE. THE MOMENT KUBARK BENDAY STEPPED FOOT ON MY ISLAND I KNEW. AND WITH YOU ON HIS ARM?
CLEARLY THE BENDAY FAMILY DESIRE MY RESOURCES, BUT NOT MY SERVICES.
SELAH.
KUBARK WILL BLOW THROUGH HIS ALLOWANCE. HE WILL LOSE IT ALL, EVEN WHEN HE WINS.
THEN YOU'LL BOTH BE ESCORTED OFF-GROUNDS AND BANNED FOR LIFE.
YOU GOT YOUR HAND CAUGHT IN THE COOKIE JAR. THIS IS SIMPLY THE COST OF DOING BUSINESS.
SHE DOESN'T KNOW SHE'S ON THE HIT LIST.
SHH.
I CAN'T LET HER LEAVE THE CASINO ALIVE.
SHH.
AFTER ALL, DARLING-- WE'RE THIEVES, NOT KILLERS.

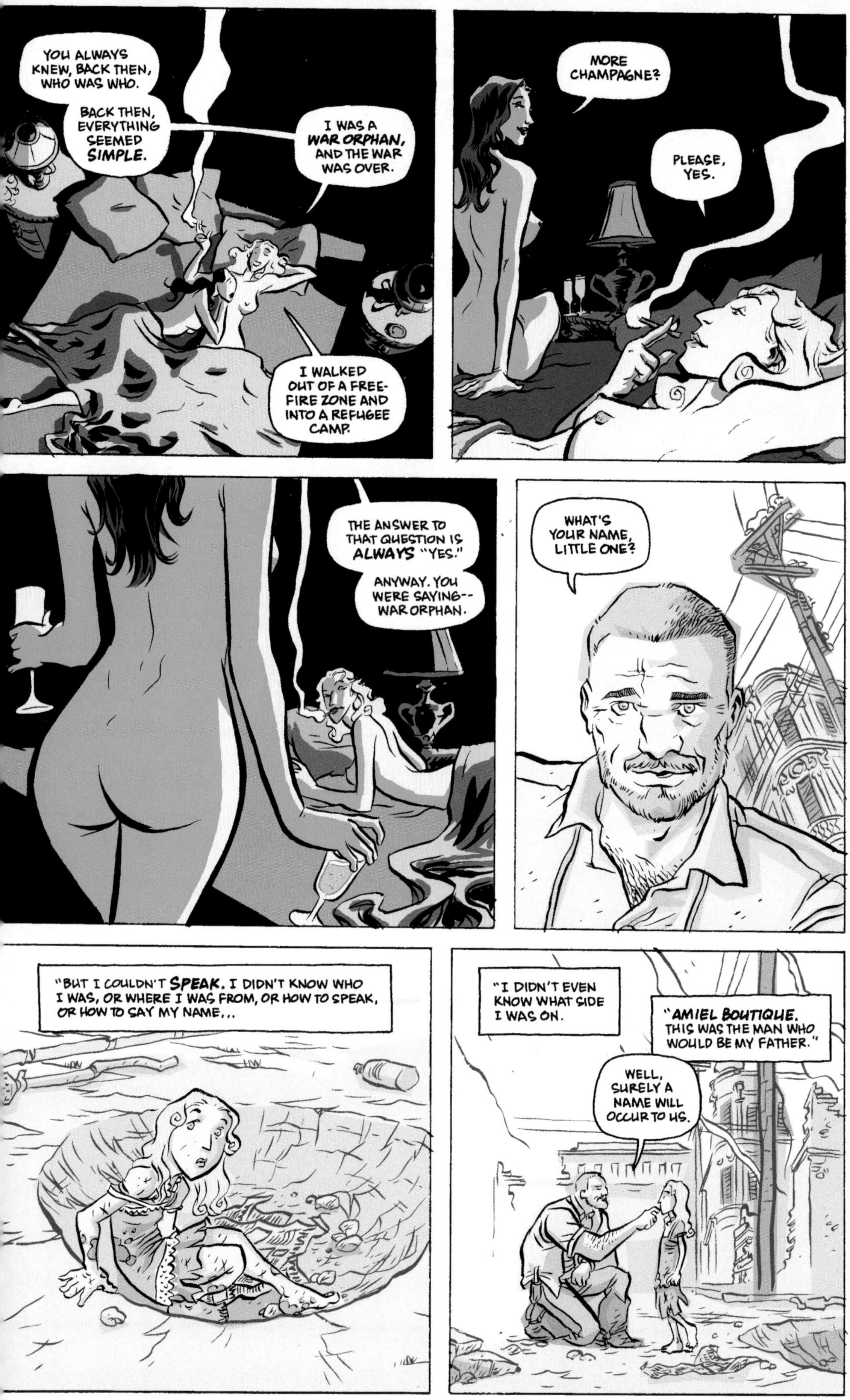
YOU ALWAYS KNEW, BACK THEN, WHO WAS WHO.
BACK THEN, EVERYTHING SEEMED SIMPLE.
I WAS A WAR ORPHAN, AND THE WAR WAS OVER.
I WALKED OUT OF A FREE-FIRE ZONE AND INTO A REFUGEE CAMP.
MORE CHAMPAGNE?
PLEASE, YES.
THE ANSWER TO THAT QUESTION IS ALWAYS "YES."
ANYWAY. YOU WERE SAYING-- WAR ORPHAN.
WHAT'S YOUR NAME, LITTLE ONE?
"BUT I COULDN'T SPEAK. I DIDN'T KNOW WHO I WAS, OR WHERE I WAS FROM, OR HOW TO SPEAK, OR HOW TO SAY MY NAME...
"I DIDN'T EVEN KNOW WHAT SIDE I WAS ON.
"AMIEL BOUTIQUE. THIS WAS THE MAN WHO WOULD BE MY FATHER."
WELL, SURELY A NAME WILL OCCUR TO US.

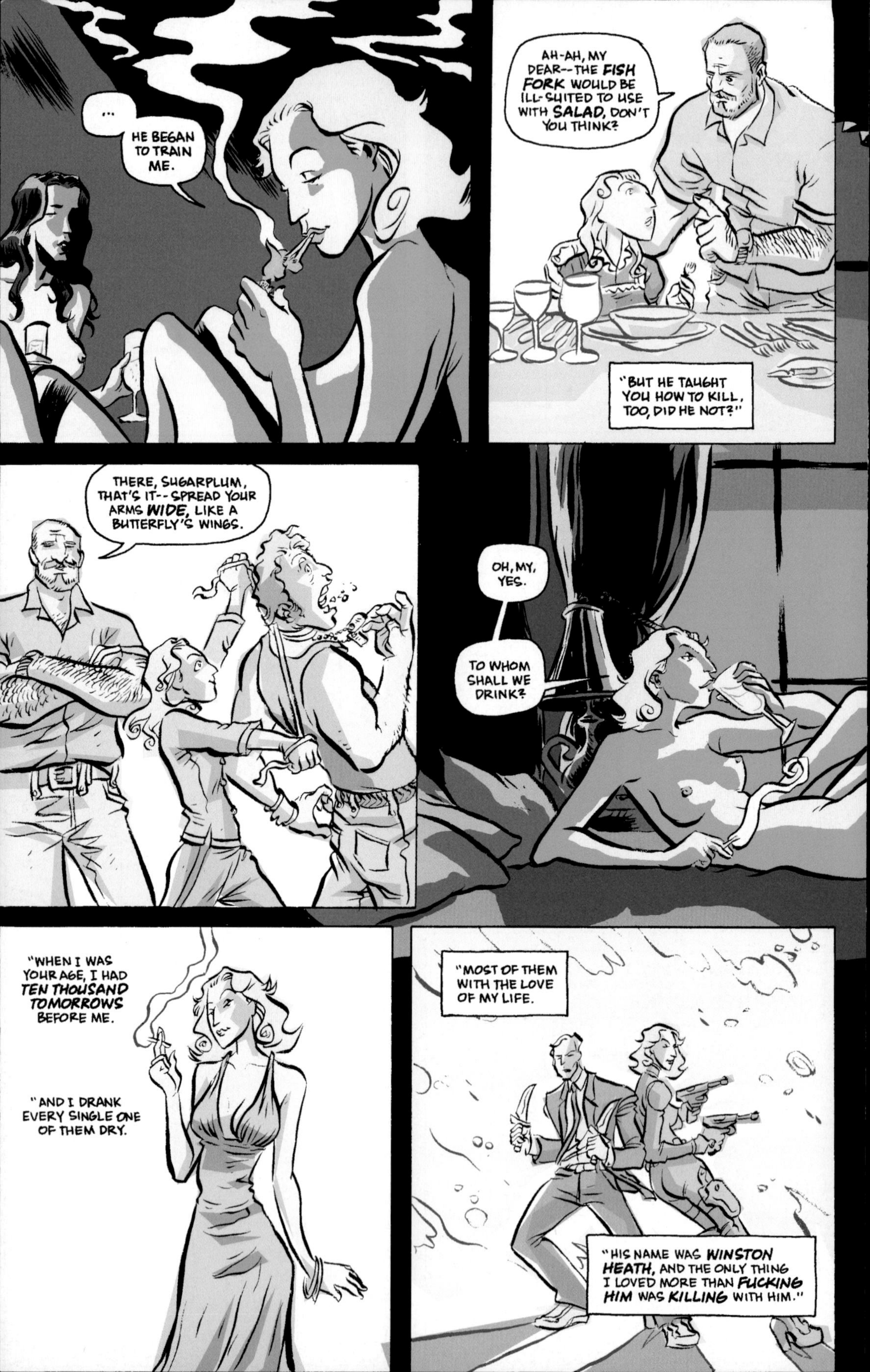
...
HE BEGAN TO TRAIN ME.
AH-AH, MY DEAR--THE FISH FORK WOULD BE ILL-SUITED TO USE WITH SALAD, DON'T YOU THINK?
"BUT HE TAUGHT YOU HOW TO KILL, TOO, DID HE NOT?"
THERE, SUGARPLUM, THAT'S IT--SPREAD YOUR ARMS WIDE, LIKE A BUTTERFLY'S WINGS.
OH, MY, YES.
TO WHOM SHALL WE DRINK?
"WHEN I WAS YOUR AGE, I HAD TEN THOUSAND TOMORROWS BEFORE ME.
"AND I DRANK EVERY SINGLE ONE OF THEM DRY.
"MOST OF THEM WITH THE LOVE OF MY LIFE.
"HIS NAME WAS WINSTON HEATH, AND THE ONLY THING I LOVED MORE THAN FUCKING HIM WAS KILLING WITH HIM."

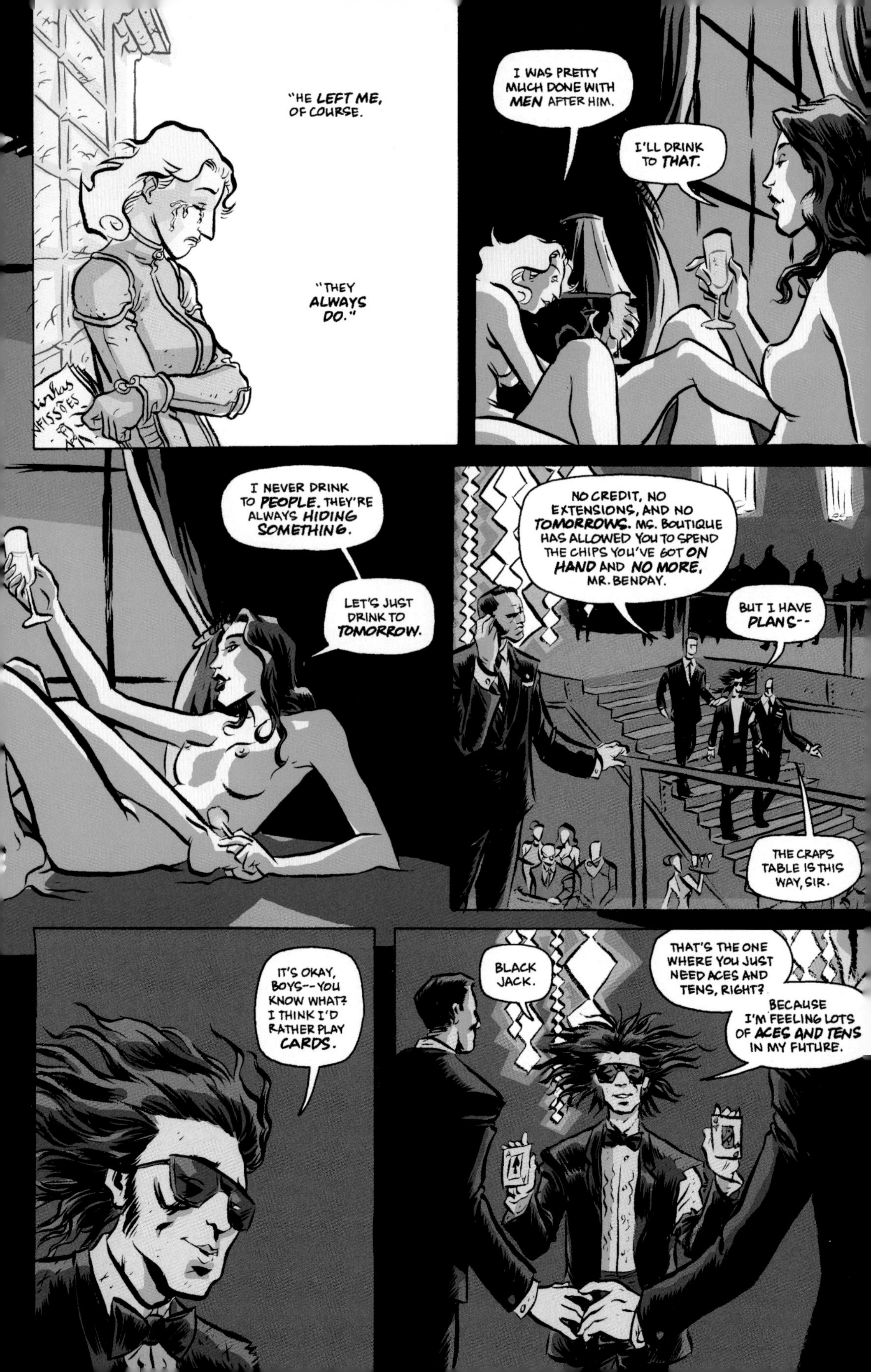
"HE LEFT ME, OF COURSE.
"THEY ALWAYS DO."
I WAS PRETTY MUCH DONE WITH MEN AFTER HIM.
I'LL DRINK TO THAT.
I NEVER DRINK TO PEOPLE. THEY'RE ALWAYS HIDING SOMETHING.
LET'S JUST DRINK TO TOMORROW.
NO CREDIT, NO EXTENSIONS, AND NO TOMORROWS. MS. BOUTIQUE HAS ALLOWED YOU TO SPEND THE CHIPS YOU'VE GOT ON HAND AND NO MORE, MR. BENDAY.
BUT I HAVE PLANS--
THE CRAPS TABLE IS THIS WAY, SIR.
IT'S OKAY, BOYS--YOU KNOW WHAT? I THINK I'D RATHER PLAY CARDS.
BLACK JACK.
THAT'S THE ONE WHERE YOU JUST NEED ACES AND TENS, RIGHT?
BECAUSE I'M FEELING LOTS OF ACES AND TENS IN MY FUTURE.

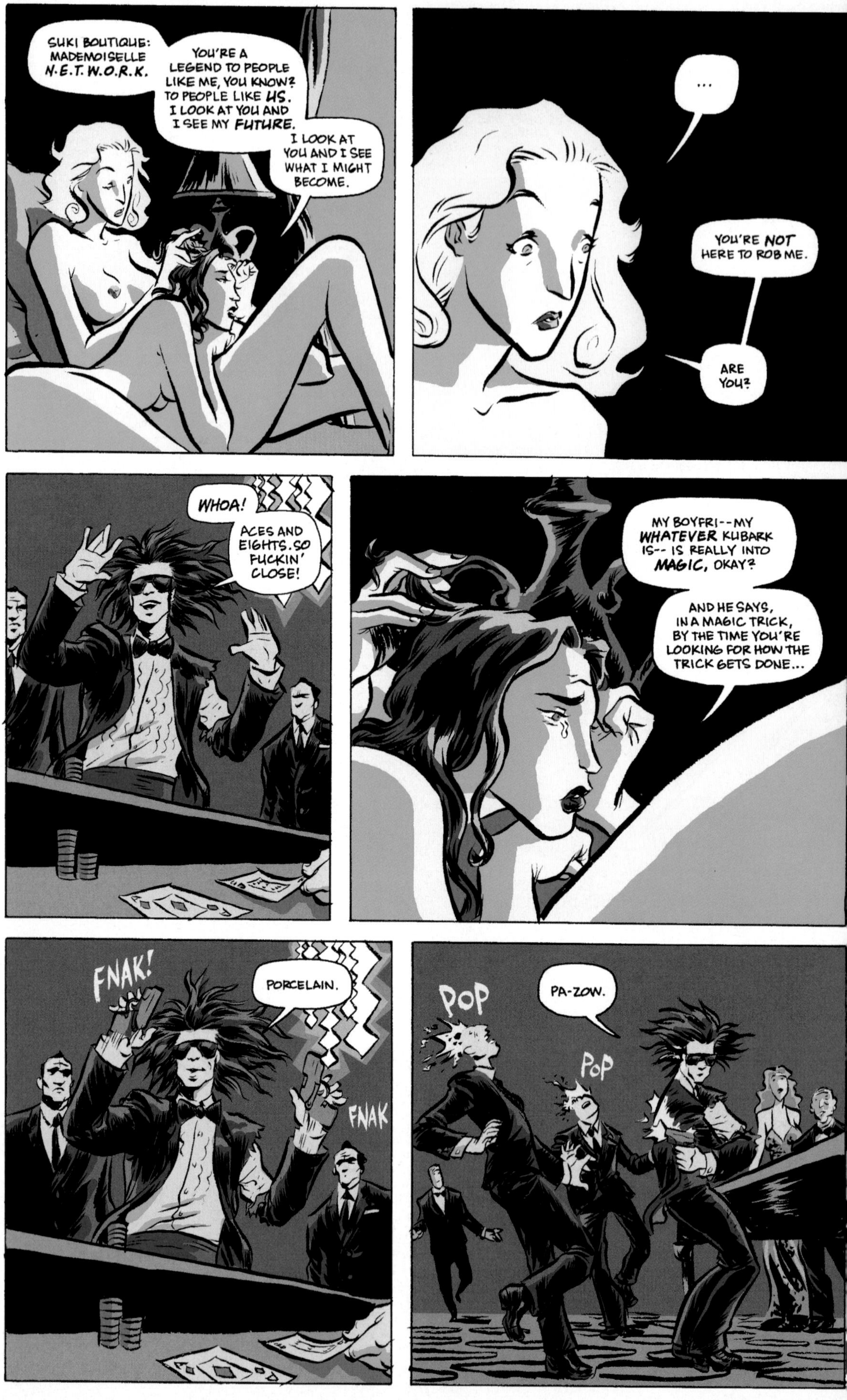
SUKI BOUTIQUE: MADEMOISELLE N.E.T.W.O.R.K.
YOU'RE A LEGEND TO PEOPLE LIKE ME, YOU KNOW? TO PEOPLE LIKE US. I LOOK AT YOU AND I SEE MY FUTURE.
I LOOK AT YOU AND I SEE WHAT I MIGHT BECOME.
...
YOU'RE NOT HERE TO ROB ME.
ARE YOU?
WHOA!
ACES AND EIGHTS. SO FUCKIN' CLOSE!
MY BOYFRI--MY WHATEVER KUBARK IS-- IS REALLY INTO MAGIC, OKAY?
AND HE SAYS, IN A MAGIC TRICK, BY THE TIME YOU'RE LOOKING FOR HOW THE TRICK GETS DONE...
FNAK!
PORCELAIN.
FNAK
POP
PA-ZOW.
POP

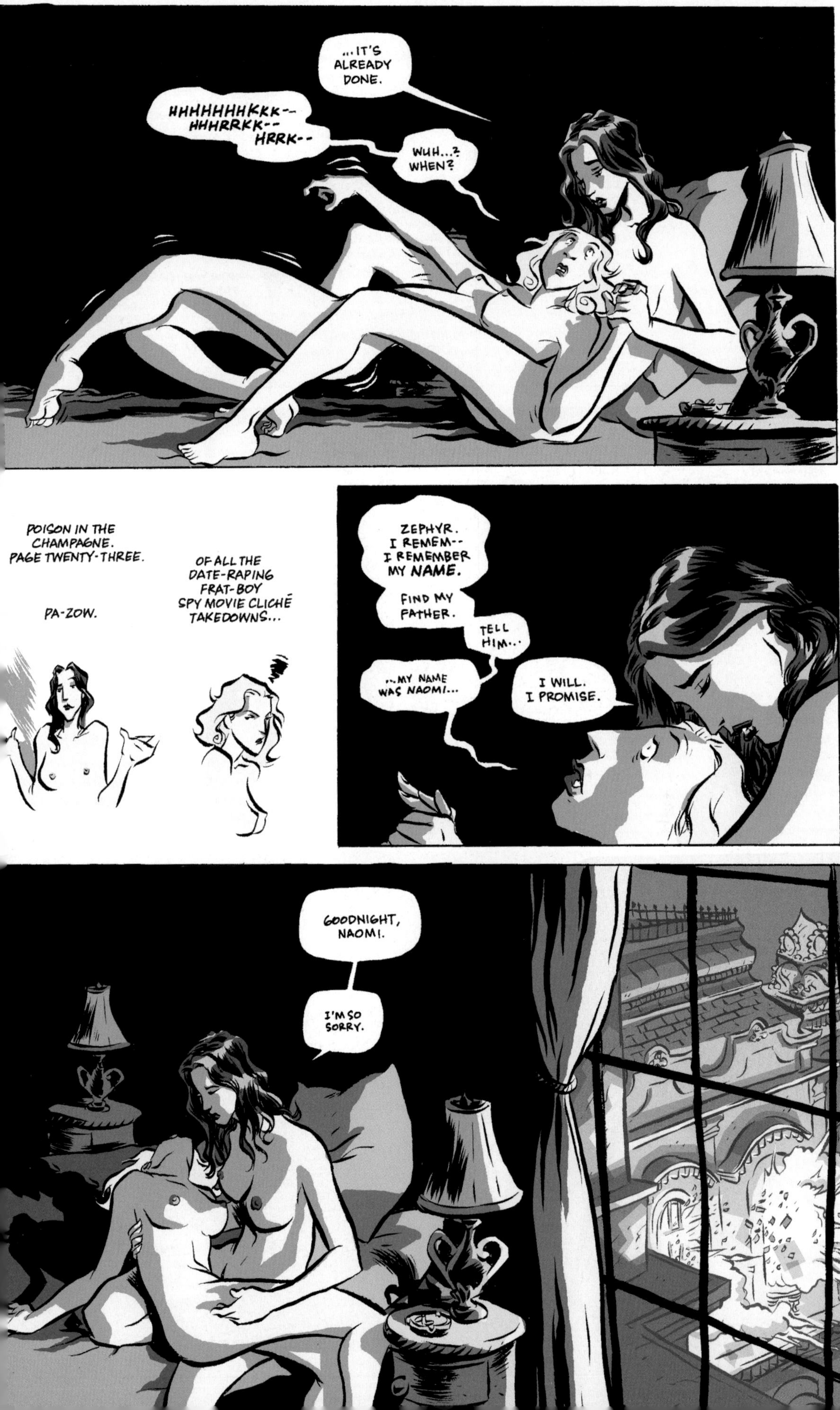
...IT'S ALREADY DONE.
HHHHHHHKKK-- HHHRRKK-- HRRK--
WUH...? WHEN?
POISON IN THE CHAMPAGNE. PAGE TWENTY-THREE.
PA-ZOW.
OF ALL THE DATE-RAPING FRAT-BOY SPY MOVIE CLICHÉ TAKEDOWNS...
ZEPHYR. I REMEM-- I REMEMBER MY NAME.
FIND MY FATHER.
TELL HIM...
...MY NAME WAS NAOMI...
I WILL. I PROMISE.
GOODNIGHT, NAOMI.
I'M SO SORRY.

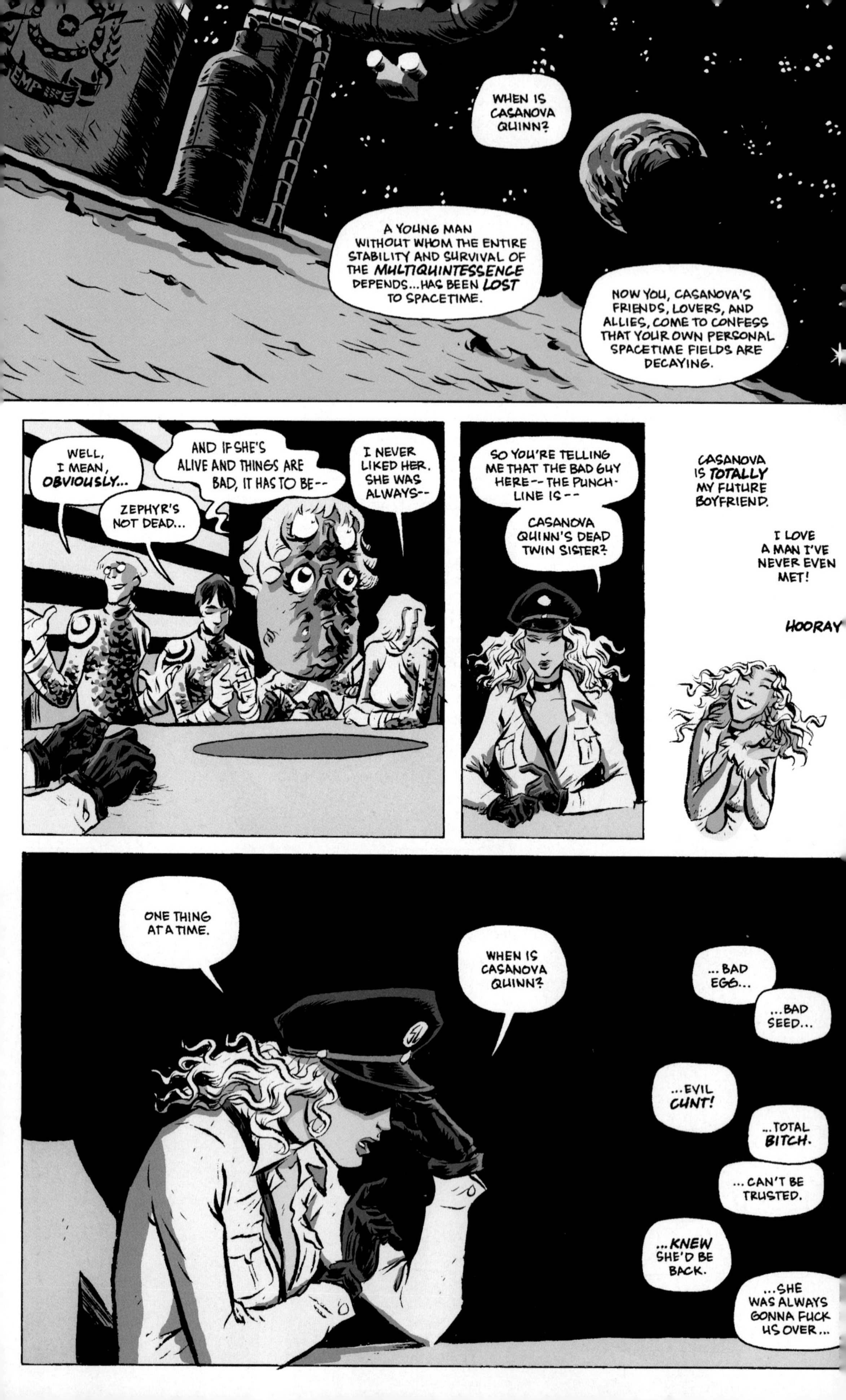

EMPIRE
WHEN IS CASANOVA QUINN?
A YOUNG MAN WITHOUT WHOM THE ENTIRE STABILITY AND SURVIVAL OF THE MULTIQUINTESSENCE DEPENDS...HAS BEEN LOST TO SPACETIME.
NOW YOU, CASANOVA'S FRIENDS, LOVERS, AND ALLIES, COME TO CONFESS THAT YOUR OWN PERSONAL SPACETIME FIELDS ARE DECAYING.
WELL, I MEAN, OBVIOUSLY...
ZEPHYR'S NOT DEAD...
AND IF SHE'S ALIVE AND THINGS ARE BAD, IT HAS TO BE--
I NEVER LIKED HER. SHE WAS ALWAYS--
SO YOU'RE TELLING ME THAT THE BAD GUY HERE-- THE PUNCH-LINE IS--
CASANOVA QUINN'S DEAD TWIN SISTER?
CASANOVA IS TOTALLY MY FUTURE BOYFRIEND.
I LOVE A MAN I'VE NEVER EVEN MET!
HOORAY
ONE THING AT A TIME.
WHEN IS CASANOVA QUINN?
...BAD EGGS...
...BAD SEED...
...EVIL CUNT!
...TOTAL BITCH.
...CAN'T BE TRUSTED.
...KNEW SHE'D BE BACK.
...SHE WAS ALWAYS GONNA FUCK US OVER...

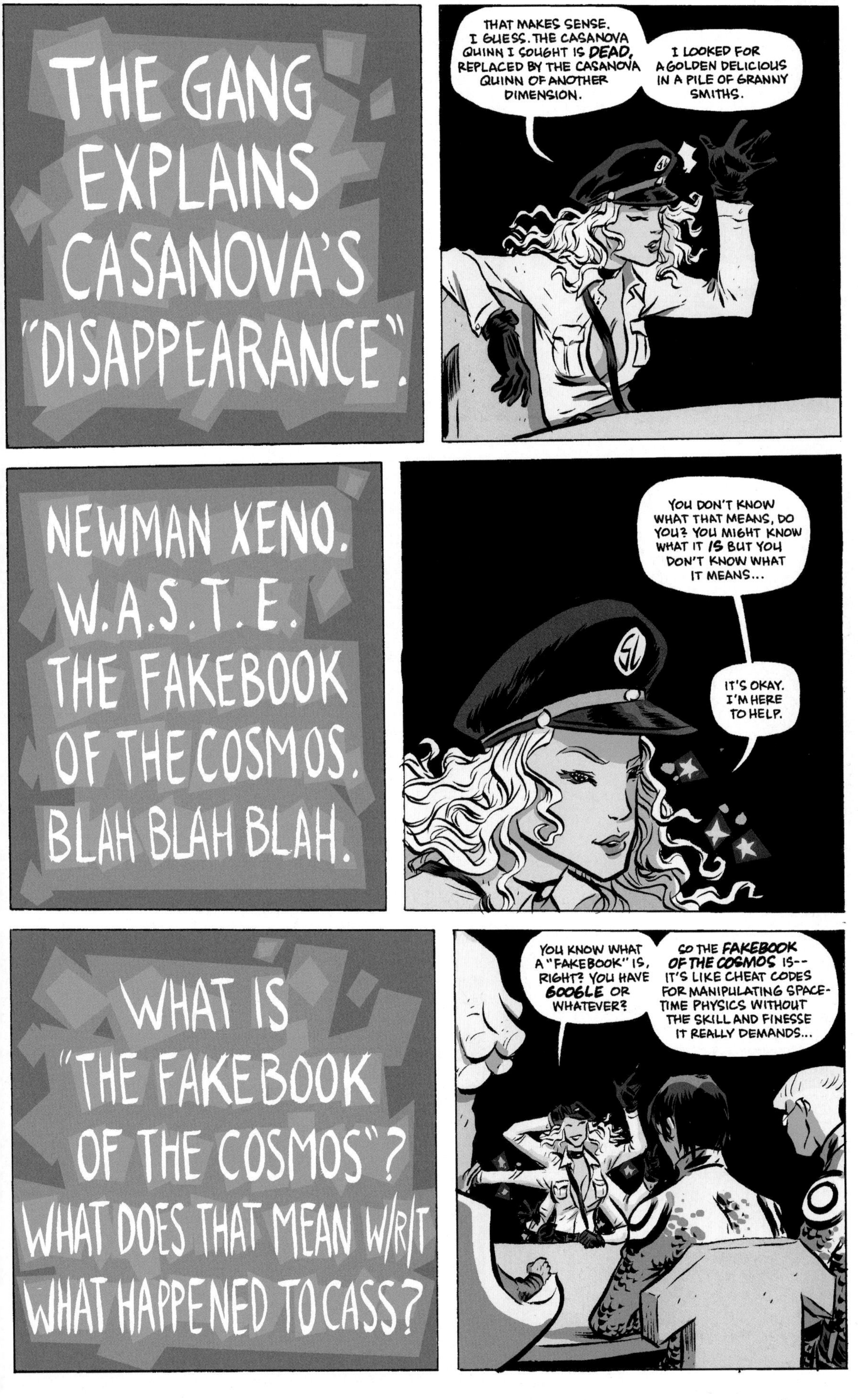
THE GANG EXPLAINS CASANOVA'S "DISAPPEARANCE".
THAT MAKES SENSE. I GUESS. THE CASANOVA QUINN I SOUGHT IS DEAD, REPLACED BY THE CASANOVA QUINN OF ANOTHER DIMENSION.
I LOOKED FOR A GOLDEN DELICIOUS IN A PILE OF GRANNY SMITHS.
NEWMAN XENO. W.A.S.T.E. THE FAKEBOOK OF THE COSMOS. BLAH BLAH BLAH.
YOU DON'T KNOW WHAT THAT MEANS, DO YOU? YOU MIGHT KNOW WHAT IT IS BUT YOU DON'T KNOW WHAT IT MEANS...
IT'S OKAY. I'M HERE TO HELP.
WHAT IS "THE FAKEBOOK OF THE COSMOS"? WHAT DOES THAT MEAN W/R/T WHAT HAPPENED TO CASS?
YOU KNOW WHAT A "FAKEBOOK" IS, RIGHT? YOU HAVE GOOGLE OR WHATEVER?
SO THE FAKEBOOK OF THE COSMOS IS-- IT'S LIKE CHEAT CODES FOR MANIPULATING SPACE-TIME PHYSICS WITHOUT THE SKILL AND FINESSE IT REALLY DEMANDS...

REPLACING CASANOVA 919 WITH CASANOVA 909 ISN'T EASY. THINK ABOUT IT: IN A **WORLD** OF INCREDIBLE THINGS, IT'S PRETTY FREAKIN' INCREDIBLE.

BUT WITH THE FAKEBOOK, SOME SMARTS, AND A SHIT-TON OF MONEY, YOU COULD DO IT.

919

909

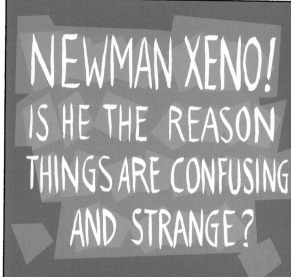

NEWMAN XENO! IS HE THE REASON THINGS ARE CONFUSING AND STRANGE?

NO. LIFE IS CONFUSING AND STRANGE, AS A RULE. EXPECT NEITHER NARRATIVE CLOSURE NOR CONTEXTUAL ILLUMINATION.

A LUNATIC WITH A POCKETKNIFE PERFORMED A DELICATE PIECE OF TRANS-DIMENSIONAL SURGERY. TRUST YOUR INTUITION: WHAT'S NEXT?

ZEPHYR?

SURE. WHY NOT? IT'S WHERE I WANT TO START.

WERE I TO **GUESS**, THERE'S A BALANCE SHE'S THROWING PROFOUNDLY OUT OF WHACK.

AND I DON'T KNOW **WHEN** CASANOVA IS. ANOTHER TIME, ANOTHER SPACE. I'LL FIND HIM ONE DAY.

WHAT IS ZEPHYR QUINN DOING, WHY, AND FOR WHOM?

I SAY WE FIND THAT BITCH AND **TEAR THE TRUTH** FROM HER LIAR'S TONGUE.

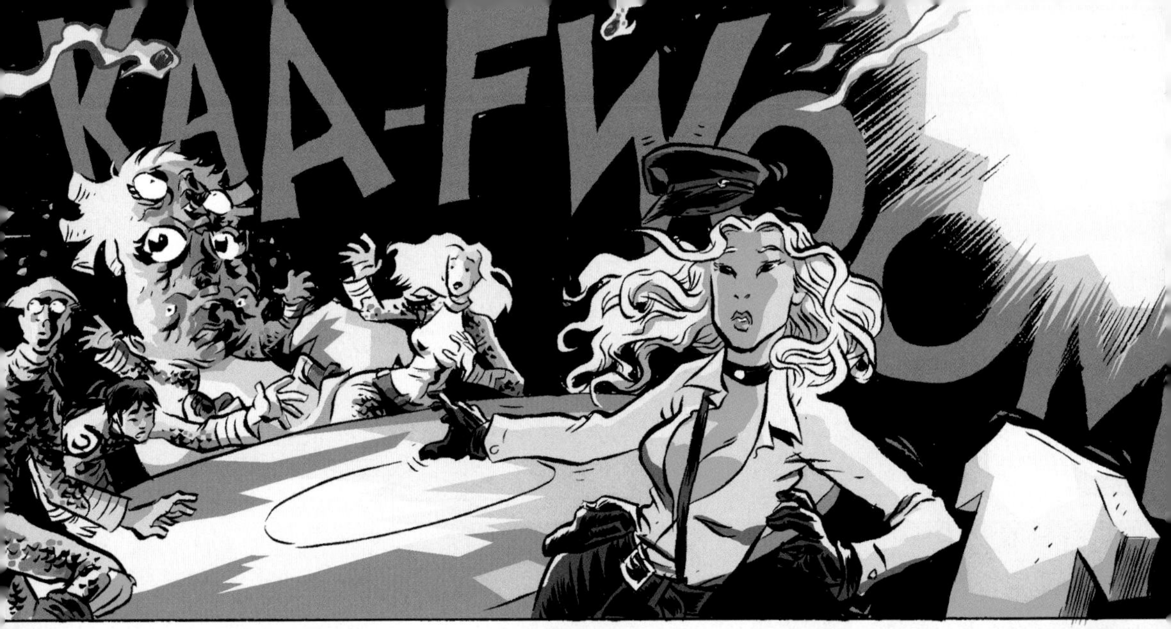
KAA-FWOOM

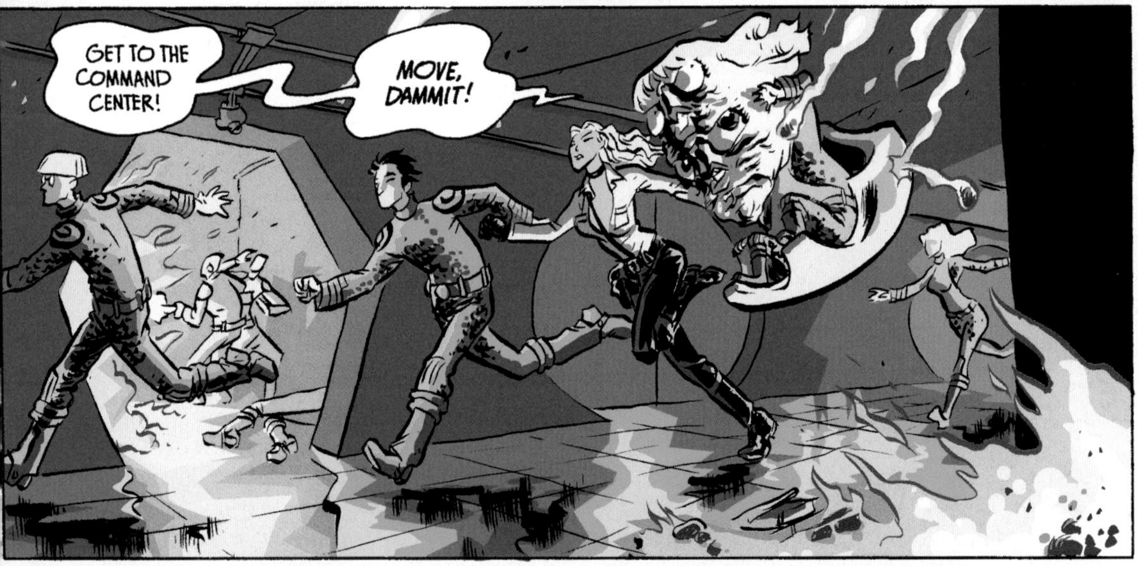
GET TO THE COMMAND CENTER!
MOVE, DAMMIT!

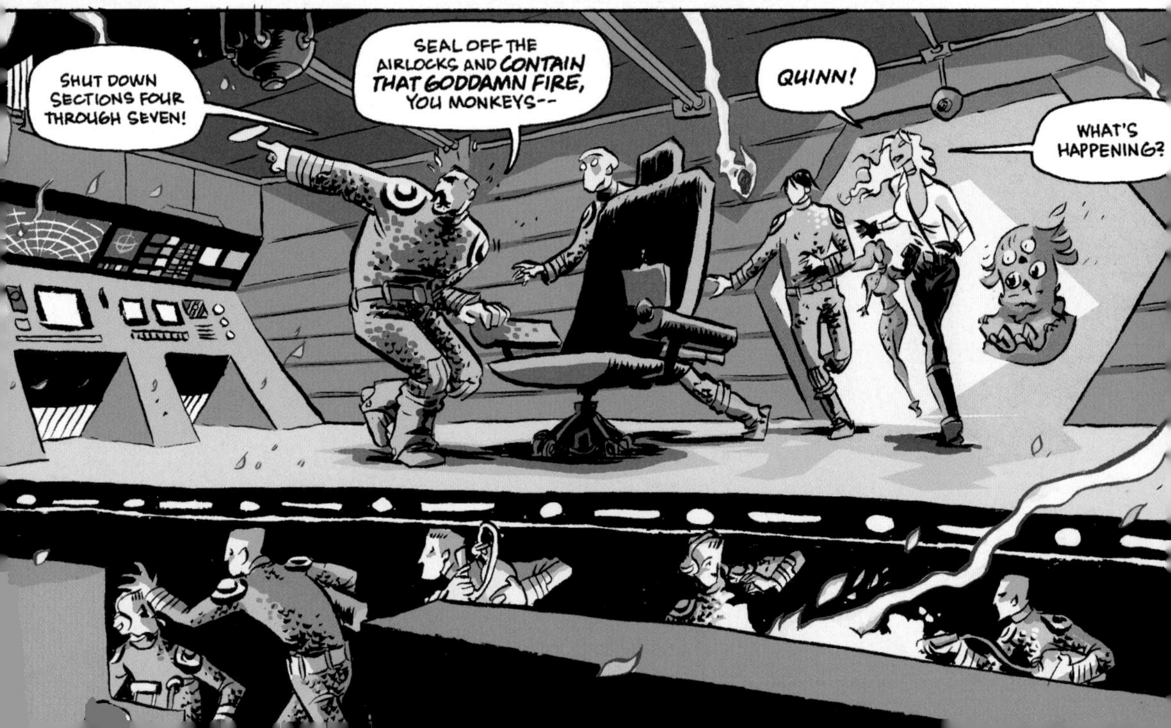
SHUT DOWN SECTIONS FOUR THROUGH SEVEN!
SEAL OFF THE AIRLOCKS AND CONTAIN THAT GODDAMN FIRE, YOU MONKEYS--
QUINN!
WHAT'S HAPPENING?

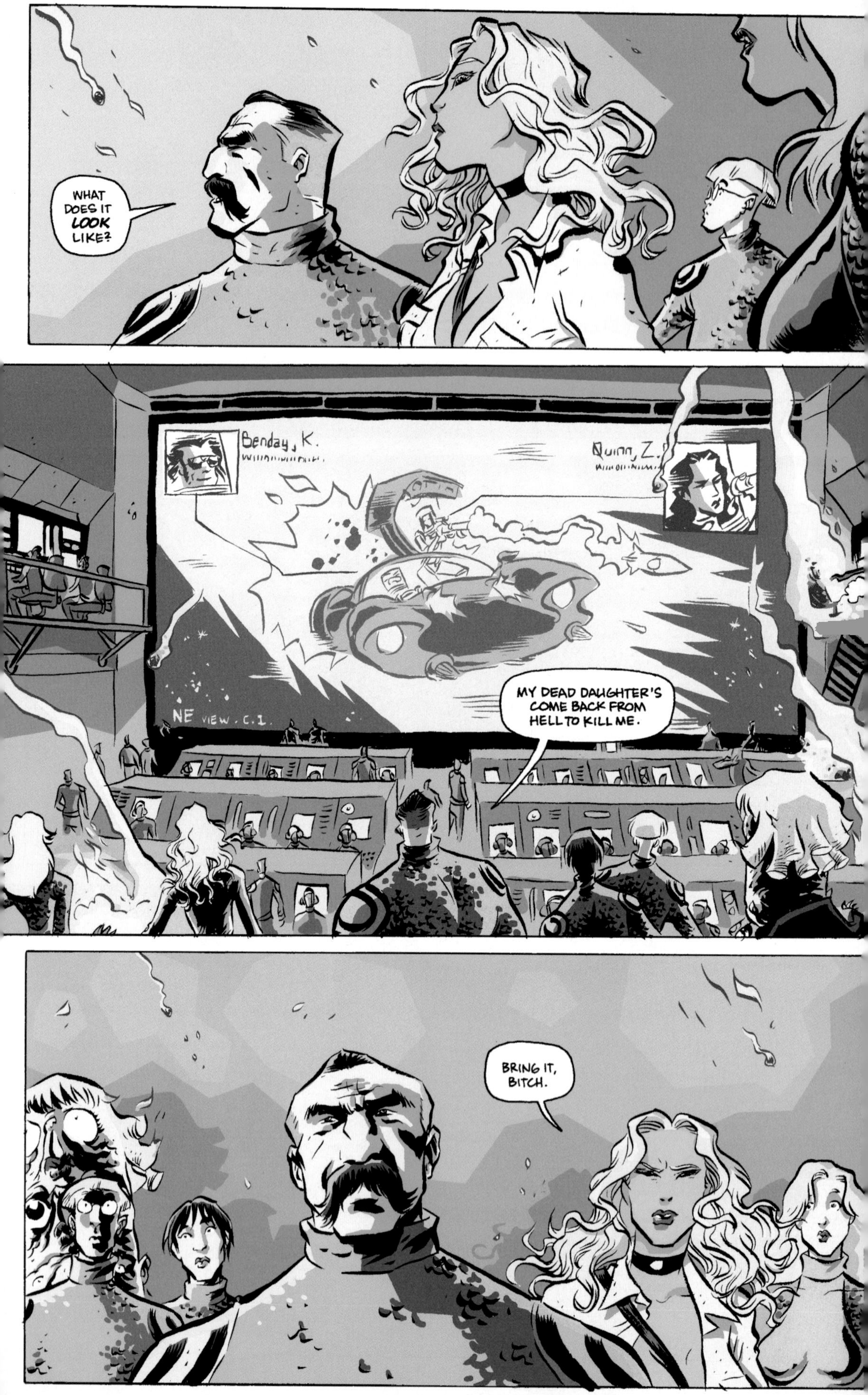
WHAT DOES IT LOOK LIKE?
Benday, K.
Quinn, Z.
NE VIEW. C.1.
MY DEAD DAUGHTER'S COME BACK FROM HELL TO KILL ME.
BRING IT, BITCH.

CHAPTER 5
FUCK SHIT UP

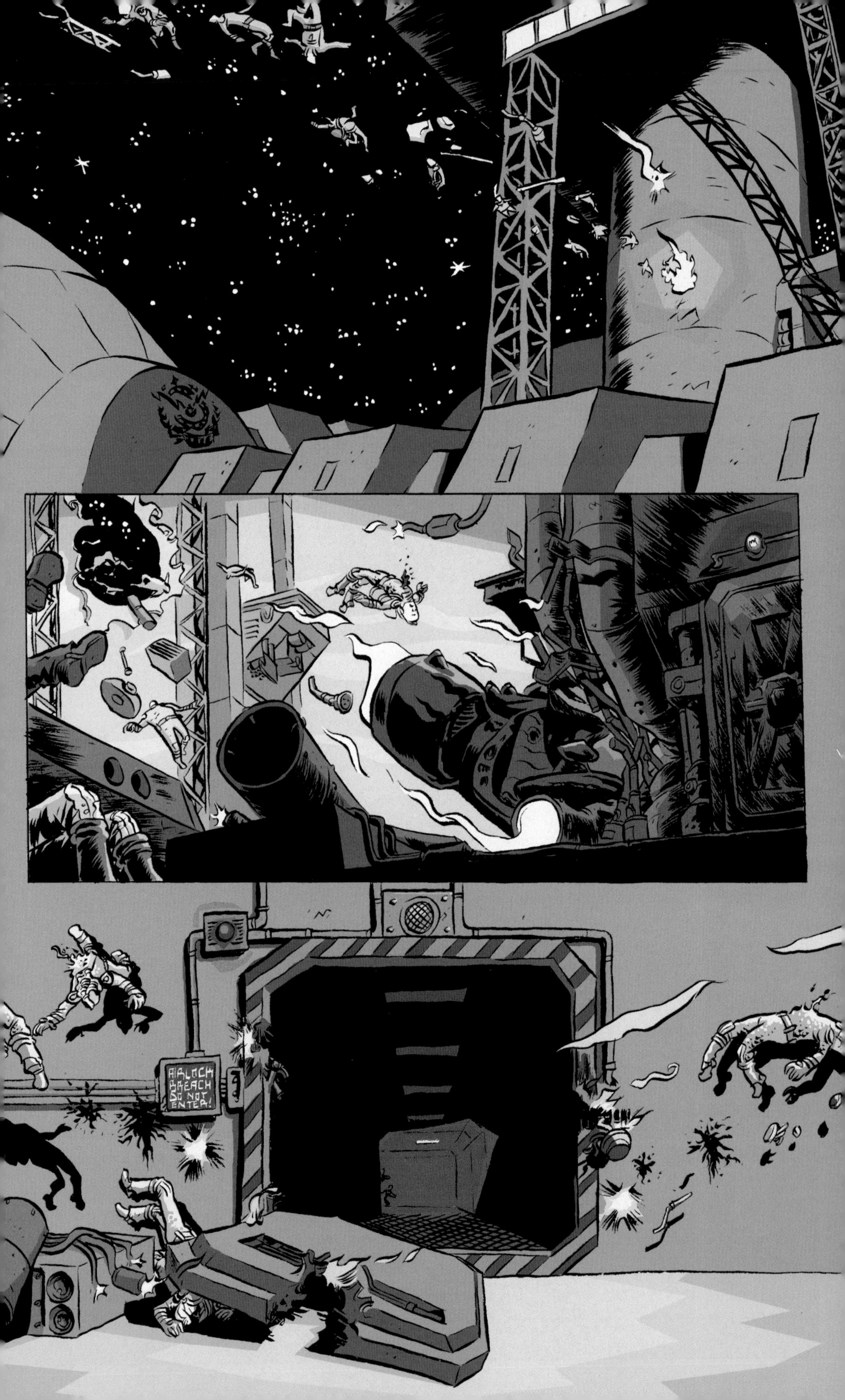
AIRLOCK BREACH DO NOT ENTER!

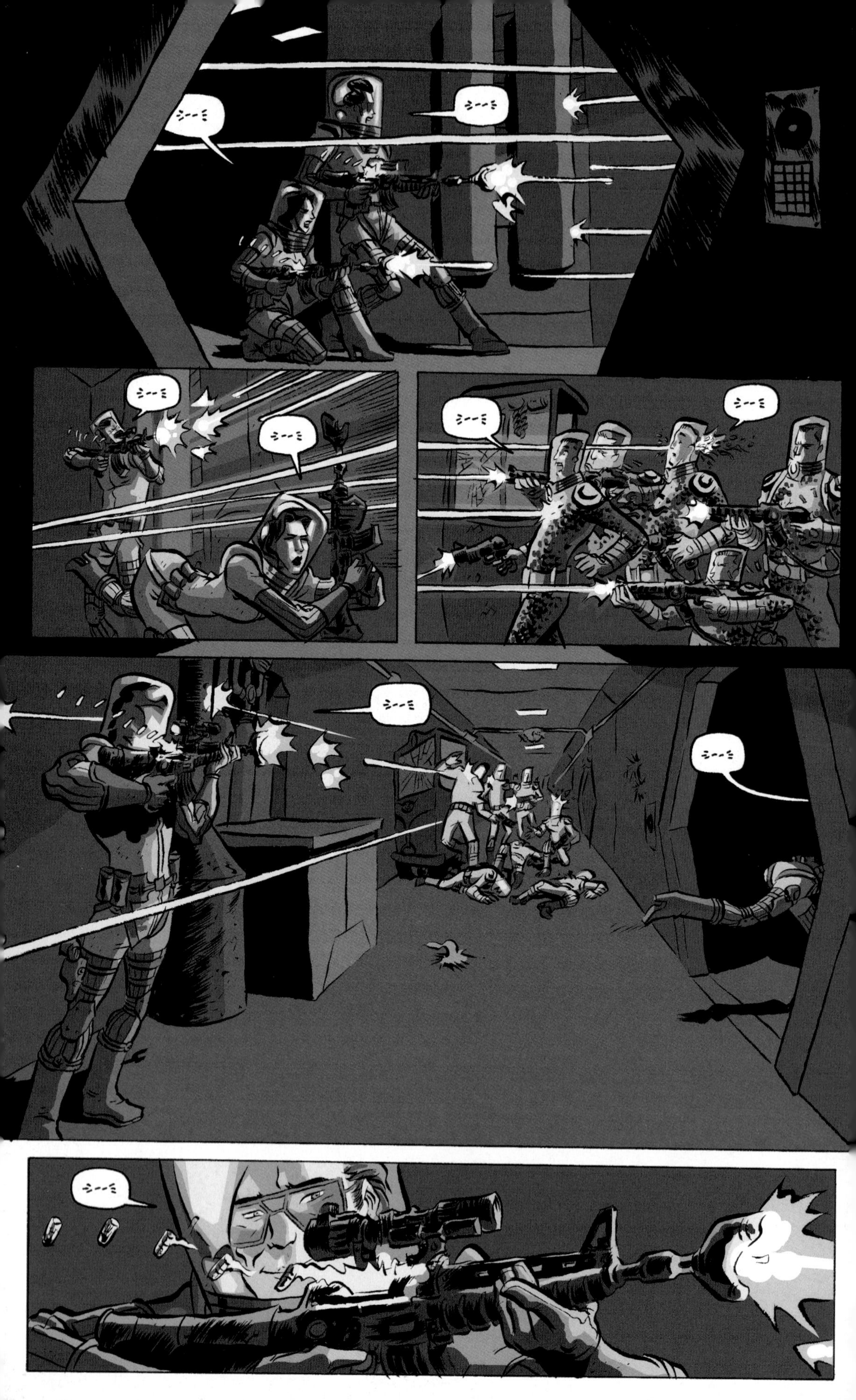

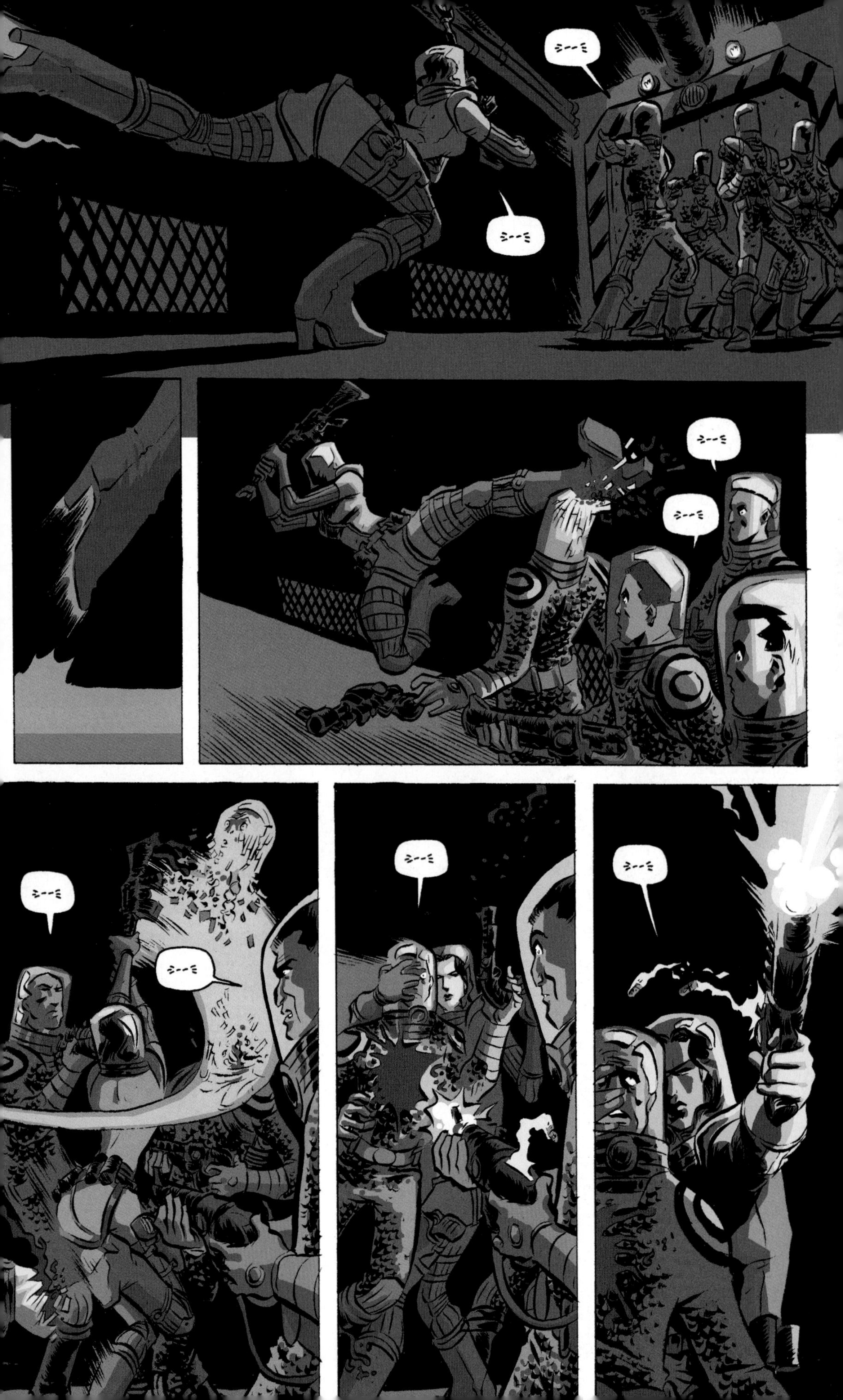

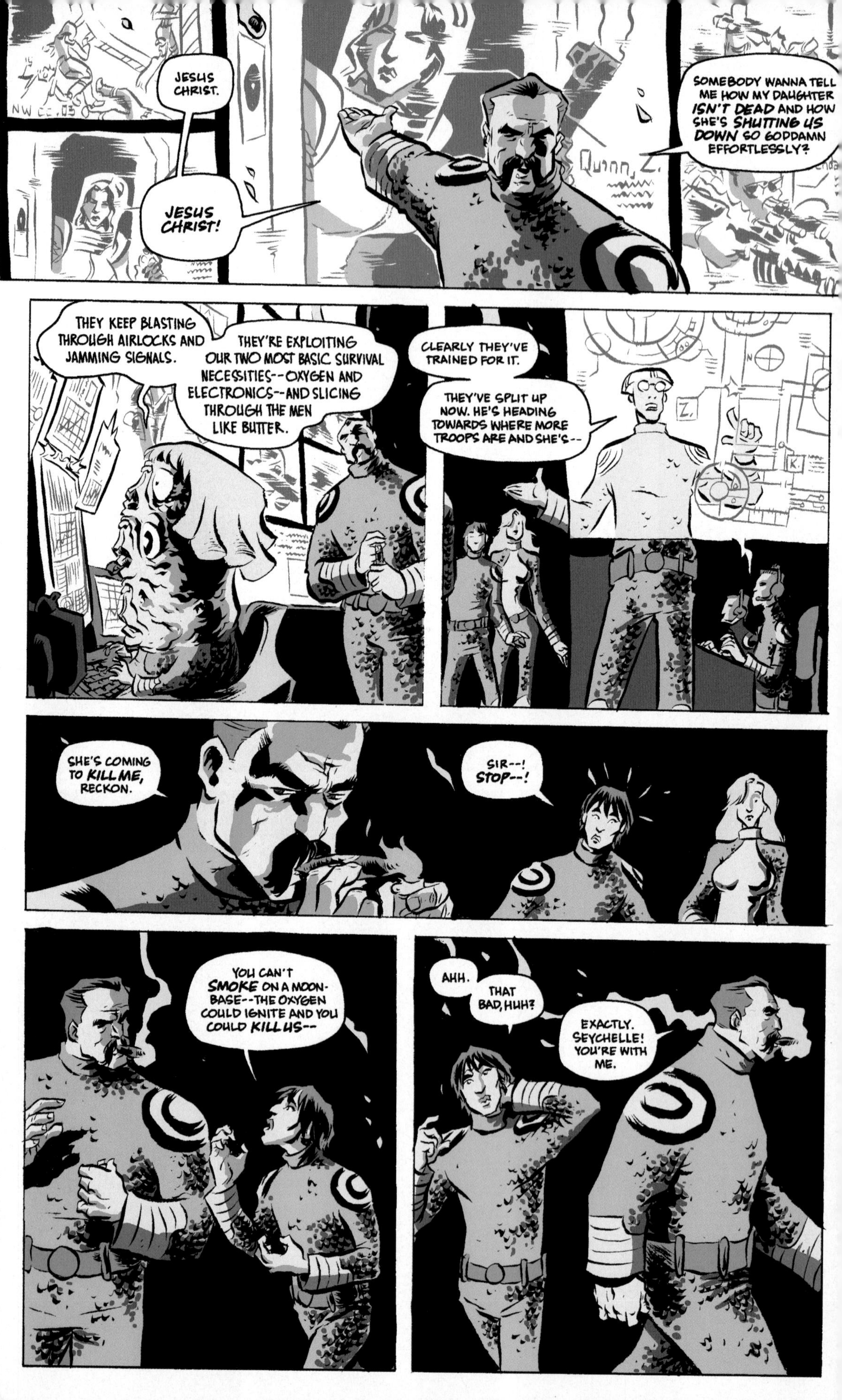
JESUS CHRIST.
JESUS CHRIST!
Quinn, Z.
SOMEBODY WANNA TELL ME HOW MY DAUGHTER ISN'T DEAD AND HOW SHE'S SHUTTING US DOWN SO GODDAMN EFFORTLESSLY?
THEY KEEP BLASTING THROUGH AIRLOCKS AND JAMMING SIGNALS.
THEY'RE EXPLOITING OUR TWO MOST BASIC SURVIVAL NECESSITIES--OXYGEN AND ELECTRONICS--AND SLICING THROUGH THE MEN LIKE BUTTER.
CLEARLY THEY'VE TRAINED FOR IT.
THEY'VE SPLIT UP NOW. HE'S HEADING TOWARDS WHERE MORE TROOPS ARE AND SHE'S--
SHE'S COMING TO KILL ME, RECKON.
SIR--! STOP--!
YOU CAN'T SMOKE ON A MOON-BASE--THE OXYGEN COULD IGNITE AND YOU COULD KILL US--
AHH.
THAT BAD, HUH?
EXACTLY. SEYCHELLE! YOU'RE WITH ME.

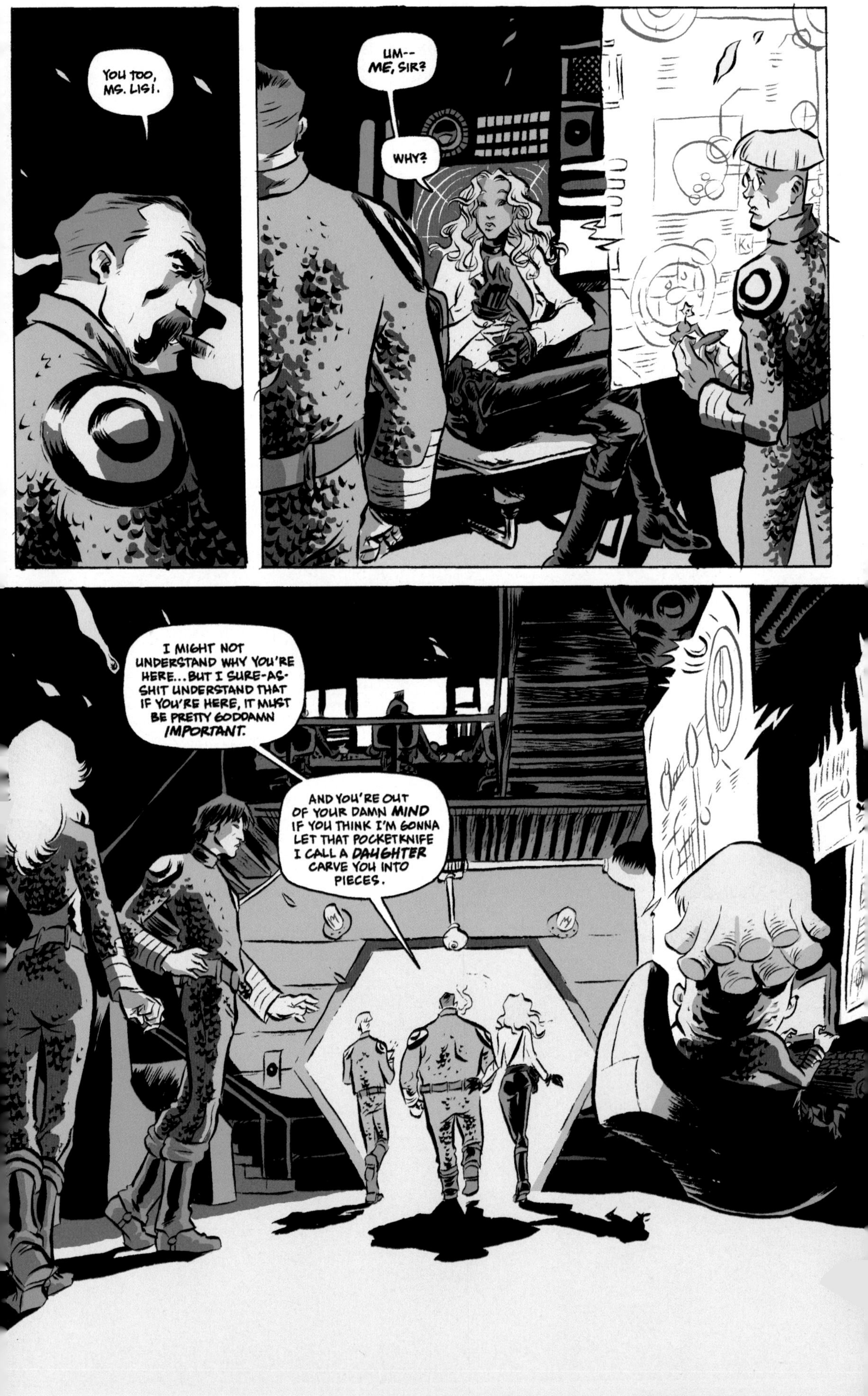
YOU TOO, MS. LISI.
UM-- ME, SIR?
WHY?
I MIGHT NOT UNDERSTAND WHY YOU'RE HERE... BUT I SURE-AS-SHIT UNDERSTAND THAT IF YOU'RE HERE, IT MUST BE PRETTY GODDAMN IMPORTANT.
AND YOU'RE OUT OF YOUR DAMN MIND IF YOU THINK I'M GONNA LET THAT POCKETKNIFE I CALL A DAUGHTER CARVE YOU INTO PIECES.

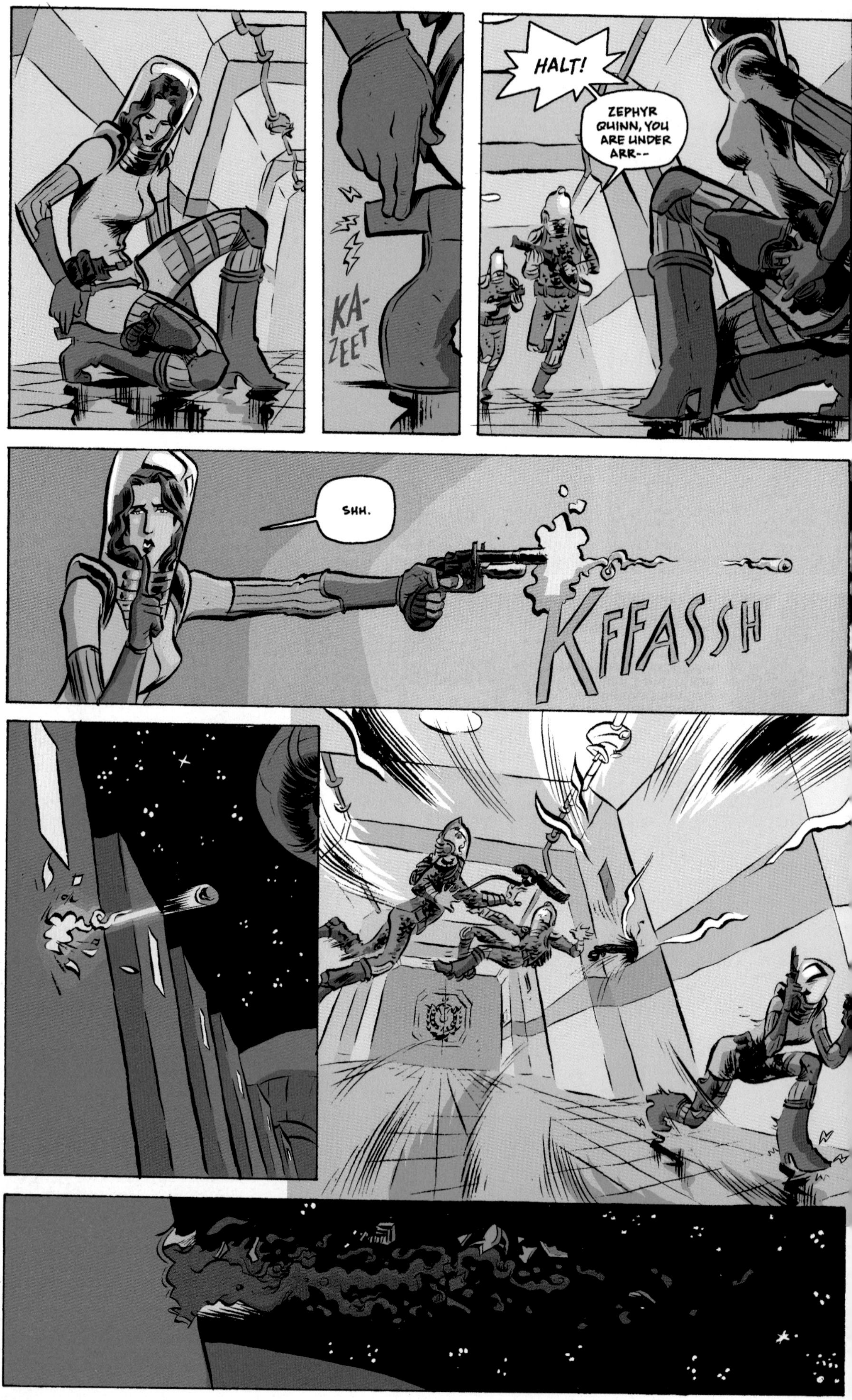
KA-ZEET
HALT!
ZEPHYR QUINN, YOU ARE UNDER ARR--
SHH.
KFFASSH

MY WORD.

SOMEBODY HAS TO *STOP* HER.

I'M JUST GOING OUTSIDE.

I MAY BE SOME TIME.

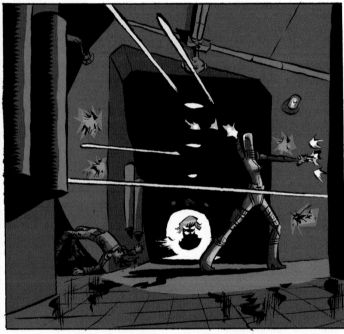

≋ WE HAD A *DEAL*. ≋

≋ NOTHING GOLD CAN STAY, PONY. ≋

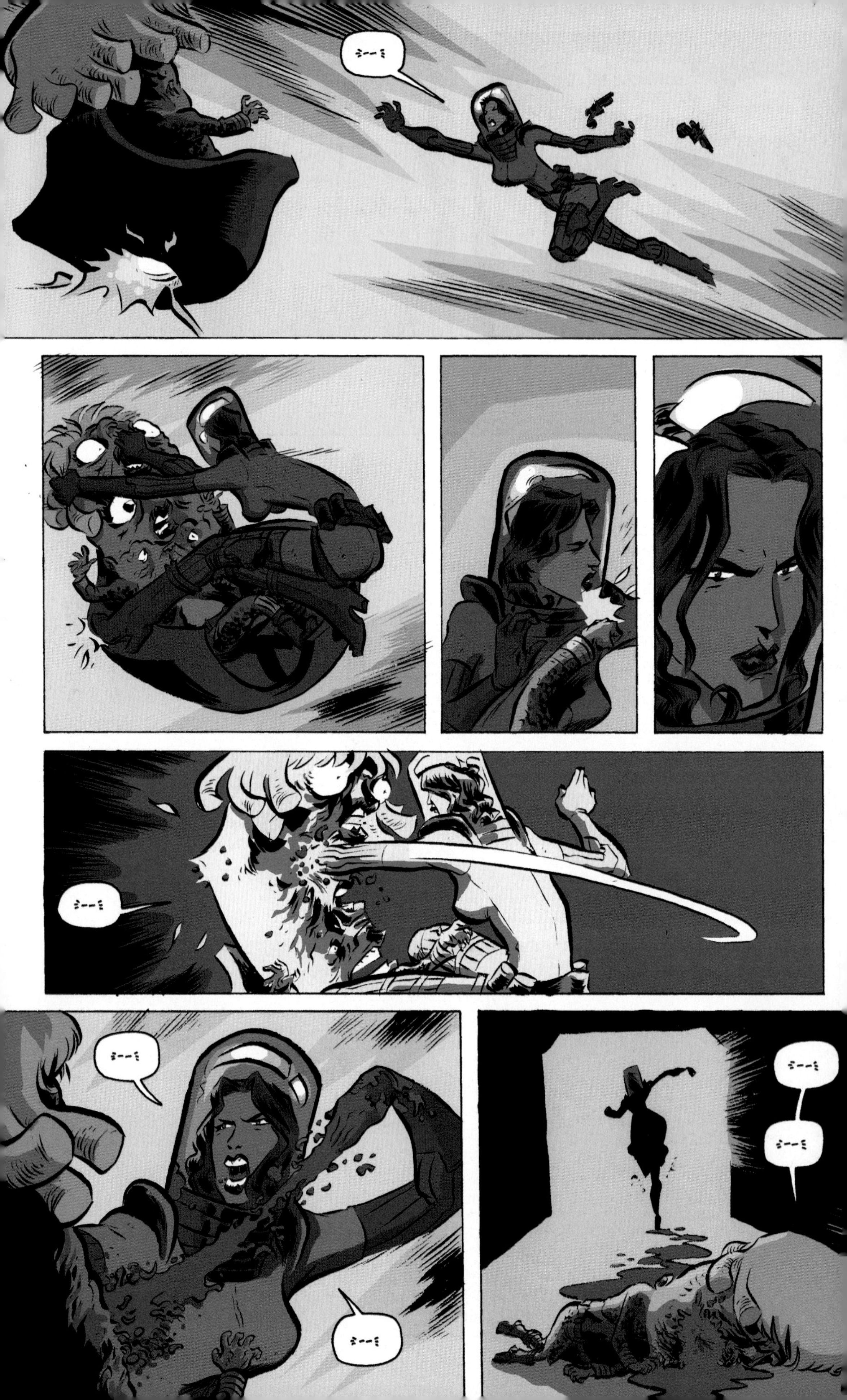

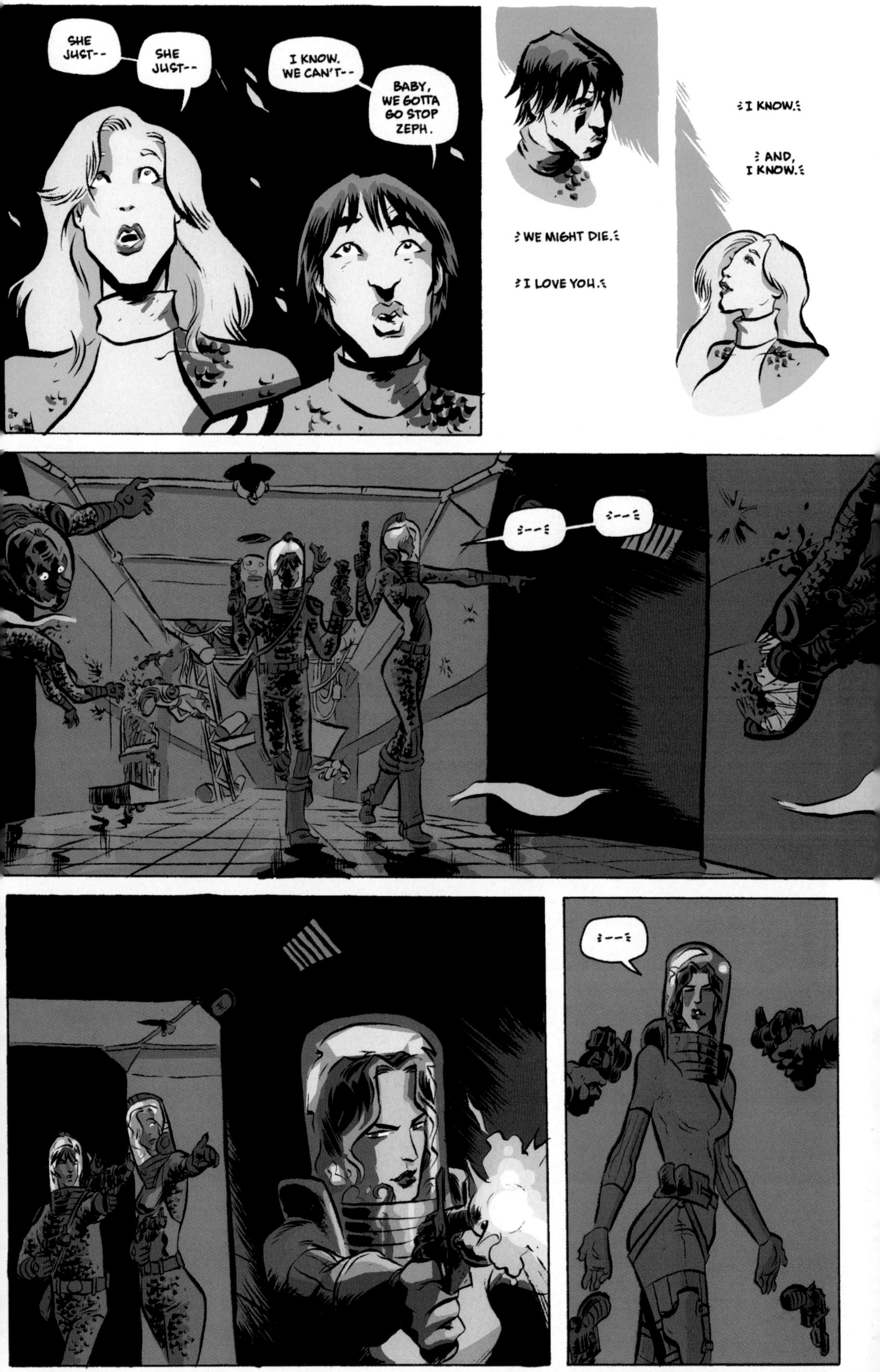
SHE JUST--
SHE JUST--
I KNOW. WE CAN'T--
BABY, WE GOTTA GO STOP ZEPH.
I KNOW.
AND, I KNOW.
WE MIGHT DIE.
I LOVE YOU.
--
--
--

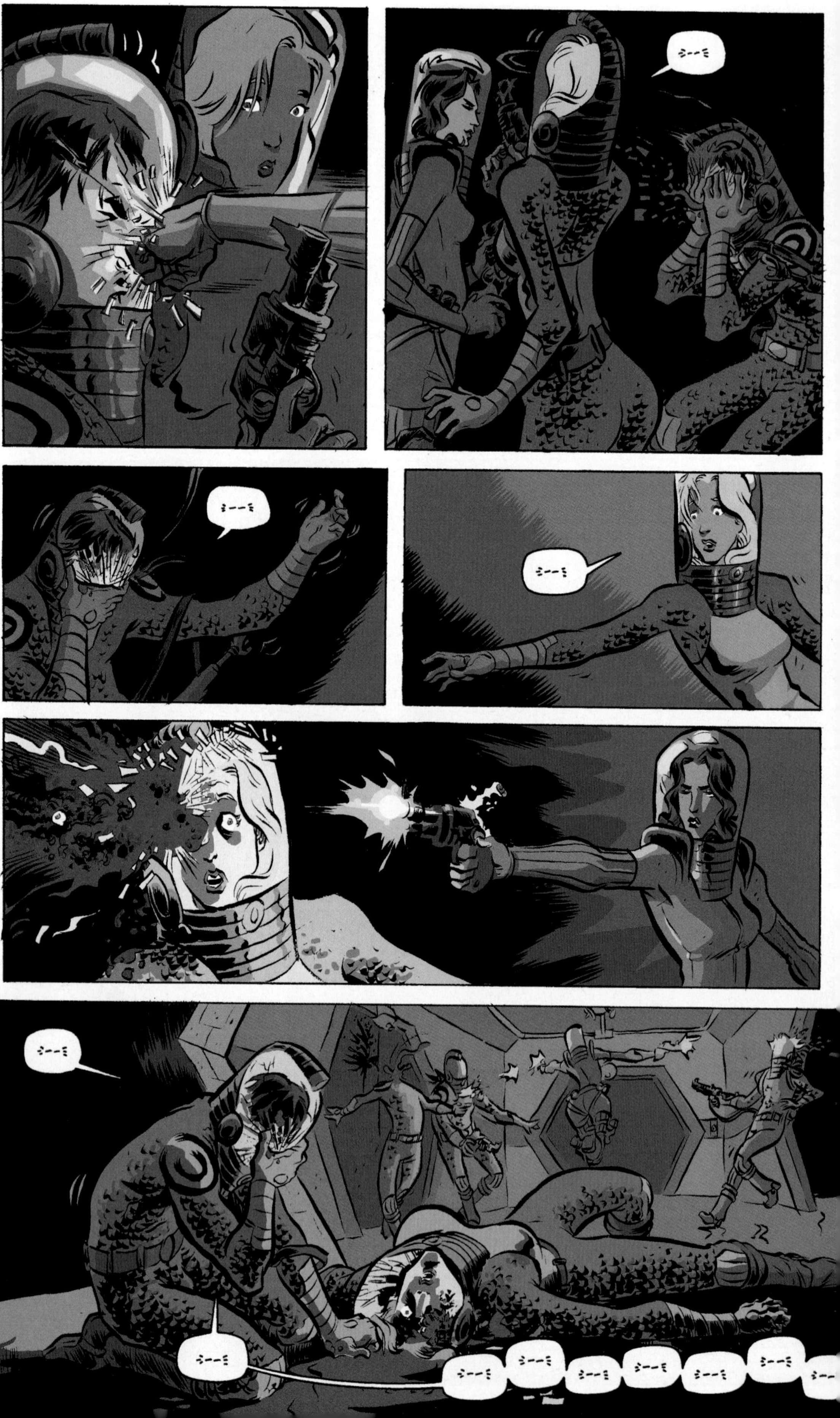

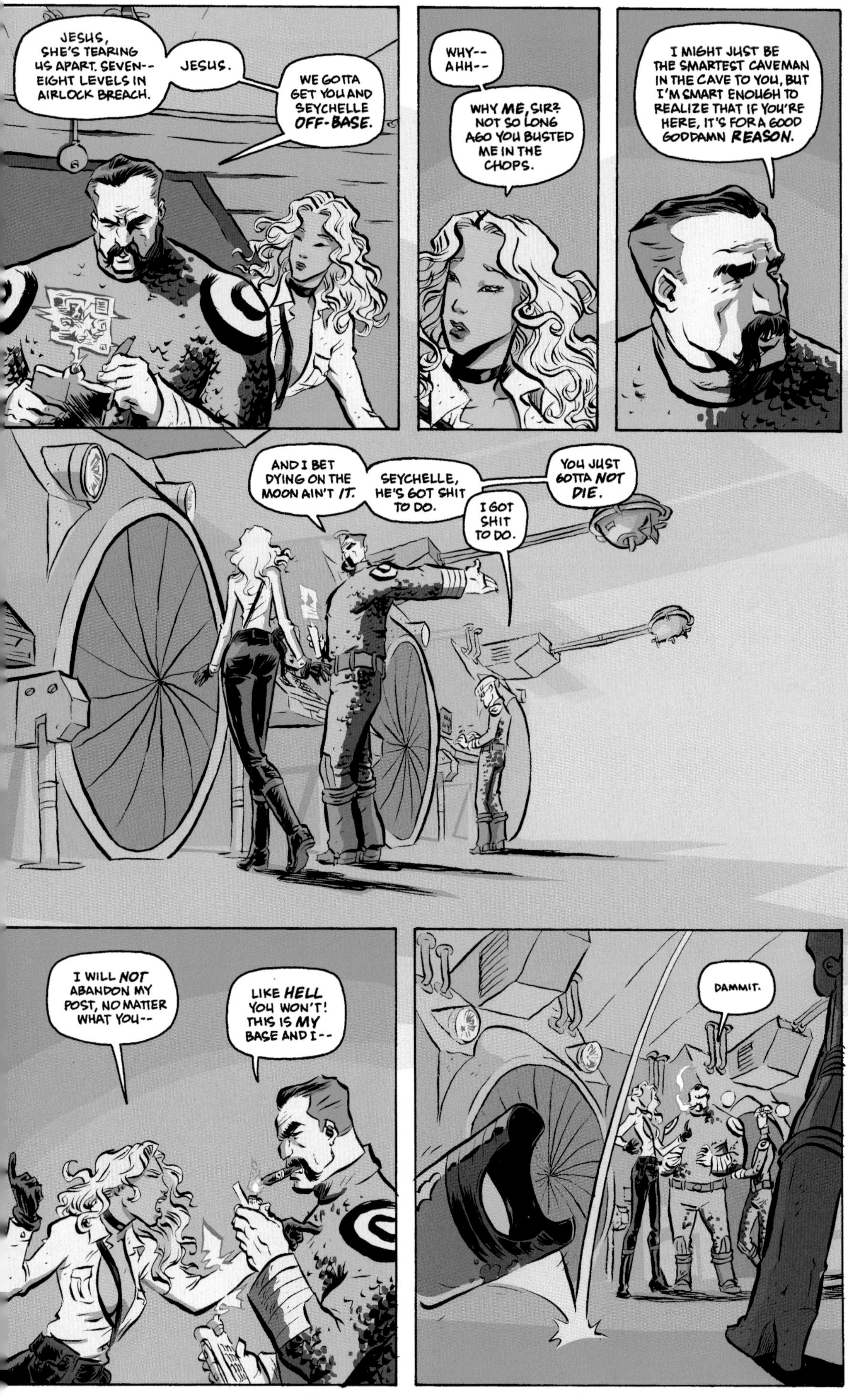
JESUS, SHE'S TEARING US APART. SEVEN--EIGHT LEVELS IN AIRLOCK BREACH.
JESUS.
WE GOTTA GET YOU AND SEYCHELLE OFF-BASE.
WHY--AHH--
WHY ME, SIR? NOT SO LONG AGO YOU BUSTED ME IN THE CHOPS.
I MIGHT JUST BE THE SMARTEST CAVEMAN IN THE CAVE TO YOU, BUT I'M SMART ENOUGH TO REALIZE THAT IF YOU'RE HERE, IT'S FOR A GOOD GODDAMN REASON.
AND I BET DYING ON THE MOON AIN'T IT.
SEYCHELLE, HE'S GOT SHIT TO DO.
YOU JUST GOTTA NOT DIE.
I GOT SHIT TO DO.
I WILL NOT ABANDON MY POST, NO MATTER WHAT YOU--
LIKE HELL YOU WON'T! THIS IS MY BASE AND I--
DAMMIT.

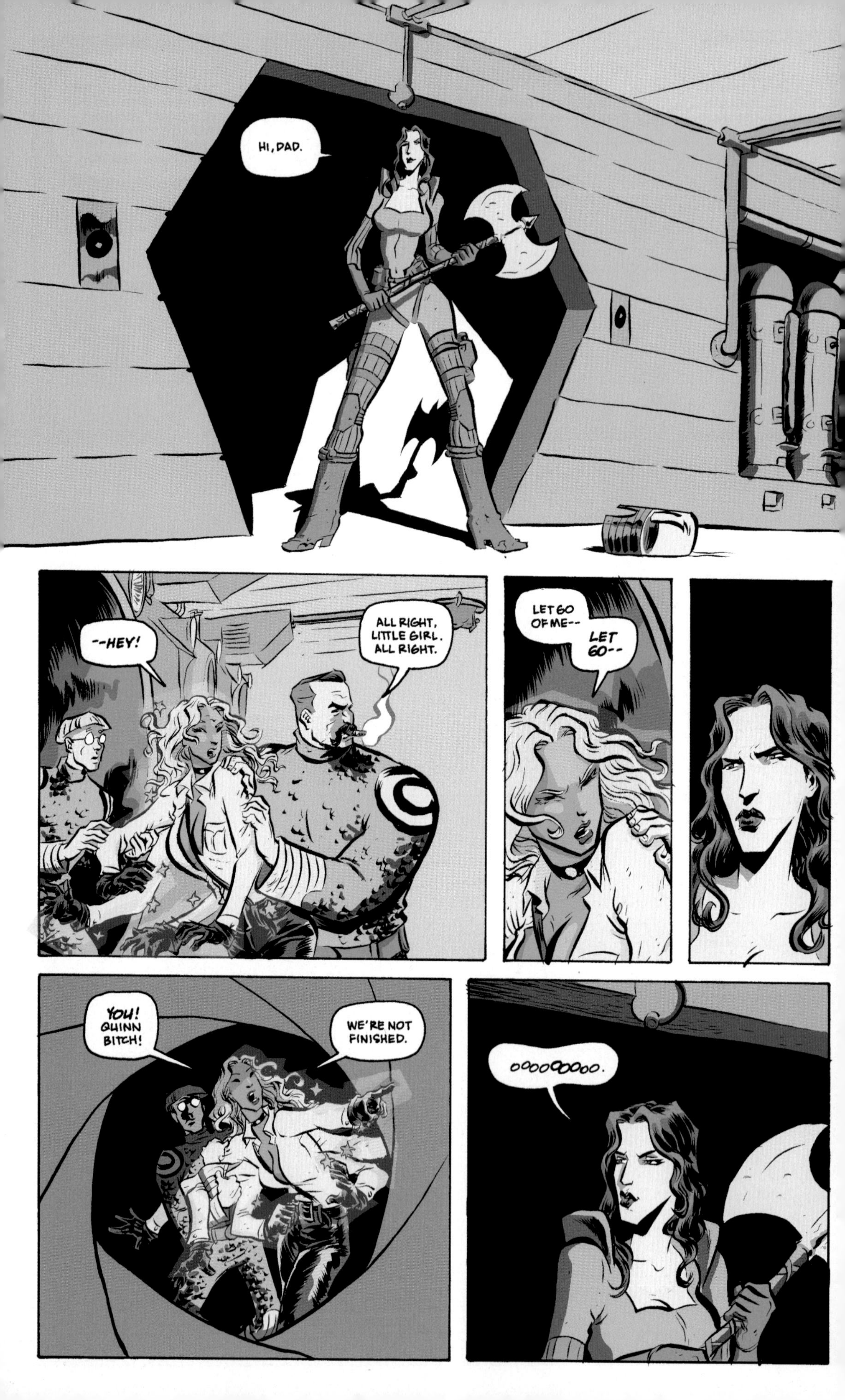
HI, DAD.
--HEY!
ALL RIGHT, LITTLE GIRL. ALL RIGHT.
LET GO OF ME--
LET GO--
YOU! QUINN BITCH!
WE'RE NOT FINISHED.
OOOOOOOOO.

SCAPE POD 2
YOU KNOW WHAT COMES NEXT, RIGHT?
OH YEAH.
SCAPE POD
SCAPE POD

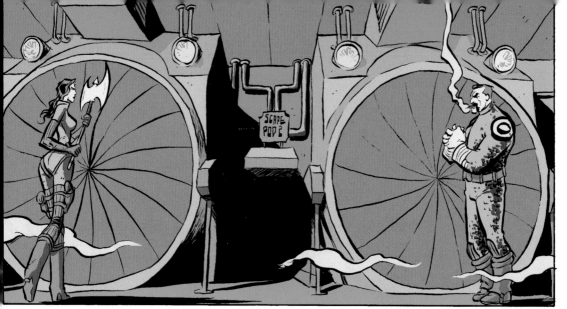

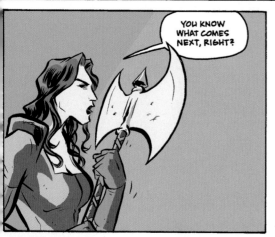

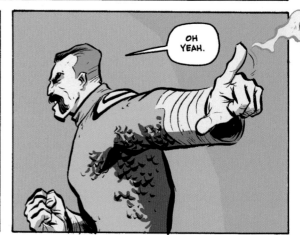

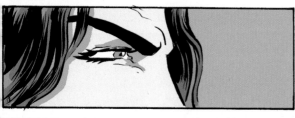

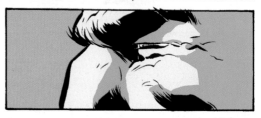

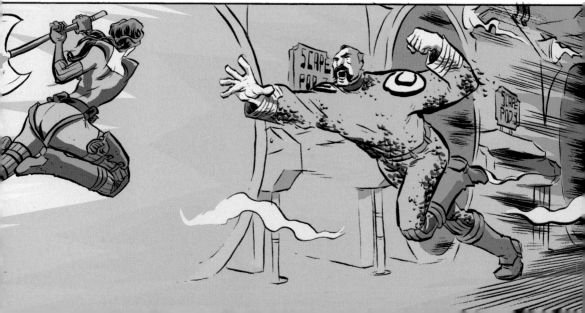

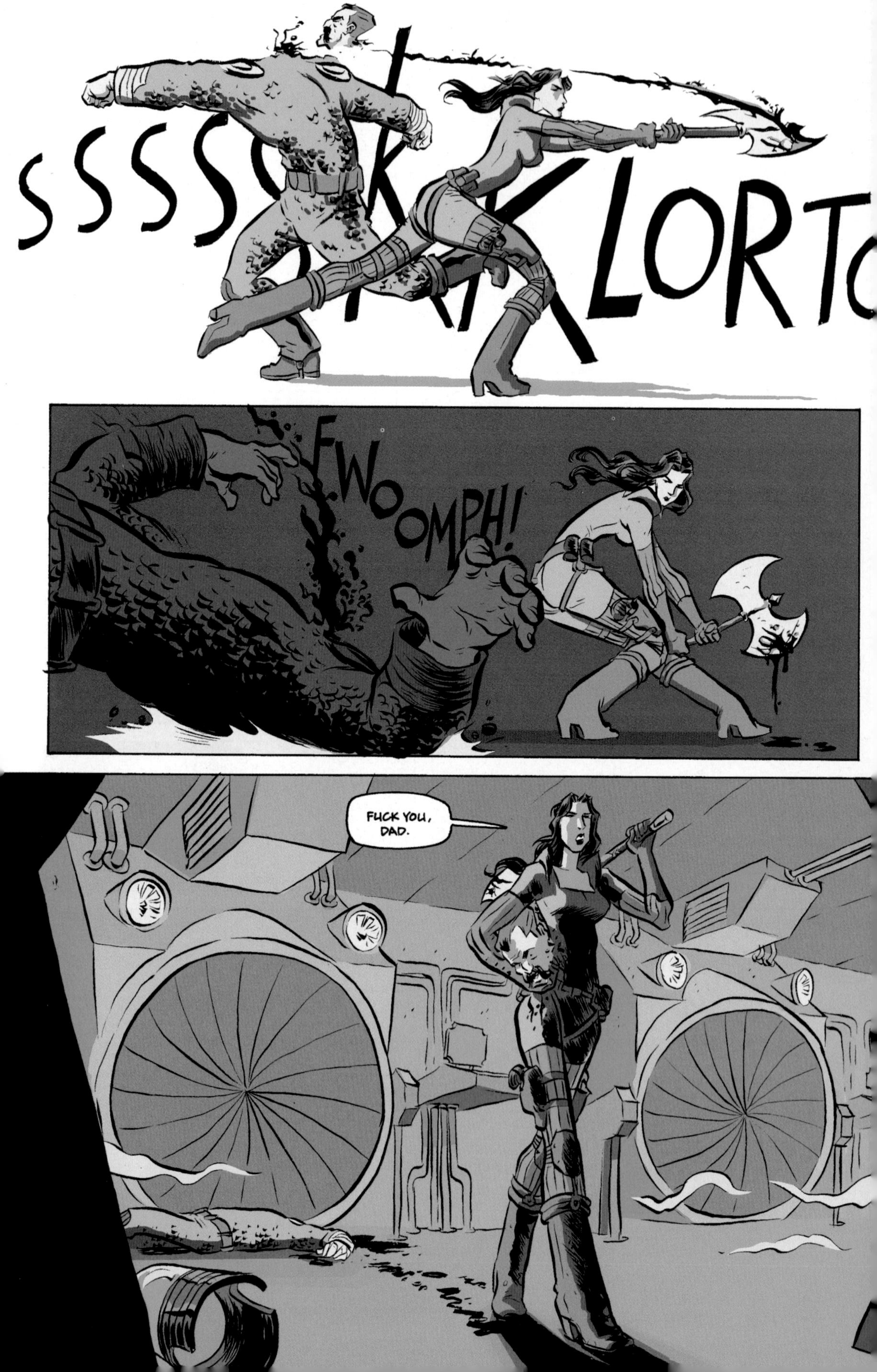
SSSSS
KLORTC
FWOOMPH!
FUCK YOU, DAD.

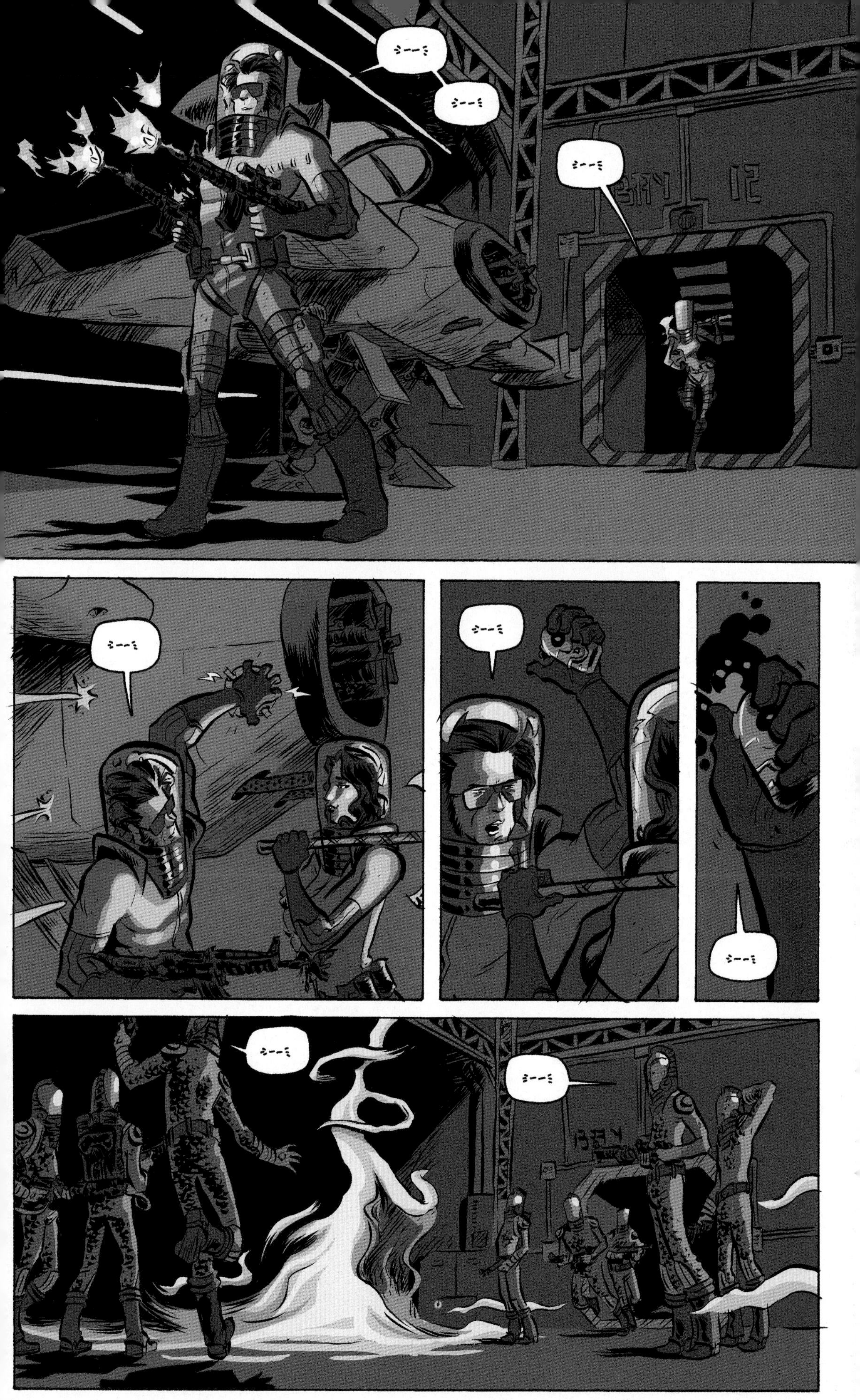

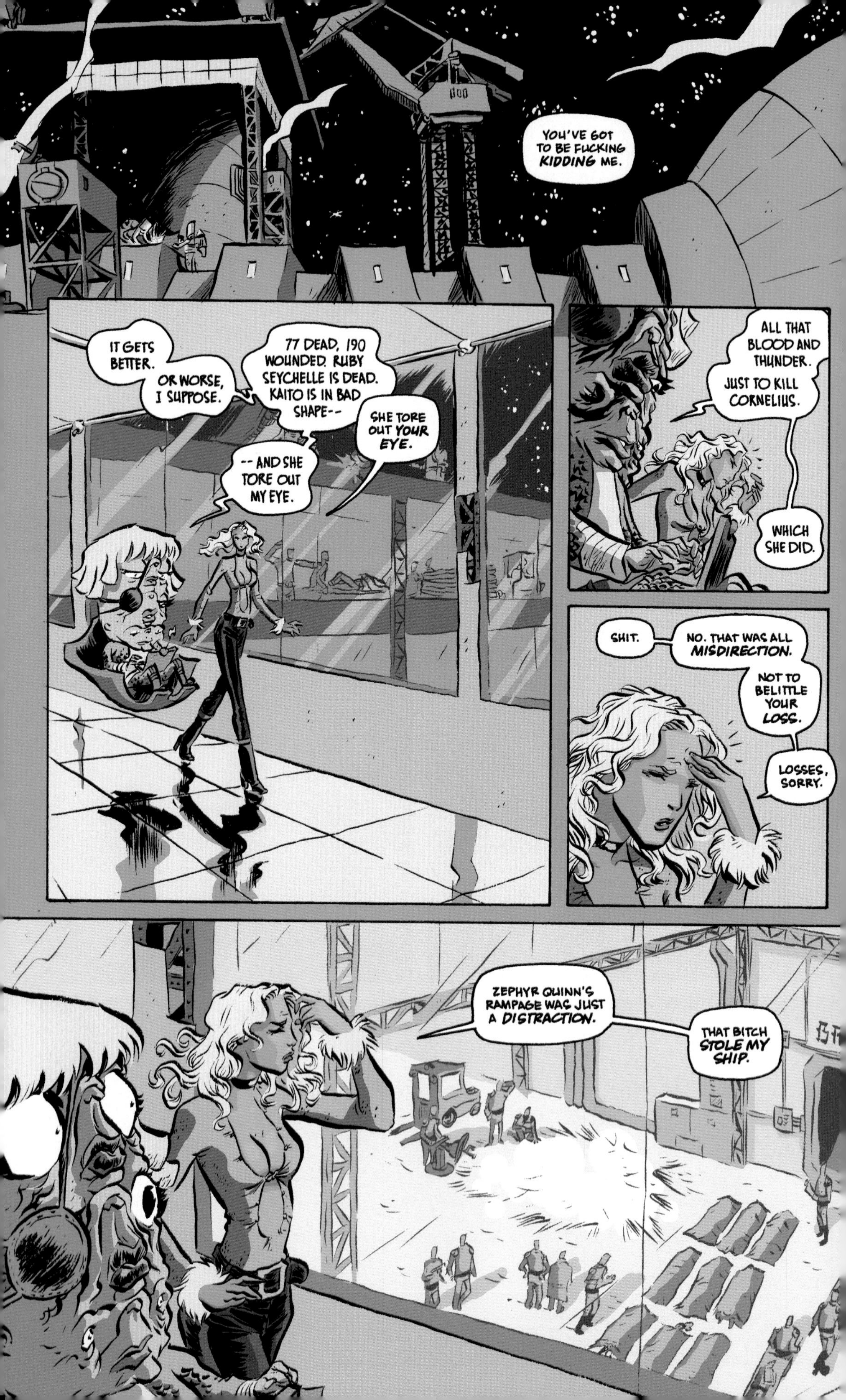

YOU'VE GOT TO BE FUCKING KIDDING ME.
IT GETS BETTER.
OR WORSE, I SUPPOSE.
77 DEAD, 190 WOUNDED. RUBY SEYCHELLE IS DEAD. KAITO IS IN BAD SHAPE--
--AND SHE TORE OUT MY EYE.
SHE TORE OUT YOUR EYE.
ALL THAT BLOOD AND THUNDER.
JUST TO KILL CORNELIUS.
WHICH SHE DID.
SHIT.
NO. THAT WAS ALL MISDIRECTION.
NOT TO BELITTLE YOUR LOSS.
LOSSES, SORRY.
ZEPHYR QUINN'S RAMPAGE WAS JUST A DISTRACTION.
THAT BITCH STOLE MY SHIP.

CHAPTER 6

SOME OF THE THINGS THAT HAPPENED TO THE MURDERERS AND MURDERED AMONG US

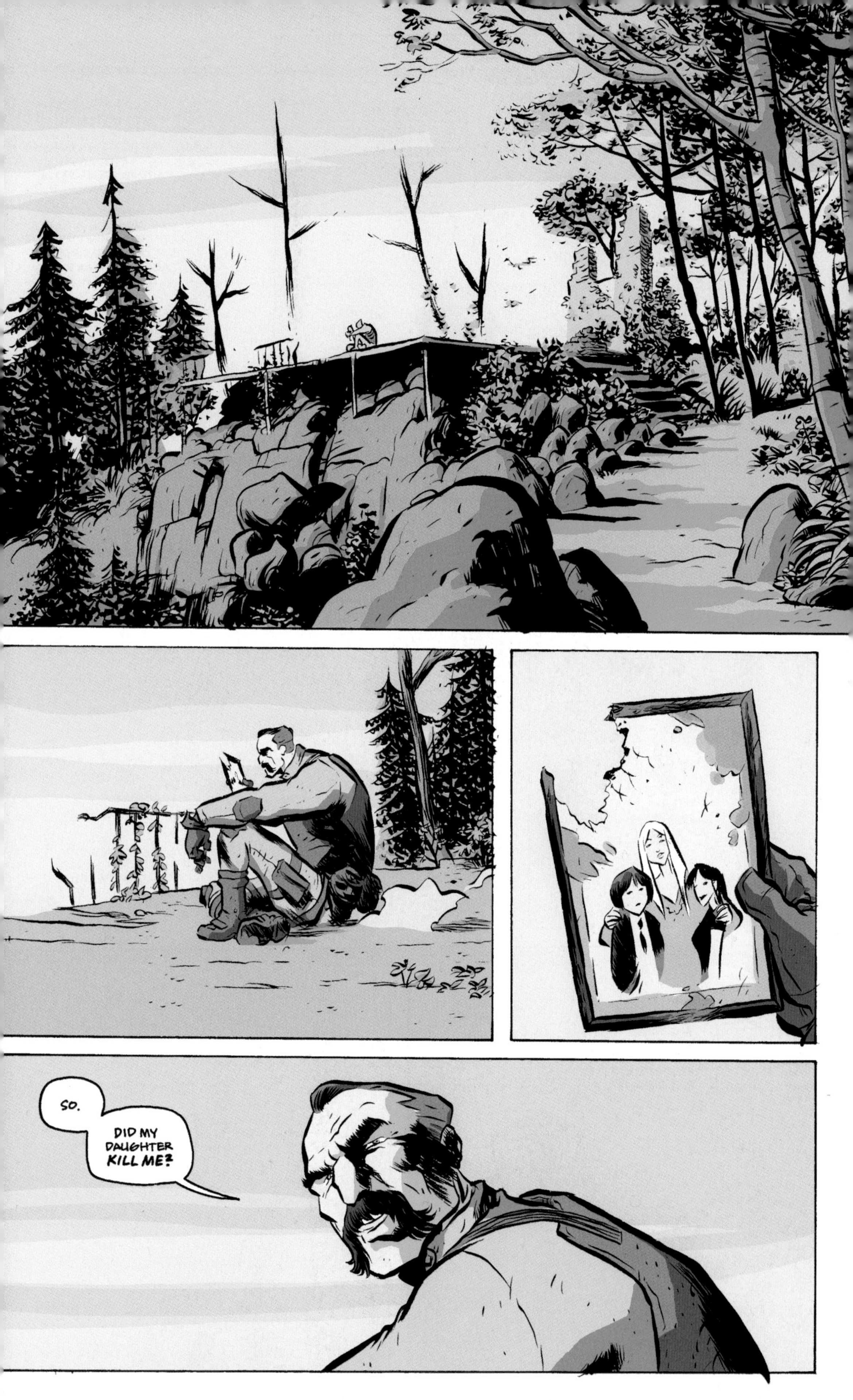
SO.
DID MY DAUGHTER KILL ME?

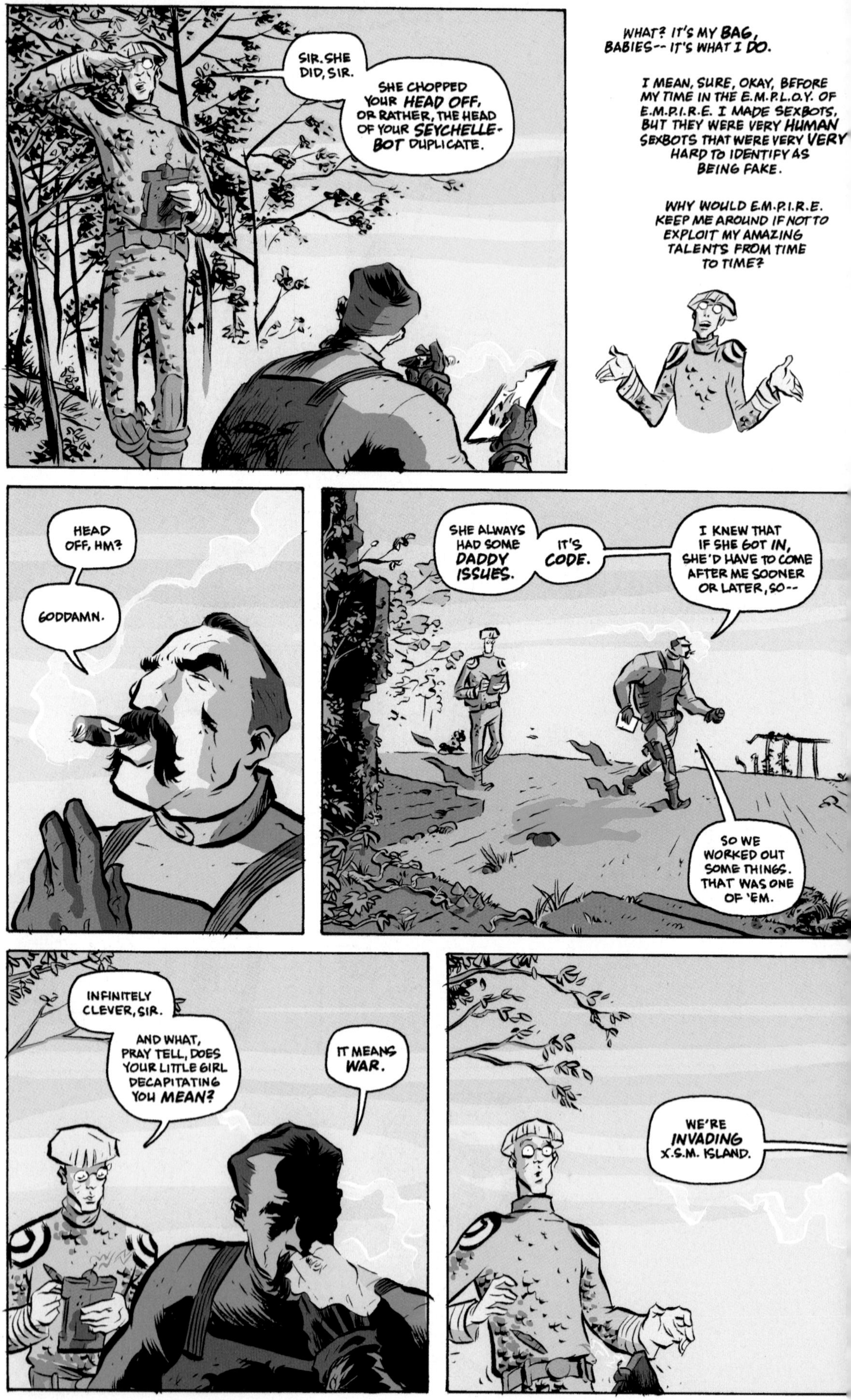
SIR. SHE DID, SIR.
SHE CHOPPED YOUR HEAD OFF, OR RATHER, THE HEAD OF YOUR SEYCHELLE-BOT DUPLICATE.
WHAT? IT'S MY BAG, BABIES-- IT'S WHAT I DO.
I MEAN, SURE, OKAY, BEFORE MY TIME IN THE E.M.P.L.O.Y. OF E.M.P.I.R.E. I MADE SEXBOTS, BUT THEY WERE VERY HUMAN SEXBOTS THAT WERE VERY VERY HARD TO IDENTIFY AS BEING FAKE.
WHY WOULD E.M.P.I.R.E. KEEP ME AROUND IF NOT TO EXPLOIT MY AMAZING TALENTS FROM TIME TO TIME?
HEAD OFF, HM?
GODDAMN.
SHE ALWAYS HAD SOME DADDY ISSUES.
IT'S CODE.
I KNEW THAT IF SHE GOT IN, SHE'D HAVE TO COME AFTER ME SOONER OR LATER, SO--
SO WE WORKED OUT SOME THINGS. THAT WAS ONE OF 'EM.
INFINITELY CLEVER, SIR.
AND WHAT, PRAY TELL, DOES YOUR LITTLE GIRL DECAPITATING YOU MEAN?
IT MEANS WAR.
WE'RE INVADING X.S.M. ISLAND.

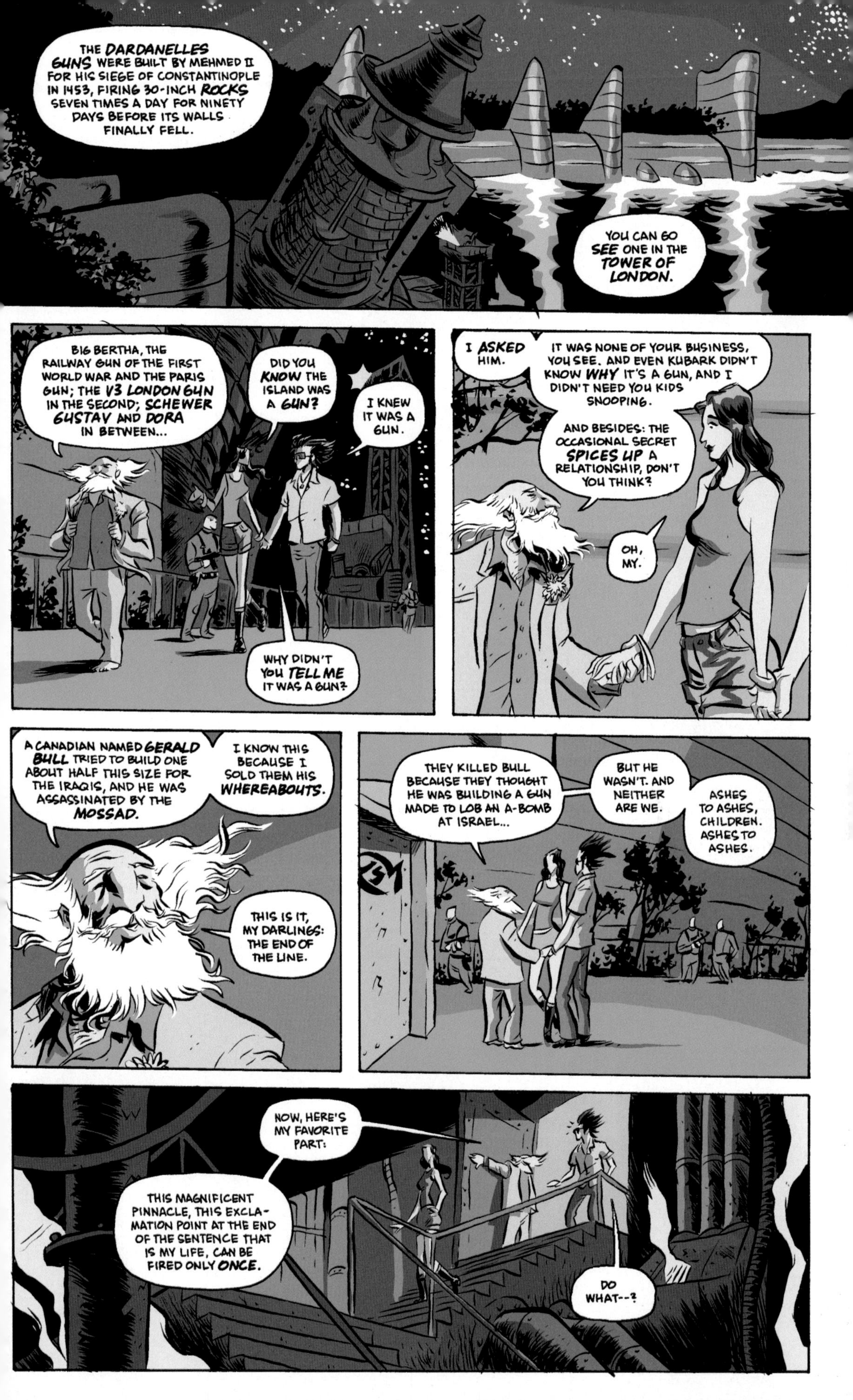
THE DARDANELLES GUNS WERE BUILT BY MEHMED II FOR HIS SIEGE OF CONSTANTINOPLE IN 1453, FIRING 30-INCH ROCKS SEVEN TIMES A DAY FOR NINETY DAYS BEFORE ITS WALLS FINALLY FELL.
YOU CAN GO SEE ONE IN THE TOWER OF LONDON.
BIG BERTHA, THE RAILWAY GUN OF THE FIRST WORLD WAR AND THE PARIS GUN; THE V3 LONDON GUN IN THE SECOND; SCHEWER GUSTAV AND DORA IN BETWEEN...
DID YOU KNOW THE ISLAND WAS A GUN?
I KNEW IT WAS A GUN.
WHY DIDN'T YOU TELL ME IT WAS A GUN?
I ASKED HIM.
IT WAS NONE OF YOUR BUSINESS, YOU SEE. AND EVEN KUBARK DIDN'T KNOW WHY IT'S A GUN, AND I DIDN'T NEED YOU KIDS SNOOPING.
AND BESIDES: THE OCCASIONAL SECRET SPICES UP A RELATIONSHIP, DON'T YOU THINK?
OH, MY.
A CANADIAN NAMED GERALD BULL TRIED TO BUILD ONE ABOUT HALF THIS SIZE FOR THE IRAQIS, AND HE WAS ASSASSINATED BY THE MOSSAD.
I KNOW THIS BECAUSE I SOLD THEM HIS WHEREABOUTS.
THIS IS IT, MY DARLINGS: THE END OF THE LINE.
THEY KILLED BULL BECAUSE THEY THOUGHT HE WAS BUILDING A GUN MADE TO LOB AN A-BOMB AT ISRAEL...
BUT HE WASN'T. AND NEITHER ARE WE.
ASHES TO ASHES, CHILDREN. ASHES TO ASHES.
NOW, HERE'S MY FAVORITE PART:
THIS MAGNIFICENT PINNACLE, THIS EXCLAMATION POINT AT THE END OF THE SENTENCE THAT IS MY LIFE, CAN BE FIRED ONLY ONCE.
DO WHAT--?

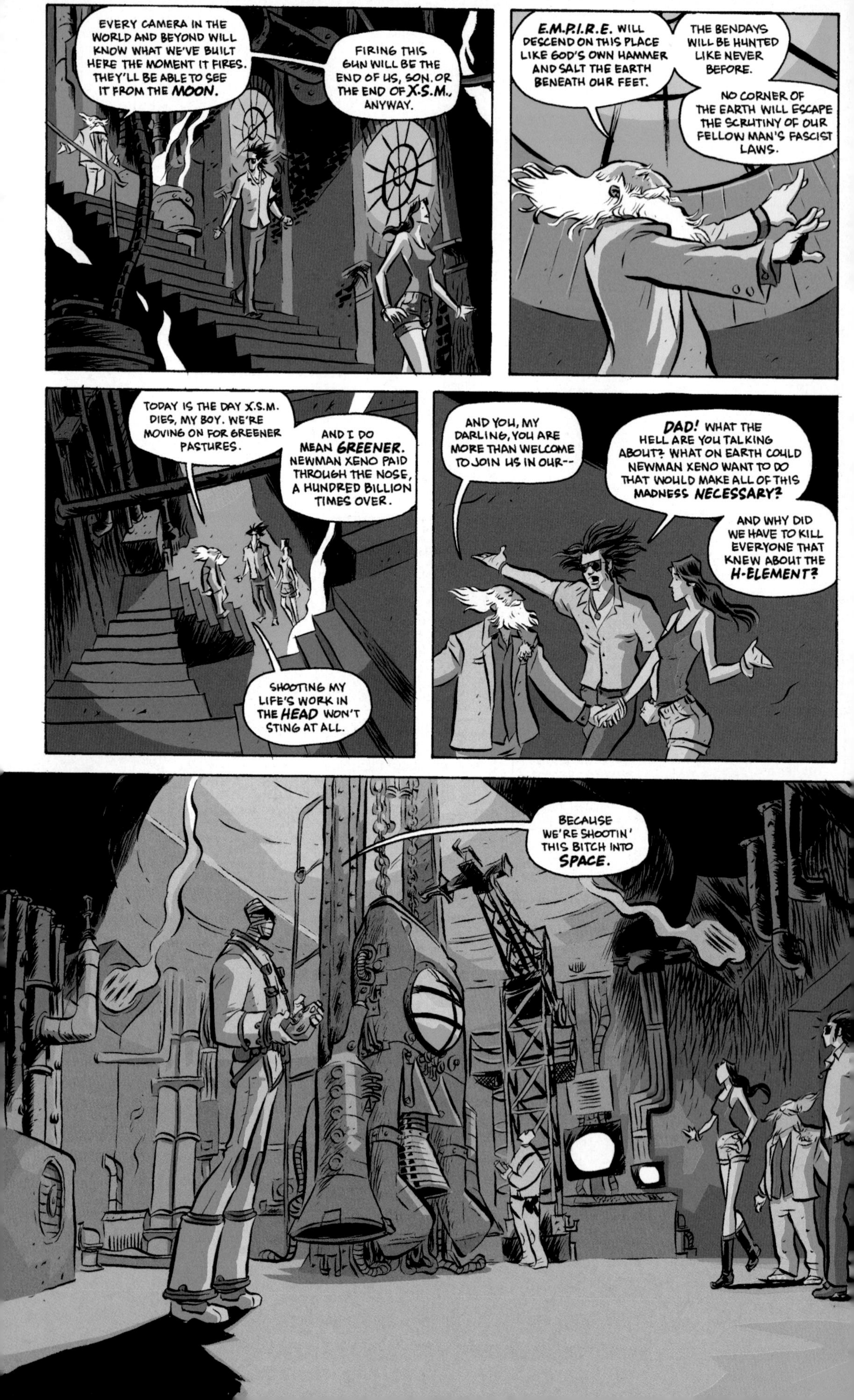
EVERY CAMERA IN THE WORLD AND BEYOND WILL KNOW WHAT WE'VE BUILT HERE THE MOMENT IT FIRES. THEY'LL BE ABLE TO SEE IT FROM THE MOON.
FIRING THIS GUN WILL BE THE END OF US, SON. OR THE END OF X.S.M., ANYWAY.
E.M.P.I.R.E. WILL DESCEND ON THIS PLACE LIKE GOD'S OWN HAMMER AND SALT THE EARTH BENEATH OUR FEET.
THE BENDAYS WILL BE HUNTED LIKE NEVER BEFORE.
NO CORNER OF THE EARTH WILL ESCAPE THE SCRUTINY OF OUR FELLOW MAN'S FASCIST LAWS.
TODAY IS THE DAY X.S.M. DIES, MY BOY. WE'RE MOVING ON FOR GREENER PASTURES.
AND I DO MEAN GREENER. NEWMAN XENO PAID THROUGH THE NOSE, A HUNDRED BILLION TIMES OVER.
SHOOTING MY LIFE'S WORK IN THE HEAD WON'T STING AT ALL.
AND YOU, MY DARLING, YOU ARE MORE THAN WELCOME TO JOIN US IN OUR--
DAD! WHAT THE HELL ARE YOU TALKING ABOUT? WHAT ON EARTH COULD NEWMAN XENO WANT TO DO THAT WOULD MAKE ALL OF THIS MADNESS NECESSARY?
AND WHY DID WE HAVE TO KILL EVERYONE THAT KNEW ABOUT THE H-ELEMENT?
BECAUSE WE'RE SHOOTIN' THIS BITCH INTO SPACE.

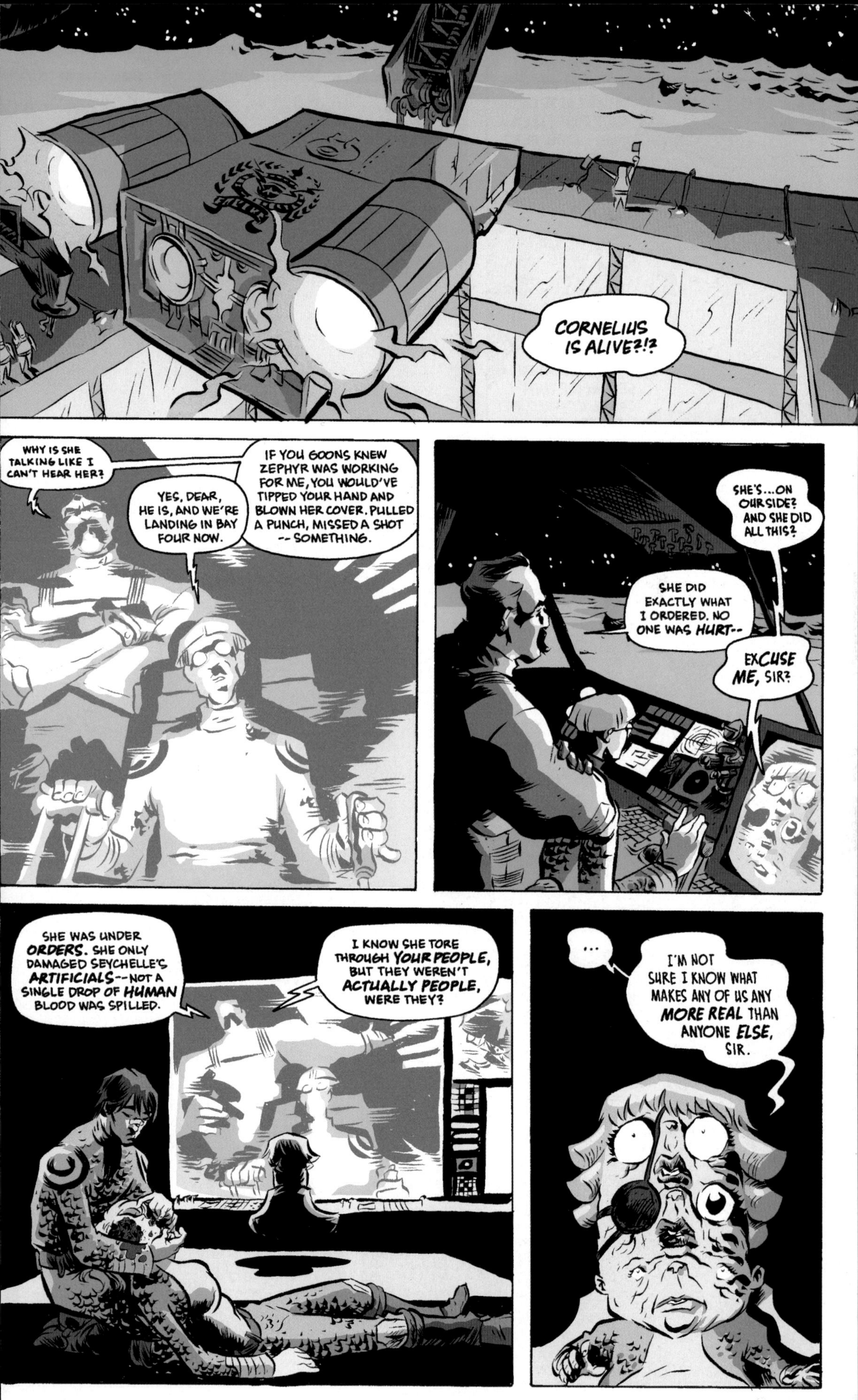
CORNELIUS IS ALIVE?!?
WHY IS SHE TALKING LIKE I CAN'T HEAR HER?
YES, DEAR, HE IS, AND WE'RE LANDING IN BAY FOUR NOW.
IF YOU GOONS KNEW ZEPHYR WAS WORKING FOR ME, YOU WOULD'VE TIPPED YOUR HAND AND BLOWN HER COVER. PULLED A PUNCH, MISSED A SHOT -- SOMETHING.
SHE'S...ON OUR SIDE? AND SHE DID ALL THIS?
SHE DID EXACTLY WHAT I ORDERED. NO ONE WAS HURT--
EXCUSE ME, SIR?
SHE WAS UNDER ORDERS. SHE ONLY DAMAGED SEYCHELLE'S ARTIFICIALS--NOT A SINGLE DROP OF HUMAN BLOOD WAS SPILLED.
I KNOW SHE TORE THROUGH YOUR PEOPLE, BUT THEY WEREN'T ACTUALLY PEOPLE, WERE THEY?
...
I'M NOT SURE I KNOW WHAT MAKES ANY OF US ANY MORE REAL THAN ANYONE ELSE, SIR.

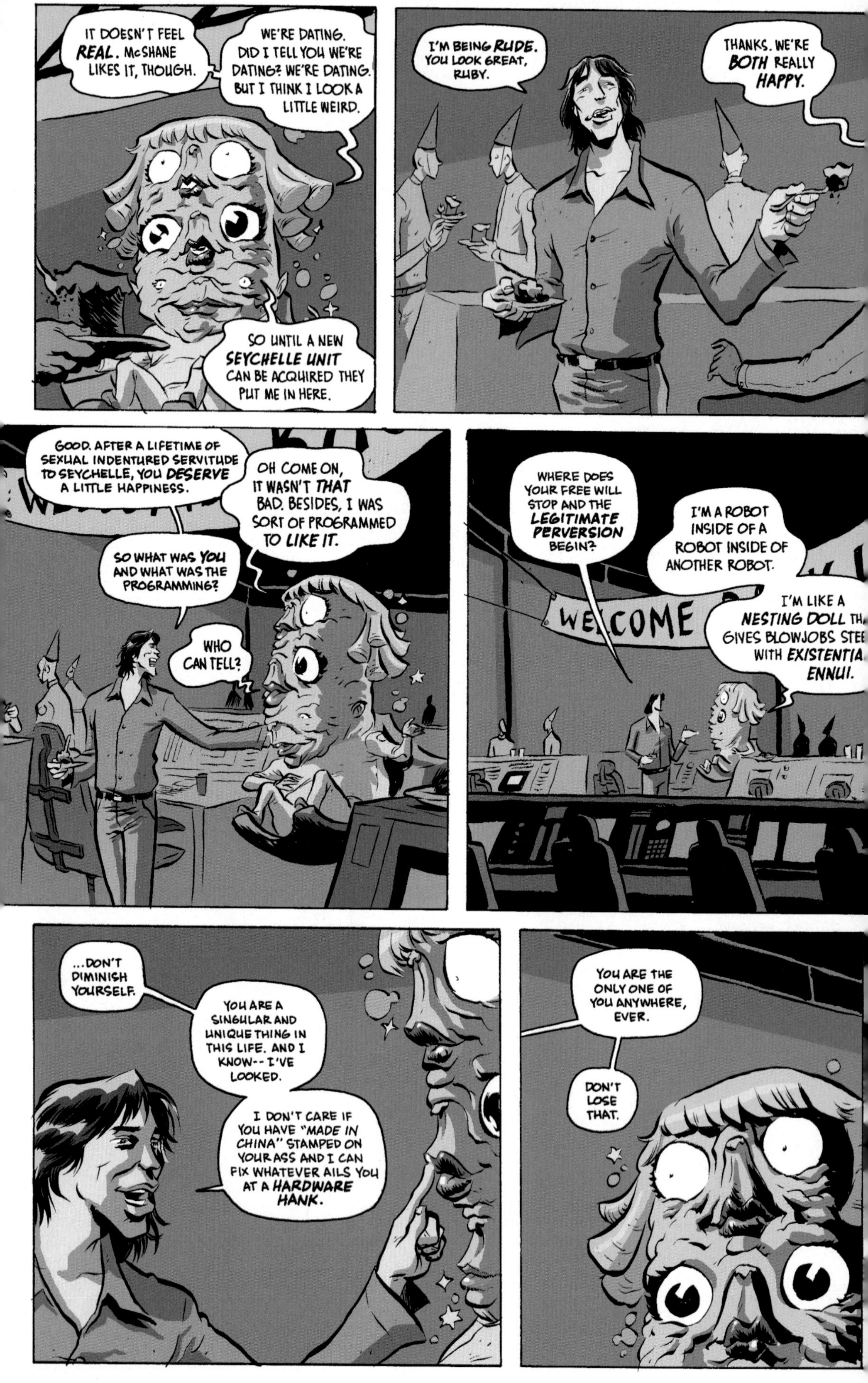
IT DOESN'T FEEL REAL. McSHANE LIKES IT, THOUGH.
WE'RE DATING. DID I TELL YOU WE'RE DATING? WE'RE DATING. BUT I THINK I LOOK A LITTLE WEIRD.
SO UNTIL A NEW SEYCHELLE UNIT CAN BE ACQUIRED THEY PUT ME IN HERE.
I'M BEING RUDE. YOU LOOK GREAT, RUBY.
THANKS. WE'RE BOTH REALLY HAPPY.
GOOD. AFTER A LIFETIME OF SEXUAL INDENTURED SERVITUDE TO SEYCHELLE, YOU DESERVE A LITTLE HAPPINESS.
OH COME ON, IT WASN'T THAT BAD. BESIDES, I WAS SORT OF PROGRAMMED TO LIKE IT.
SO WHAT WAS YOU AND WHAT WAS THE PROGRAMMING?
WHO CAN TELL?
WHERE DOES YOUR FREE WILL STOP AND THE LEGITIMATE PERVERSION BEGIN?
I'M A ROBOT INSIDE OF A ROBOT INSIDE OF ANOTHER ROBOT.
WELCOME
I'M LIKE A NESTING DOLL TH
GIVES BLOWJOBS STE
WITH EXISTENTIA
ENNUI.
...DON'T DIMINISH YOURSELF.
YOU ARE A SINGULAR AND UNIQUE THING IN THIS LIFE. AND I KNOW-- I'VE LOOKED.
I DON'T CARE IF YOU HAVE "MADE IN CHINA" STAMPED ON YOUR ASS AND I CAN FIX WHATEVER AILS YOU AT A HARDWARE HANK.
YOU ARE THE ONLY ONE OF YOU ANYWHERE, EVER.
DON'T LOSE THAT.

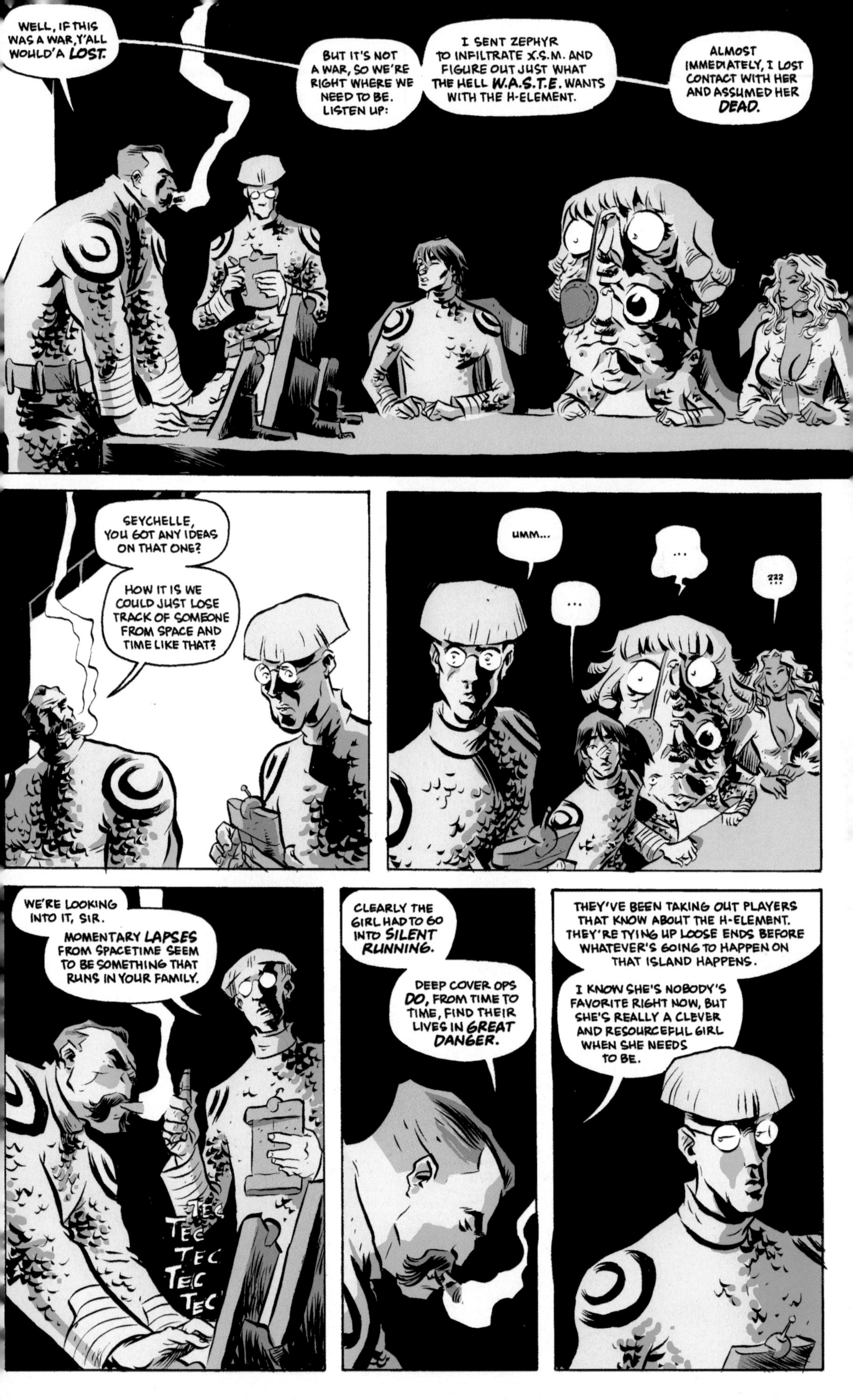

WELL, IF THIS WAS A WAR, Y'ALL WOULD'A LOST.
BUT IT'S NOT A WAR, SO WE'RE RIGHT WHERE WE NEED TO BE. LISTEN UP:
I SENT ZEPHYR TO INFILTRATE X.S.M. AND FIGURE OUT JUST WHAT THE HELL W.A.S.T.E. WANTS WITH THE H-ELEMENT.
ALMOST IMMEDIATELY, I LOST CONTACT WITH HER AND ASSUMED HER DEAD.
SEYCHELLE, YOU GOT ANY IDEAS ON THAT ONE?
HOW IT IS WE COULD JUST LOSE TRACK OF SOMEONE FROM SPACE AND TIME LIKE THAT?
UMM...
...
...
???
WE'RE LOOKING INTO IT, SIR.
MOMENTARY LAPSES FROM SPACETIME SEEM TO BE SOMETHING THAT RUNS IN YOUR FAMILY.
TEC TEC TEC TEC TEC
CLEARLY THE GIRL HAD TO GO INTO SILENT RUNNING.
DEEP COVER OPS DO, FROM TIME TO TIME, FIND THEIR LIVES IN GREAT DANGER.
THEY'VE BEEN TAKING OUT PLAYERS THAT KNOW ABOUT THE H-ELEMENT. THEY'RE TYING UP LOOSE ENDS BEFORE WHATEVER'S GOING TO HAPPEN ON THAT ISLAND HAPPENS.
I KNOW SHE'S NOBODY'S FAVORITE RIGHT NOW, BUT SHE'S REALLY A CLEVER AND RESOURCEFUL GIRL WHEN SHE NEEDS TO BE.

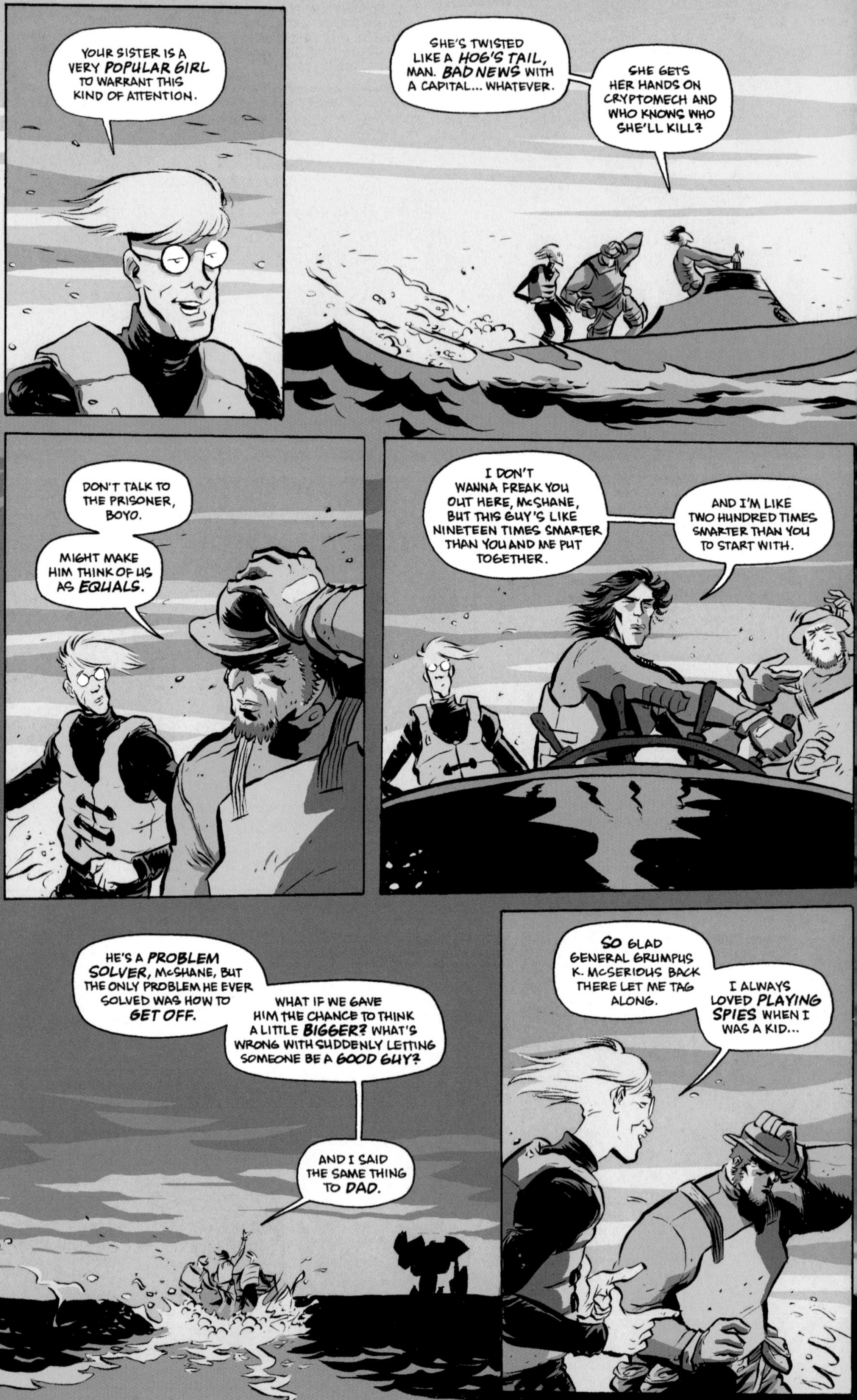
YOUR SISTER IS A VERY POPULAR GIRL TO WARRANT THIS KIND OF ATTENTION.
SHE'S TWISTED LIKE A HOG'S TAIL, MAN. BAD NEWS WITH A CAPITAL... WHATEVER.
SHE GETS HER HANDS ON CRYPTOMECH AND WHO KNOWS WHO SHE'LL KILL?
DON'T TALK TO THE PRISONER, BOYO.
MIGHT MAKE HIM THINK OF US AS EQUALS.
I DON'T WANNA FREAK YOU OUT HERE, McSHANE, BUT THIS GUY'S LIKE NINETEEN TIMES SMARTER THAN YOU AND ME PUT TOGETHER.
AND I'M LIKE TWO HUNDRED TIMES SMARTER THAN YOU TO START WITH.
HE'S A PROBLEM SOLVER, McSHANE, BUT THE ONLY PROBLEM HE EVER SOLVED WAS HOW TO GET OFF.
WHAT IF WE GAVE HIM THE CHANCE TO THINK A LITTLE BIGGER? WHAT'S WRONG WITH SUDDENLY LETTING SOMEONE BE A GOOD GUY?
AND I SAID THE SAME THING TO DAD.
SO GLAD GENERAL GRUMPUS K. McSERIOUS BACK THERE LET ME TAG ALONG.
I ALWAYS LOVED PLAYING SPIES WHEN I WAS A KID...

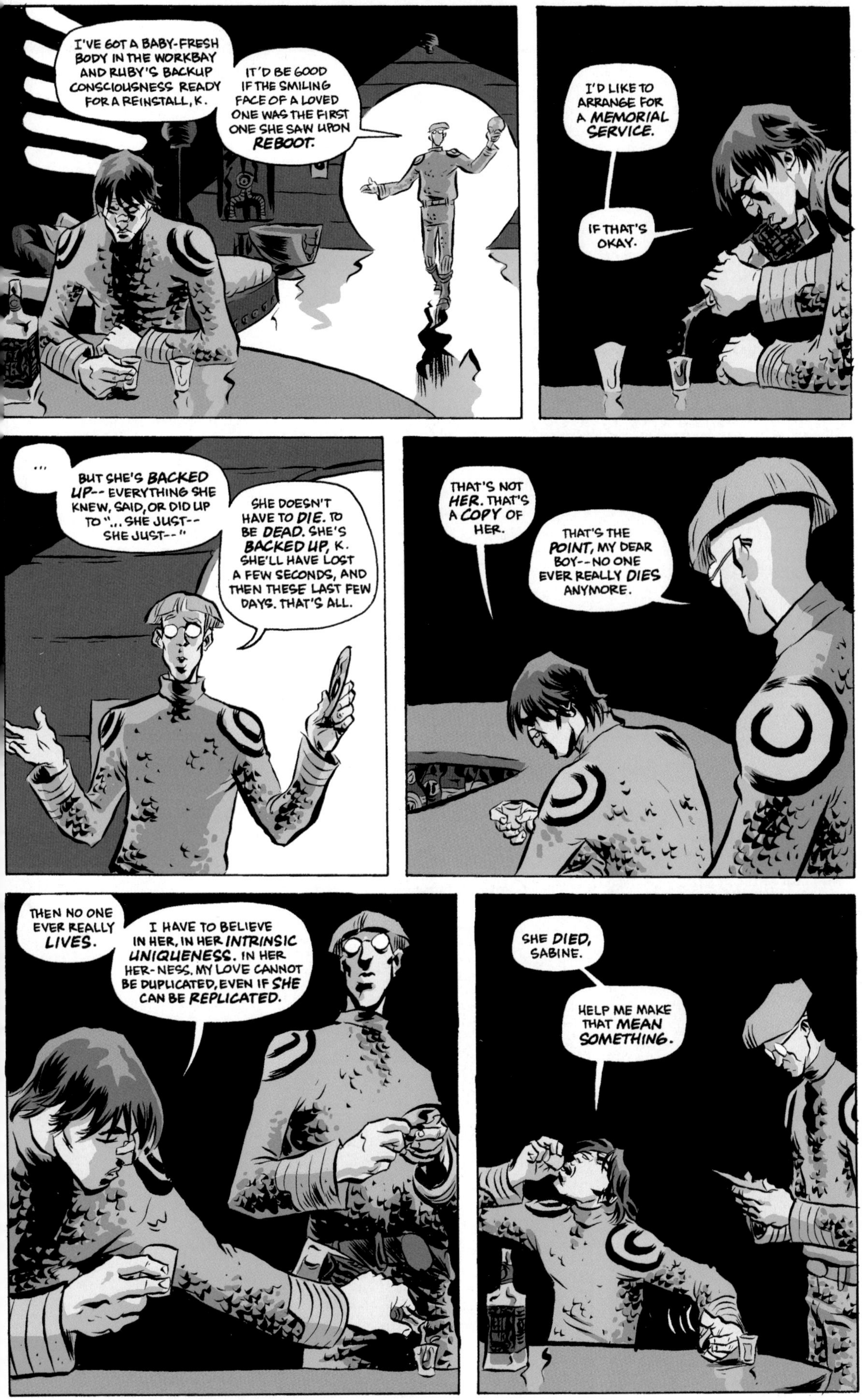
I'VE GOT A BABY-FRESH BODY IN THE WORKBAY AND RUBY'S BACKUP CONSCIOUSNESS READY FOR A REINSTALL, K.
IT'D BE GOOD IF THE SMILING FACE OF A LOVED ONE WAS THE FIRST ONE SHE SAW UPON REBOOT.
I'D LIKE TO ARRANGE FOR A MEMORIAL SERVICE.
IF THAT'S OKAY.
...
BUT SHE'S BACKED UP-- EVERYTHING SHE KNEW, SAID, OR DID UP TO "... SHE JUST-- SHE JUST--"
SHE DOESN'T HAVE TO DIE. TO BE DEAD. SHE'S BACKED UP, K. SHE'LL HAVE LOST A FEW SECONDS, AND THEN THESE LAST FEW DAYS. THAT'S ALL.
THAT'S NOT HER. THAT'S A COPY OF HER.
THAT'S THE POINT, MY DEAR BOY-- NO ONE EVER REALLY DIES ANYMORE.
THEN NO ONE EVER REALLY LIVES.
I HAVE TO BELIEVE IN HER, IN HER INTRINSIC UNIQUENESS. IN HER HER-NESS. MY LOVE CANNOT BE DUPLICATED, EVEN IF SHE CAN BE REPLICATED.
SHE DIED, SABINE.
HELP ME MAKE THAT MEAN SOMETHING.

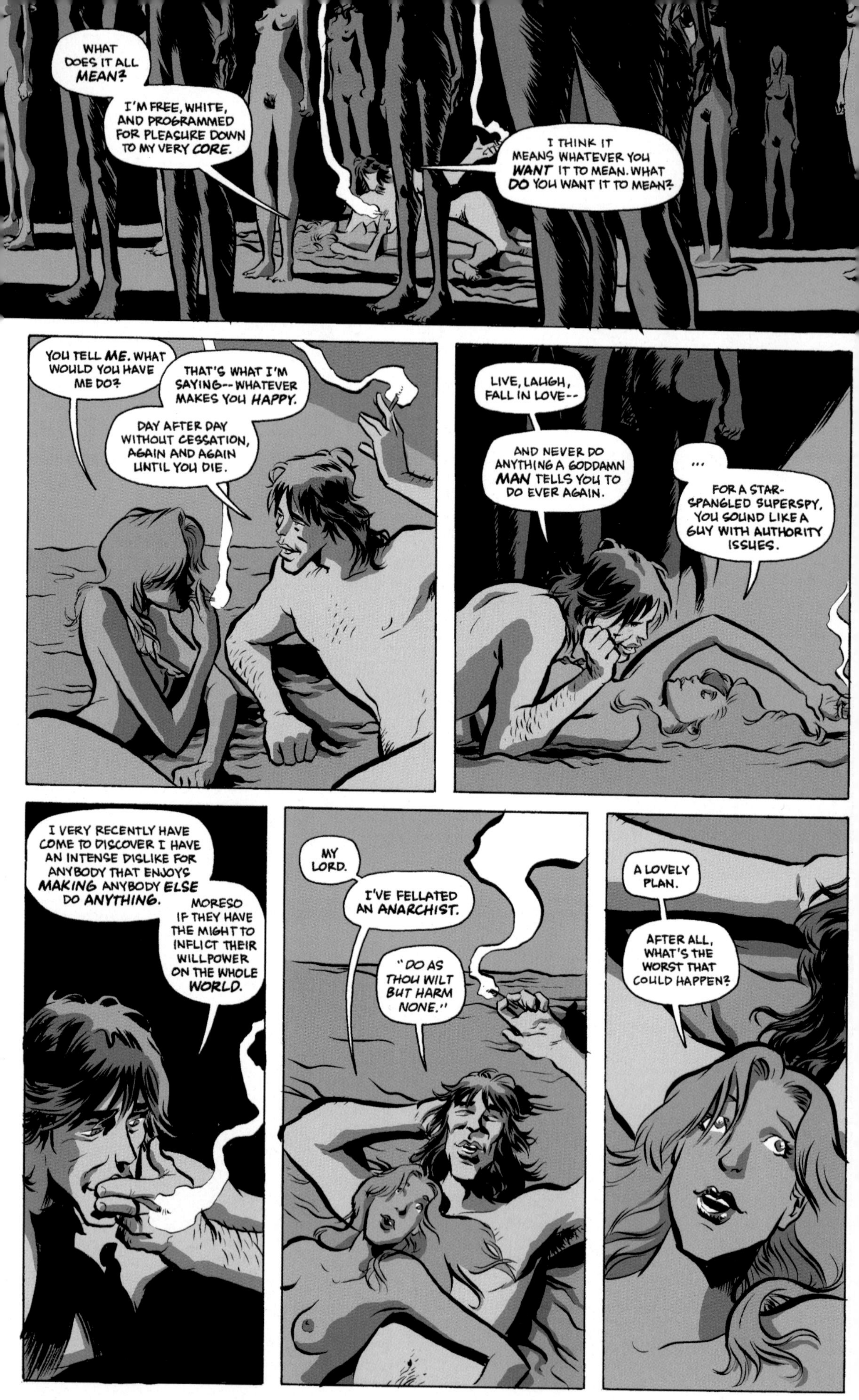
WHAT DOES IT ALL MEAN?
I'M FREE, WHITE, AND PROGRAMMED FOR PLEASURE DOWN TO MY VERY CORE.
I THINK IT MEANS WHATEVER YOU WANT IT TO MEAN. WHAT DO YOU WANT IT TO MEAN?
YOU TELL ME. WHAT WOULD YOU HAVE ME DO?
THAT'S WHAT I'M SAYING--WHATEVER MAKES YOU HAPPY.
DAY AFTER DAY WITHOUT CESSATION, AGAIN AND AGAIN UNTIL YOU DIE.
LIVE, LAUGH, FALL IN LOVE--
AND NEVER DO ANYTHING A GODDAMN MAN TELLS YOU TO DO EVER AGAIN.
...
FOR A STAR-SPANGLED SUPERSPY, YOU SOUND LIKE A GUY WITH AUTHORITY ISSUES.
I VERY RECENTLY HAVE COME TO DISCOVER I HAVE AN INTENSE DISLIKE FOR ANYBODY THAT ENJOYS MAKING ANYBODY ELSE DO ANYTHING.
MORESO IF THEY HAVE THE MIGHT TO INFLICT THEIR WILLPOWER ON THE WHOLE WORLD.
MY LORD.
I'VE FELLATED AN ANARCHIST.
"DO AS THOU WILT BUT HARM NONE."
A LOVELY PLAN.
AFTER ALL, WHAT'S THE WORST THAT COULD HAPPEN?

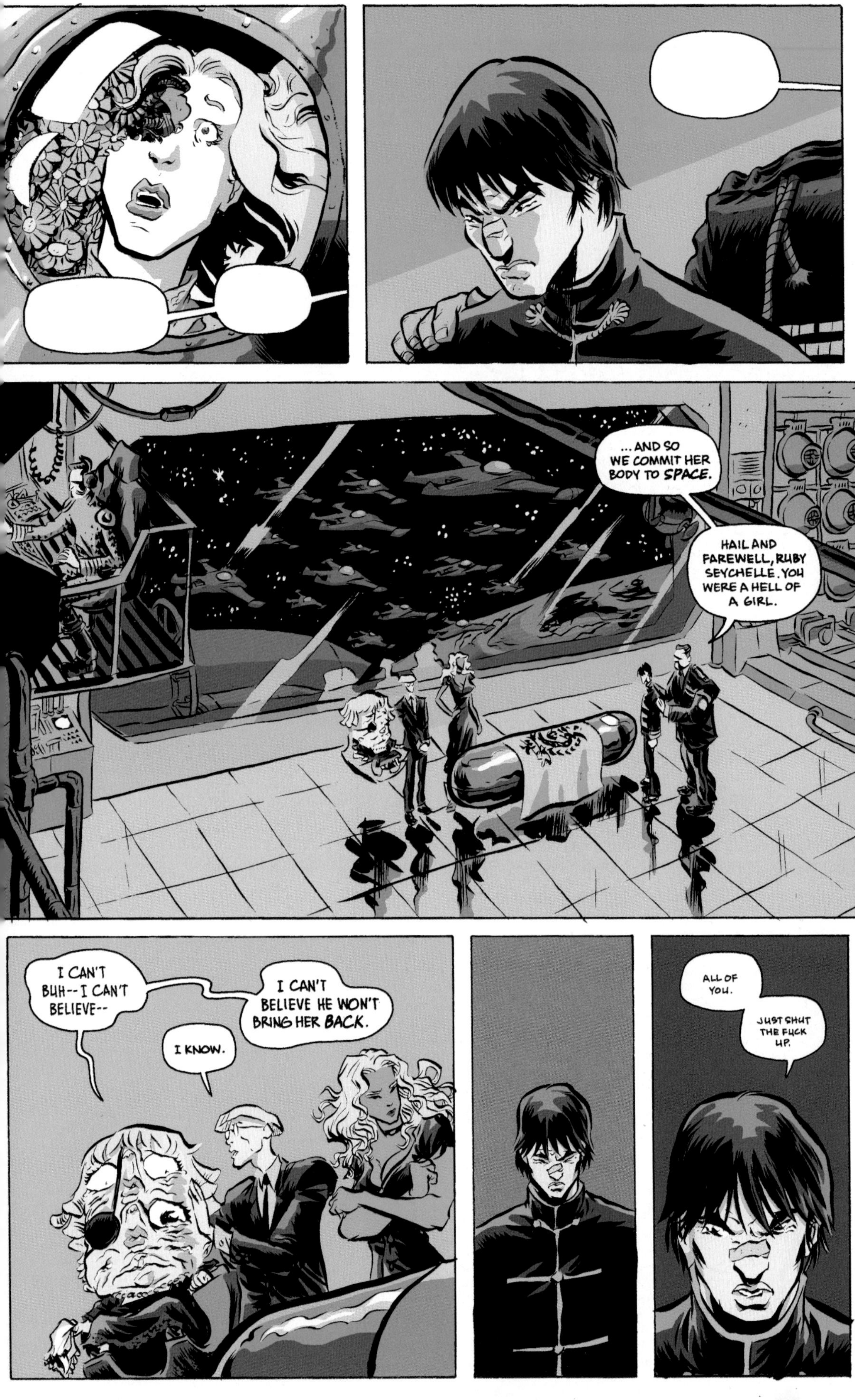
...AND SO WE COMMIT HER BODY TO SPACE.
HAIL AND FAREWELL, RUBY SEYCHELLE. YOU WERE A HELL OF A GIRL.
I CAN'T BUH--I CAN'T BELIEVE--
I CAN'T BELIEVE HE WON'T BRING HER BACK.
I KNOW.
ALL OF YOU.
JUST SHUT THE FUCK UP.

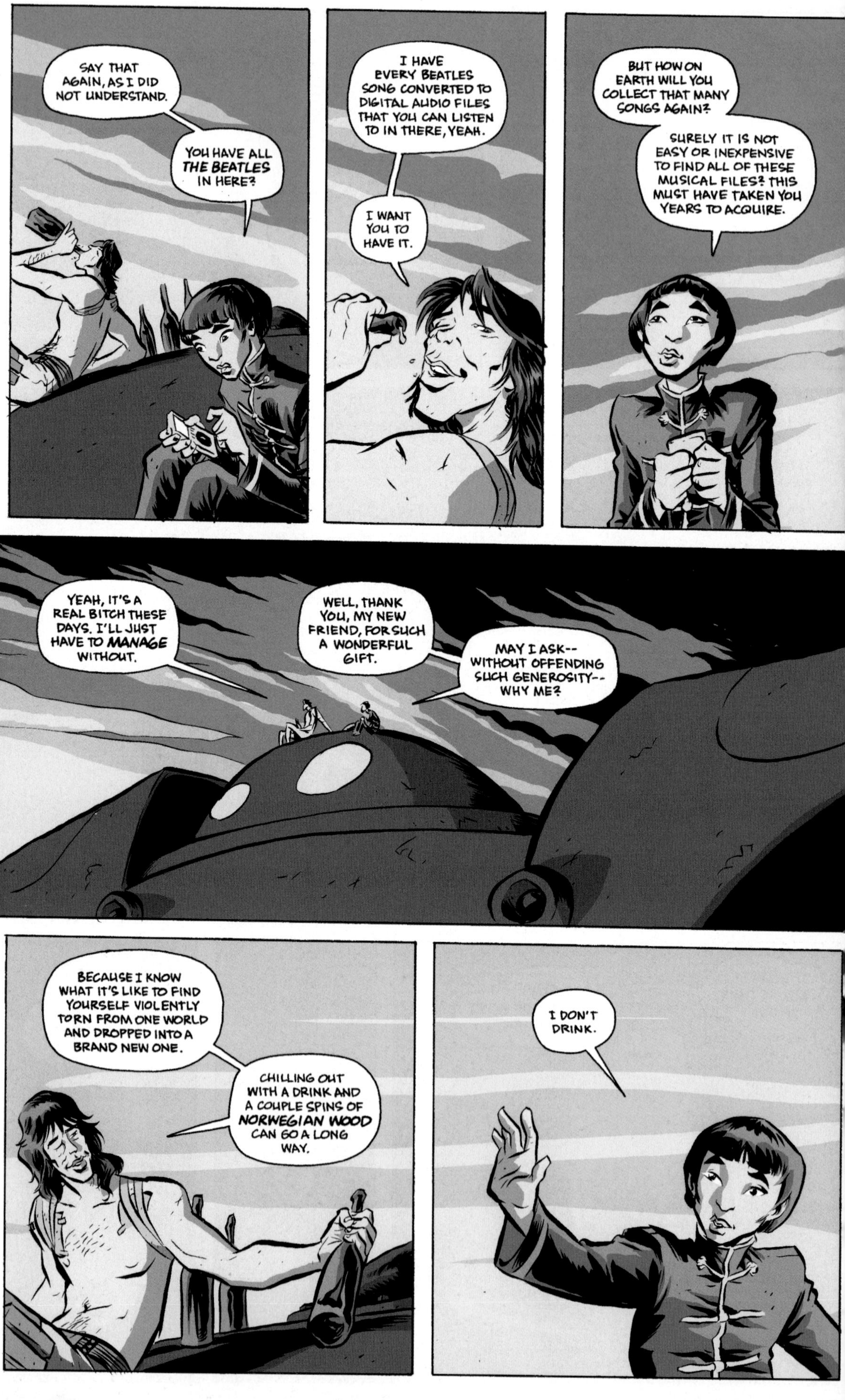
SAY THAT AGAIN, AS I DID NOT UNDERSTAND.
YOU HAVE ALL THE BEATLES IN HERE?
I HAVE EVERY BEATLES SONG CONVERTED TO DIGITAL AUDIO FILES THAT YOU CAN LISTEN TO IN THERE, YEAH.
I WANT YOU TO HAVE IT.
BUT HOW ON EARTH WILL YOU COLLECT THAT MANY SONGS AGAIN?
SURELY IT IS NOT EASY OR INEXPENSIVE TO FIND ALL OF THESE MUSICAL FILES? THIS MUST HAVE TAKEN YOU YEARS TO ACQUIRE.
YEAH, IT'S A REAL BITCH THESE DAYS. I'LL JUST HAVE TO MANAGE WITHOUT.
WELL, THANK YOU, MY NEW FRIEND, FOR SUCH A WONDERFUL GIFT.
MAY I ASK-- WITHOUT OFFENDING SUCH GENEROSITY-- WHY ME?
BECAUSE I KNOW WHAT IT'S LIKE TO FIND YOURSELF VIOLENTLY TORN FROM ONE WORLD AND DROPPED INTO A BRAND NEW ONE.
CHILLING OUT WITH A DRINK AND A COUPLE SPINS OF NORWEGIAN WOOD CAN GO A LONG WAY.
I DON'T DRINK.

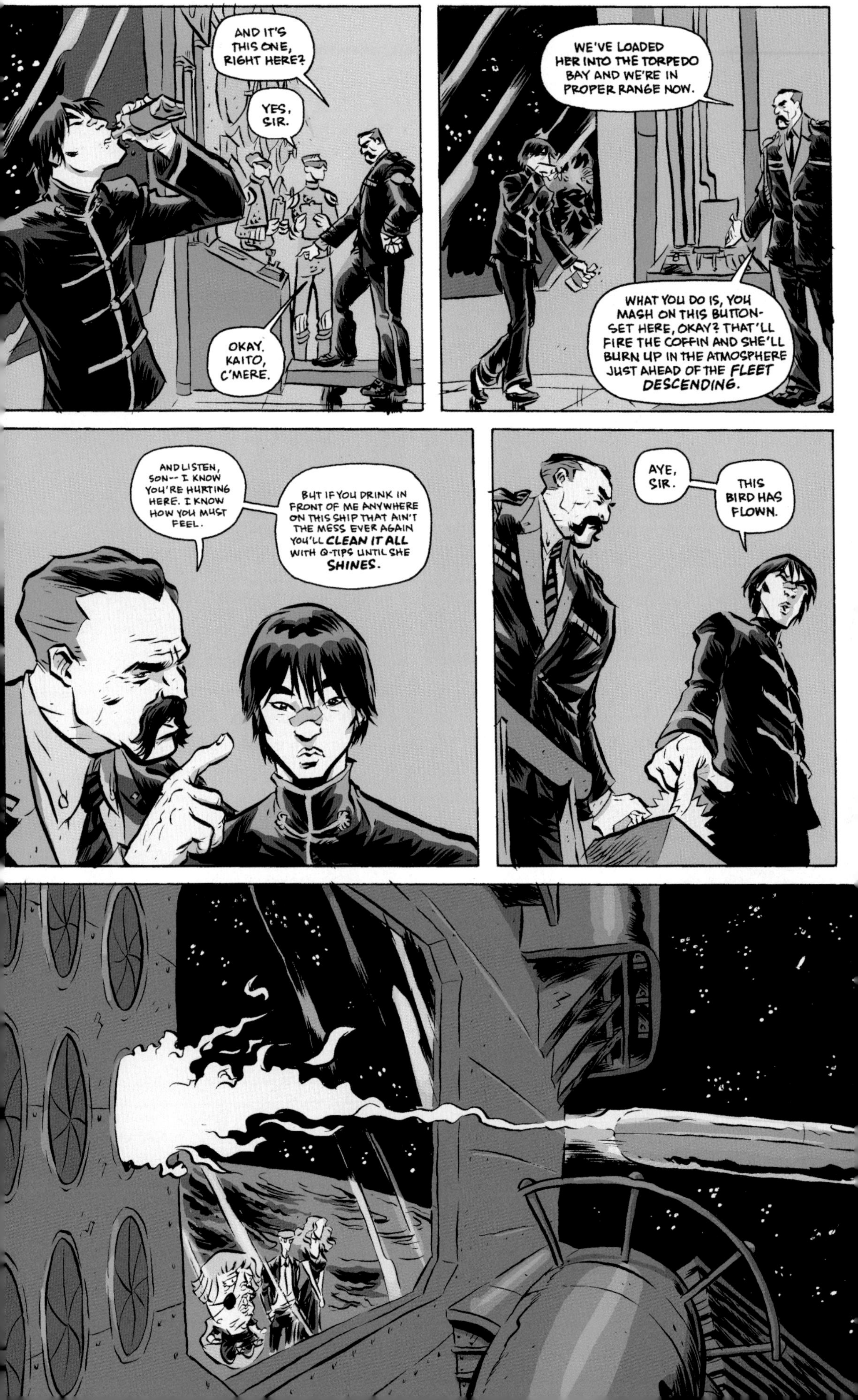

AND IT'S THIS ONE, RIGHT HERE?
YES, SIR.
OKAY. KAITO, C'MERE.
WE'VE LOADED HER INTO THE TORPEDO BAY AND WE'RE IN PROPER RANGE NOW.
WHAT YOU DO IS, YOU MASH ON THIS BUTTON-SET HERE, OKAY? THAT'LL FIRE THE COFFIN AND SHE'LL BURN UP IN THE ATMOSPHERE JUST AHEAD OF THE FLEET DESCENDING.
AND LISTEN, SON-- I KNOW YOU'RE HURTING HERE. I KNOW HOW YOU MUST FEEL.
BUT IF YOU DRINK IN FRONT OF ME ANYWHERE ON THIS SHIP THAT AIN'T THE MESS EVER AGAIN YOU'LL CLEAN IT ALL WITH Q-TIPS UNTIL SHE SHINES.
AYE, SIR.
THIS BIRD HAS FLOWN.

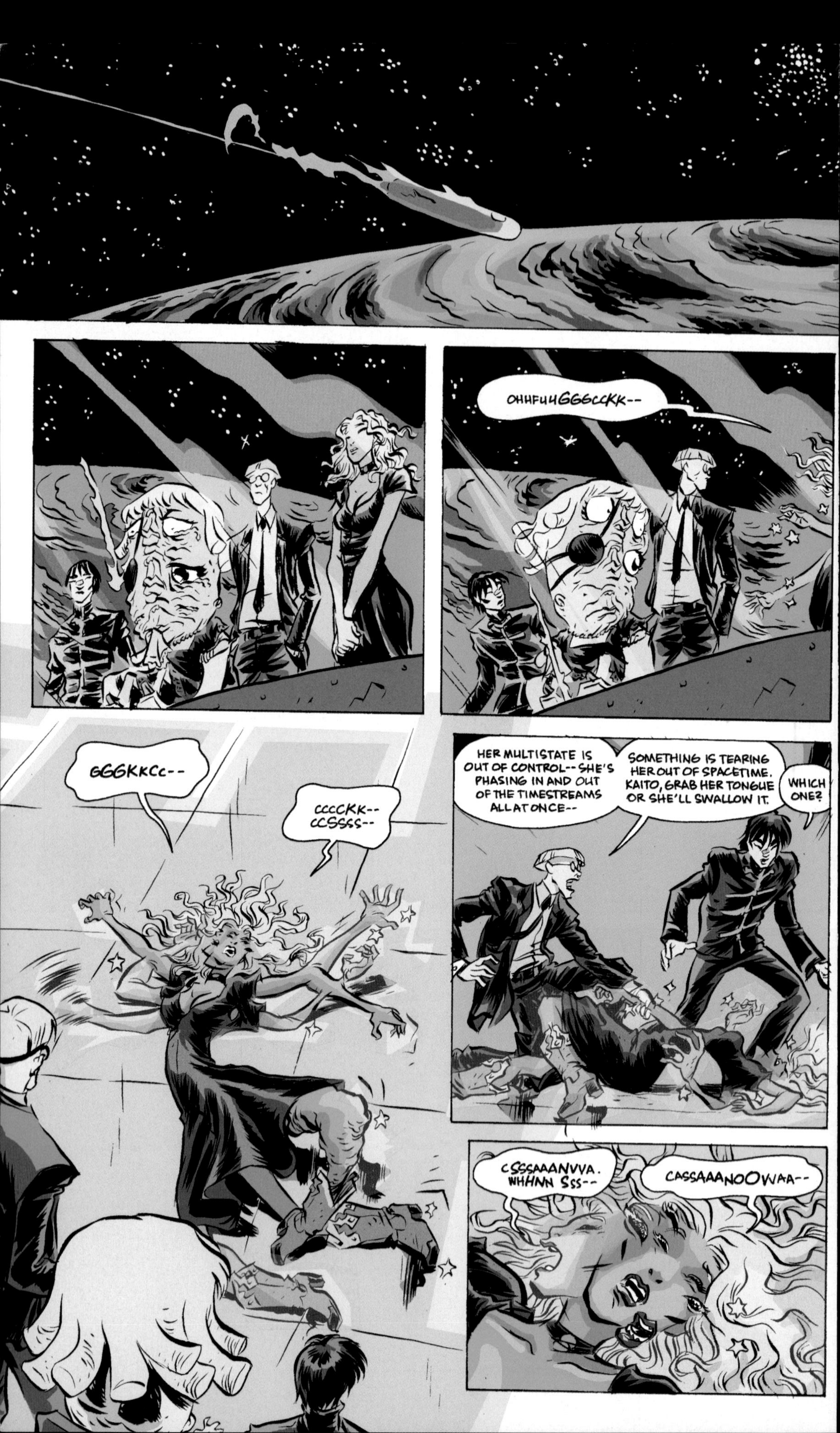

OHHFUUGGGCCKK--
GGGKKCc--
CCCCKK--
CCSSSS--
HER MULTISTATE IS OUT OF CONTROL--SHE'S PHASING IN AND OUT OF THE TIMESTREAMS ALL AT ONCE--
SOMETHING IS TEARING HER OUT OF SPACETIME. KAITO, GRAB HER TONGUE OR SHE'LL SWALLOW IT.
WHICH ONE?
CSSSAAANVVA. WHHNN SSS--
CASSAAANOOVVAA--

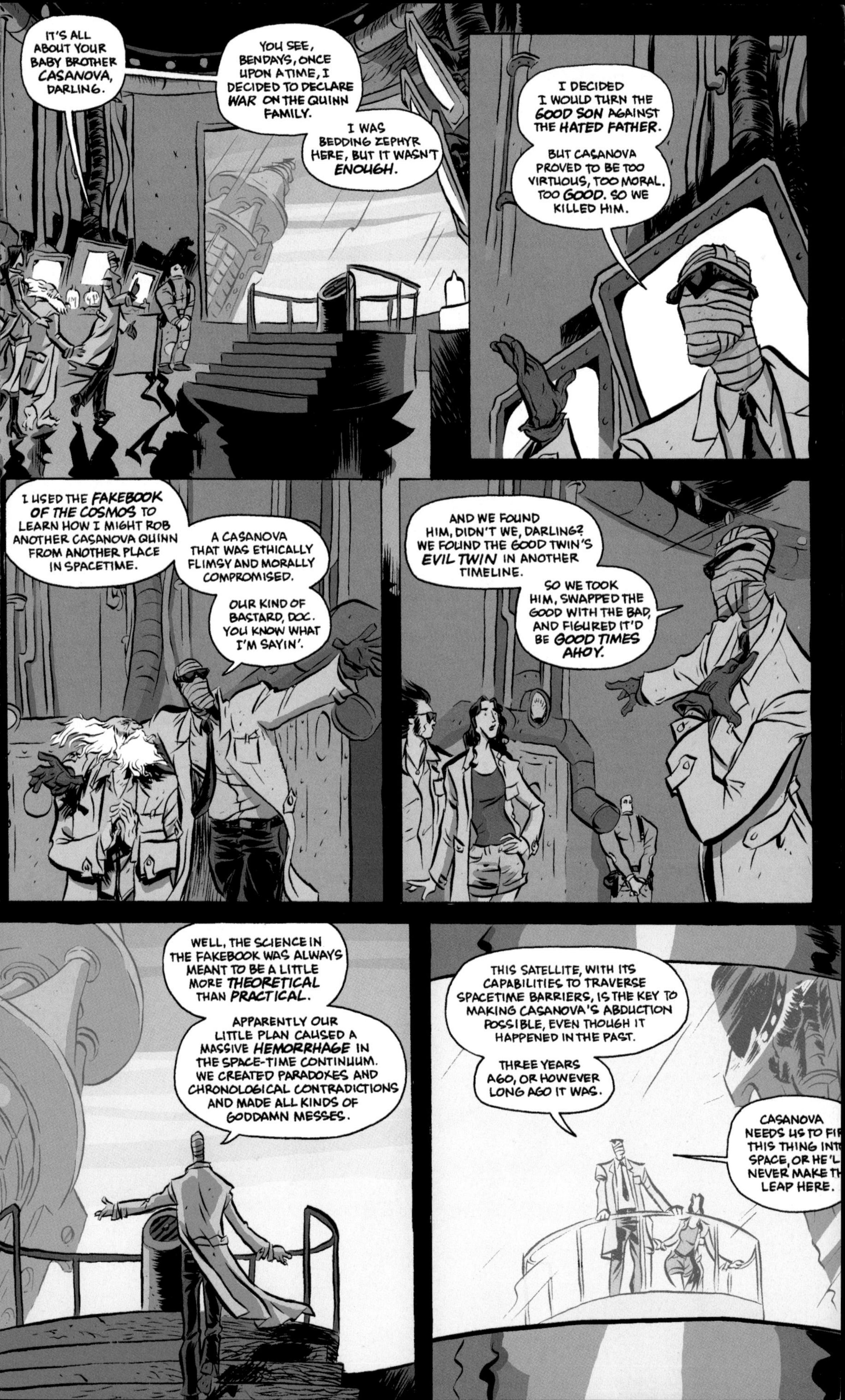
IT'S ALL ABOUT YOUR BABY BROTHER CASANOVA, DARLING.
YOU SEE, BENDAYS, ONCE UPON A TIME, I DECIDED TO DECLARE WAR ON THE QUINN FAMILY.
I WAS BEDDING ZEPHYR HERE, BUT IT WASN'T ENOUGH.
I DECIDED I WOULD TURN THE GOOD SON AGAINST THE HATED FATHER.
BUT CASANOVA PROVED TO BE TOO VIRTUOUS, TOO MORAL. TOO GOOD. SO WE KILLED HIM.
I USED THE FAKEBOOK OF THE COSMOS TO LEARN HOW I MIGHT ROB ANOTHER CASANOVA QUINN FROM ANOTHER PLACE IN SPACETIME.
A CASANOVA THAT WAS ETHICALLY FLIMSY AND MORALLY COMPROMISED.
OUR KIND OF BASTARD, DOC. YOU KNOW WHAT I'M SAYIN'.
AND WE FOUND HIM, DIDN'T WE, DARLING? WE FOUND THE GOOD TWIN'S EVIL TWIN IN ANOTHER TIMELINE.
SO WE TOOK HIM, SWAPPED THE GOOD WITH THE BAD, AND FIGURED IT'D BE GOOD TIMES AHOY.
WELL, THE SCIENCE IN THE FAKEBOOK WAS ALWAYS MEANT TO BE A LITTLE MORE THEORETICAL THAN PRACTICAL.
APPARENTLY OUR LITTLE PLAN CAUSED A MASSIVE HEMORRHAGE IN THE SPACE-TIME CONTINUUM. WE CREATED PARADOXES AND CHRONOLOGICAL CONTRADICTIONS AND MADE ALL KINDS OF GODDAMN MESSES.
THIS SATELLITE, WITH ITS CAPABILITIES TO TRAVERSE SPACETIME BARRIERS, IS THE KEY TO MAKING CASANOVA'S ABDUCTION POSSIBLE, EVEN THOUGH IT HAPPENED IN THE PAST.
THREE YEARS AGO, OR HOWEVER LONG AGO IT WAS.
CASANOVA NEEDS US TO FI THIS THING INT SPACE, OR HE'L NEVER MAKE T LEAP HERE.

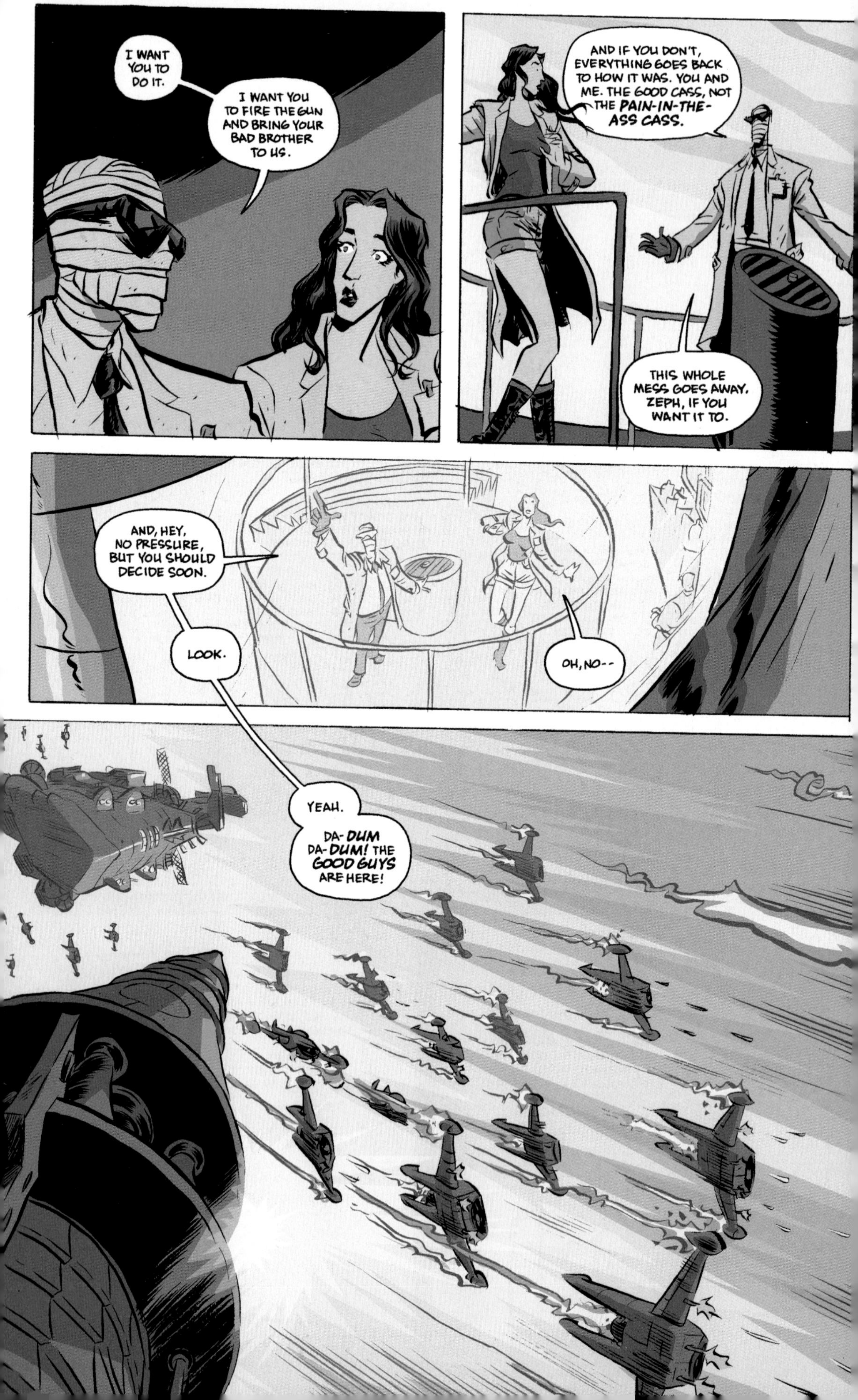
I WANT YOU TO DO IT.
I WANT YOU TO FIRE THE GUN AND BRING YOUR BAD BROTHER TO US.
AND IF YOU DON'T, EVERYTHING GOES BACK TO HOW IT WAS. YOU AND ME. THE GOOD CASS, NOT THE PAIN-IN-THE-ASS CASS.
THIS WHOLE MESS GOES AWAY, ZEPH, IF YOU WANT IT TO.
AND, HEY, NO PRESSURE, BUT YOU SHOULD DECIDE SOON.
LOOK.
OH, NO--
YEAH.
DA-DUM DA-DUM! THE GOOD GUYS ARE HERE!

CHAPTER 7
HALLO SPACEBOY

1: PAPER PLANES (3:24)

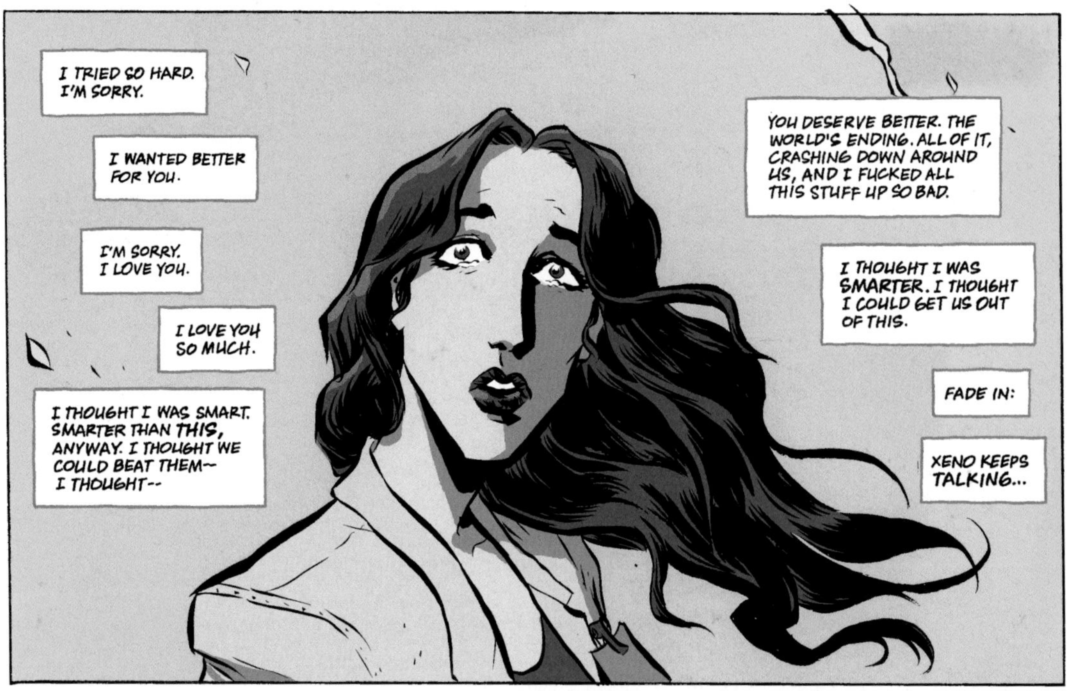

I TRIED SO HARD. I'M SORRY.
I WANTED BETTER FOR YOU.
I'M SORRY. I LOVE YOU.
I LOVE YOU SO MUCH.
I THOUGHT I WAS SMART. SMARTER THAN THIS, ANYWAY. I THOUGHT WE COULD BEAT THEM-- I THOUGHT--
YOU DESERVE BETTER. THE WORLD'S ENDING. ALL OF IT, CRASHING DOWN AROUND US, AND I FUCKED ALL THIS STUFF UP SO BAD.
I THOUGHT I WAS SMARTER. I THOUGHT I COULD GET US OUT OF THIS.
FADE IN:
XENO KEEPS TALKING...

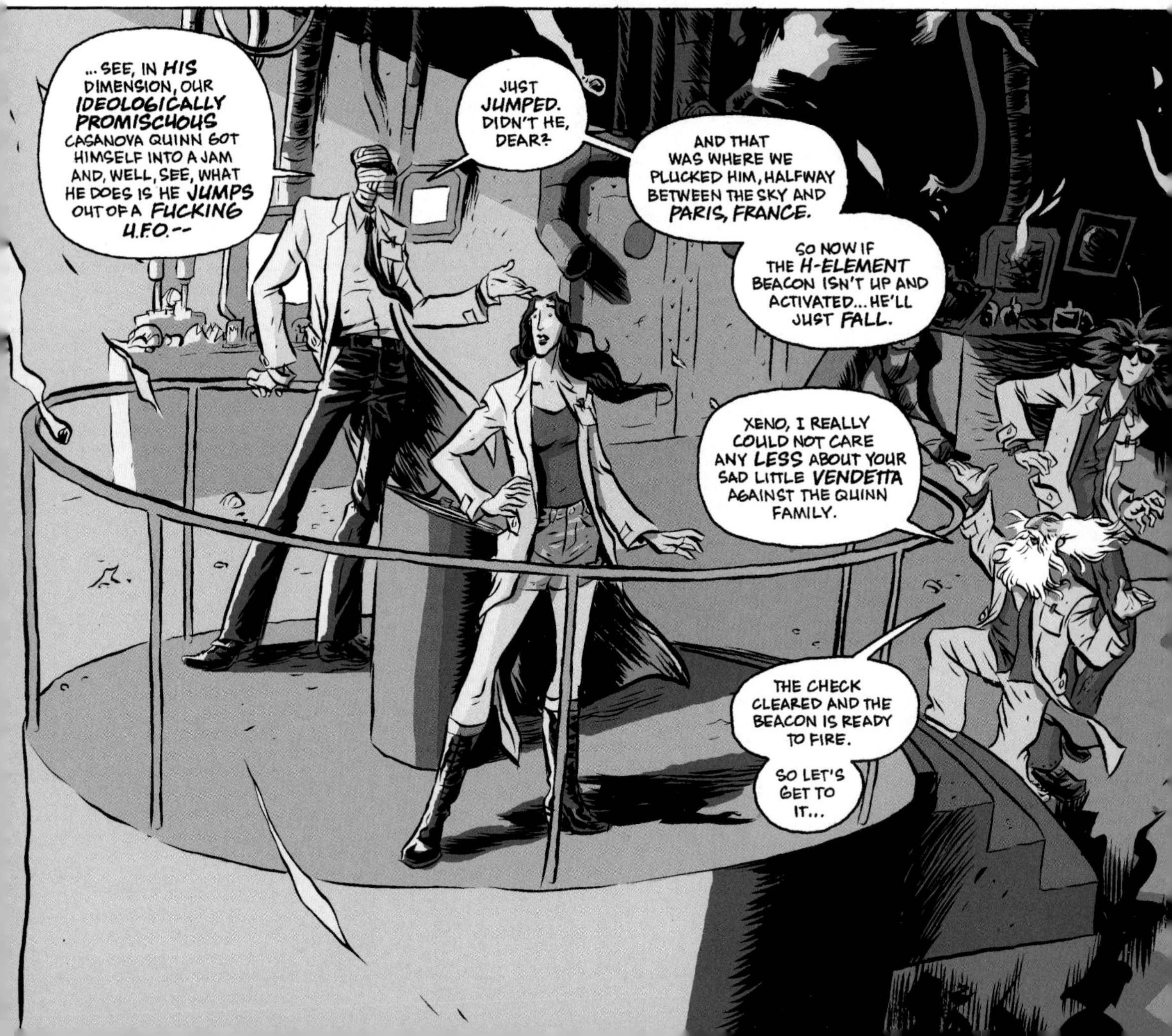

... SEE, IN HIS DIMENSION, OUR IDEOLOGICALLY PROMISCUOUS CASANOVA QUINN GOT HIMSELF INTO A JAM AND, WELL, SEE, WHAT HE DOES IS HE JUMPS OUT OF A FUCKING U.F.O.--
JUST JUMPED. DIDN'T HE, DEAR?
AND THAT WAS WHERE WE PLUCKED HIM, HALFWAY BETWEEN THE SKY AND PARIS, FRANCE.
SO NOW IF THE H-ELEMENT BEACON ISN'T UP AND ACTIVATED... HE'LL JUST FALL.
XENO, I REALLY COULD NOT CARE ANY LESS ABOUT YOUR SAD LITTLE VENDETTA AGAINST THE QUINN FAMILY.
THE CHECK CLEARED AND THE BEACON IS READY TO FIRE.
SO LET'S GET TO IT...

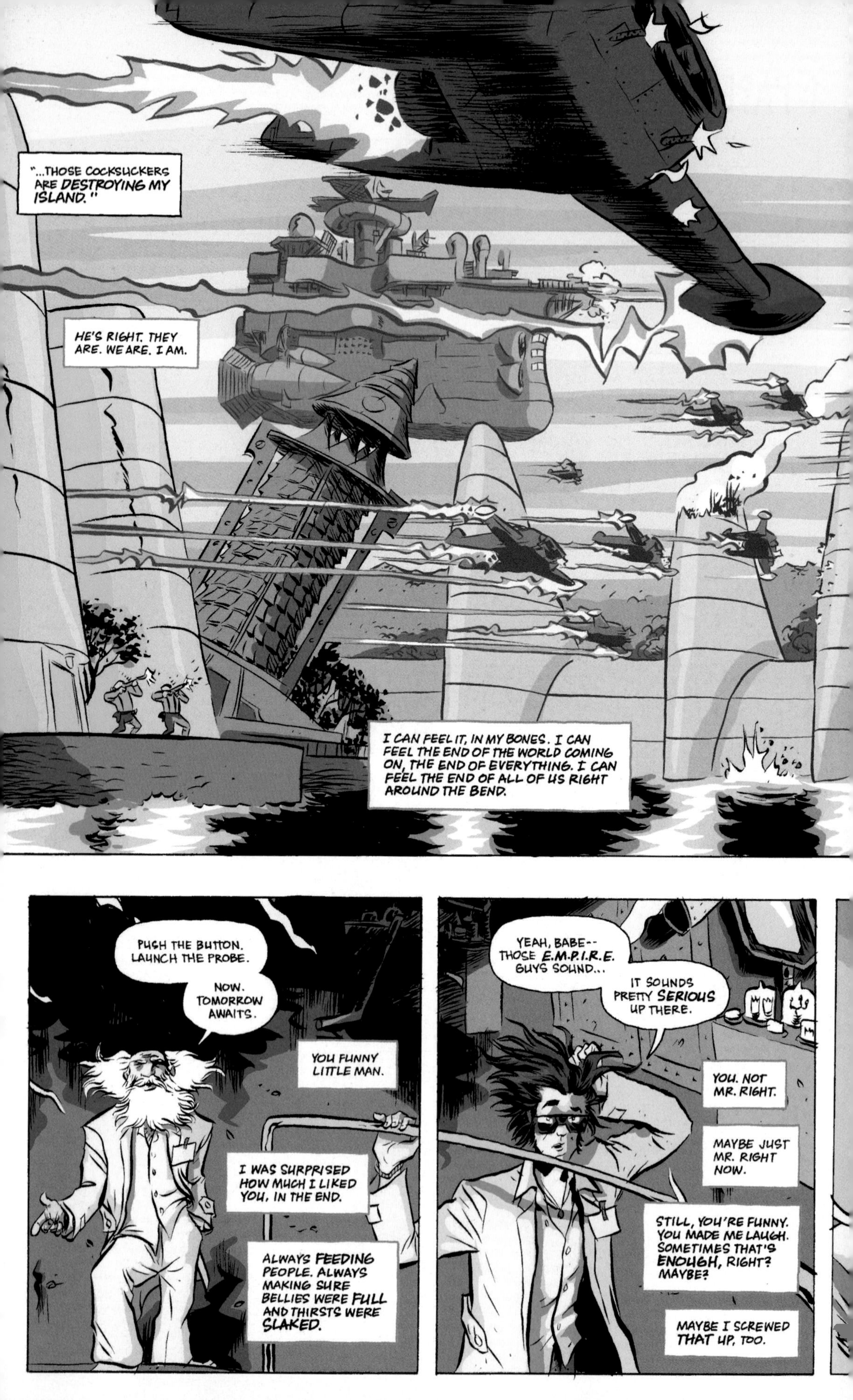
"...THOSE COCKSUCKERS ARE DESTROYING MY ISLAND."
HE'S RIGHT. THEY ARE. WE ARE. I AM.
I CAN FEEL IT, IN MY BONES. I CAN FEEL THE END OF THE WORLD COMING ON, THE END OF EVERYTHING. I CAN FEEL THE END OF ALL OF US RIGHT AROUND THE BEND.
PUSH THE BUTTON. LAUNCH THE PROBE.
NOW. TOMORROW AWAITS.
YOU FUNNY LITTLE MAN.
I WAS SURPRISED HOW MUCH I LIKED YOU, IN THE END.
ALWAYS FEEDING PEOPLE. ALWAYS MAKING SURE BELLIES WERE FULL AND THIRSTS WERE SLAKED.
YEAH, BABE-- THOSE E.M.P.I.R.E. GUYS SOUND...
IT SOUNDS PRETTY SERIOUS UP THERE.
YOU. NOT MR. RIGHT.
MAYBE JUST MR. RIGHT NOW.
STILL, YOU'RE FUNNY. YOU MADE ME LAUGH. SOMETIMES THAT'S ENOUGH, RIGHT? MAYBE?
MAYBE I SCREWED THAT UP, TOO.

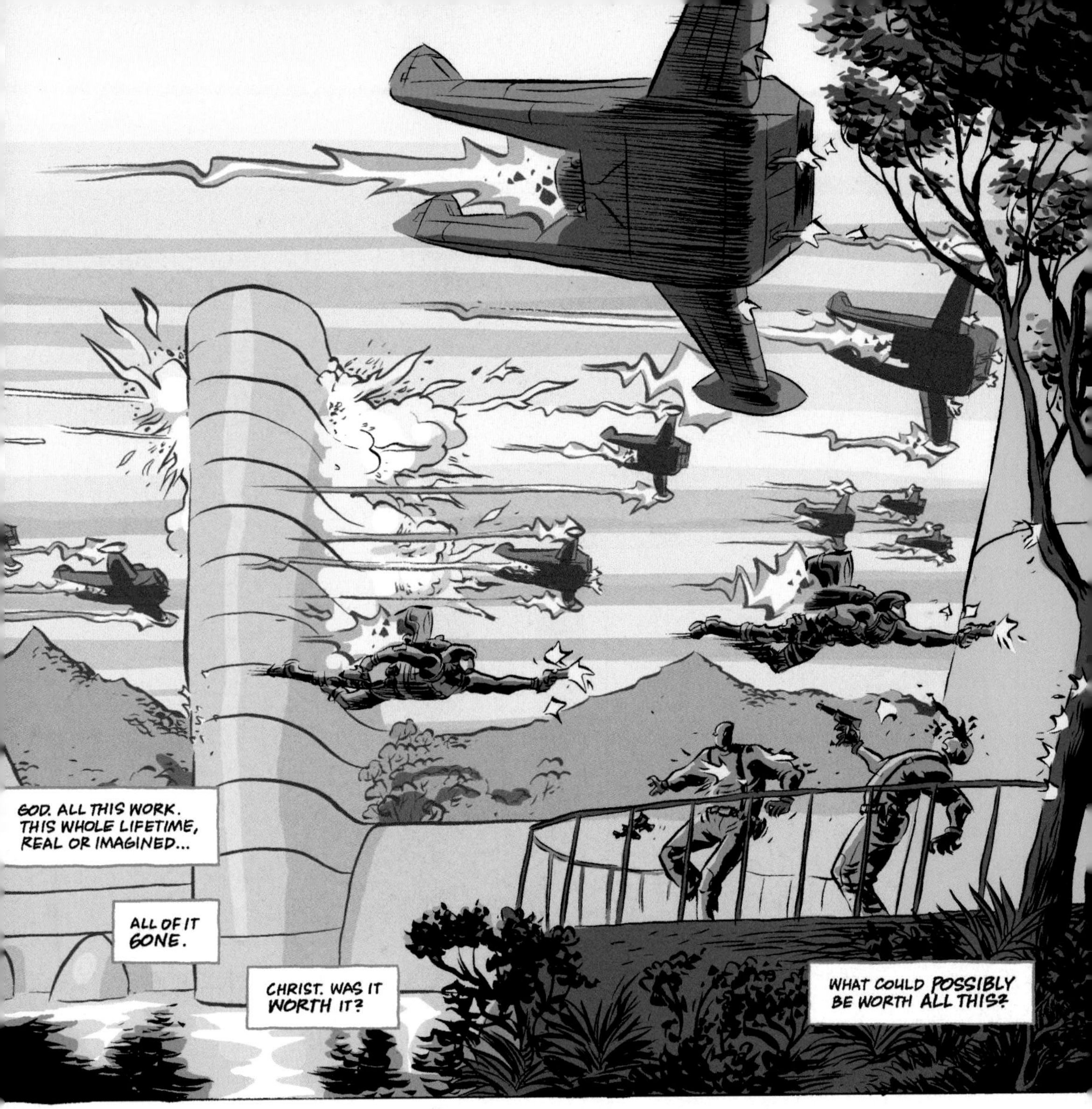
GOD. ALL THIS WORK. THIS WHOLE LIFETIME, REAL OR IMAGINED...
ALL OF IT GONE.
CHRIST. WAS IT WORTH IT?
WHAT COULD POSSIBLY BE WORTH ALL THIS?

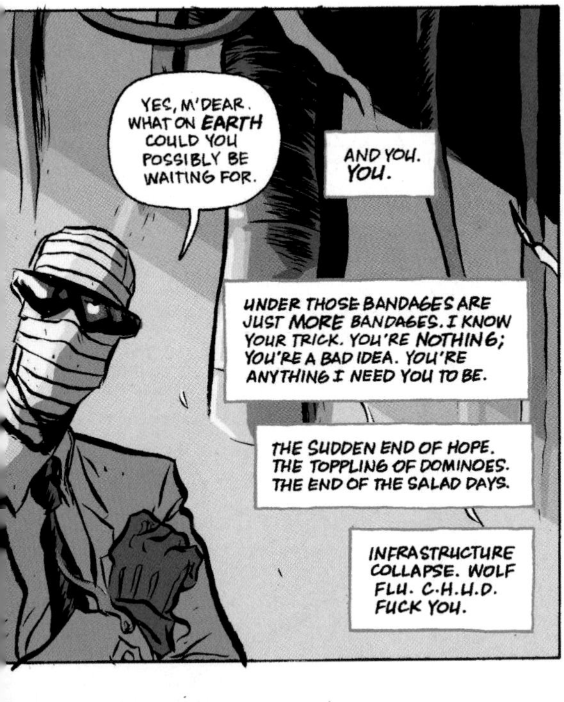
YES, M'DEAR. WHAT ON EARTH COULD YOU POSSIBLY BE WAITING FOR.
AND YOU. YOU.
UNDER THOSE BANDAGES ARE JUST MORE BANDAGES. I KNOW YOUR TRICK. YOU'RE NOTHING; YOU'RE A BAD IDEA. YOU'RE ANYTHING I NEED YOU TO BE.
THE SUDDEN END OF HOPE. THE TOPPLING OF DOMINOES. THE END OF THE SALAD DAYS.
INFRASTRUCTURE COLLAPSE. WOLF FLU. C.H.U.D. FUCK YOU.

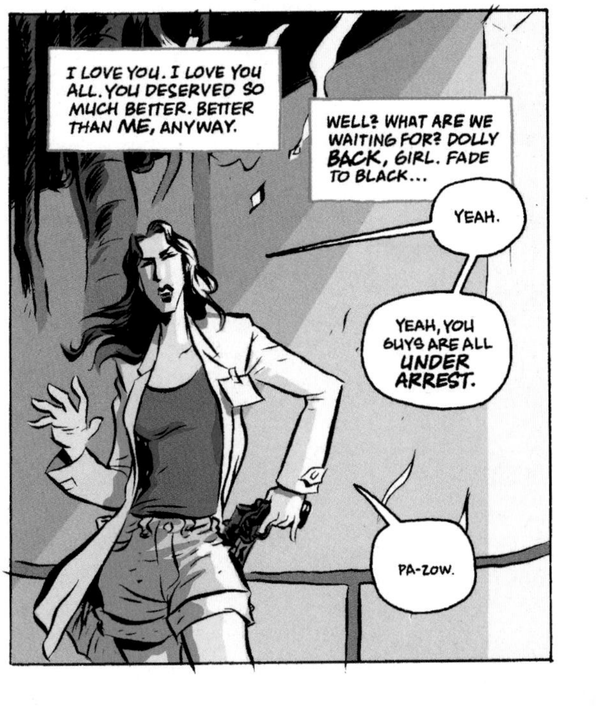
I LOVE YOU. I LOVE YOU ALL. YOU DESERVED SO MUCH BETTER. BETTER THAN ME, ANYWAY.
WELL? WHAT ARE WE WAITING FOR? DOLLY BACK, GIRL. FADE TO BLACK...
YEAH.
YEAH, YOU GUYS ARE ALL UNDER ARREST.
PA-ZOW.

2: YOUNG FOLKS (4:39)

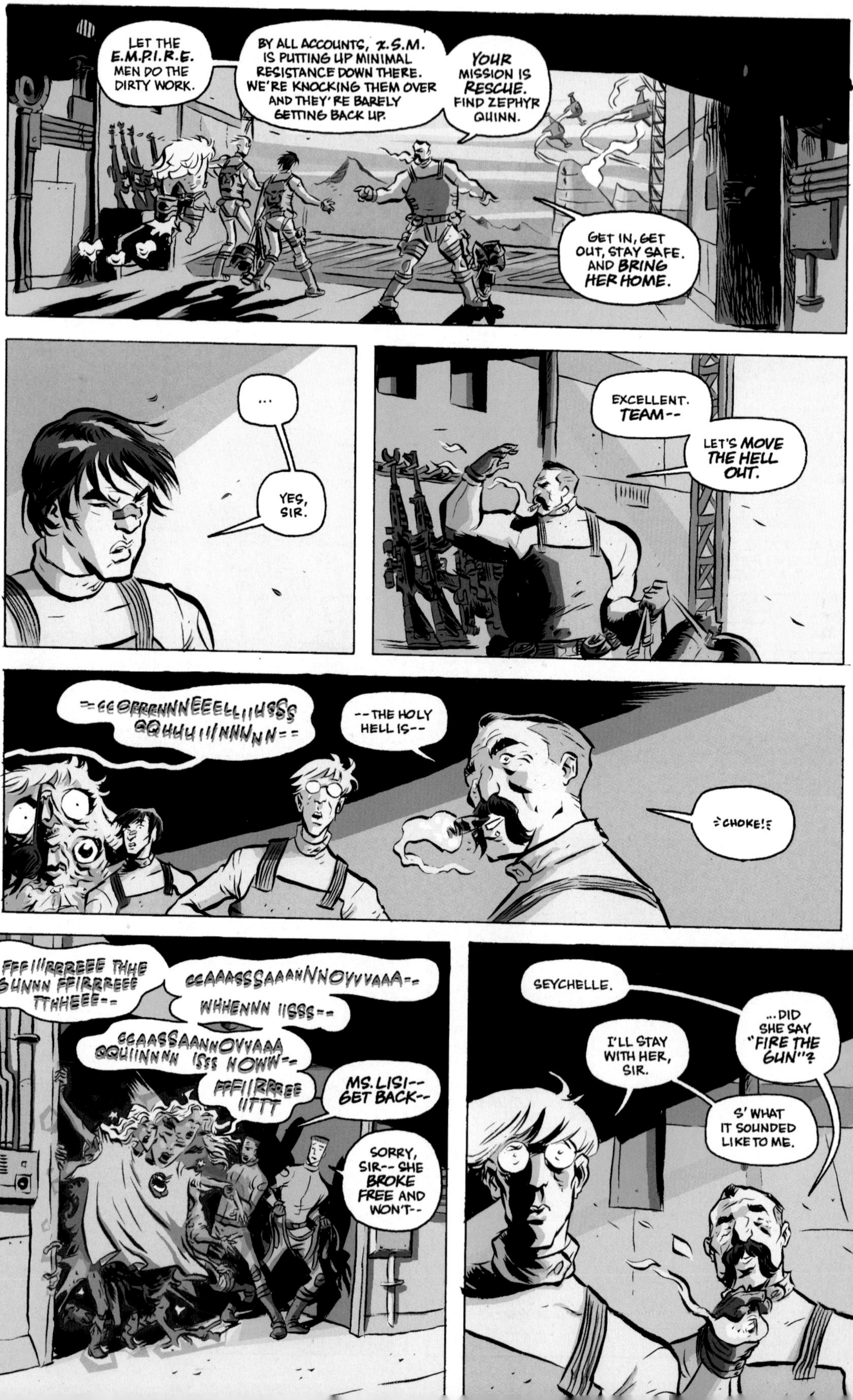
LET THE E.M.P.I.R.E. MEN DO THE DIRTY WORK.
BY ALL ACCOUNTS, Z.S.M. IS PUTTING UP MINIMAL RESISTANCE DOWN THERE. WE'RE KNOCKING THEM OVER AND THEY'RE BARELY GETTING BACK UP.
YOUR MISSION IS RESCUE. FIND ZEPHYR QUINN.
GET IN, GET OUT, STAY SAFE. AND BRING HER HOME.
...
YES, SIR.
EXCELLENT. TEAM--
LET'S MOVE THE HELL OUT.
==CCOPPRRNNNEEELLIIUSSS QQUUUIIINNNNNN==
--THE HOLY HELL IS--
=CHOKE!=
FFFIIIRRREEE THHE GGUNNN FFIRRREEE TTHHEEE--
CCAAASSSAAANNNOVVVAAA-- WHHENNN IISSS--
CCAASSAANNOVVAAA QQUIINNNN ISSS NOWW-- FFFIIRRREE IITTT
MS. LISI-- GET BACK--
SORRY, SIR-- SHE BROKE FREE AND WON'T--
SEYCHELLE.
I'LL STAY WITH HER, SIR.
...DID SHE SAY "FIRE THE GUN"?
S' WHAT IT SOUNDED LIKE TO ME.

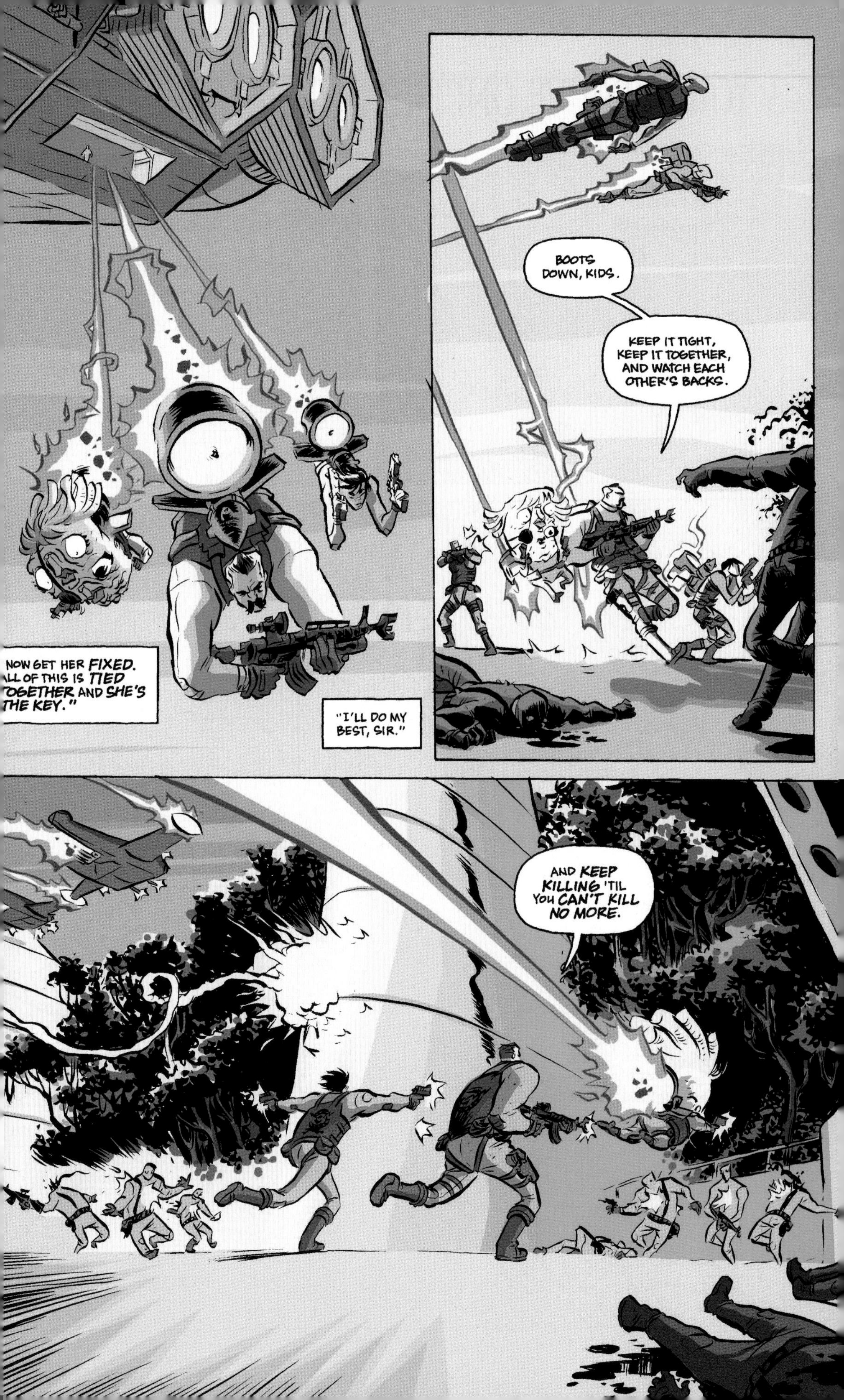
NOW GET HER FIXED. ALL OF THIS IS TIED TOGETHER AND SHE'S THE KEY."
"I'LL DO MY BEST, SIR."
BOOTS DOWN, KIDS.
KEEP IT TIGHT, KEEP IT TOGETHER, AND WATCH EACH OTHER'S BACKS.
AND KEEP KILLING 'TIL YOU CAN'T KILL NO MORE.

3: YOU ONLY LIVE ONCE (3:05)

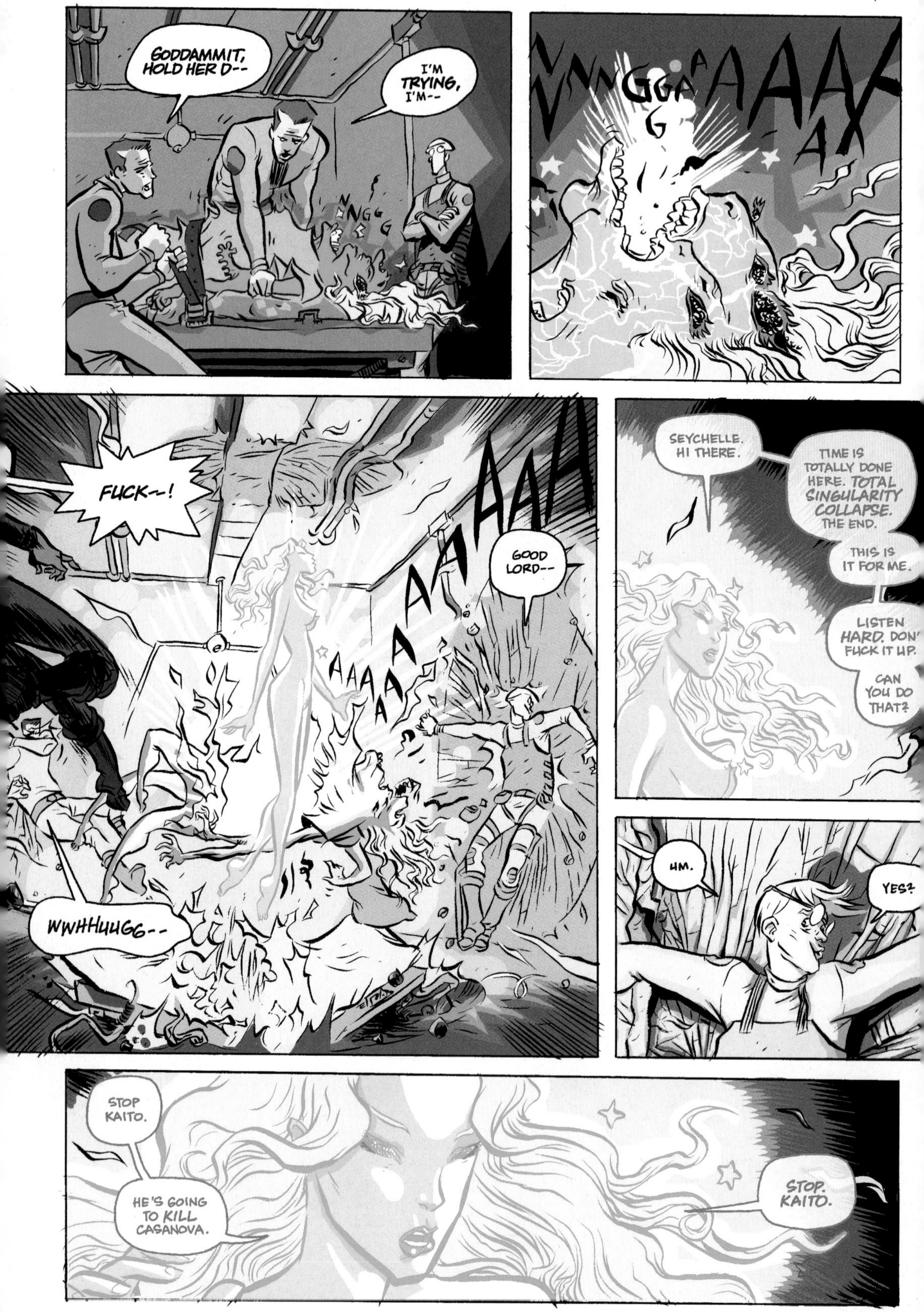
GODDAMMIT, HOLD HER D--
I'M TRYING, I'M--
NNGG G
NNNGGA G AAAAK AX
FUCK--!
GOOD LORD--
AAAAAAAAAAA
WWHHUUGG--
SEYCHELLE. HI THERE.
TIME IS TOTALLY DONE HERE. TOTAL SINGULARITY COLLAPSE. THE END.
THIS IS IT FOR ME.
LISTEN HARD, DON' FUCK IT UP.
CAN YOU DO THAT?
UM.
YES?
STOP KAITO.
HE'S GOING TO KILL CASANOVA.
STOP. KAITO.

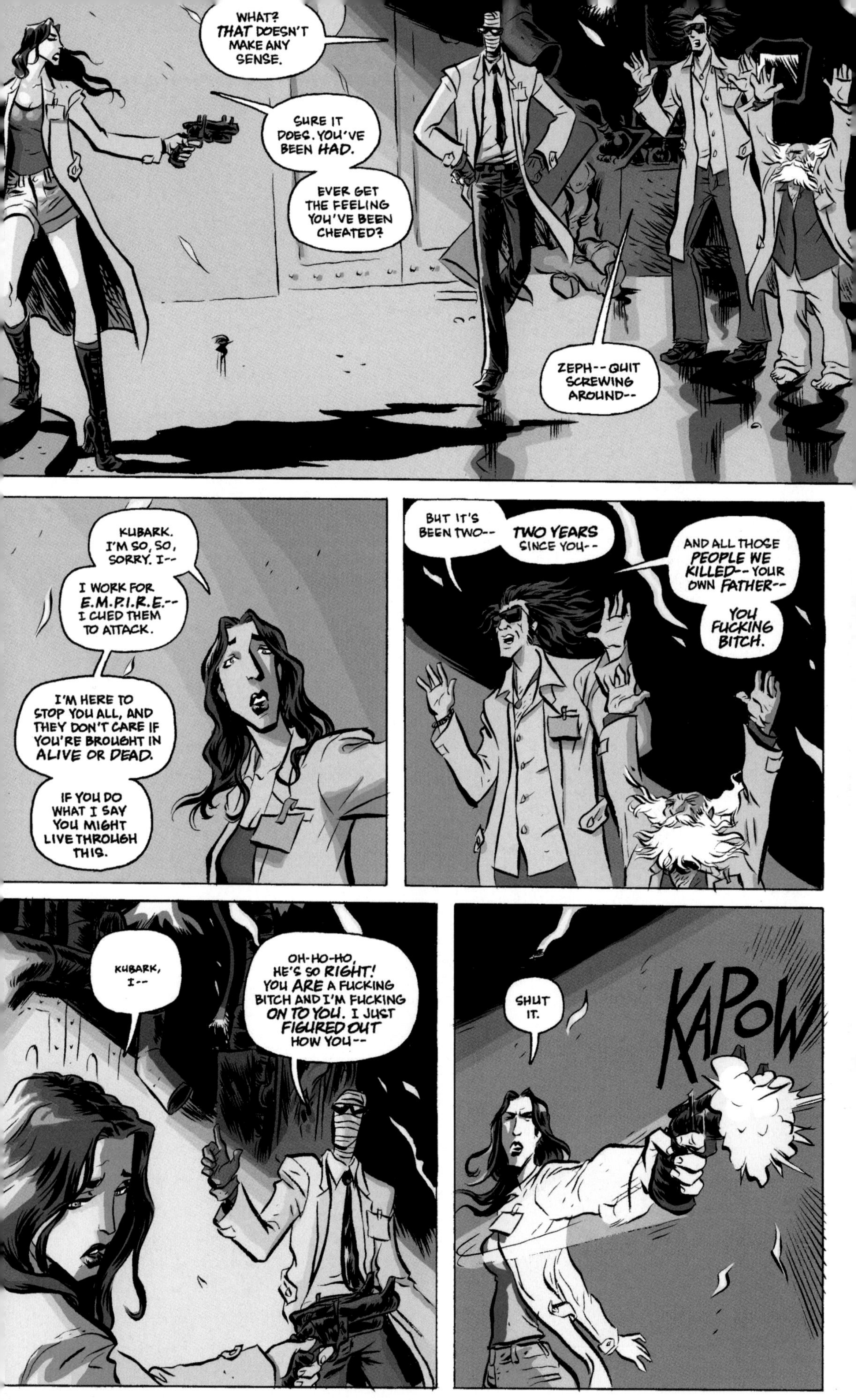
WHAT? THAT DOESN'T MAKE ANY SENSE.
SURE IT DOES. YOU'VE BEEN HAD.
EVER GET THE FEELING YOU'VE BEEN CHEATED?
ZEPH--QUIT SCREWING AROUND--
KUBARK. I'M SO, SO, SORRY. I--
I WORK FOR E.M.P.I.R.E.-- I CUED THEM TO ATTACK.
I'M HERE TO STOP YOU ALL, AND THEY DON'T CARE IF YOU'RE BROUGHT IN ALIVE OR DEAD.
IF YOU DO WHAT I SAY YOU MIGHT LIVE THROUGH THIS.
BUT IT'S BEEN TWO--
TWO YEARS SINCE YOU--
AND ALL THOSE PEOPLE WE KILLED--YOUR OWN FATHER--
YOU FUCKING BITCH.
KUBARK, I--
OH-HO-HO, HE'S SO RIGHT! YOU ARE A FUCKING BITCH AND I'M FUCKING ON TO YOU. I JUST FIGURED OUT HOW YOU--
SHUT IT.
KAPOW

4: THE BEAT THAT MY HEART SKIPPED (3:48)

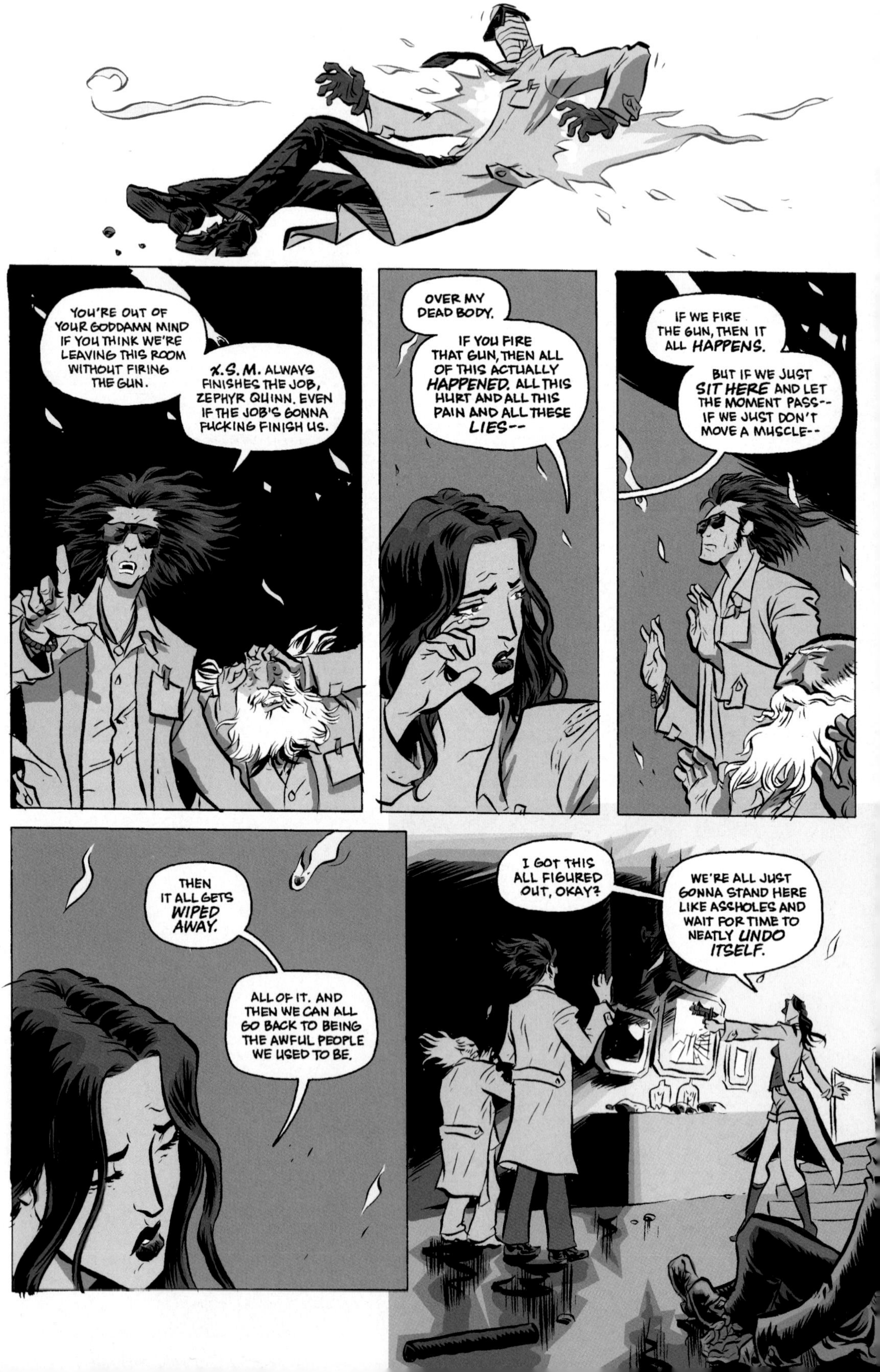

YOU'RE OUT OF YOUR GODDAMN MIND IF YOU THINK WE'RE LEAVING THIS ROOM WITHOUT FIRING THE GUN.
X.S.M. ALWAYS FINISHES THE JOB, ZEPHYR QUINN. EVEN IF THE JOB'S GONNA FUCKING FINISH US.
OVER MY DEAD BODY.
IF YOU FIRE THAT GUN, THEN ALL OF THIS ACTUALLY HAPPENED. ALL THIS HURT AND ALL THIS PAIN AND ALL THESE LIES--
IF WE FIRE THE GUN, THEN IT ALL HAPPENS.
BUT IF WE JUST SIT HERE AND LET THE MOMENT PASS-- IF WE JUST DON'T MOVE A MUSCLE--
THEN IT ALL GETS WIPED AWAY.
ALL OF IT. AND THEN WE CAN ALL GO BACK TO BEING THE AWFUL PEOPLE WE USED TO BE.
I GOT THIS ALL FIGURED OUT, OKAY?
WE'RE ALL JUST GONNA STAND HERE LIKE ASSHOLES AND WAIT FOR TIME TO NEATLY UNDO ITSELF.

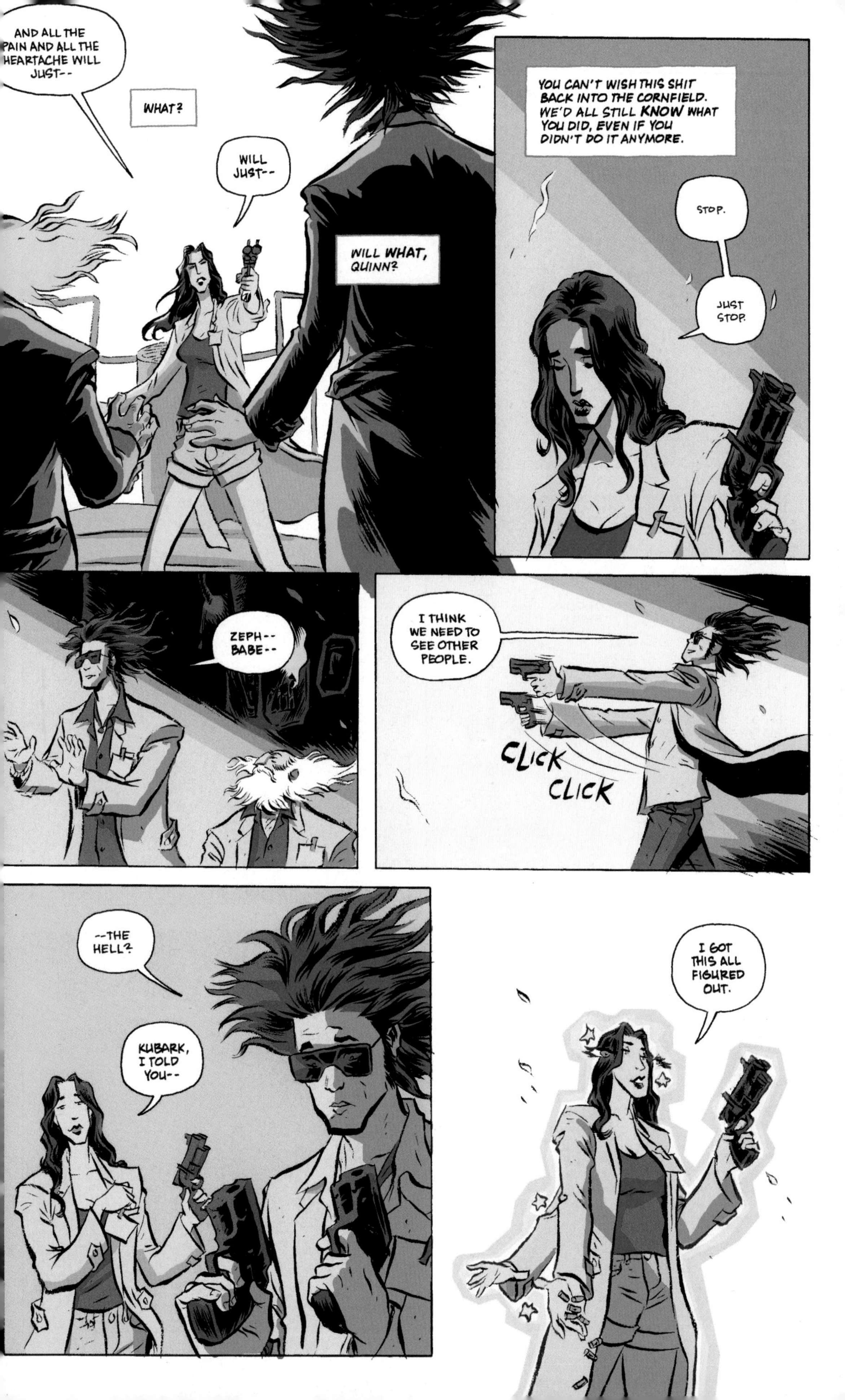
AND ALL THE PAIN AND ALL THE HEARTACHE WILL JUST--
WHAT?
WILL JUST--
WILL WHAT, QUINN?
YOU CAN'T WISH THIS SHIT BACK INTO THE CORNFIELD. WE'D ALL STILL KNOW WHAT YOU DID, EVEN IF YOU DIDN'T DO IT ANYMORE.
STOP.
JUST STOP.
ZEPH-- BABE--
I THINK WE NEED TO SEE OTHER PEOPLE.
CLICK
CLICK
--THE HELL?
KUBARK, I TOLD YOU--
I GOT THIS ALL FIGURED OUT.

5: ASHES TO ASHES (4:28)

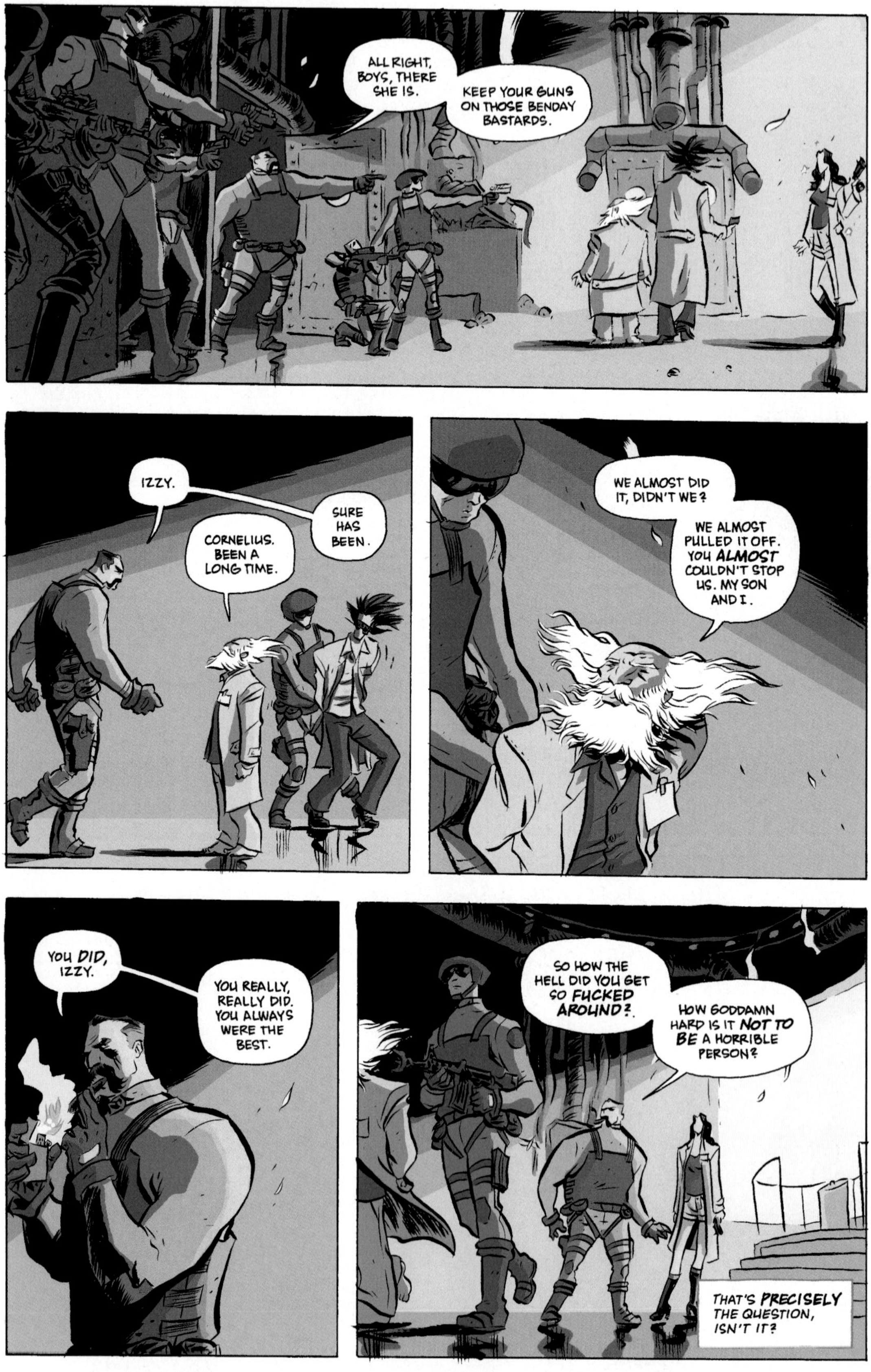
ALL RIGHT, BOYS, THERE SHE IS.
KEEP YOUR GUNS ON THOSE BENDAY BASTARDS.
IZZY.
SURE HAS BEEN.
CORNELIUS. BEEN A LONG TIME.
WE ALMOST DID IT, DIDN'T WE?
WE ALMOST PULLED IT OFF. YOU ALMOST COULDN'T STOP US. MY SON AND I.
YOU DID, IZZY.
YOU REALLY, REALLY DID. YOU ALWAYS WERE THE BEST.
SO HOW THE HELL DID YOU GET SO FUCKED AROUND?
HOW GODDAMN HARD IS IT NOT TO BE A HORRIBLE PERSON?
THAT'S PRECISELY THE QUESTION, ISN'T IT?

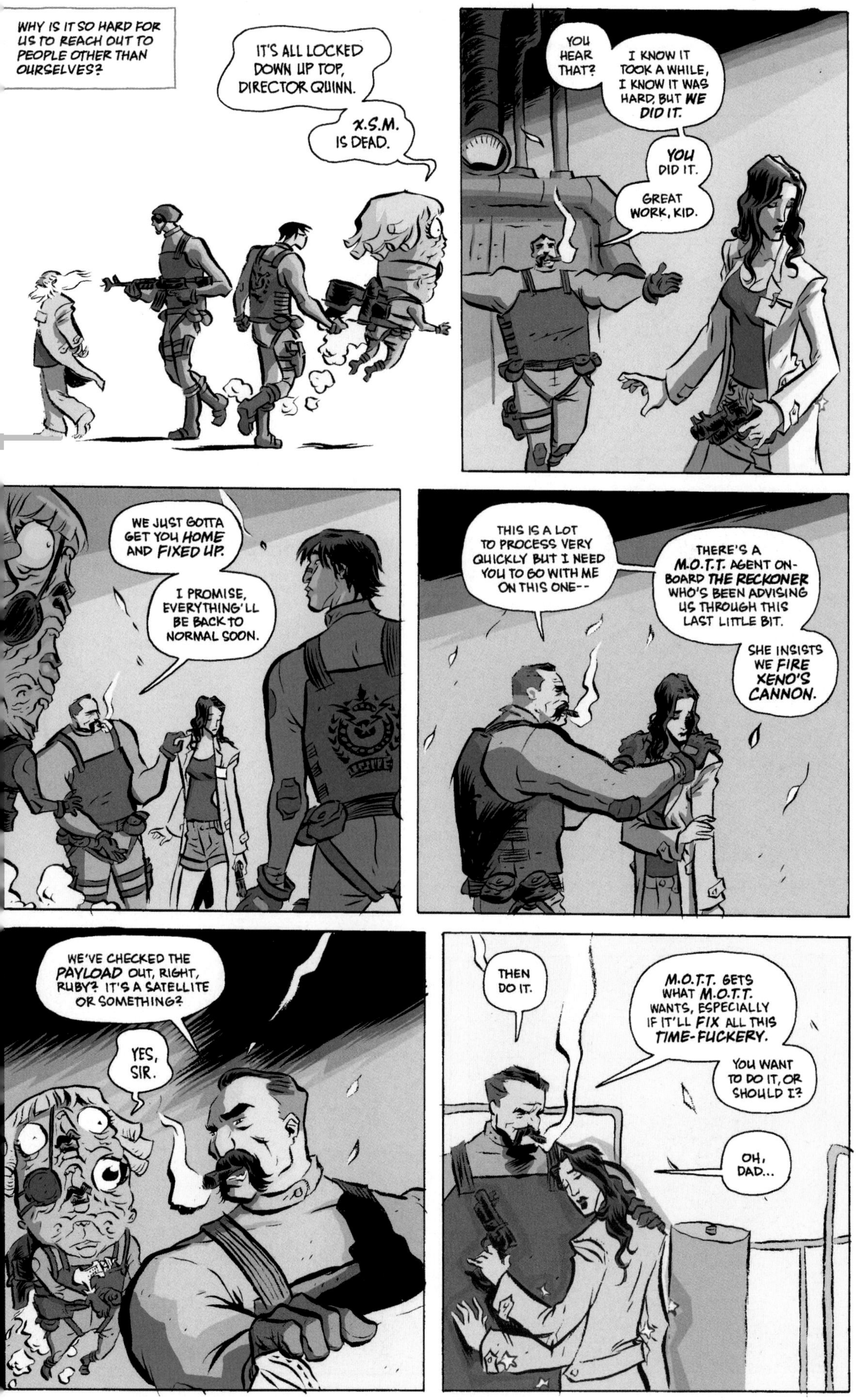
WHY IS IT SO HARD FOR US TO REACH OUT TO PEOPLE OTHER THAN OURSELVES?
IT'S ALL LOCKED DOWN UP TOP, DIRECTOR QUINN.
X.S.M. IS DEAD.
YOU HEAR THAT?
I KNOW IT TOOK A WHILE, I KNOW IT WAS HARD, BUT WE DID IT.
YOU DID IT.
GREAT WORK, KID.
WE JUST GOTTA GET YOU HOME AND FIXED UP.
I PROMISE, EVERYTHING'LL BE BACK TO NORMAL SOON.
THIS IS A LOT TO PROCESS VERY QUICKLY BUT I NEED YOU TO GO WITH ME ON THIS ONE--
THERE'S A M.O.T.T. AGENT ON-BOARD THE RECKONER WHO'S BEEN ADVISING US THROUGH THIS LAST LITTLE BIT.
SHE INSISTS WE FIRE XENO'S CANNON.
WE'VE CHECKED THE PAYLOAD OUT, RIGHT, RUBY? IT'S A SATELLITE OR SOMETHING?
YES, SIR.
THEN DO IT.
M.O.T.T. GETS WHAT M.O.T.T. WANTS, ESPECIALLY IF IT'LL FIX ALL THIS TIME-FUCKERY.
YOU WANT TO DO IT, OR SHOULD I?
OH, DAD...

6: 7 STARS (3:47)

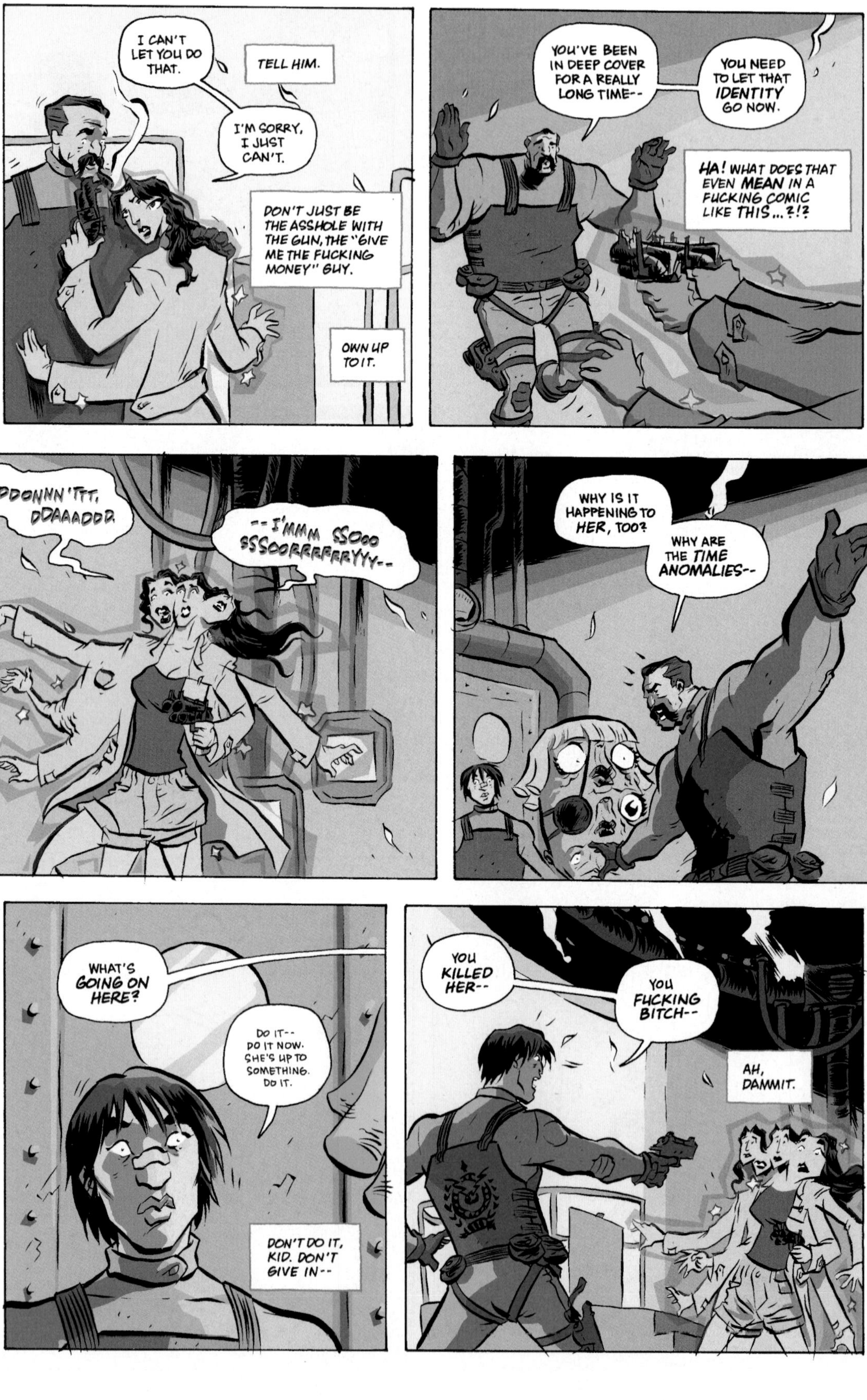

I CAN'T LET YOU DO THAT.
TELL HIM.
I'M SORRY, I JUST CAN'T.
DON'T JUST BE THE ASSHOLE WITH THE GUN, THE "GIVE ME THE FUCKING MONEY" GUY.
OWN UP TO IT.
YOU'VE BEEN IN DEEP COVER FOR A REALLY LONG TIME--
YOU NEED TO LET THAT IDENTITY GO NOW.
HA! WHAT DOES THAT EVEN MEAN IN A FUCKING COMIC LIKE THIS...?!?
DDONNN'TTT, DDAAADDD.
--I'MMM SSOoo SSSOORRRRRRRYYY--
WHY IS IT HAPPENING TO HER, TOO?
WHY ARE THE TIME ANOMALIES--
WHAT'S GOING ON HERE?
DO IT-- DO IT NOW. SHE'S UP TO SOMETHING. DO IT.
DON'T DO IT, KID. DON'T GIVE IN--
YOU KILLED HER--
YOU FUCKING BITCH--
AH, DAMMIT.

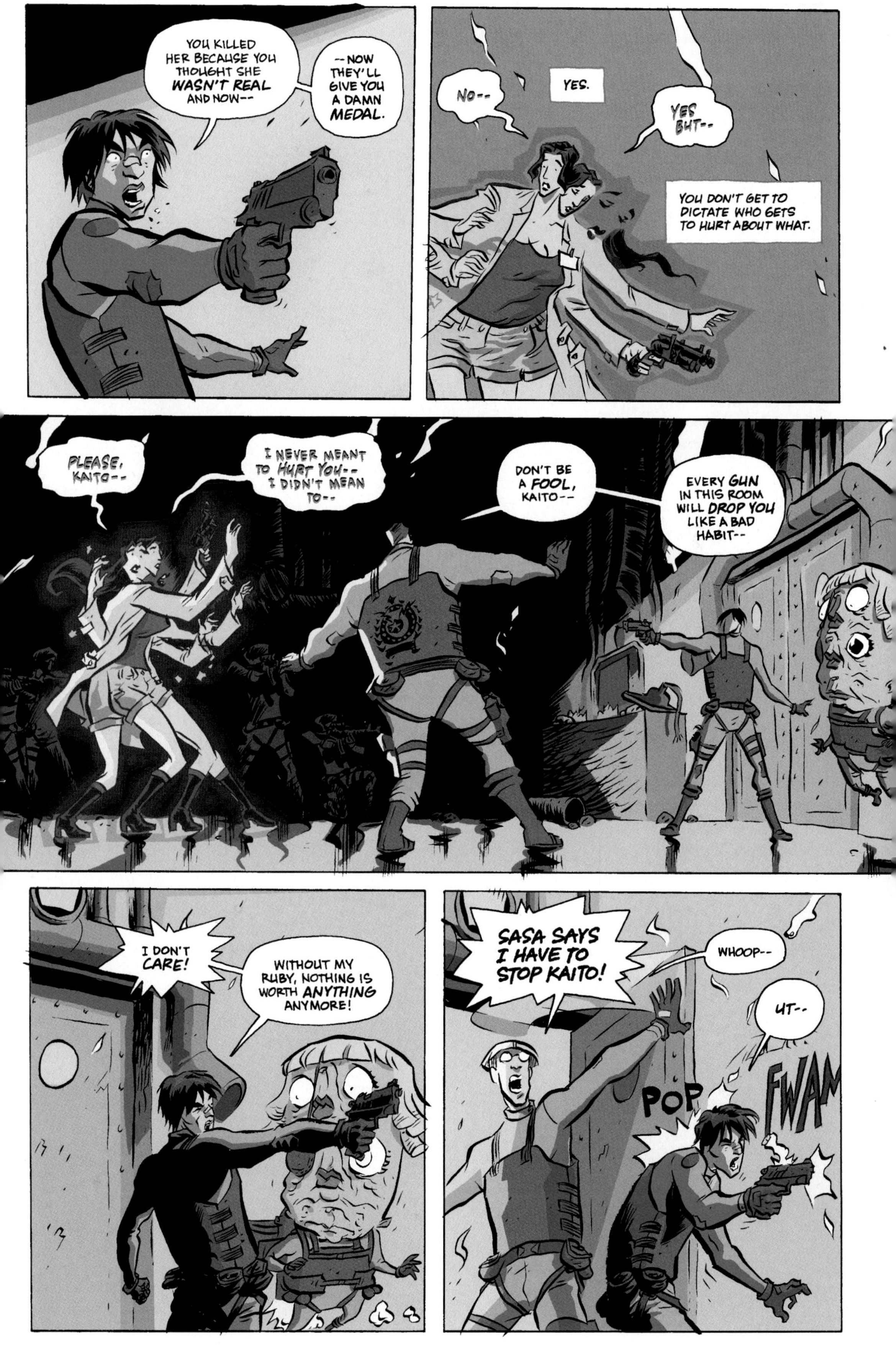

YOU KILLED HER BECAUSE YOU THOUGHT SHE WASN'T REAL AND NOW--
--NOW THEY'LL GIVE YOU A DAMN MEDAL.
NO--
YES.
YES BUT--
YOU DON'T GET TO DICTATE WHO GETS TO HURT ABOUT WHAT.
PLEASE, KAITO--
I NEVER MEANT TO HURT YOU-- I DIDN'T MEAN TO--
DON'T BE A FOOL, KAITO--
EVERY GUN IN THIS ROOM WILL DROP YOU LIKE A BAD HABIT--
I DON'T CARE!
WITHOUT MY RUBY, NOTHING IS WORTH ANYTHING ANYMORE!
SASA SAYS I HAVE TO STOP KAITO!
WHOOP--
UT--
POP
FWAM

7: WOKE UP NEW (2:57)

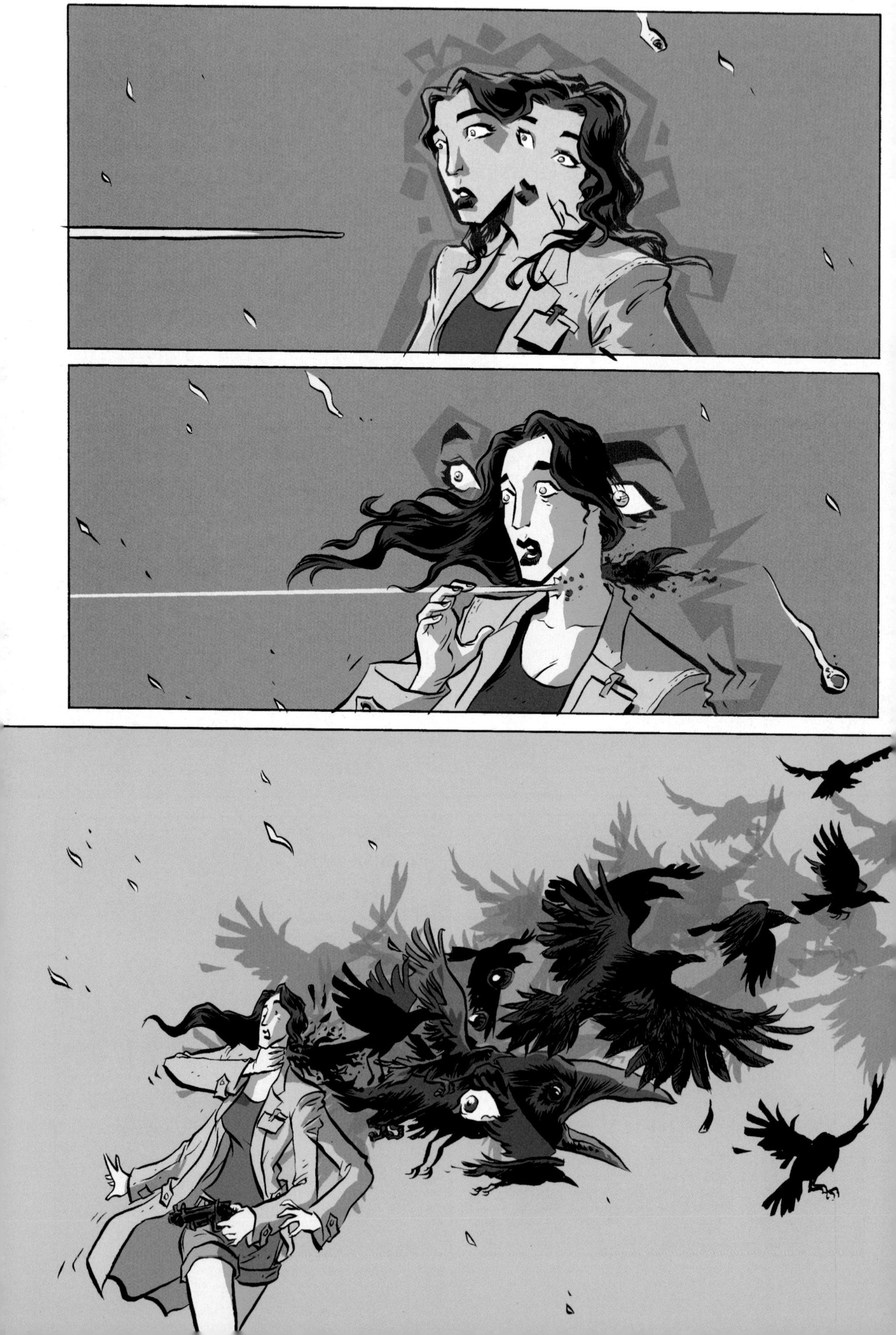

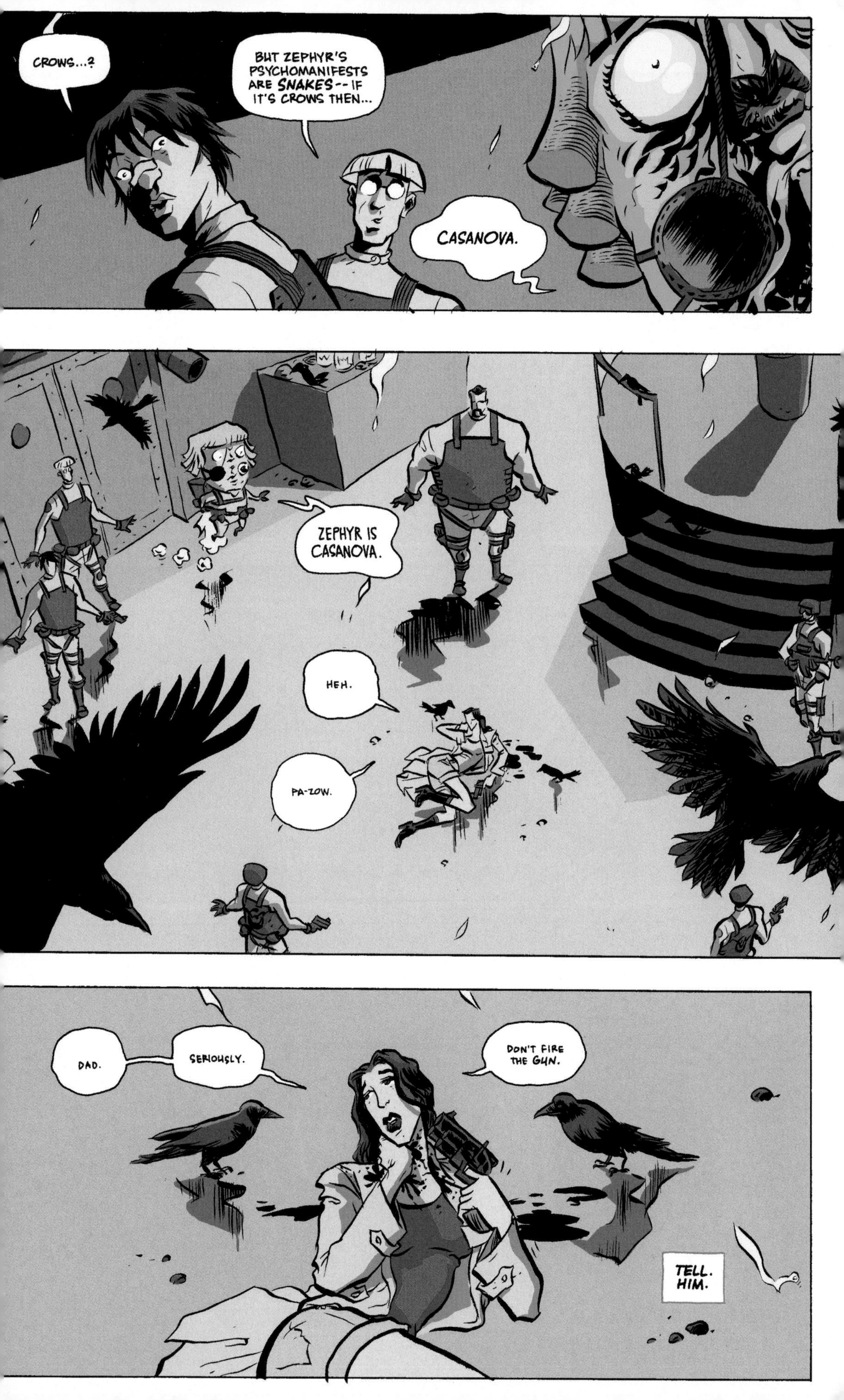
CROWS...?
BUT ZEPHYR'S PSYCHOMANIFESTS ARE SNAKES-- IF IT'S CROWS THEN...
CASANOVA.
ZEPHYR IS CASANOVA.
HEH.
PA-ZOW.
DAD.
SERIOUSLY.
DON'T FIRE THE GUN.
TELL. HIM.

8: EVIL WILL PREVAIL (3:46)

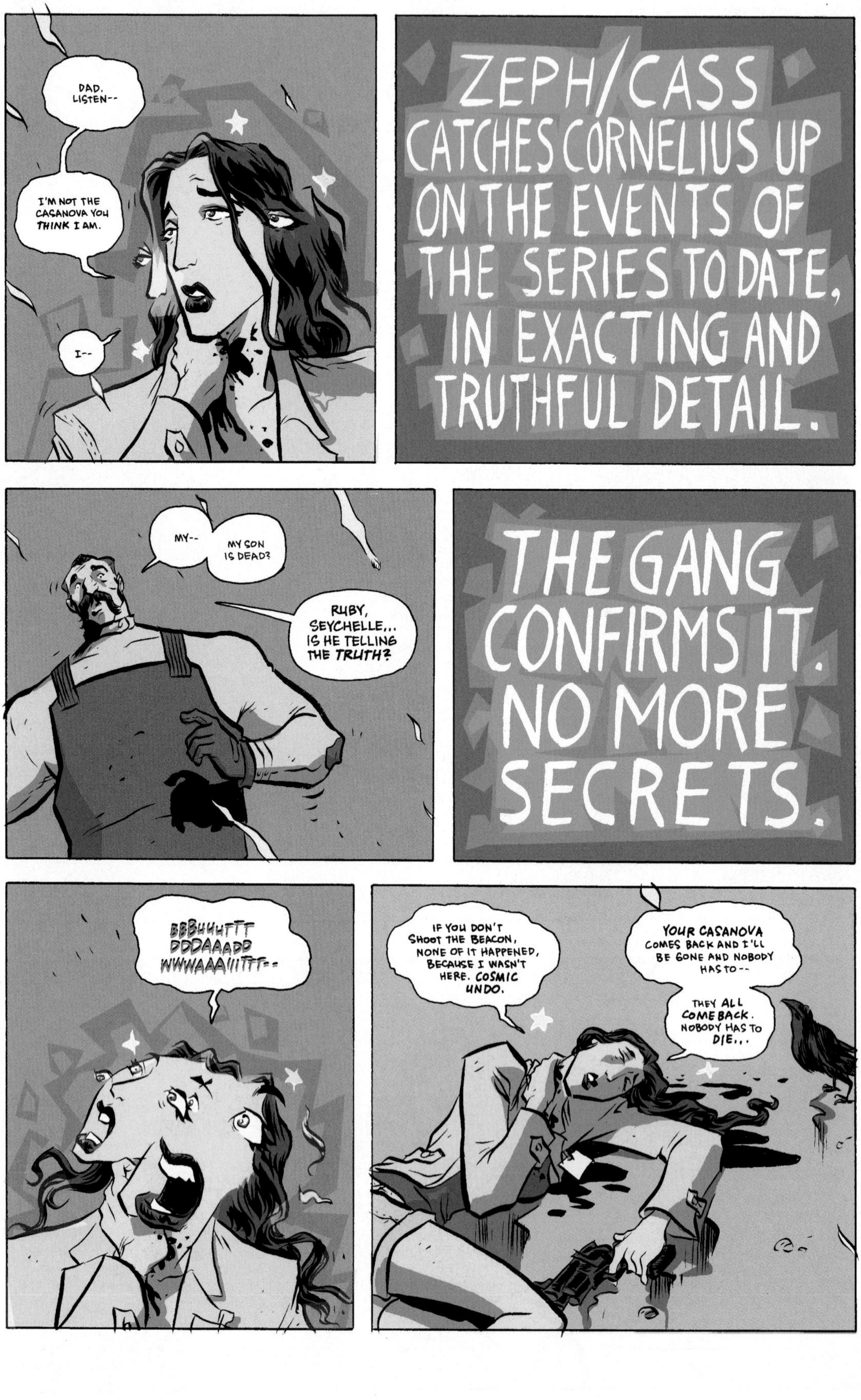
DAD. LISTEN--
I'M NOT THE CASANOVA YOU THINK I AM.
I--
ZEPH/CASS CATCHES CORNELIUS UP ON THE EVENTS OF THE SERIES TO DATE, IN EXACTING AND TRUTHFUL DETAIL.
MY--
MY SON IS DEAD?
RUBY, SEYCHELLE... IS HE TELLING THE TRUTH?
THE GANG CONFIRMS IT. NO MORE SECRETS.
BBBUUUTTT DDDAAADD WWWAAAIIITTT--
IF YOU DON'T SHOOT THE BEACON, NONE OF IT HAPPENED, BECAUSE I WASN'T HERE. COSMIC UNDO.
YOUR CASANOVA COMES BACK AND I'LL BE GONE AND NOBODY HAS TO--
THEY ALL COME BACK. NOBODY HAS TO DIE...

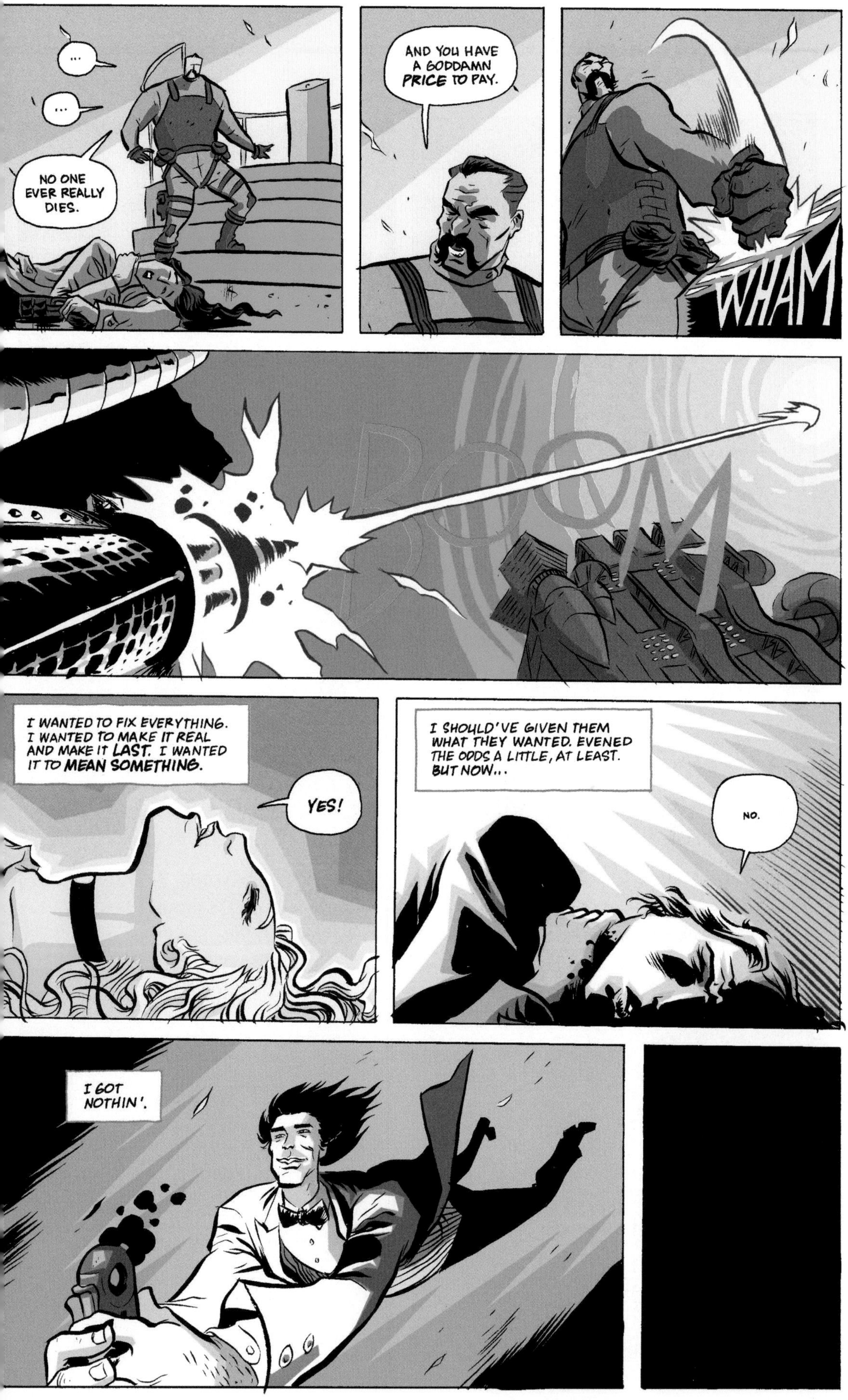
...
...
NO ONE EVER REALLY DIES.
AND YOU HAVE A GODDAMN PRICE TO PAY.
WHAM
BOOM
I WANTED TO FIX EVERYTHING. I WANTED TO MAKE IT REAL AND MAKE IT LAST. I WANTED IT TO MEAN SOMETHING.
YES!
I SHOULD'VE GIVEN THEM WHAT THEY WANTED. EVENED THE ODDS A LITTLE, AT LEAST. BUT NOW...
NO.
I GOT NOTHIN'.

9: SIX DAYS (5:02)

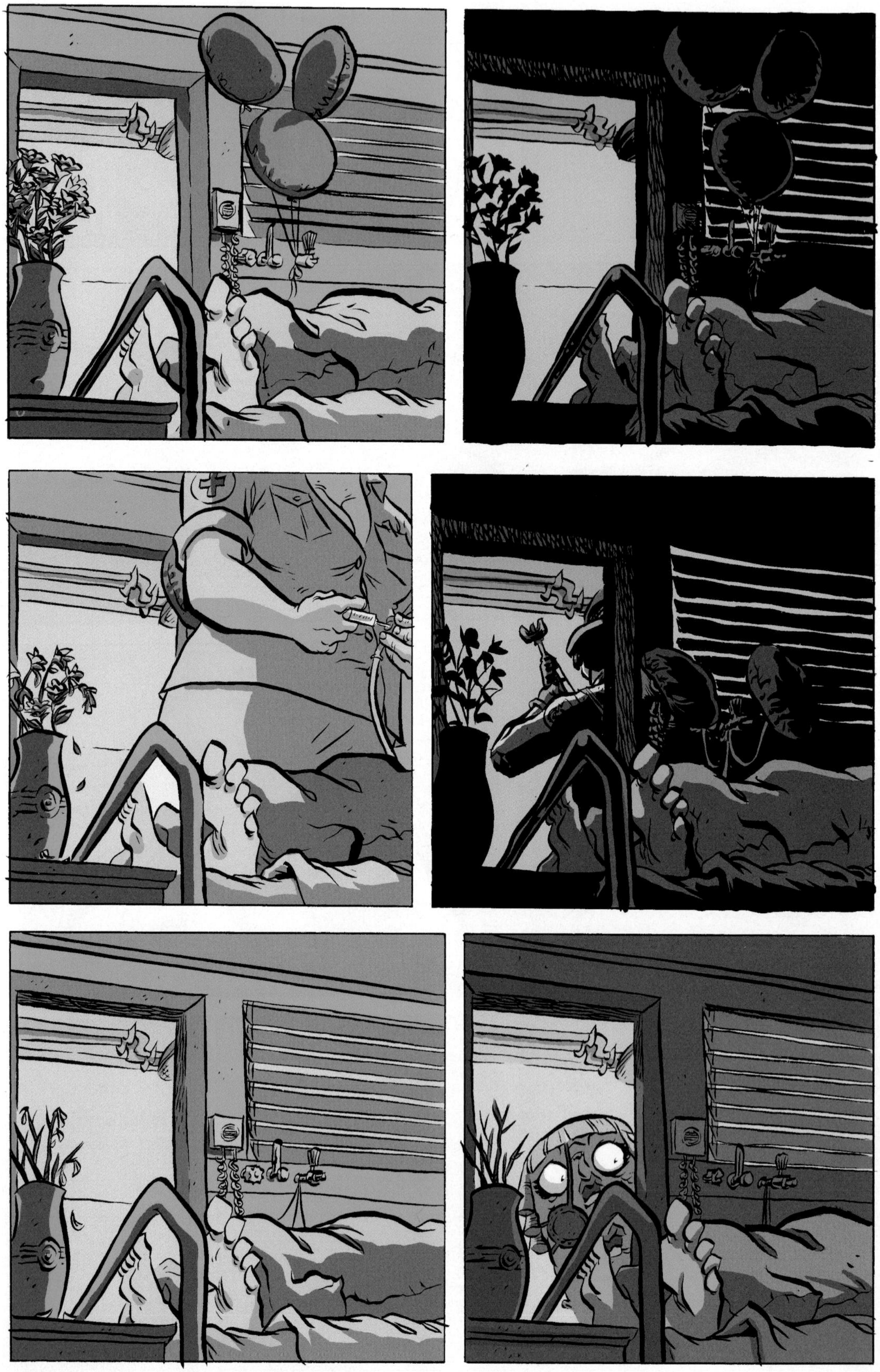

WELL, FOR A GUY THAT WAS A GIRL AND NOW IS A GUY AGAIN, I GOTTA SAY, YOU *ABSOLUTELY* LOOK LIKE A GUY AGAIN.

THEY GET YOUR *JUNK* WORKING, TOO?

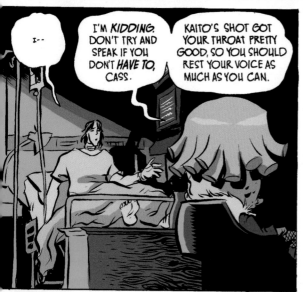

I--

I'M *KIDDING*. DON'T TRY AND SPEAK IF YOU DON'T *HAVE TO*, CASS.

KAITO'S SHOT GOT YOUR THROAT PRETTY GOOD, SO YOU SHOULD REST YOUR VOICE AS MUCH AS YOU CAN.

RUBY, I'M SO--

YEAH.

YOU'RE NOT SUCH A BAD SHOT YOURSELF, ARE YOU?

SEYCHELLE OFFERED TO MAKE ME A *REPLACEMENT EYE* BUT I--

BUT I WANT TO REMEMBER.

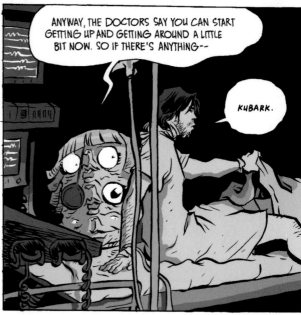

ANYWAY, THE DOCTORS SAY YOU CAN START GETTING UP AND GETTING AROUND A LITTLE BIT NOW. SO IF THERE'S ANYTHING--

KUBARK.

10: RIVER DEEP, MOUNTAIN HIGH (3:39)

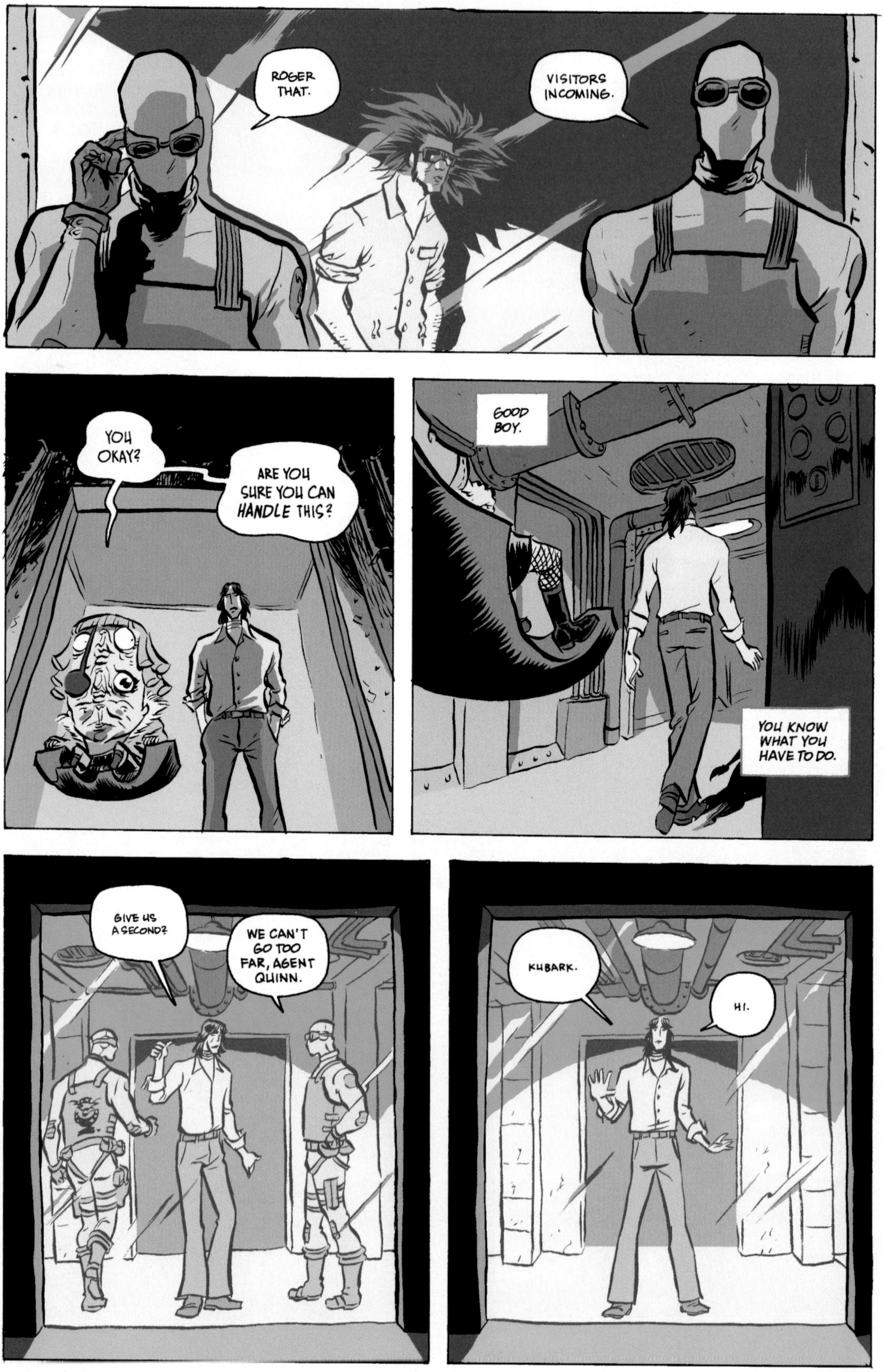
ROGER THAT.
VISITORS INCOMING.
YOU OKAY?
ARE YOU SURE YOU CAN HANDLE THIS?
GOOD BOY.
YOU KNOW WHAT YOU HAVE TO DO.
GIVE US A SECOND?
WE CAN'T GO TOO FAR, AGENT QUINN.
KUBARK.
HI.

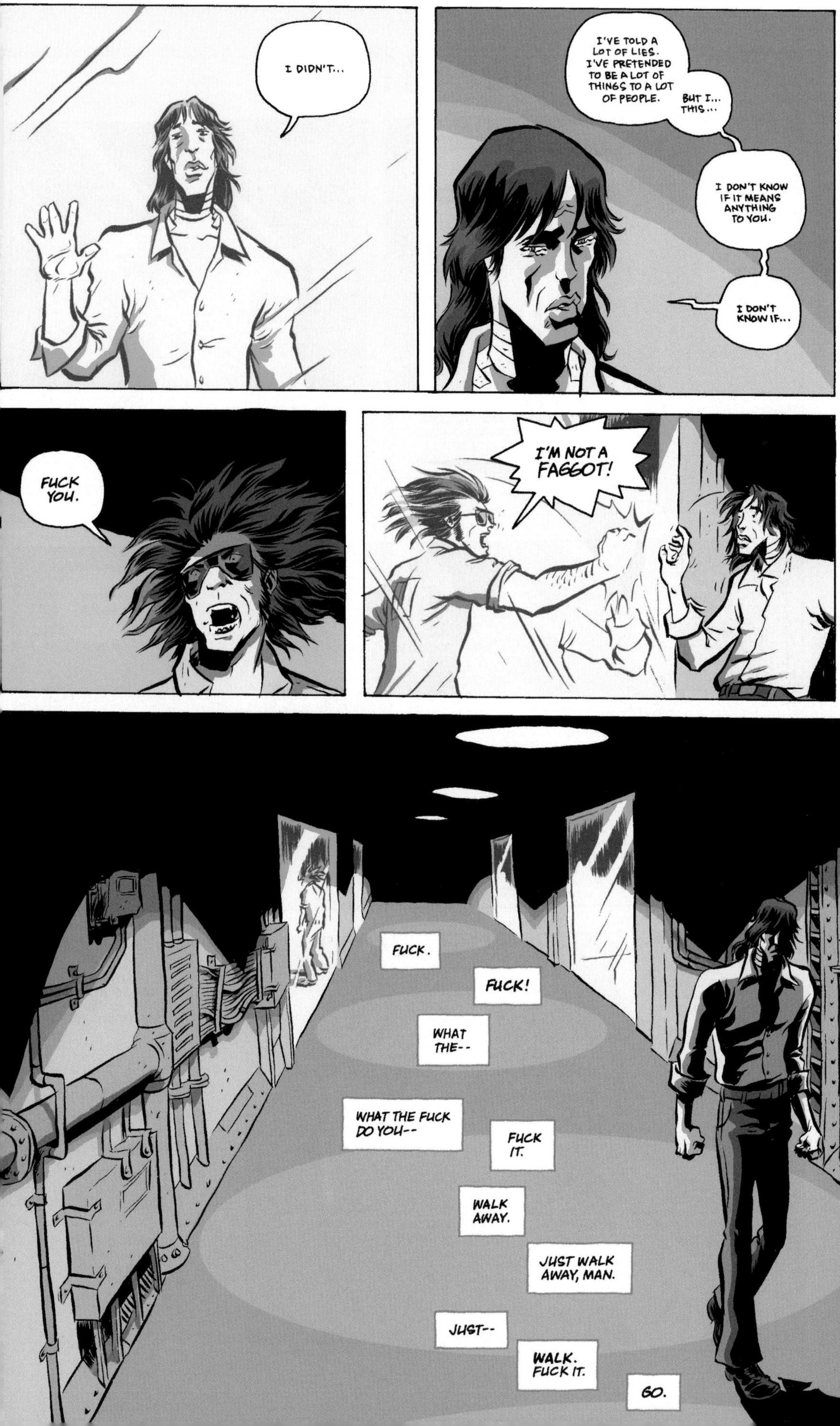
I DIDN'T...
I'VE TOLD A LOT OF LIES. I'VE PRETENDED TO BE A LOT OF THINGS TO A LOT OF PEOPLE.
BUT I... THIS...
I DON'T KNOW IF IT MEANS ANYTHING TO YOU.
I DON'T KNOW IF...
FUCK YOU.
I'M NOT A FAGGOT!
FUCK.
FUCK!
WHAT THE--
WHAT THE FUCK DO YOU--
FUCK IT.
WALK AWAY.
JUST WALK AWAY, MAN.
JUST--
WALK. FUCK IT.
GO.

11: TO CATCH A THIEF (3:17)

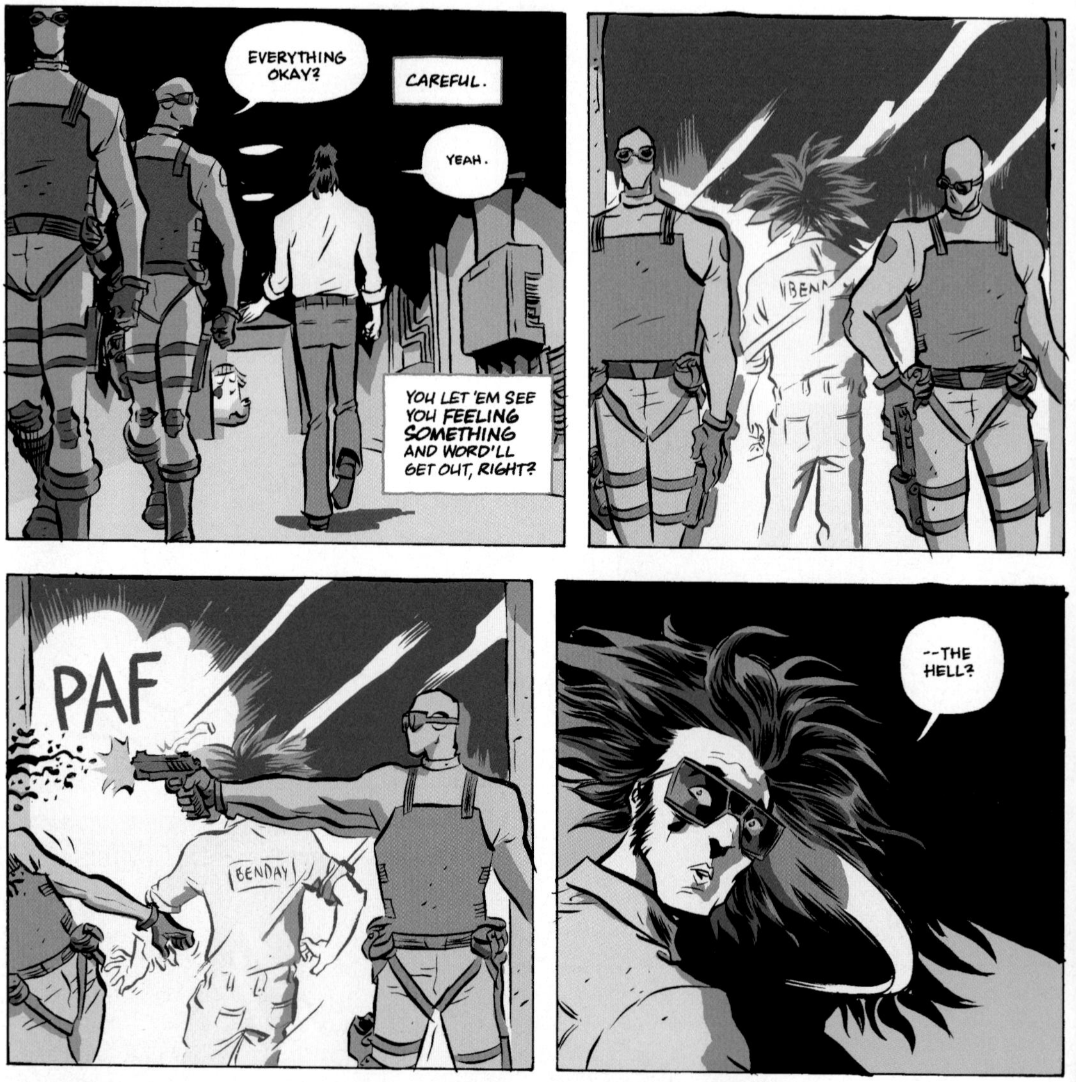

EVERYTHING OKAY?
CAREFUL.
YEAH.
YOU LET 'EM SEE YOU FEELING SOMETHING AND WORD'LL GET OUT, RIGHT?
BENDAY
PAF
BENDAY
--THE HELL?

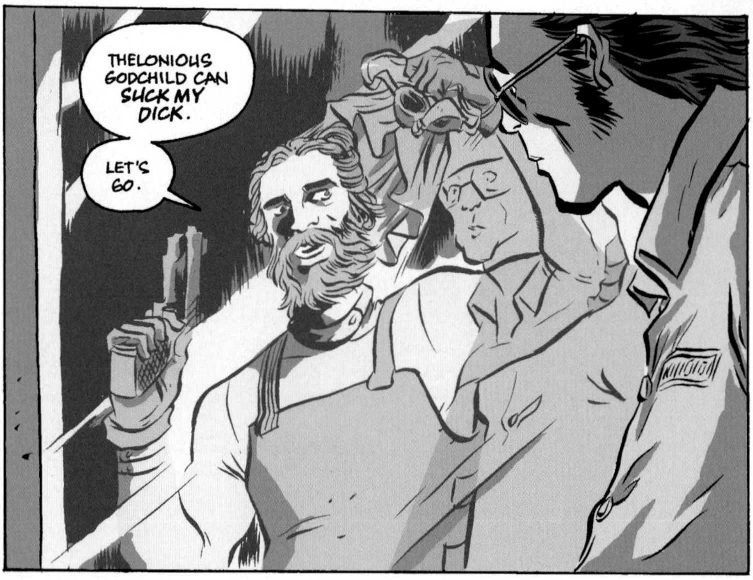

THELONIOUS GODCHILD CAN SUCK MY DICK.
LET'S GO.

HI, EVERYBODY. DAVID X, ESCAPE MESSIAH EXTRAORDINAIRE.

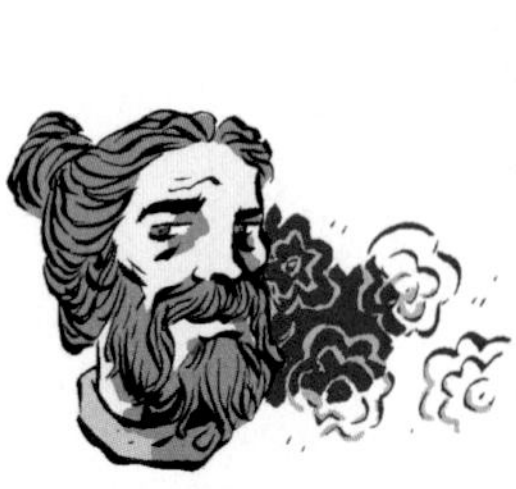

YOU LAST SAW ME GETTING MURDERED IN GULA #1. AND BEFORE THAT, I WAS IN... LUXURIA #3 MAYBE? I THINK IT WAS #3.

ANYWAY. HI.

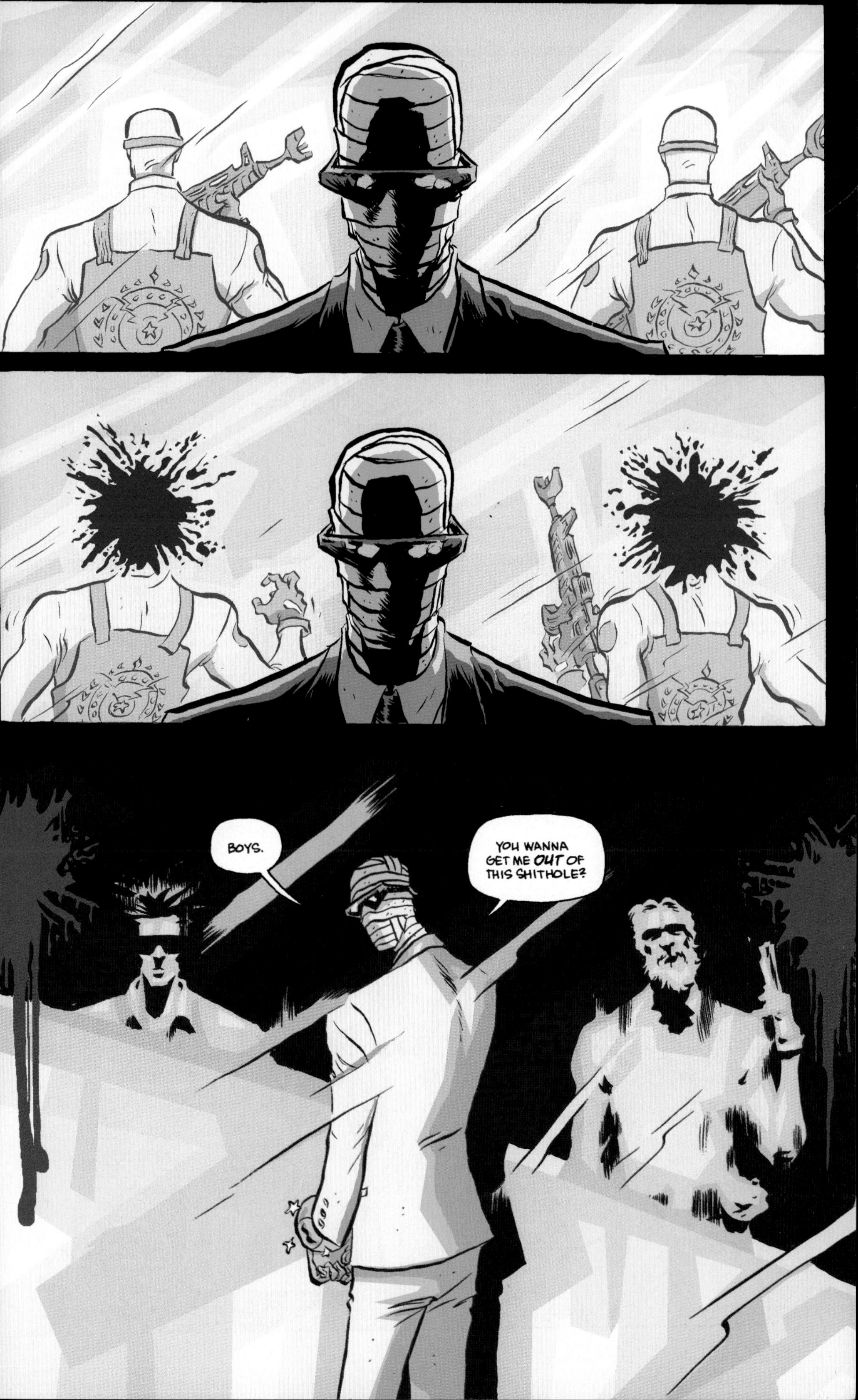
BOYS.
YOU WANNA GET ME OUT OF THIS SHITHOLE?

12: SHE WILL ONLY BRING YOU HAPPINESS (3:28)

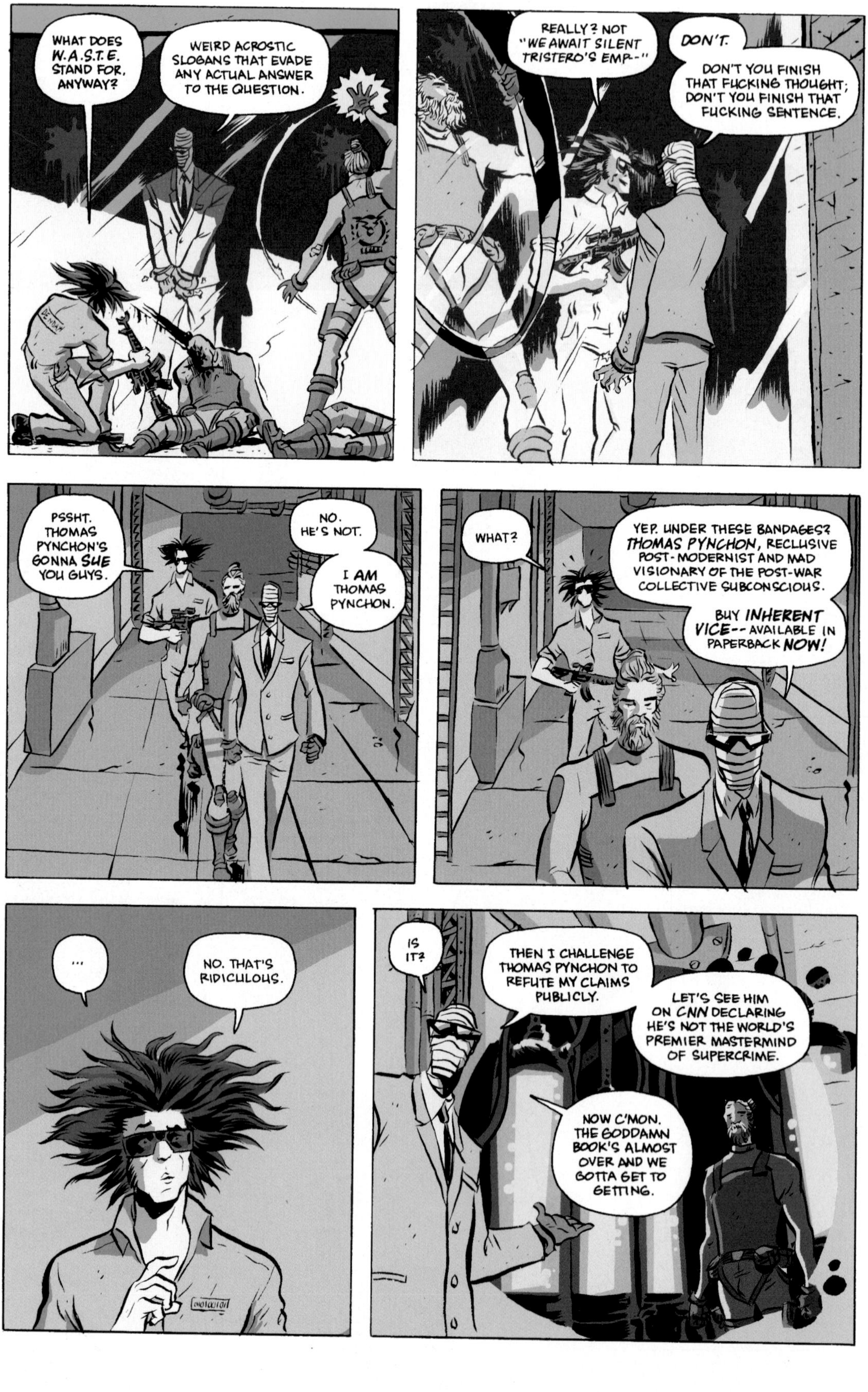

WHAT DOES W.A.S.T.E. STAND FOR, ANYWAY?
WEIRD ACROSTIC SLOGANS THAT EVADE ANY ACTUAL ANSWER TO THE QUESTION.
REALLY? NOT "WE AWAIT SILENT TRISTERO'S EMP--"
DON'T.
DON'T YOU FINISH THAT FUCKING THOUGHT; DON'T YOU FINISH THAT FUCKING SENTENCE.
PSSHT. THOMAS PYNCHON'S GONNA SUE YOU GUYS.
NO. HE'S NOT.
I AM THOMAS PYNCHON.
WHAT?
YEP. UNDER THESE BANDAGES? THOMAS PYNCHON, RECLUSIVE POST-MODERNIST AND MAD VISIONARY OF THE POST-WAR COLLECTIVE SUBCONSCIOUS.
BUY INHERENT VICE-- AVAILABLE IN PAPERBACK NOW!
...
NO. THAT'S RIDICULOUS.
IS IT?
THEN I CHALLENGE THOMAS PYNCHON TO REFUTE MY CLAIMS PUBLICLY.
LET'S SEE HIM ON CNN DECLARING HE'S NOT THE WORLD'S PREMIER MASTERMIND OF SUPERCRIME.
NOW C'MON. THE GODDAMN BOOK'S ALMOST OVER AND WE GOTTA GET TO GETTING.

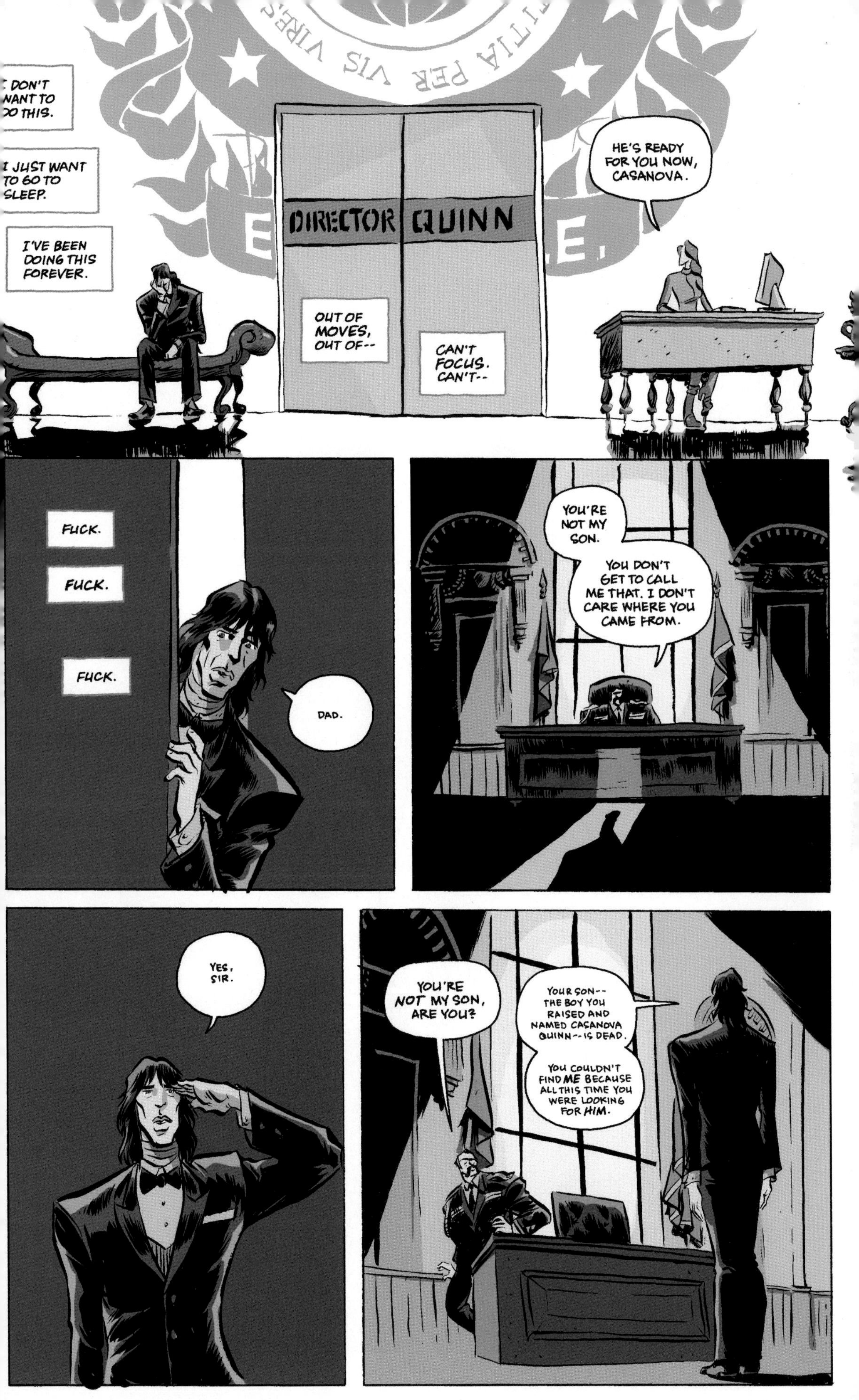

TITIA PER VIS VIRES
DON'T WANT TO DO THIS.
I JUST WANT TO GO TO SLEEP.
I'VE BEEN DOING THIS FOREVER.
DIRECTOR QUINN
OUT OF MOVES, OUT OF--
CAN'T FOCUS. CAN'T--
HE'S READY FOR YOU NOW, CASANOVA.
FUCK.
FUCK.
FUCK.
DAD.
YOU'RE NOT MY SON.
YOU DON'T GET TO CALL ME THAT. I DON'T CARE WHERE YOU CAME FROM.
YES, SIR.
YOU'RE NOT MY SON, ARE YOU?
YOUR SON-- THE BOY YOU RAISED AND NAMED CASANOVA QUINN--IS DEAD.
YOU COULDN'T FIND ME BECAUSE ALL THIS TIME YOU WERE LOOKING FOR HIM.

13: TAYMAN (2:39)

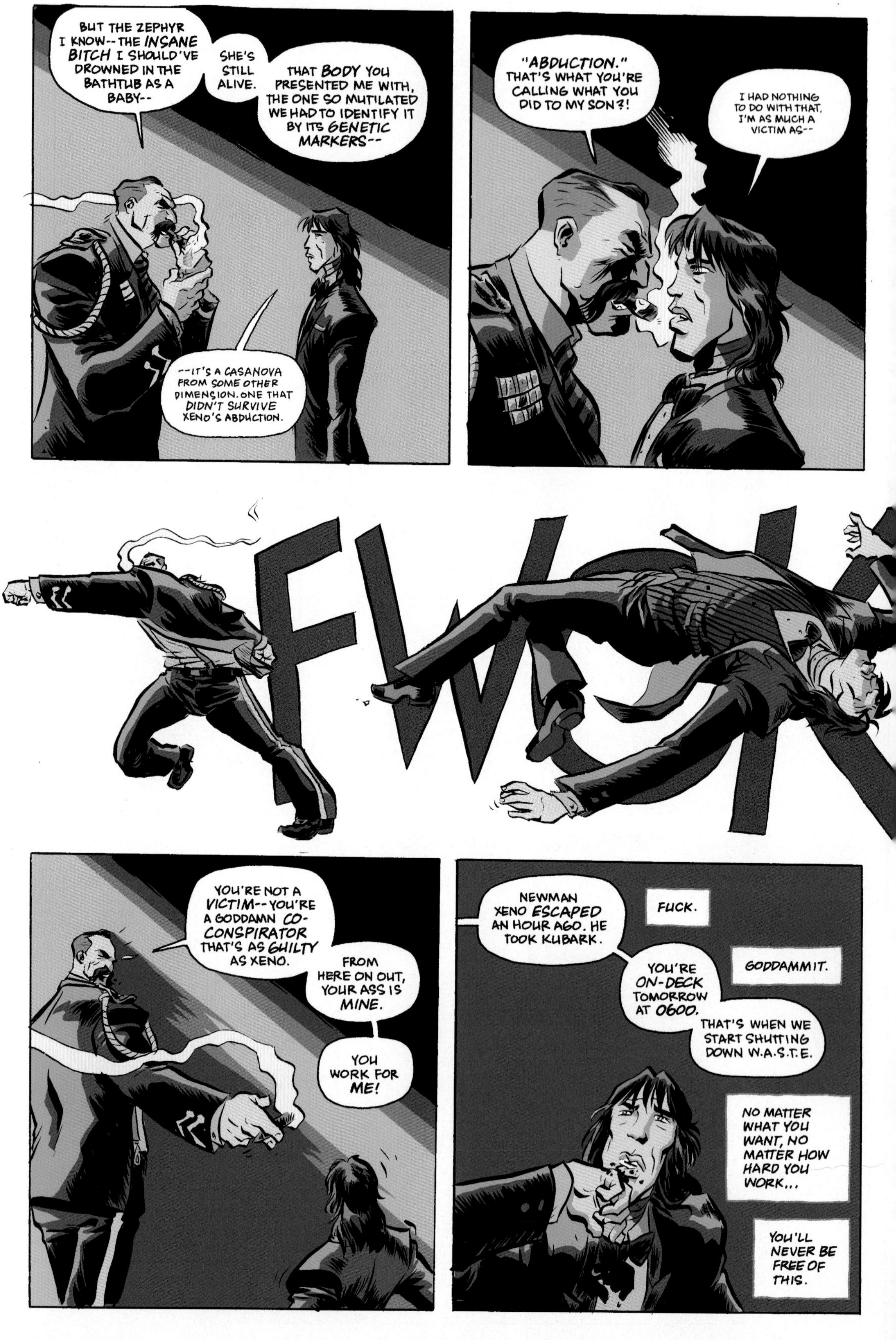
BUT THE ZEPHYR I KNOW-- THE INSANE BITCH I SHOULD'VE DROWNED IN THE BATHTUB AS A BABY--
SHE'S STILL ALIVE.
THAT BODY YOU PRESENTED ME WITH, THE ONE SO MUTILATED WE HAD TO IDENTIFY IT BY ITS GENETIC MARKERS--
--IT'S A CASANOVA FROM SOME OTHER DIMENSION. ONE THAT DIDN'T SURVIVE XENO'S ABDUCTION.
"ABDUCTION." THAT'S WHAT YOU'RE CALLING WHAT YOU DID TO MY SON?!
I HAD NOTHING TO DO WITH THAT. I'M AS MUCH A VICTIM AS--
FWOK
YOU'RE NOT A VICTIM-- YOU'RE A GODDAMN CO-CONSPIRATOR THAT'S AS GUILTY AS XENO.
FROM HERE ON OUT, YOUR ASS IS MINE.
YOU WORK FOR ME!
NEWMAN XENO ESCAPED AN HOUR AGO. HE TOOK KUBARK.
FUCK.
YOU'RE ON-DECK TOMORROW AT 0600.
GODDAMMIT.
THAT'S WHEN WE START SHUTTING DOWN W.A.S.T.E.
NO MATTER WHAT YOU WANT, NO MATTER HOW HARD YOU WORK...
YOU'LL NEVER BE FREE OF THIS.

GOD FUCKING DAMMIT.

WELL, THERE'S ALWAYS THAT ONE LAST THING, ISN'T THERE?

ONE LAST THING THAT CAN BE TAKEN AWAY.

HALLO, SPACEBOY.

SASA LISI.

THE GIRL FROM M.O.T.T.

THE GIRL FROM THE FUTURE.

THE GIRL WHO TELLS ANYONE WHO'LL LISTEN THAT WE'LL ONE DAY BE IN LOVE WITH EACH OTHER.

YES.

YES.

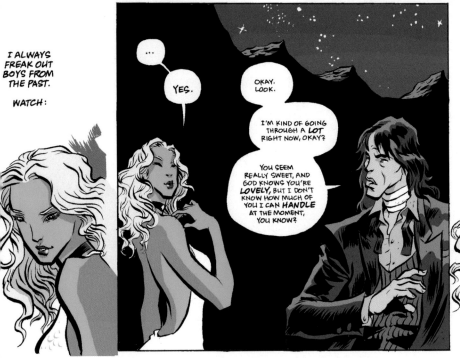

I ALWAYS FREAK OUT BOYS FROM THE PAST.

WATCH:

...

YES.

OKAY. LOOK.

I'M KIND OF GOING THROUGH A LOT RIGHT NOW, OKAY?

YOU SEEM REALLY SWEET, AND GOD KNOWS YOU'RE LOVELY, BUT I DON'T KNOW HOW MUCH OF YOU I CAN HANDLE AT THE MOMENT, YOU KNOW?

IT'S OKAY.

WE HAVE ALL THE TIME IN THE WORLD.

JUST YOU WAIT.

14: EXECUTION DAY (3:00)

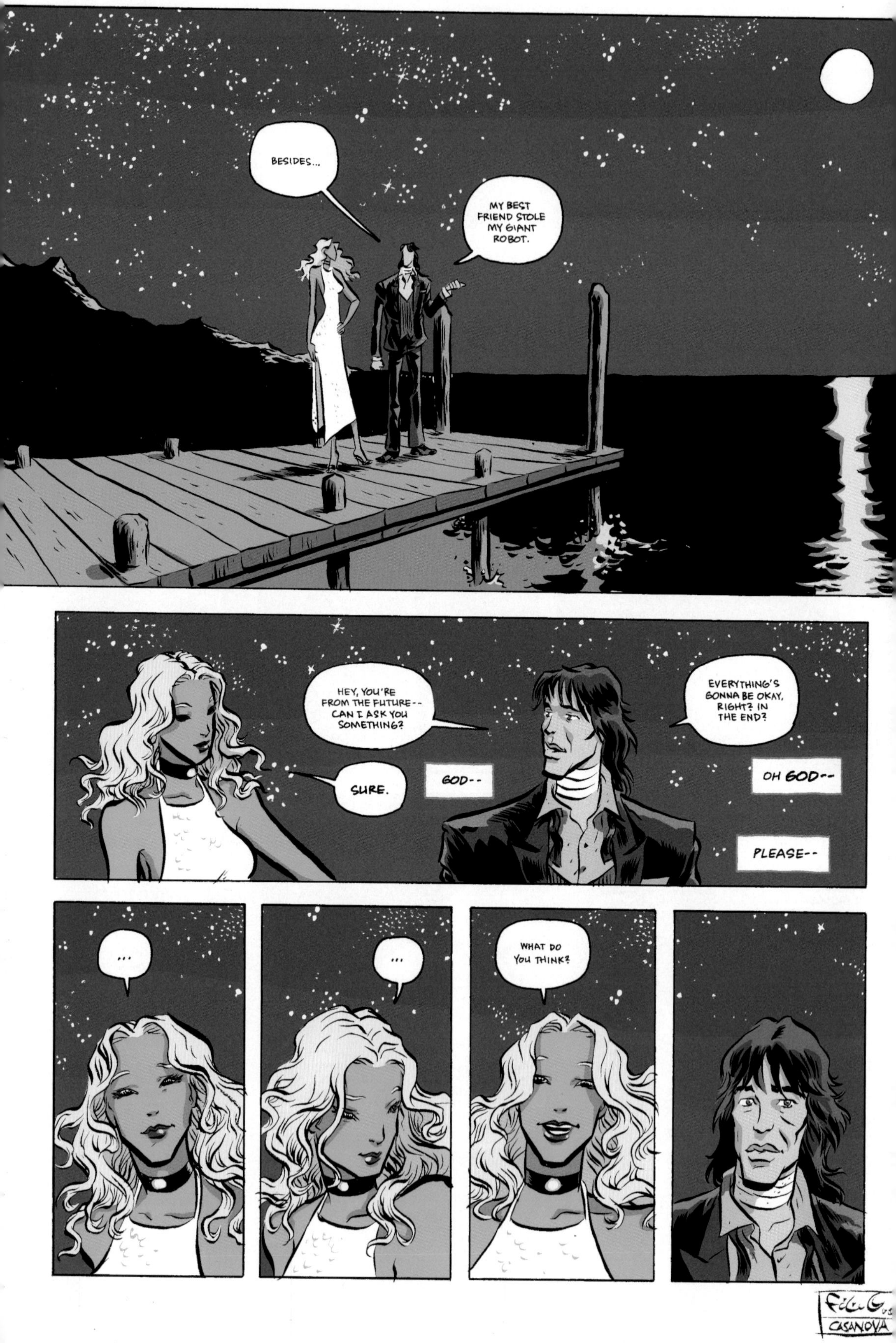
BESIDES...
MY BEST FRIEND STOLE MY GIANT ROBOT.
HEY, YOU'RE FROM THE FUTURE-- CAN I ASK YOU SOMETHING?
SURE.
GOD--
EVERYTHING'S GONNA BE OKAY, RIGHT? IN THE END?
OH GOD--
PLEASE--
...
...
WHAT DO YOU THINK?
CASANOVA

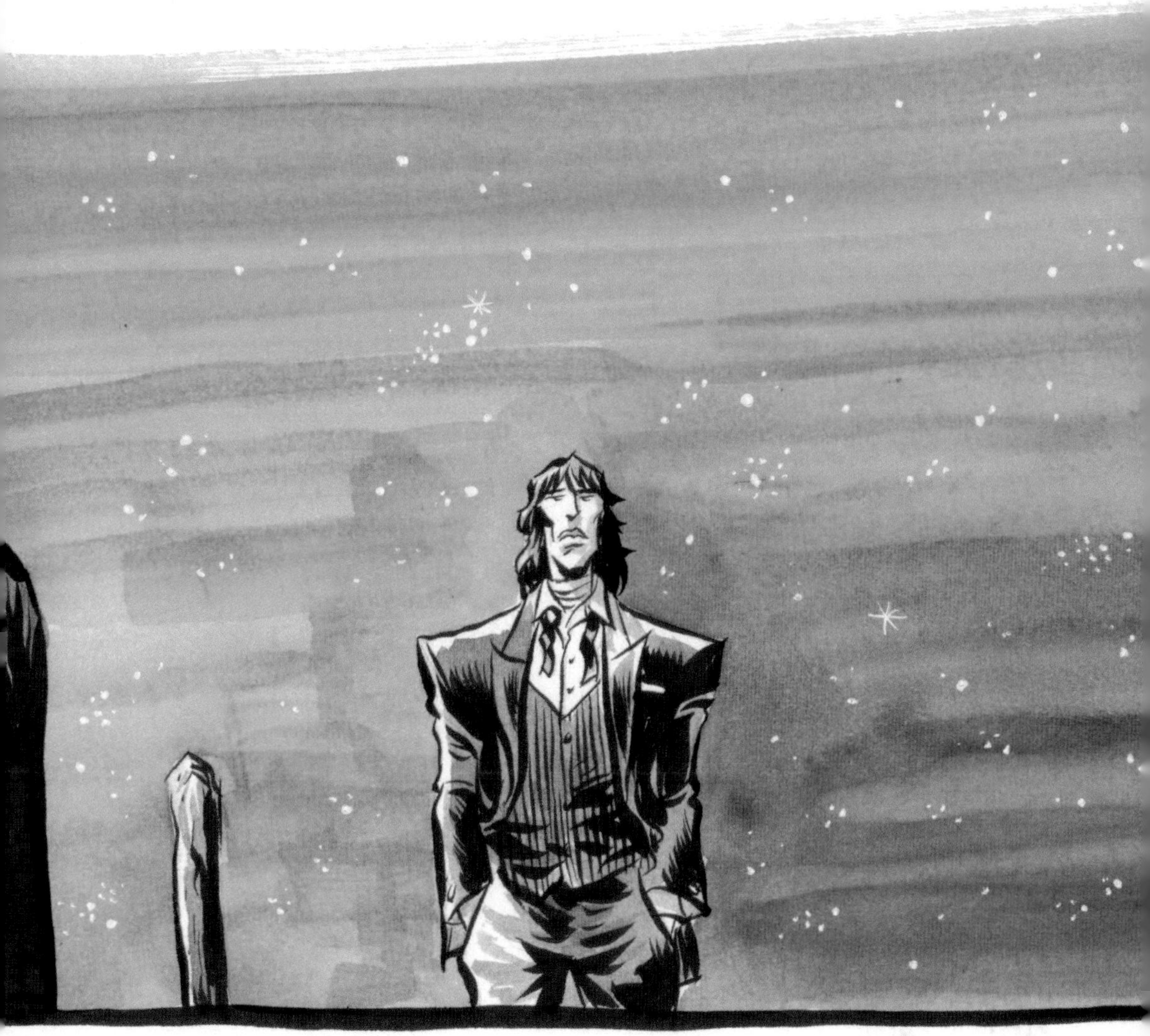

BONUS STORY
DIT DIT DIT
DAH DAH DAH
DIT DIT

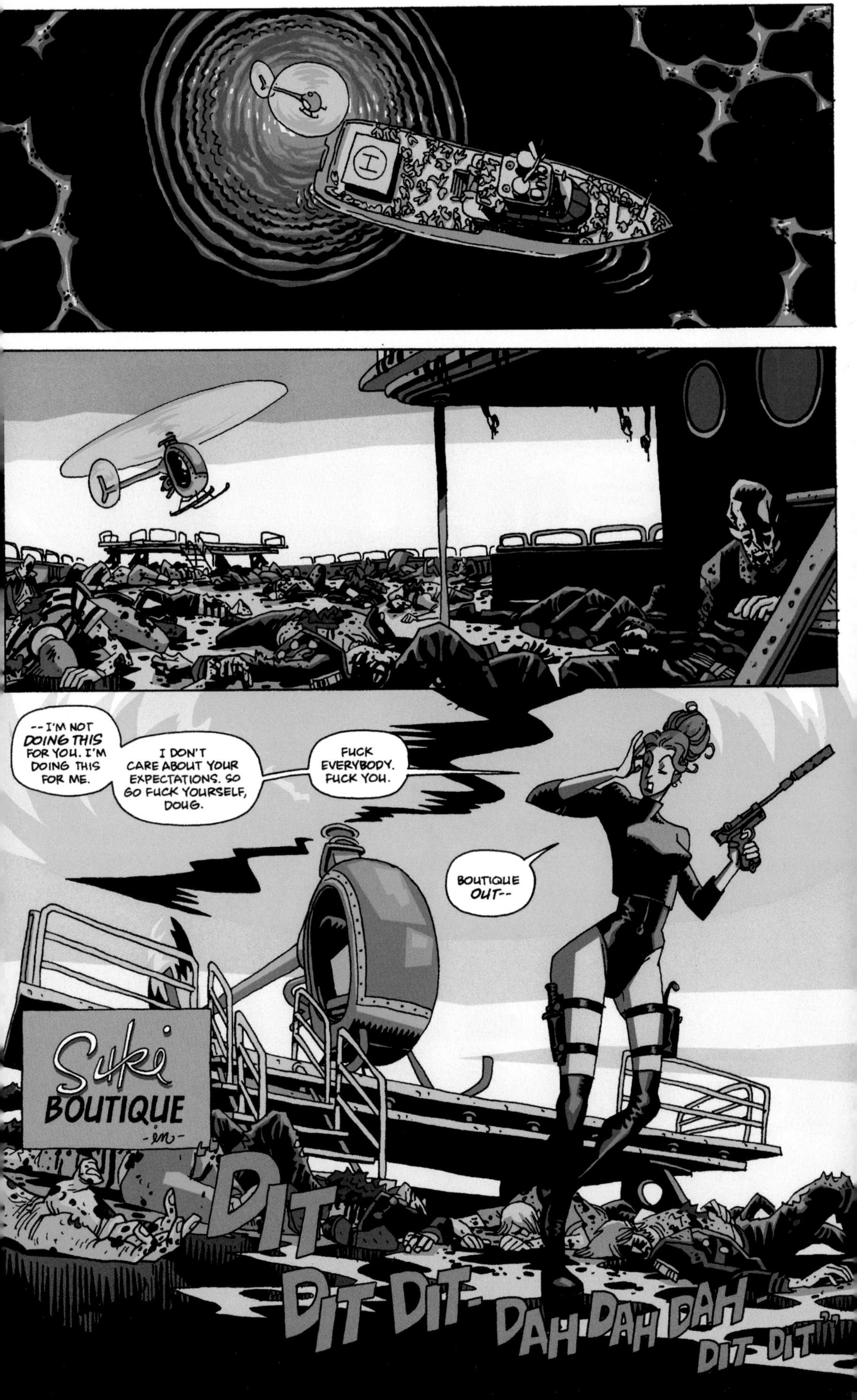
--I'M NOT DOING THIS FOR YOU. I'M DOING THIS FOR ME.
I DON'T CARE ABOUT YOUR EXPECTATIONS. SO GO FUCK YOURSELF, DOUG.
FUCK EVERYBODY. FUCK YOU.
BOUTIQUE OUT--
Suki BOUTIQUE -in-
DIT DIT DIT- DAH DAH DAH DIT DIT

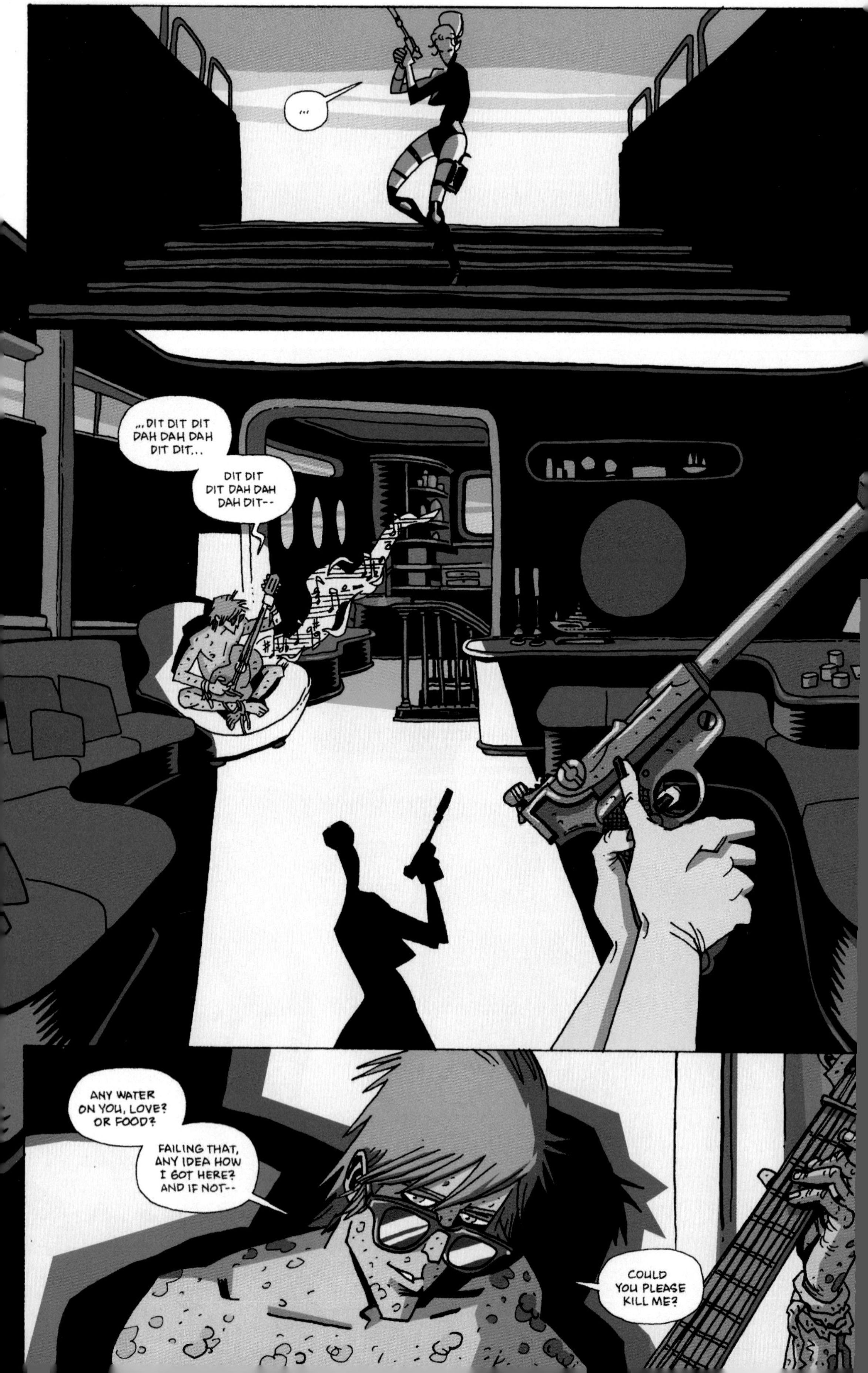
...
...DIT DIT DIT DAH DAH DAH DIT DIT...
DIT DIT DIT DAH DAH DAH DIT--
ANY WATER ON YOU, LOVE? OR FOOD?
FAILING THAT, ANY IDEA HOW I GOT HERE? AND IF NOT--
COULD YOU PLEASE KILL ME?

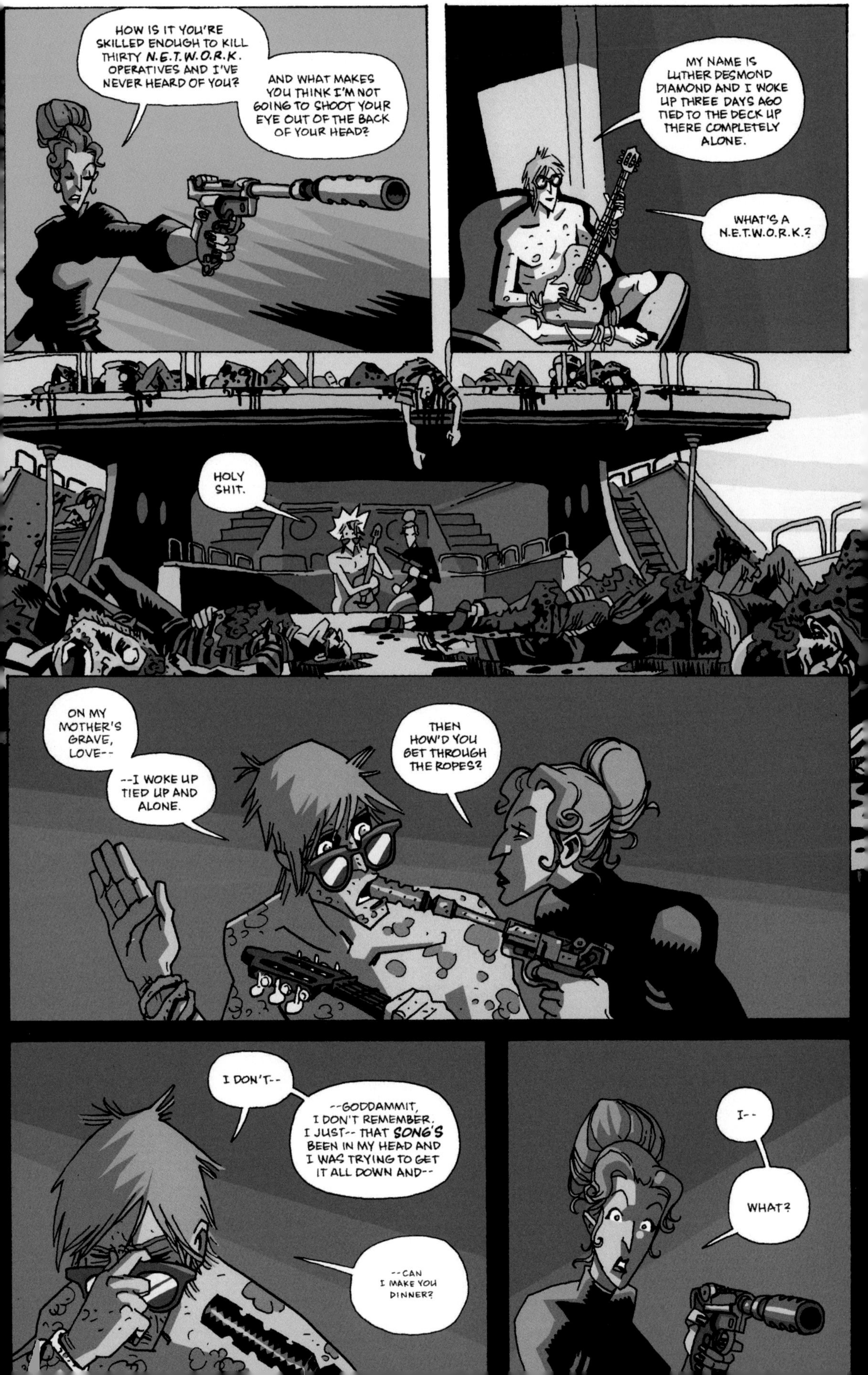
HOW IS IT YOU'RE SKILLED ENOUGH TO KILL THIRTY N.E.T.W.O.R.K. OPERATIVES AND I'VE NEVER HEARD OF YOU?
AND WHAT MAKES YOU THINK I'M NOT GOING TO SHOOT YOUR EYE OUT OF THE BACK OF YOUR HEAD?
MY NAME IS LUTHER DESMOND DIAMOND AND I WOKE UP THREE DAYS AGO TIED TO THE DECK UP THERE COMPLETELY ALONE.
WHAT'S A N.E.T.W.O.R.K.?
HOLY SHIT.
ON MY MOTHER'S GRAVE, LOVE--
--I WOKE UP TIED UP AND ALONE.
THEN HOW'D YOU GET THROUGH THE ROPES?
I DON'T--
--GODDAMMIT, I DON'T REMEMBER. I JUST-- THAT SONG'S BEEN IN MY HEAD AND I WAS TRYING TO GET IT ALL DOWN AND--
--CAN I MAKE YOU DINNER?
I--
WHAT?

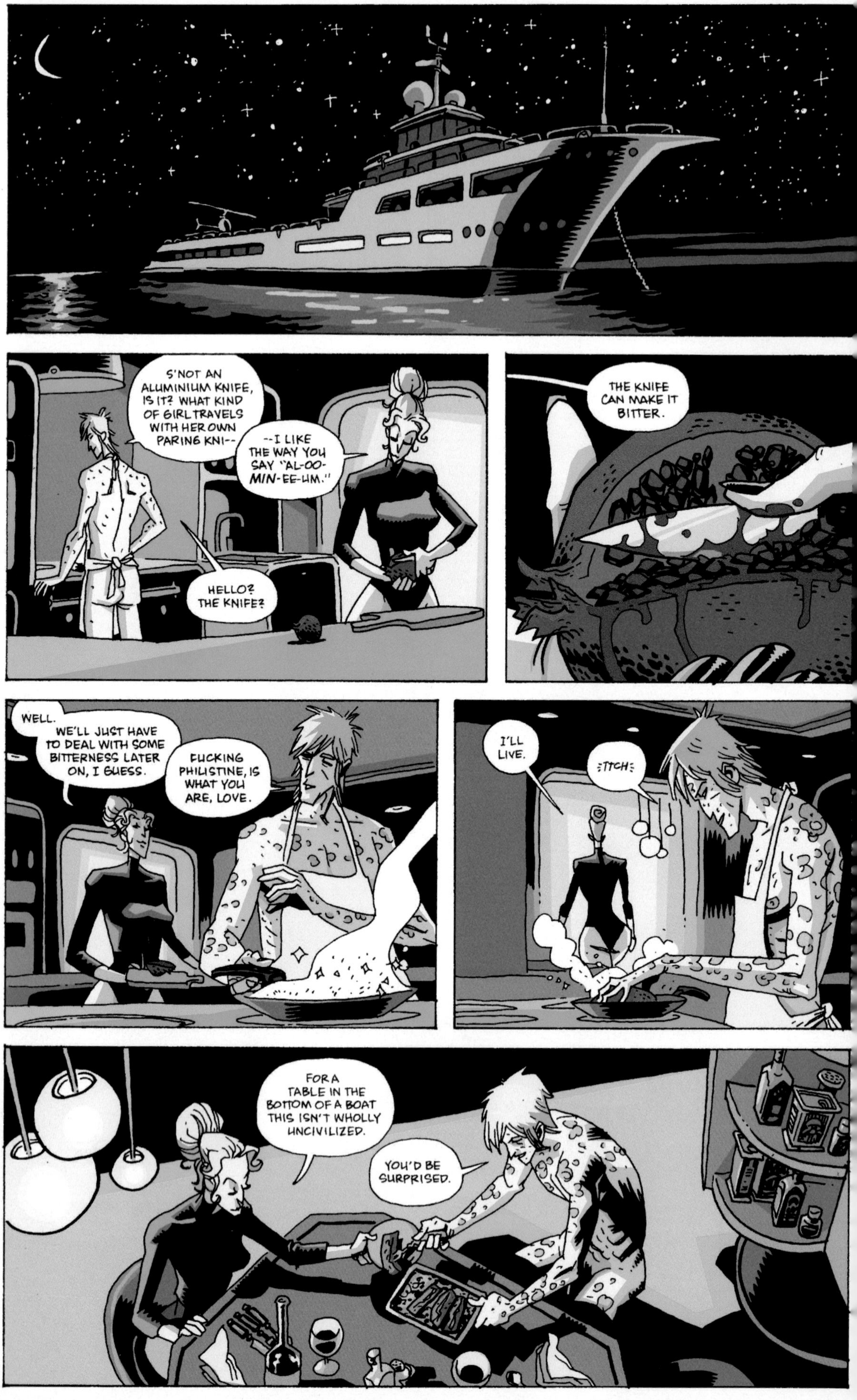

S'NOT AN ALUMINIUM KNIFE, IS IT? WHAT KIND OF GIRL TRAVELS WITH HER OWN PARING KNI--
--I LIKE THE WAY YOU SAY "AL-OO-MIN-EE-UM."
HELLO? THE KNIFE?
THE KNIFE CAN MAKE IT BITTER.
WELL.
WE'LL JUST HAVE TO DEAL WITH SOME BITTERNESS LATER ON, I GUESS.
FUCKING PHILISTINE, IS WHAT YOU ARE, LOVE.
I'LL LIVE.
TTCH
FOR A TABLE IN THE BOTTOM OF A BOAT THIS ISN'T WHOLLY UNCIVILIZED.
YOU'D BE SURPRISED.

Y'KNOW, I'M *ENGLISH*--I'VE NEVER REALLY HAD A PROPER TROPICAL SUNBURN BEFORE.

YOU SAY THAT LIKE IT'S AN ACQUISITIVE ACHIEVEMENT.

WELL, AN *EXPERIENTIAL* ACHIEVEMENT, ANYWAY.

S'WHAT IT'S ABOUT, RIGHT?

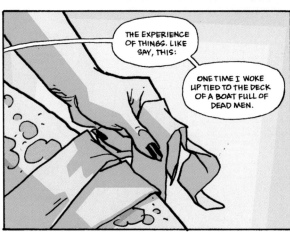

THE EXPERIENCE OF THINGS. LIKE SAY, THIS:

ONE TIME I WOKE UP TIED TO THE DECK OF A BOAT FULL OF DEAD MEN.

NO CLUE HOW I GOT THERE.

I SWEAR. BUT THEN--

THEN THIS CRAZY BIRD LANDS IN A HELICHIPPER AND SAYS I DID IT. AND I'M TELLING YOU, I CAN'T REMEMBER SHIT ABOUT FUCK RIGHT NOW BUT SO--

SO-- SO THEN I--

SO THEN I POISON HER. I SUDDENLY REMEMBER I KNOW HOW TO DO THAT.

I POISON HER AND SHE DOESN'T DIE.

ISN'T THAT THE CRAZIEST THING YOU'VE EVER HEARD?

TRADE SECRET.

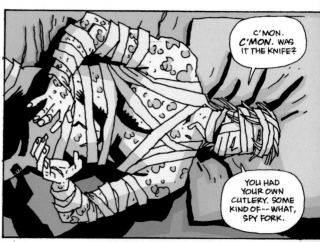

C'MON. *C'MON.* WAS IT THE KNIFE?

YOU HAD YOUR OWN CUTLERY. SOME KIND OF-- WHAT, SPY FORK.

RIGHT? SPY FORK. IT WAS A SPY FORK.

HELLO?

HOW DID YOU KILL THIRTY N.E.T.W.O.R.K. MEN?

I DON'T KNOW. SPY FORK? I DON'T EVEN REMEMBER HOW I KNEW HOW TO POISON PEOPLE. IT CAME AND WENT.

WHATEVER GETS YOU THROUGH THE NIGHT.

YOU.

YOU CAN GET ME THROUGH THE NIGHT.

PLEASE.

YOU THINK I'M SO DUMB I'D LET MYSELF GET *POISONED.*

YOU'RE NOT MY TYPE.

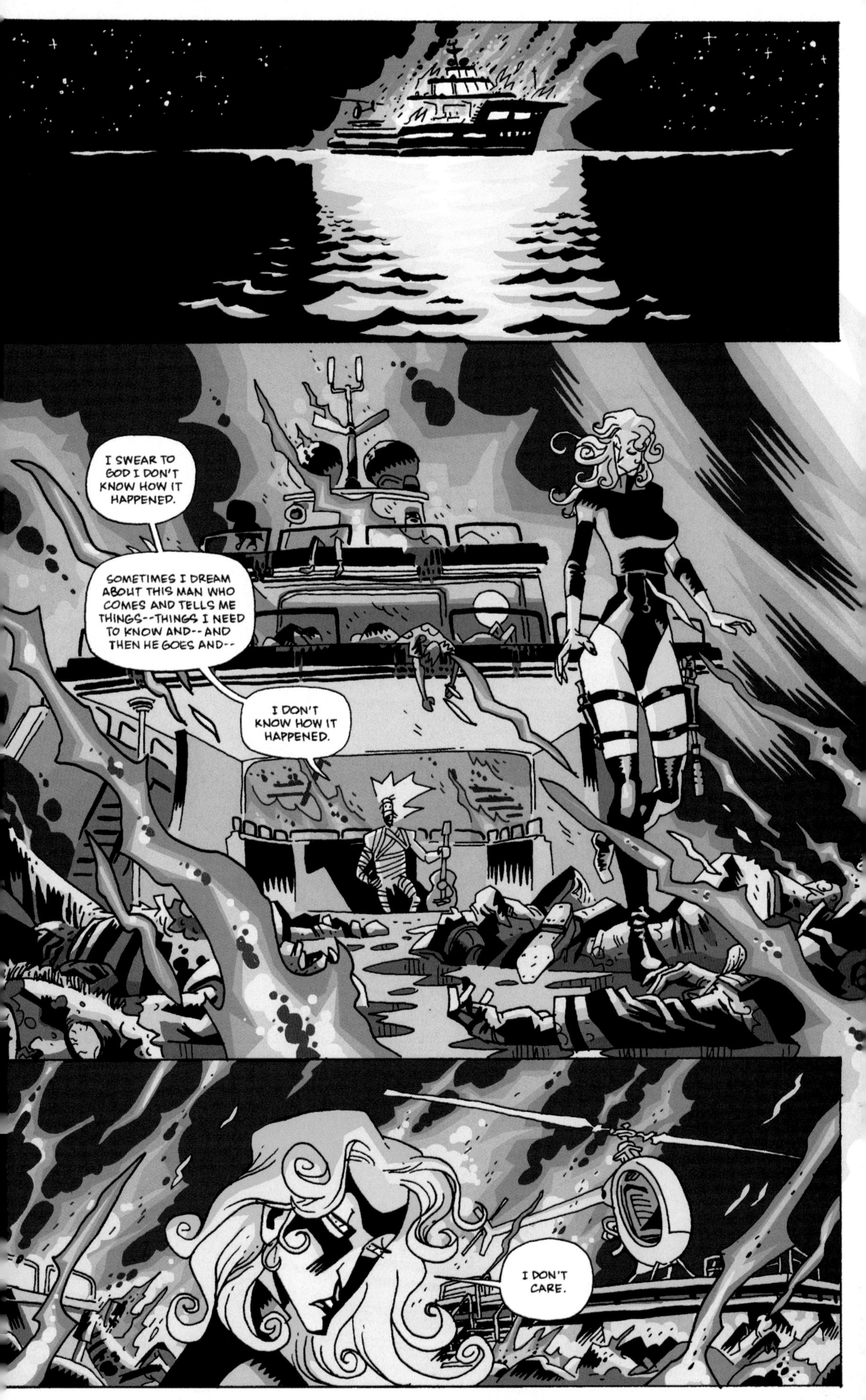
I SWEAR TO GOD I DON'T KNOW HOW IT HAPPENED.
SOMETIMES I DREAM ABOUT THIS MAN WHO COMES AND TELLS ME THINGS--THINGS I NEED TO KNOW AND--AND THEN HE GOES AND--
I DON'T KNOW HOW IT HAPPENED.
I DON'T CARE.

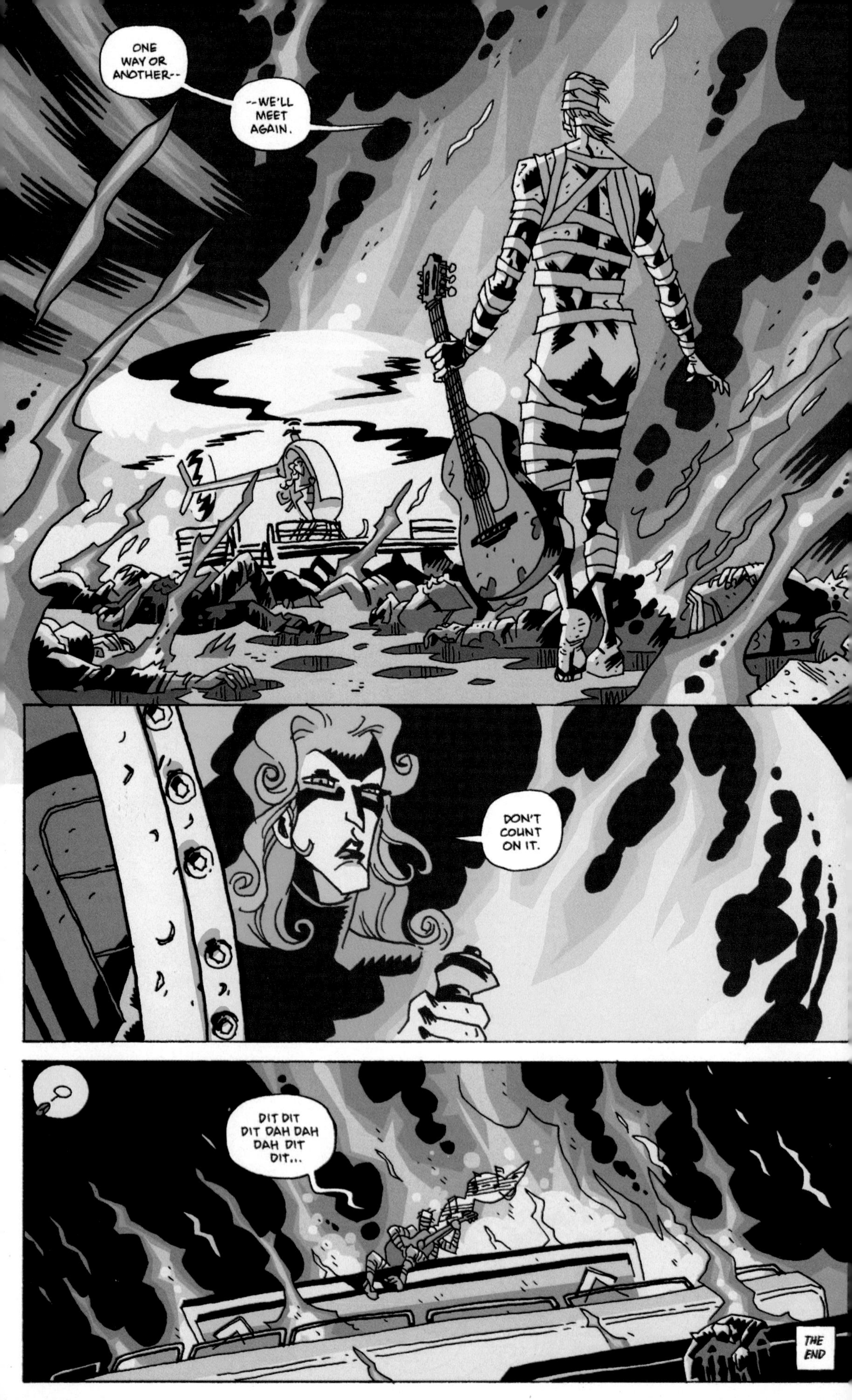
ONE WAY OR ANOTHER--
--WE'LL MEET AGAIN.
DON'T COUNT ON IT.
DIT DIT DIT DAH DAH DAH DIT DIT...
THE END

the good news is yr not paralyzed

i've just lost his wife...
awful, isnt it? abuse + suicides are
through the roof today - that's my
relate christmas here.

FIRST WORDS

On Christmas Day, 2006, I was admitted to the emergency room at Fawcett Memorial Hospital in New Port Richey, Florida. During triage, the above was said to me more or less as it would later be said to Casanova on the second page of the first chapter. I grabbed another intake form and transcribed as quick as I could and that was the start of the writing of CASANOVA: GULA.

It was, as they say, all true.

James Brown died that day, too; it was on the TV. What kind of god takes James Brown on Christmas?

Matt Fraction

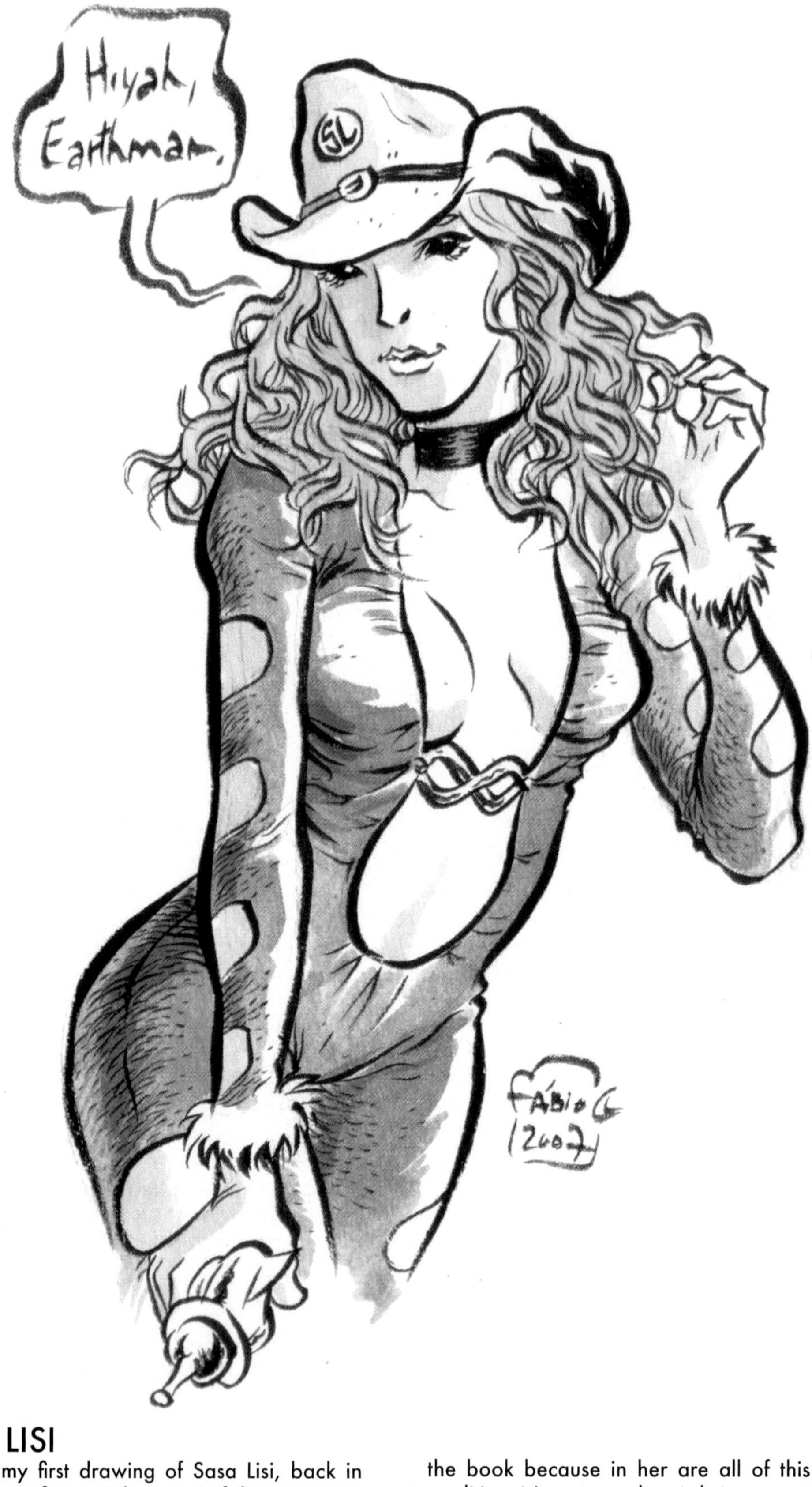
Hiyah, Earthman.
FÁBIO
2007

SASA LISI

This was my first drawing of Sasa Lisi, back in 2007 when I first got the script of this story. On the next page, the image and the initial sketch I did for the cover of this collection. Smaller, a loose watercolor sketch I did just for fun. Without a doubt, she's still my favorite character in the book because in her are all of this story's qualities: it's sexy and weird, it seems to come from a strange place you're not familiar with and, as you know more, it only gets sexier and weirder. She comes from another planet, and from the future no less, but still she could have

come from Europe. From one of the many sexy erotic French bandes dessinées or Italian fumetti that inspired an entire generation of artists, to be more precise.

One of the greatest advantages of collaborating on a project is the unintentional mix of influences that end up inspiring the work. Matt's Sasa is Barbarella, both the comic book and the movie versions, mixed with all those cosmic Jim Starlin comics, and then mine was a super-model from fashion week, and she was my Druuna and she was my Leia.

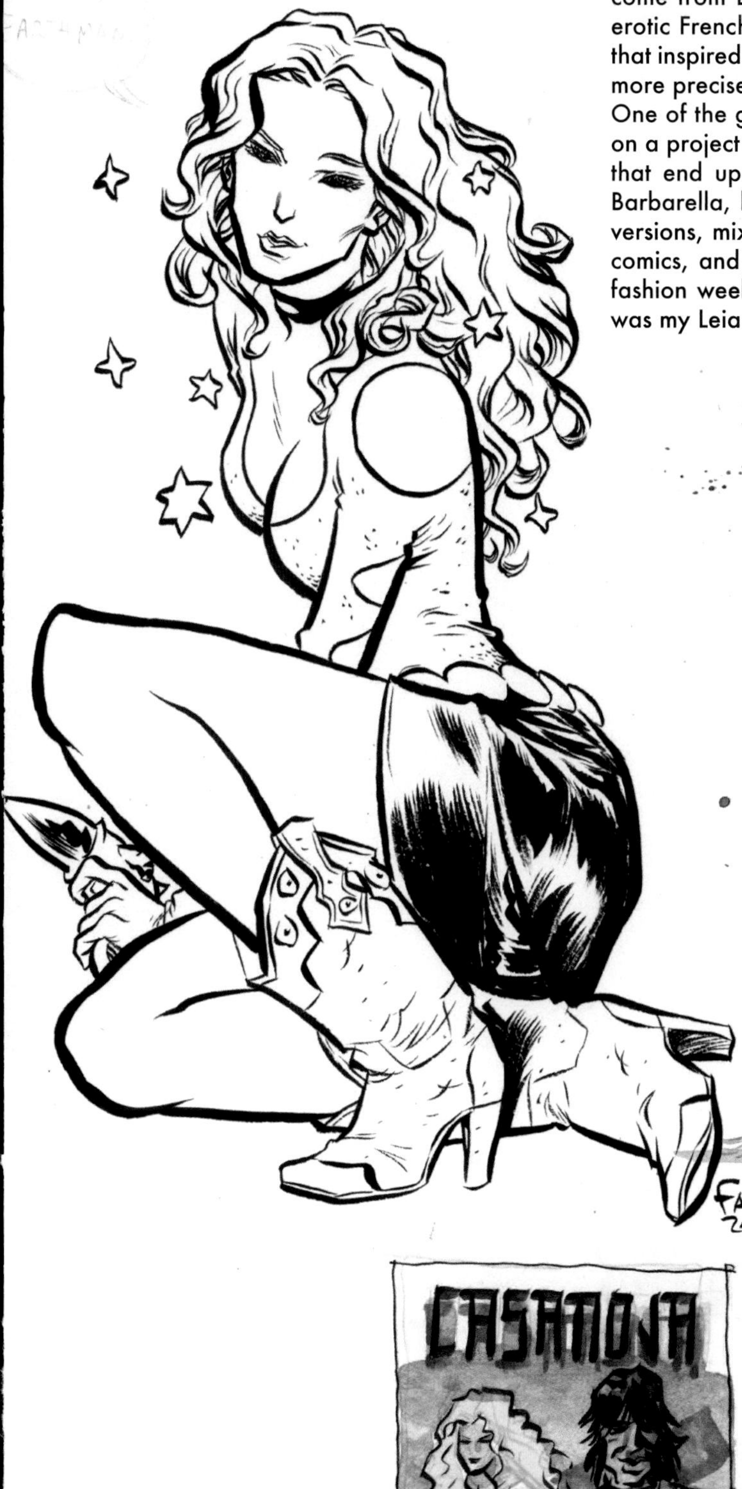
FÁBIO C
2011-SP

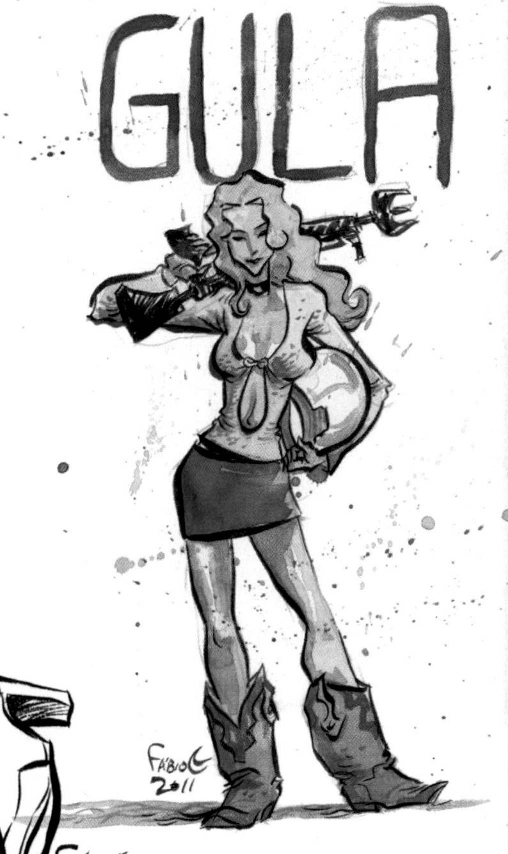
GULA
FÁBIO C
2011

16·FEV·2011

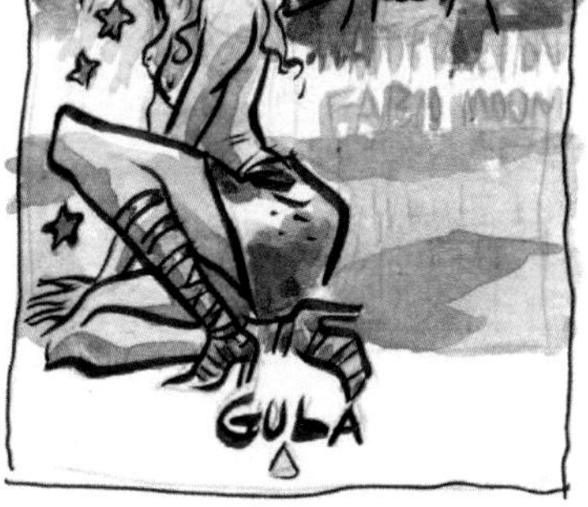
CASANOVA
GULA

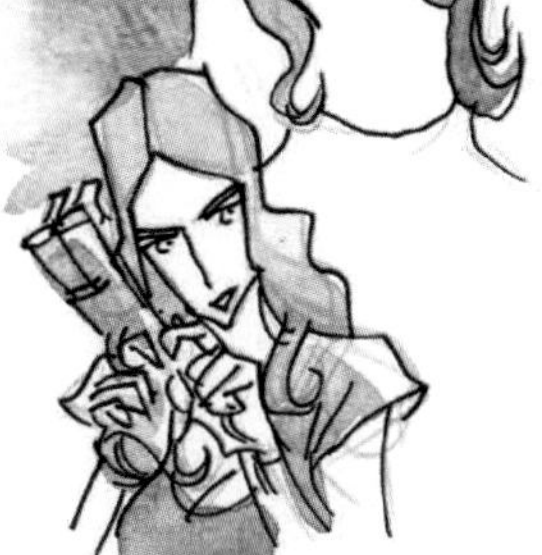

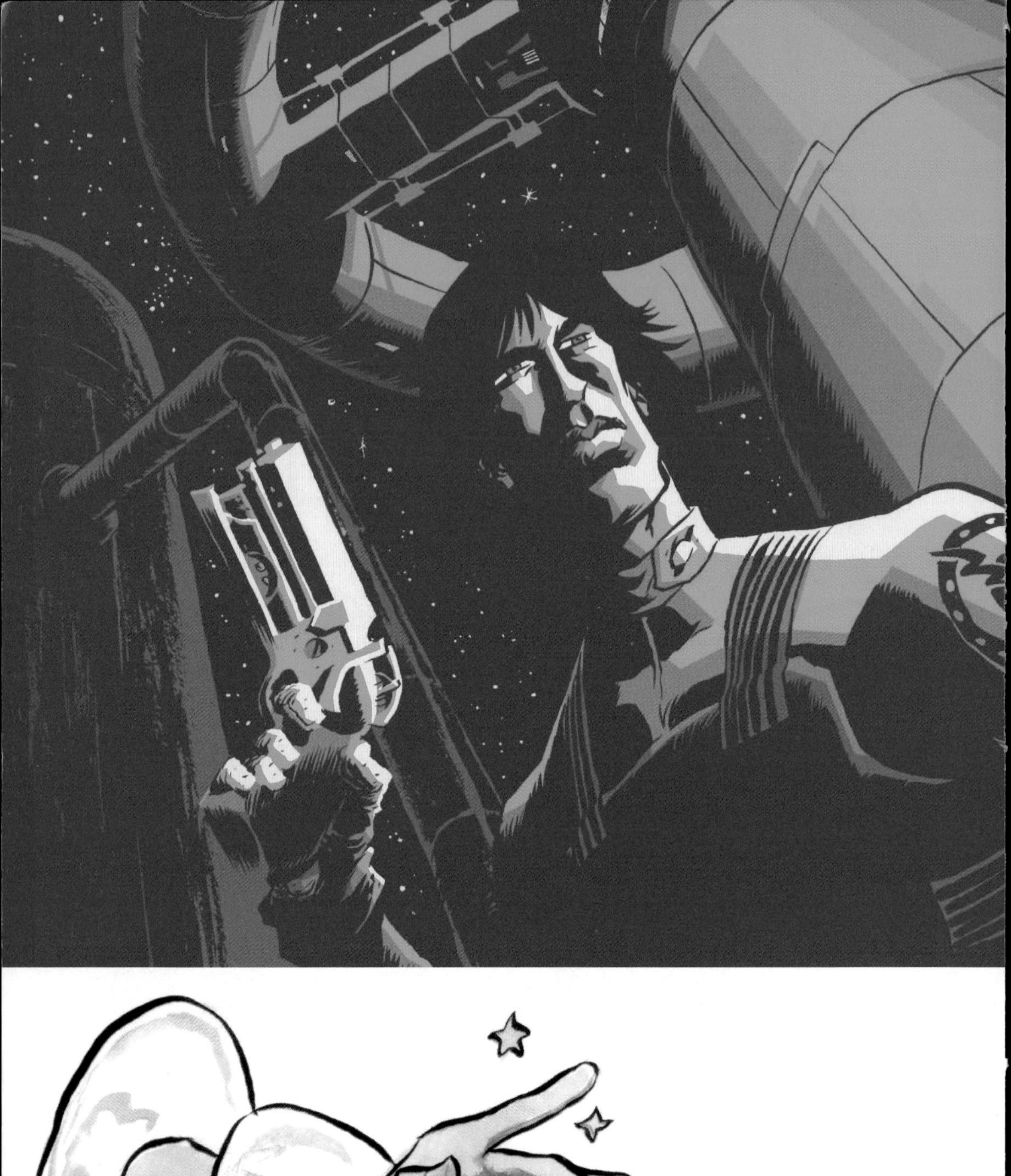

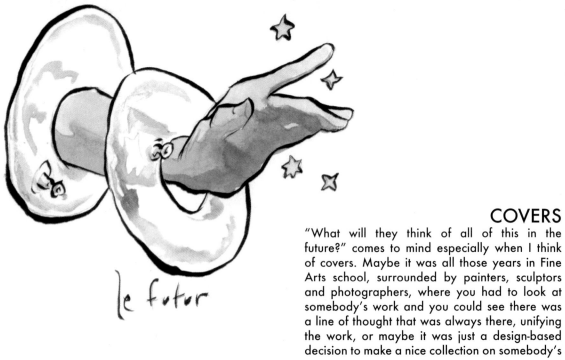

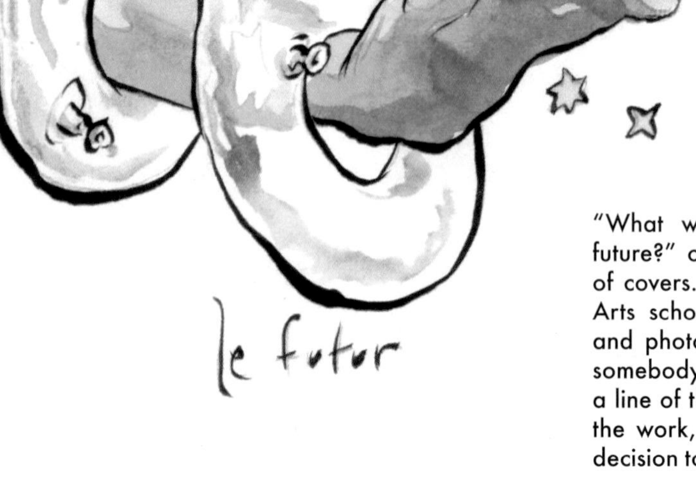
le futur

COVERS

"What will they think of all of this in the future?" comes to mind especially when I think of covers. Maybe it was all those years in Fine Arts school, surrounded by painters, sculptors and photographers, where you had to look at somebody's work and you could see there was a line of thought that was always there, unifying the work, or maybe it was just a design-based decision to make a nice collection on somebody's

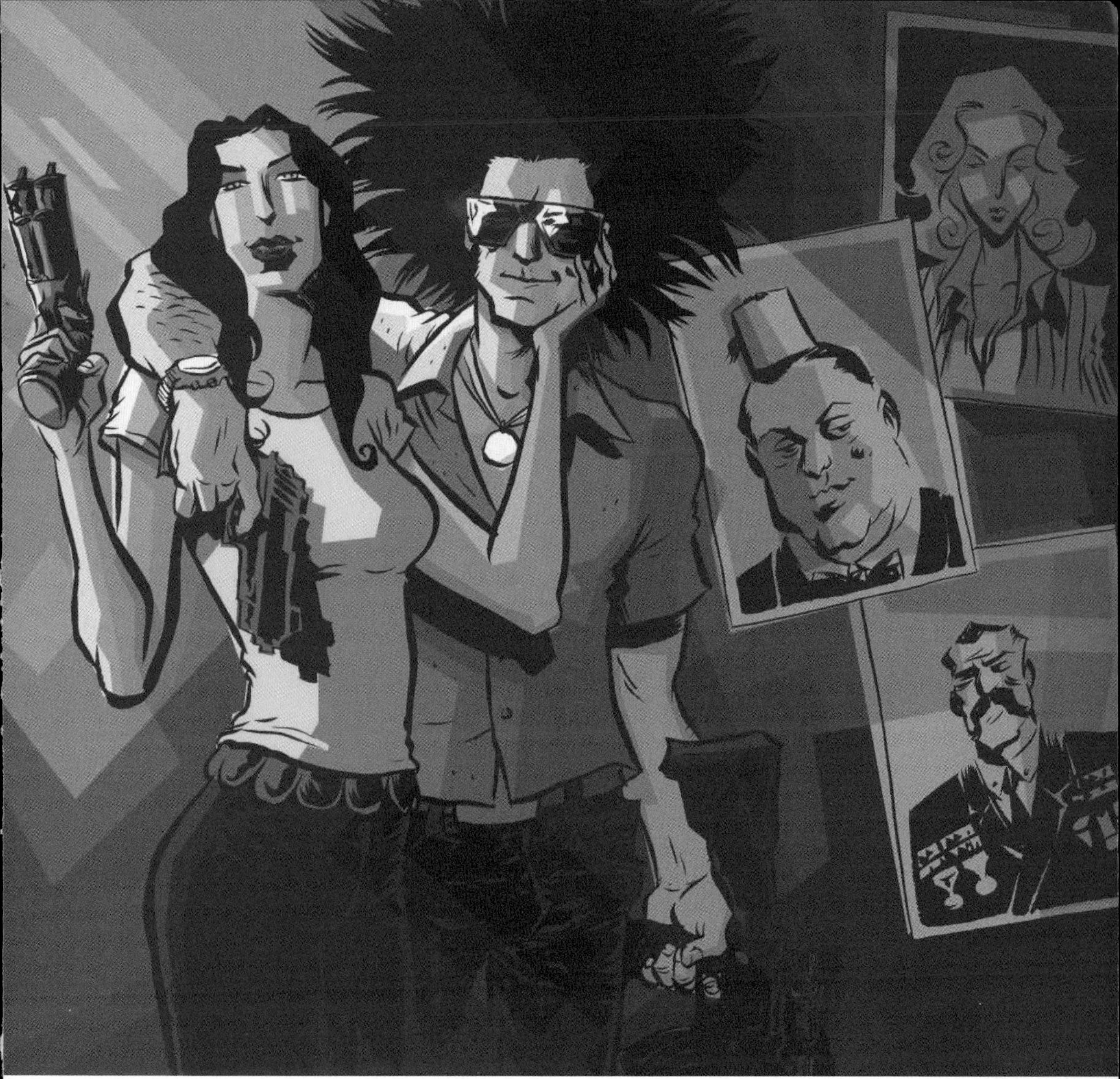

bookshelf, but covers have to work together. "In the future," when they bump into any of the covers from this series, they'll go "Ah, that was a Casanova cover." Bá did four amazing covers for the LUXURIA story arc and set the model the covers would follow. My job, still trying to maintain the unity of the collection, was to keep the covers interesting and dynamic instead of repetitive.

The best sensation you get when you're creating a cover is when you do the sketch and you see it working right there in those simple scribbles. I was lucky to be able to do the covers after the entire story was done, so I could do all four sketches at

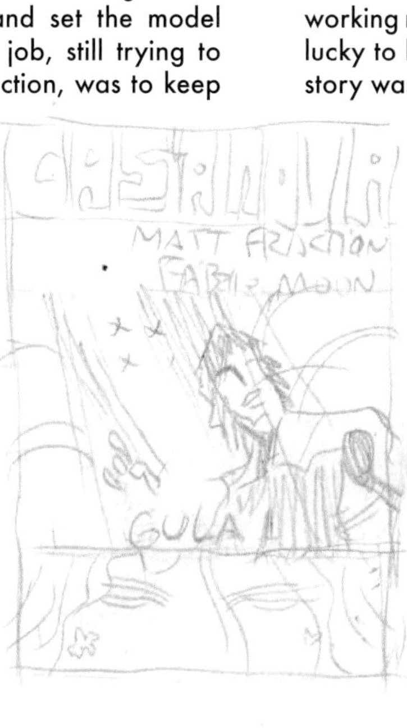
MATT FRACTION
GULA

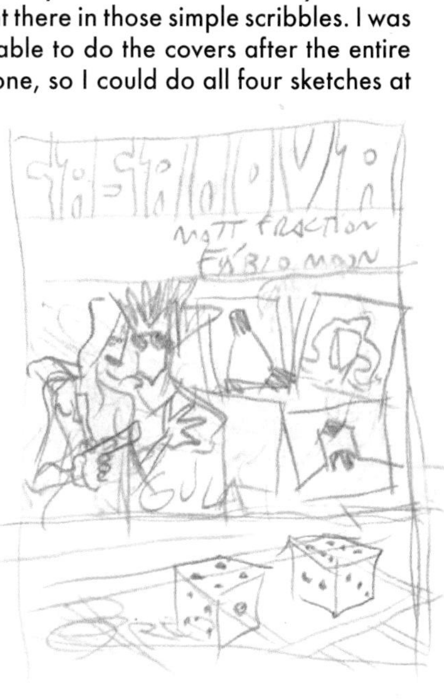
MATT FRACTION
GULA

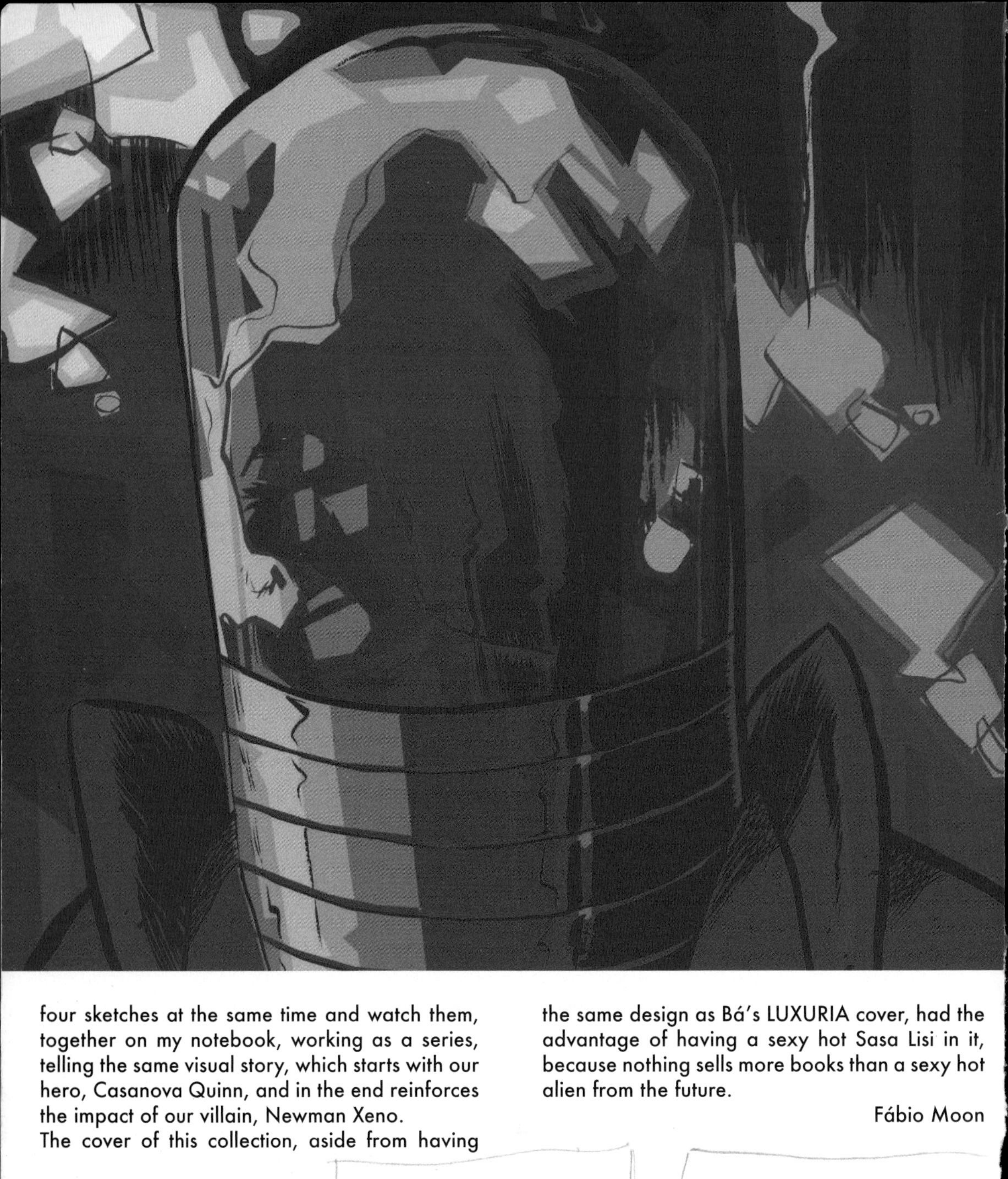

four sketches at the same time and watch them, together on my notebook, working as a series, telling the same visual story, which starts with our hero, Casanova Quinn, and in the end reinforces the impact of our villain, Newman Xeno.
The cover of this collection, aside from having the same design as Bá's LUXURIA cover, had the advantage of having a sexy hot Sasa Lisi in it, because nothing sells more books than a sexy hot alien from the future.

Fábio Moon

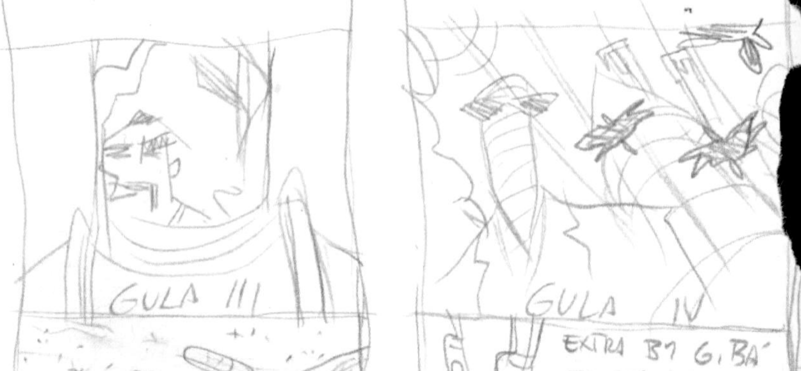
GULA III
GULA IV
EXTRA BY G. BÁ

CASANOVA - GULA

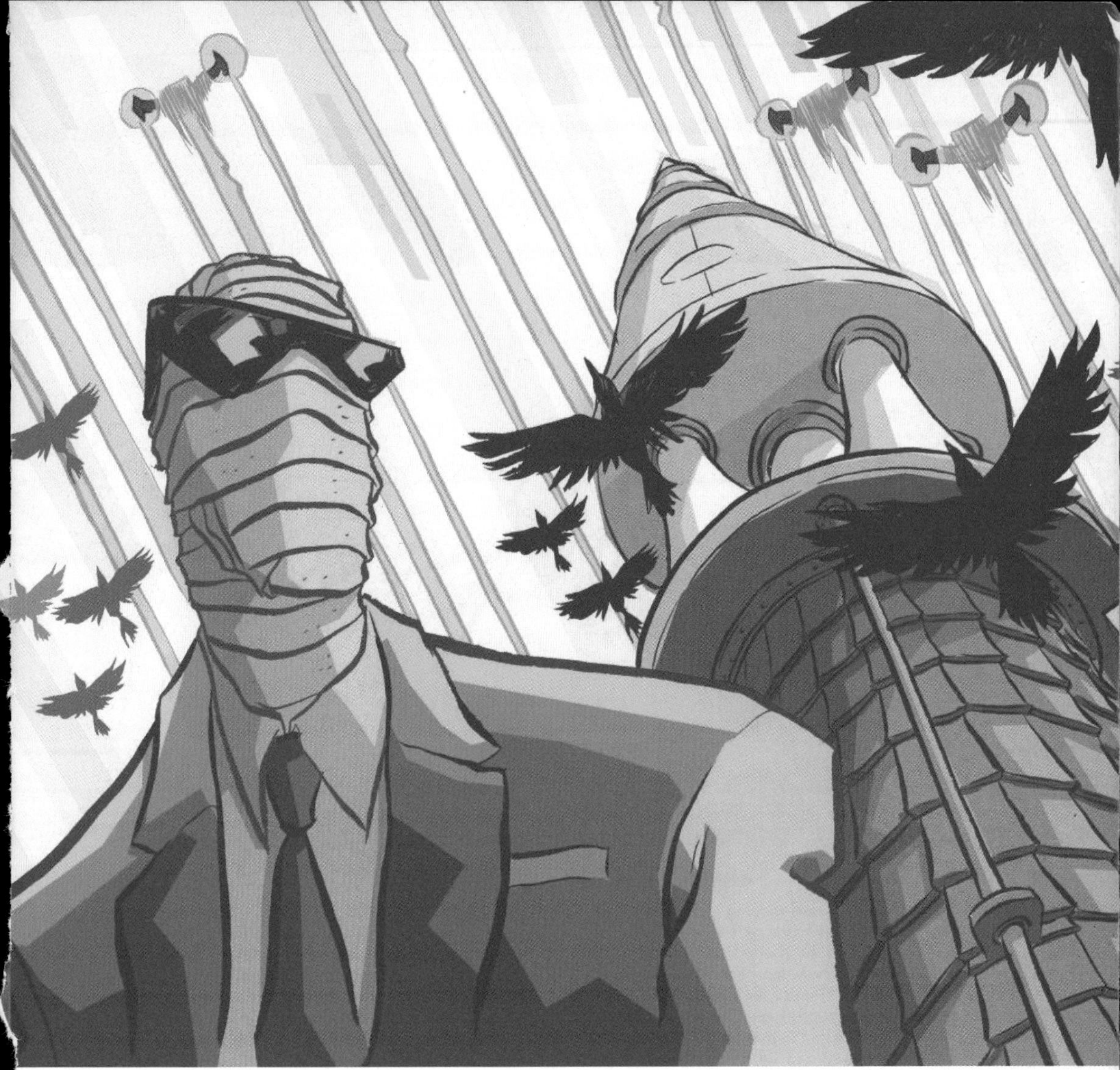

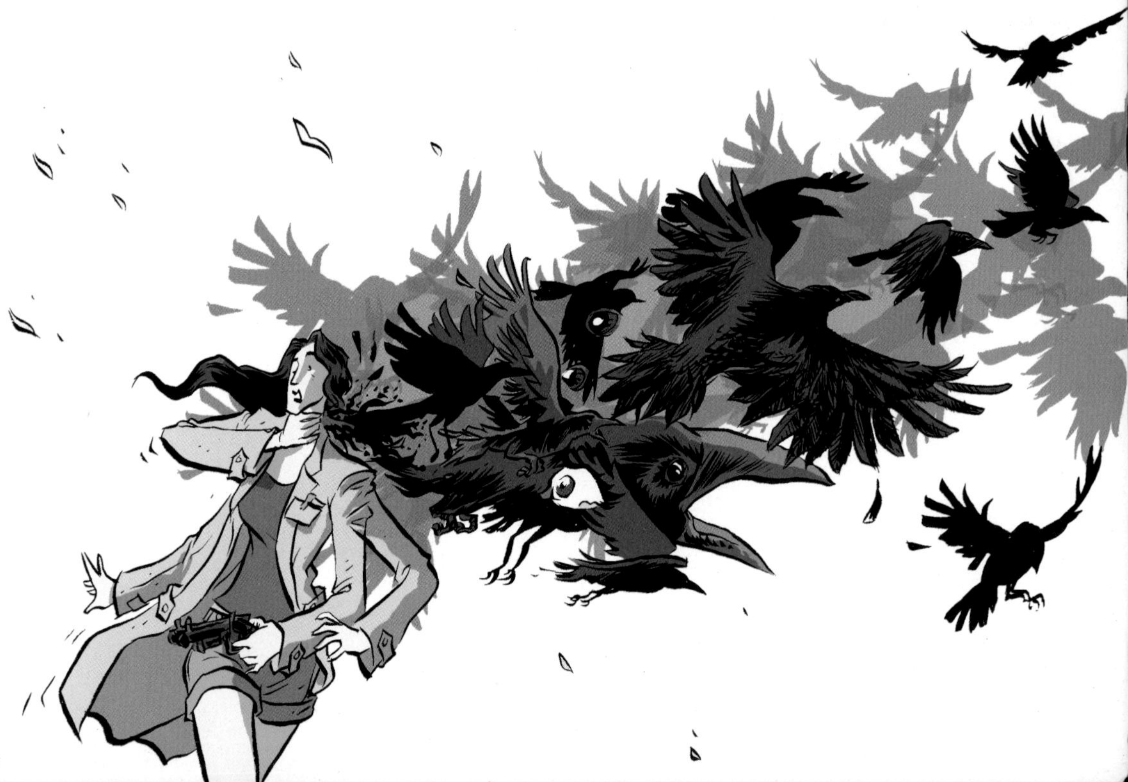

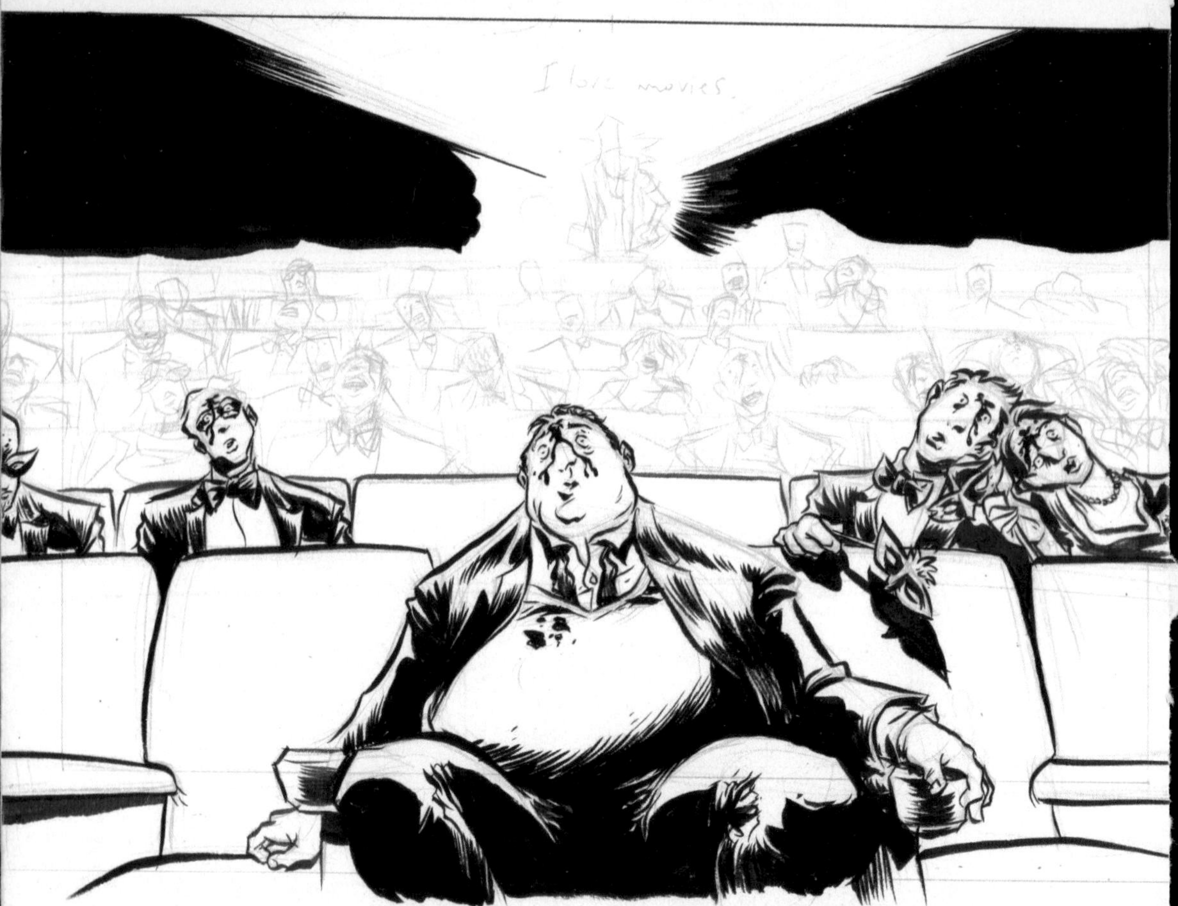
I love movies.

Matt Fraction is an Eisner Award-winning American comic book writer, known for his work on THE INVINCIBLE IRON MAN, THE MIGHTY THOR, and the Marvel mega-event FEAR ITSELF. He's written THE IMMORTAL IRON FIST, UNCANNY X-MEN, and others for Marvel Comics; he's written the graphic novels LAST OF THE INDEPENDENTS and THE FIVE FISTS OF SCIENCE. He's recently contributed to the storylines and dialogue of both the IRON MAN 2 and THOR video games for Sega, and was a consultant on the IRON MAN 2 film. He lives in Portland, Oregon, with his wife, the writer Kelly Sue DeConnick, and his two children, two dogs, two cats, and the ghosts of two frogs.

Fábio Moon is Gabriel Bá's Eisner Award-winning evil twin whose world domination plans include creating great comics, be it with great authors like Joss Whedon and Mike Mignola (and Matt, of course), be it only with his twin brother Bá doing their weird twinnery in such books as DAYTRIPPER and DE:TALES. He lives in São Paulo, but his stories live all over the world in the minds of his readers.

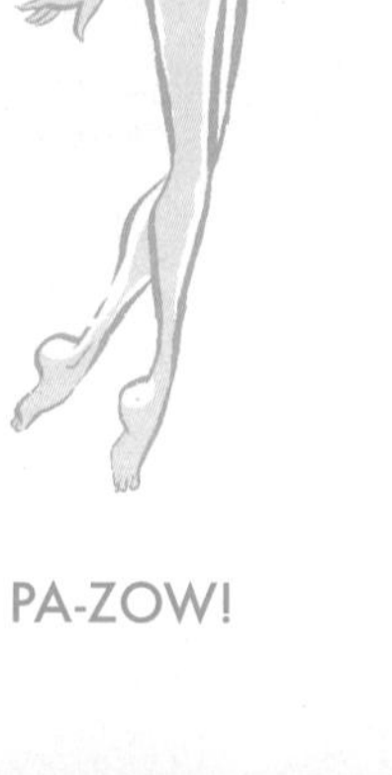

PA-ZOW!